BUSINESS ISSUES, COMPETITION AND ENTREPRENEURSHIP

ECONOMIC AND FINANCIAL MODELING OF MARKETS, INSTITUTIONS AND INSTRUMENTS

BUSINESS ISSUES, COMPETITION AND ENTREPRENEURSHIP

Additional books in this series can be found on Nova's website under the Series tab.

Additional e-books in this series can be found on Nova's website under the e-book tab.

BUSINESS ISSUES, COMPETITION AND ENTREPRENEURSHIP

ECONOMIC AND FINANCIAL MODELING OF MARKETS, INSTITUTIONS AND INSTRUMENTS

ANDREW C. WORTHINGTON
EDITOR

nova
publishers
New York

Library of Congress Cataloging-in-Publication Data

Economic and financial modeling of markets, institutions and instruments / editor, Andrew C. Worthington.
pages cm. -- (Business issues, competition and entrepreneurship)
Includes index.
ISBN 978-1-63463-111-2 (hardcover)
1. Finance--Mathematical models. 2. Finance--Econometric models. 3. Capital markets. I. Worthington, Andrew C.
HG106.E35 2014
332.01'5195--dc23
2014036530

Published by Nova Science Publishers, Inc. † New York

CONTENTS

Chapter 1	Introduction to the Economic and Financial Modeling of Markets, Institutions and Instruments *Andrew C. Worthington*	**1**
Chapter 2	Modeling the Pricing of Initial Public Offerings *Jirapun Chorruk and Andrew C. Worthington*	**9**
Chapter 3	Trading/Trading-Restricted and Business/Nonbusiness Days in Market Return Models *Mitesh Mistry, Andrew C. Worthington, Dionigi Gerace and Chandra Gulati*	**29**
Chapter 4	The Theory and Practice of Credit Risk Modeling *Mohamed Habara and Andrew C. Worthington*	**45**
Chapter 5	Modeling Firm-Specific Determinants of Initial Public Offerings *Jirapun Chorruk and Andrew C. Worthington*	**73**
Chapter 6	Models of Political Cycles and Market Risk and Return *Andrew C. Worthington*	**97**
Chapter 7	A Combined Conceptual, Theoretical and Empirical Review of Credit-Scoring Models *Mohamed Habara and Andrew C. Worthington*	**113**
Chapter 8	Contextual Factors in Social and Environmental Accounting Disclosure Models *Omer Elsakit and Andrew C. Worthington*	**161**
Chapter 9	Modeling Factor Price Elasticities and Factor Substitution *Andrew C. Worthington and Helen Higgs*	**185**
Chapter 10	Performance Models for Initial Public Offerings *Nancy Vu, Andrew C. Worthington and Phillip Laird*	**197**
Chapter 11	Nonparametric Models of Technical Efficiency in Urban Water Utilities *Andrew C. Worthington*	**217**

Chapter 12	An Application of Credit Score Modeling *Mohamed Habara and Andrew C. Worthington*	**235**
Editor's Contact Information		**267**
Index		**269**

In: Economic and Financial Modeling
Editor: Andrew C. Worthington
ISBN: 978-1-63463-111-2

Chapter 1

INTRODUCTION TO THE ECONOMIC AND FINANCIAL MODELING OF MARKETS, INSTITUTIONS AND INSTRUMENTS

Andrew C. Worthington*
Griffith University, Australia

A model is a simplified representation of a real object or situation that facilitates our understanding and manipulation of the real thing. There are four main categories of models. First, a *verbal (or logical) model* is the simplest type and the one usually used first in any field of inquiry. This approach uses verbal analogies, such as metaphors (a term applied to something to which it does not literally apply) and similes (something is like another), and produces a type of model called a paradigm. For example, great Scottish economist Adam Smith used a pin factory to illustrate the division of labor, and spoke of an invisible hand directing individual decisions for the benefit of society. Second, an *iconic model* is a physical replica of the real thing. These are very common, and include scale models for a shopping center, highway or an airport, a model aircraft or automobile in a wind tunnel, and even most children's toys, including dolls and action figures, toy soldiers, and toy cars. Third, an *analog model* is a physical representation of objects or situations that do not look like the real thing. An organizational chart is representative of analog models. Finally, a *symbolic (or mathematical or algebraic) model* is a set of symbols and mathematical relationships that represent a real situation. For example, break-even analyses and plots of supply and demand or aggregate expenditure are representative of symbolic models, as are regression equations and linear programs describing production and cost functions, asset price determination and valuation, and human behavior. In this volume, we concentrate on analog and symbolic (mathematical) models and their use in academic and industry research.

Analog models such as graphs and charts are very useful in research. First, they are able to summarize large amounts of information. In many cases a graph can be used illustrate numerical data from a large table or database. For example, we may use a line graph to

---

* Department of Accounting, Finance and Economics, Griffith University, Nathan QLD 4111, Australia. Email. a.worthington@griffith.edu.au.

illustrate the daily changes in a stock's price over a two-year period. Likewise, a chart can illustrate aspects of firm's financing function and show the breakup between debt and equity. Second, analog models also enhance our understanding of complex situations. Building a chart can enhance our understanding of complex situations. For example, the environment of financial decision-making is the complex interaction of taxation, financial institutions, firm operations, etc. Similarly, analog models facilitate comparison between financial items. We can use a graph to compare numerical financial data over time, or to facilitate comparisons among items. For example, we could graph firm profits over time, or examine firm profits and sales amongst a number of firms at a single point in time. Third, analog models are also useful for conveying information difficult to communicate using raw data. For instance, we could use a graph to identify trends and patterns that we might otherwise overlook. For example, if we plotted merchandise sales over a year we can usually identify a clear seasonal trend. Lastly, analog models enhance the representation of financial reports. Graphs can help place data in a clear logical sequence within a report and can force the reader to examine the most pertinent details in the report.

All analog models share some common characteristics. The first characteristic is an objective. That is, we must define clearly and concisely the objective of the model. The second characteristic is the presence of assumptions. Given analog models are abstractions from reality we must define and present these assumptions clearly. Simplicity is necessary to make the model workable; comprehensiveness is required to make it realistic. The third characteristic is the model components. In a chart, the components are normally boxes, circles, lines, and labels. Behind these are the sets of data employed. For instance, a bar graph of yearly sales will consist of a sequence of years and a sequence of sales in dollars. The third and final characteristic is the clear elaboration of the relationships between a model's components. In a chart, we may identify relationships with arrows and lines. In a graph, we may use points, lines, and bars.

Let us take the simple example of the functions of corporate finance, as depicted by Figure 1. The objective here is to provide a chart illustrating the finance function and the fact that we should carry on this function in such a way as to achieve the firm's objective. The assumptions, components, and relationships are such that we classify the finance function into three groups: short-term financial management, long-term investment decisions, and long-term financing decisions. We know the conventional objective of the firm is to maximize shareholder wealth, so by definition, we also know the finance function, including these three different areas of financial decision-making, should be used to maximize shareholder wealth.

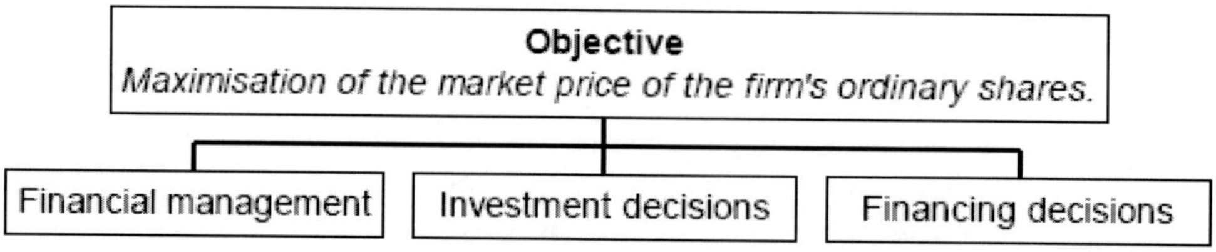

Figure 1. A simple analog model.

The second type of model we discuss in this volume is symbolic or mathematical models. Invariably, most of the models we use in economics and finance have their basis in an analog model with nearly all used to help us solve problems or to make decisions, as shown in Figures 2 and 3, respectively. All of the cases we examine in this volume have followed this basic modeling process. In fact, most of the empirical research published in refereed journals and book chapters is of this form. These have a number of advantages. First, mathematical models are clear. We can readily view the solution of a mathematical model in terms of the approach used, the assumptions of the model, the components of the model and the relationships between them extremely clearly. Second, there are standard mathematical models. In many cases, we can analyze different sets of data with a standard function. For example, we can use discounted cash flow techniques consistently for the evaluation of investments. In addition, we can use regression analysis to examine the relationships between economic and financial variables. Third, mathematical models can provide quantitative results. By being largely numerical, we can use mathematical models to provide results that are uniform and easy to analyze.

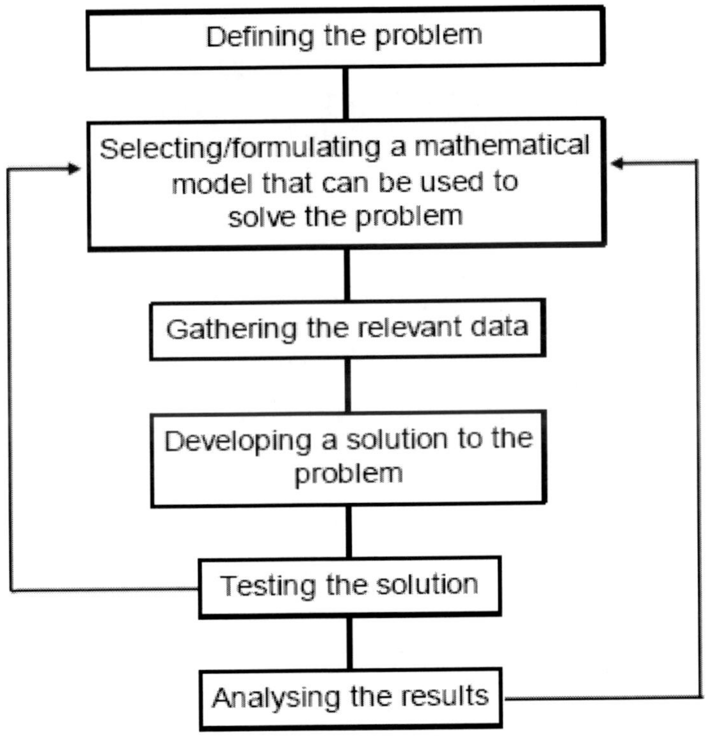

Figure 2. A problem-solving model process.

Fourth, we can use computer hardware and software to solve mathematical models. Software is widely, easily, and cheaply available to facilitate the solving of numerical problems, i.e. spreadsheets like Microsoft Excel or statistical programs like STATA, S+, EViews, and SPSS. Even when data is not necessarily quantitative, such as open responses from a questionnaire, data analysis may be possible with a small number of assumptions using appropriate software, i.e. Nudist and NVivo. Fifth, mathematical models increase the user's understanding of the decision-making process. For example, by modelling an investment project using the net present value method, the user can clearly identify the impact on the firm of the selection criteria. This means that modelling techniques can help the user make the 'best' decision.

Sixth, mathematical models are transparent. Any relationships and assumptions employed in a mathematical model are readily available for comment and critique. In many cases, we can modify the assumptions used for constructing models to make them more accurate and thus making better decisions. For example, in financial modelling, we may drop the assumption of certainty and consider risk. Seventh, mathematical models and computer applications can help to evaluate different alternatives. For example, using 'what if' (or simulation) analysis we can assess a model's sensitivity to a particular variable and assess the extent of this sensitivity. In a regression model, we could likewise change a restriction on some coefficient estimate, or add or remove variables or observations from the analysis. Finally, using modelling (that is, a mathematical description of a situation) facilitates the manipulation, understanding, experimentation, and analysis of an economic or financial situation. We can divide the types of ways we are likely to use this information into two types, namely, problem solving and decision making.

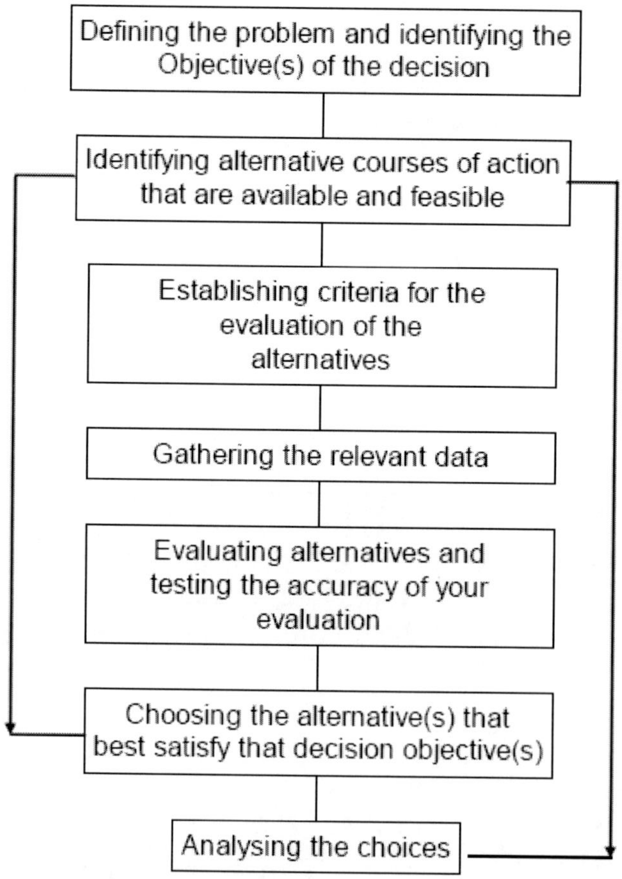

Figure 3. A decision-making model process.

The purpose of this volume is to present eleven modelling exercises relating to markets, institutions, and instruments that help to illustrate the practical application of these concepts.

They are then of value not only in terms of responding to a specific problem, but also the details of the modeling techniques, approaches, and methods employed. In Chapter 2, Jirapun Chorruk and Andrew Worthington examine the pricing and performance of initial public offerings (IPOs) in the Stock Exchange of Thailand. This is important, not least in developing economies, because how well an IPO is priced determines how much capital will flow to the firm from listing, while performance determines how much investors gain from taking up the new stock. In their model, underpricing is calculated using headline underpricing, underpricing issuer loss, underpricing loss by market value, and underpricing loss by issuer price. The results indicate average underpricing of 17.60%, 5.01%, 6.94%, 6.68%, and 16.10%, respectively. This is a significantly lower level of underpricing than previously documented in Thailand before the 1997 Asian financial crisis and reflects money being 'left on the table' by the listing firm. The authors then model post-listing performance using monthly cumulative abnormal returns, buy-and-hold returns, and wealth relatives, and find that Thai IPOs generally outperform market benchmarks up to 24 months and underperform thereafter up to 36 months. However, there is much variation in long-run performance among industries. For example, multiple regression analysis shows that IPOs in the financial services industry perform relatively better in the longer run. The key modelling challenge in this analysis was the gathering of the relevant data in a developing market context.

In Chapter 3, Mitesh Mistry, Andrew Worthington, Dionigi Gerace and Chandra Gulati provide an empirical analysis of trading-restricted, business days and trading, non-business days on the Australian Securities Exchange (ASX). In this, the authors make the argument that it is not possible to model the returns on a stock market in the same way for the majority of ordinary trading and business days as for days when trading and/or clearing and settlement is restricted. Seven of these days are included in the analysis, namely, the Bank Holiday in NSW (non-business), Labor Day in NSW (non-business), Easter Thursday (early close), Labor Day in Victoria (non-business), Melbourne Cup Day in Melbourne (non-business), the last business day before Christmas (early close) and the last business day of the calendar year (early close). Three indexes provide different daily return measures, being the All Ordinaries (market), the Small Ordinaries (small-cap), and the ASX100 (large-cap). The findings indicate return abnormalities on three days when trading and/or business activity is restricted: Melbourne Cup Day, the last business day before Christmas and the last business day of the calendar year. The key modeling challenge here was dealing with the large amount of data available for market in most developed economies.

In Chapter 4, Mohamed Habara and Andrew Worthington review the various models that quantify credit decision making. The first set of models is models of standalone credit risk that attempt to assess credit risk at the firm or individual borrower level. These models include expert and credit rating systems. The second set of models is models of portfolio credit risk that measure credit risk at the portfolio level, including structural models, explicit factor models, and reduced form models. Each model has its own strengths and weaknesses and it is therefore useful to be aware of these in their chosen context. This chapter exemplifies that in modelling many different approaches and methods are sometimes available, and thus there is a need to be fully aware of their advantages and disadvantages in a given context.

In Chapter 5, Jirapun Chorruk and Andrew Worthington return to the Thai IPO market, but instead examine the firm-specific determinants and outcomes of IPOs using data on 5,228 private and newly publicly listed firms. The key modeling question here is to identify what firm-specific factors are influential in encouraging unlisted Thai firm to list. They use the listing requirements of the Stock Exchange of Thailand to identify all private firms compulsorily registered with the Department of Business Development, Thai Ministry of Commerce as potential IPOs. Analysis of the determinants of IPOs reveals that firms that are younger, larger, more leveraged and with lower interest rates from borrowing are more likely to list. Analysis of post-IPO performance suggests that Thai firms going public succeed in lowering their borrowing rates, and that unlike comparable findings elsewhere, profitability does not decline after listing. However, despite these findings, the rate of listing in Thailand remains relatively low, and the paper hypothesizes that relatively high listing costs and the availability of alternative cheaper debt financing sources, the large shares of foreign subsidiary and small and medium-sized business operating in Thailand, along with market and political instability and cultural factors act against Thai IPOs.

In Chapter 6, Andrew Worthington tests for the presence of a political cycle in Australian daily stock returns over a 47-year period. Anecdotal evidence abounds of the link between securities markets and politics. The financial media analyzes economic and social policy for possible market reactions, and industry and consumer groups comment on anticipated and hoped for changes in policy. At election time, politicians are frequently accused of pork barreling, with firms and investors alike anticipating the heady mix of tax breaks, consumption and production subsidies and fiscal and monetary stimulation that accompanies changes in the political party in power, while parties are seen as pro- or anti-business and pro- or anti-investor. The author defines the political cycle in terms of the party in power, the time since the last election and election information effects. The results indicate returns are highest during the ministries of Holt–McEwen and Hawke and lowest during Whitlam and Fraser, while risk is highest during Whitlam and Hawke and lowest during Menzies and Holt–McEwen. However, regression analysis shows that Liberal–National and Labor governments more generally differ in the volatility of returns such that political cycle-sourced return volatility increases at a decreasing rate with the time in power. Such risk differences potentially arise from the different parties' economic and social policies, uncertainty among investors about these policies, or doubt among voters concerning future election outcomes.

In Chapter 7, Mohamed Habara and Andrew Worthington review credit-scoring models as quantitative tools used by lenders to evaluate credit risk. The authors provide a wide-ranging review of existing and novel parametric and nonparametric techniques used in credit score modelling. They also include a comprehensive survey of empirical work in the literature on credit-scoring models. This is a particularly useful contribution to our knowledge of modelling in that they include specific details of the samples and variables used by recent studies in this area. The main purpose of the chapter is to facilitate the selection of the variables and techniques used in constructing credit-scoring models by industry practitioners and academic researchers.

In Chapter 8, Omer Elsakit and Andrew Worthington discuss the modeling of social and environmental accounting disclosure practice throughout the world. The authors conclude that a range of determinants affect the motivation of firms to provide social and environmental information, and the adequacy and suitability of this type of information to assist decision makers. These include the impact on corporate governance and firm characteristics on differences in social and environmental disclosure practices by firms operating in similar or different sectors in terms of the level and quality of disclosure. Moreover, contextual factors are of significance when it comes to justifying these differences in disclosure practices by firms in different countries acting in similar and dissimilar sectors. The importance of contextual factors is evident by their impact on the expected influence of corporate governance and firm characteristics, which has prevented researchers generalizing the results of studies in countries not included in their samples and, thus, creating the need to conduct more research in different countries to consolidate these results. The most important contribution of this chapter is that it casts useful light on those factors suitable for modelling these behaviors, including include political, economic and cultural factors.

In Chapter 9, Andrew Worthington and Helen Higgs employ a multiple-input, multiple-output translog cost function model to calculate Allen–Uzawa and Morishima elasticities of substitution for Australian universities. The input prices are academic and nonacademic labor and capital. The six outputs are undergraduate, postgraduate and PhD completions, national competitive and industry grants, and publications. The results suggest that the derived demand for academic labor in the Australian university sector is highly price inelastic while the demand for nonacademic labor and capital is highly price elastic. This suggests that the cost drivers in the Australian university sector are presently price-related for academic inputs and technology-related for nonacademic and capital inputs. Moreover, the opportunities for input substitution are not symmetric, with the sector generally finding it easier to switch to capital than academic and nonacademic labor. Finally, while the Allen–Uzawa measures indicate that academic and nonacademic labor is a substitute, the less-restrictive Morishima measures suggest neither complementarity nor substitutability at the aggregate level.

In Chapter 10, Nancy Vu, Andrew C. Worthington, and Phillip Laird model the pricing and performance of ordinary, venture capital, and private equity-backed initial public offerings in the Australian stock market. The authors use headline underpricing, underpricing issuer loss, underpricing loss by market value, and underpricing loss by issue price to measure underpricing, and cumulative buy-and-hold abnormal returns with equal and value-weighted market indexes, market and book-to-market value quintile adjustments, and the Fama–French three-factor model to compare performance. The measures of underpricing indicate that venture capital and private equity-backed issues are underpriced less than ordinary issues. Further, all three forms of issuance outperform the nominal performance benchmarks. However, there is no statistically significant difference in the risk-adjusted performance of initial public offerings, regardless of backing.

In Chapter 11, Andrew Worthington models the technical operating and capital efficiency of major Australian urban water utilities using data envelopment analysis. After specifying different inputs and outputs for each measure of efficiency, the author makes allowance in his model for the inclusion of uncontrollable contextual inputs thought to impact upon the observed efficiency of utilities but largely outside their control. The results indicate that a relatively high level of relative operating and capital efficiency prevails across the sector. Measured efficiency is even higher after allowance for the scale of operations. However, a number of utilities exhibit inefficient behavior in operations and, to a lesser extent, in capital activities, and this is useful for providing target inputs, outputs, and sets of best-practice peers that utilities can focus on when making decisions affecting performance.

Finally, in Chapter 12, Mohamed Habara and Andrew Worthington use three standard statistical techniques, namely, discriminant analysis, logistic regression and survival analysis, to construct and evaluate a credit-scoring model for the Al-Wahada Bank in Libya. They randomly select 400 hundred loans for the analysis and specify 21 independent variables along with measures indicating loan default. The results indicate that five independent variables are common to all three models, which they consider the most important variables affecting the probability of loan default. With regard to a comparison of model performance, the results indicate that logistic regression performs better than either discriminant or survival analysis in this particular context. This chapter exemplifies the decisions modelers need to take in identifying better-performing models that best suit their decision-making needs.

The topics addressed in this volume are broad and range across a large number of different contexts. However, they share a common focus in the use of economic and financial modeling techniques in helping researchers to solve problems and make decisions concerning markets, institutions, and instruments. Each of the chapters illustrates well the complexity of modeling and some of the challenges faced when trying to simplify complex real world behavior and outcomes using models.

In: Economic and Financial Modeling
Editor: Andrew C. Worthington

ISBN: 978-1-63463-111-2

Chapter 2

Modeling the Pricing of Initial Public Offerings

Jirapun Chorruk[1] and Andrew C. Worthington[2*]
[1]Mahasarakham University, Thailand
[2]Griffith University, Australia

Abstract

This chapter examines the pricing and performance of initial public offerings (IPOs) in the Stock Exchange of Thailand (SET) from February 1997 to October 2008. Underpricing is calculated using headline underpricing, underpricing issuer loss, underpricing loss by market value, and underpricing loss by issuer price. The results show that average underpricing of 17.60%, 5.01%, 6.94%, 6.68%, and 16.10%, respectively. This is a significantly lower level of underpricing than previously documented in Thailand before the 1997 Asian financial crisis. We assess postlisting performance using monthly cumulative abnormal returns, buy-and-hold returns, and wealth relatives. These findings indicate that Thai IPOs generally outperform market benchmarks up to 24 months and underperform thereafter up to 36 months. However, there is much variation in long-run performance among industries. For example, multiple regression analysis shows that IPOs in the financial services industry perform relatively better in the longer run.

1. Introduction

From record highs in the fourth quarter of 2007, in terms of both the number of deals and capital raised, the global initial public offering (IPO) market has experienced successive dramatic declines and now lies at its lowest level in more than a decade. However, despite experiencing parallel impacts to developed markets in the aftermath of the global financial crisis, emerging markets are continuing to drive what little activity remains in the IPO market.

* Corresponding author: Department of Accounting, Finance and Economics, Griffith University, 170 Kessels Road, Nathan QLD 4111, Australia. Email. a.worthington@griffith.edu.au.

For example, in the March 2009 quarter developing economies made up 68% of the number of deals globally (albeit only 33% of total global capital raised) compared to developed economies, and six of the top ten IPOs and 12 of the top 20 IPOs by capital raised were from emerging markets. Of these, the Asia-Pacific was the leading region with a 72% market share with the Far East (South Korea, Japan, China/Hong Kong, Thailand, Singapore and Vietnam) accounting for the majority (Ernst and Young, 2009).

It is likely that the outcomes generated by the current economic situation will provide a similar watershed for emerging markets as the 1997 Asian financial crisis, of which Thailand represents an interesting case. From humble beginnings in 1975, the Stock Exchange of Thailand (SET) (2009a) experienced moderate IPO growth in its startup phase until 1987. From then until 1997, IPOs grew strongly in a period of rapid expansion, at which time the market entered a period of maturity and stabilization. By 2006, Thailand ranked highest in South-East Asia for total capital raised and the total number of completed IPOs (before Malaysia, Singapore, the Philippines, and Indonesia) and sixth in the Asia-Pacific (after China, Japan, India, South Korea and Australia (Ernst and Young, 2006).

However, there is considerable uncertainty in the current outlook, with both internal and external factors severely affecting the Thai capital market. In the first half of 2008, the global financial and oil price crises, and internal political instability negatively affected the capital market, with the Bank of Thailand failing to adequately stimulate the market. In the second half of 2008, the subprime loan crisis caused many local financial institutions to face a liquidity crisis with on flows to other sectors. In response, foreign investors have repatriated funds to meet margin calls and fund redemptions, with foreign investors in Thailand now net sellers (SET, 2009b). Overall, and in little more than a year, the SET has fallen by more than forty percent in market capitalization, dividend yields have doubled and price-earnings ratios halved, and local investors (institutional and otherwise) are accounting for an increasing share of turnover. It is therefore an opportune time to reflect on the most recent IPO development phase in this regionally important emerging market. Unfortunately, although a substantial amount of research of this type exists in the United States and elsewhere, Thai studies concerning principal aspects of IPOs, especially pricing and performance, are scarce and limited in scope. This chapter's principal objective is then to increase the depth of Thai research by examining the pricing and performance of initial public offers during the period 1997 to 2007.

The chapter is organized as follows. Section 2 discusses the Thai IPO market. Section 3 provides a brief literature review. Section 4 explains the methodology and Section 5 presents the empirical results. Section 6 contains some brief concluding remarks.

2. THAI IPO MARKET

The Thai equity market, as elsewhere, comprises a primary market and a secondary market. The primary market is where IPOs and subsequent issues are first made available to the public and lies under the supervision of the Thai Securities and Exchange Commission (SEC) (2009). A company wishing to issue an IPO must first apply for SEC approval and satisfy its filing requirements prior to allowing the company to list and trade on this market. However, in contrast to many other national markets, there are two primary markets in

Thailand: the Stock Exchange of Thailand (SET) (2009a) and the Market for Alternative Investments (mai) (2009). The SET is the main board for large public limited companies with at least 300 million baht (USD1 = THB35) of paid-up capital (SET 2008), while IPOs for small-and-medium-sized enterprises (SMEs) with paid-up capital between 20 and 300 million baht are generally able to list on the mai (mai 2008).

The SET was established in 1961 as an outcome of the Thai government's five-year National Economic and Social Development plan. The objective of this plan was to support the economic growth and stability of the country in addition to developing a higher standard of living. When the basic legislative framework was in place, the SET officially commenced trading on April 30, 1975. Since then, the SET has grown significantly in size and trading activities, with the total number of listed companies increasing from 21 in 1975 to 475 in 2007. Securities traded on the SET include common stock, preferred stock, depository receipts, unit trusts, warrants, derivative warrants, and transferable subscription rights. Trading of common stocks, however, dominates all other securities. By the end of 2007, the number of common stock issues had grown to 491 alongside 10 issues of preferred stock, 1 depository receipt, 8 unit trusts, and 71 warrants of various types; a total of 581 individual securities. The market value of trading reached 6,636,068.73 million baht with a daily average of 17,097.05 million baht over this same period. Currently in the Asia-Pacific, the SET is the fourteenth-largest market by capitalization, thirteenth largest in terms of the number of listed companies and twelfth fastest by turnover velocity (WFE, 2007).

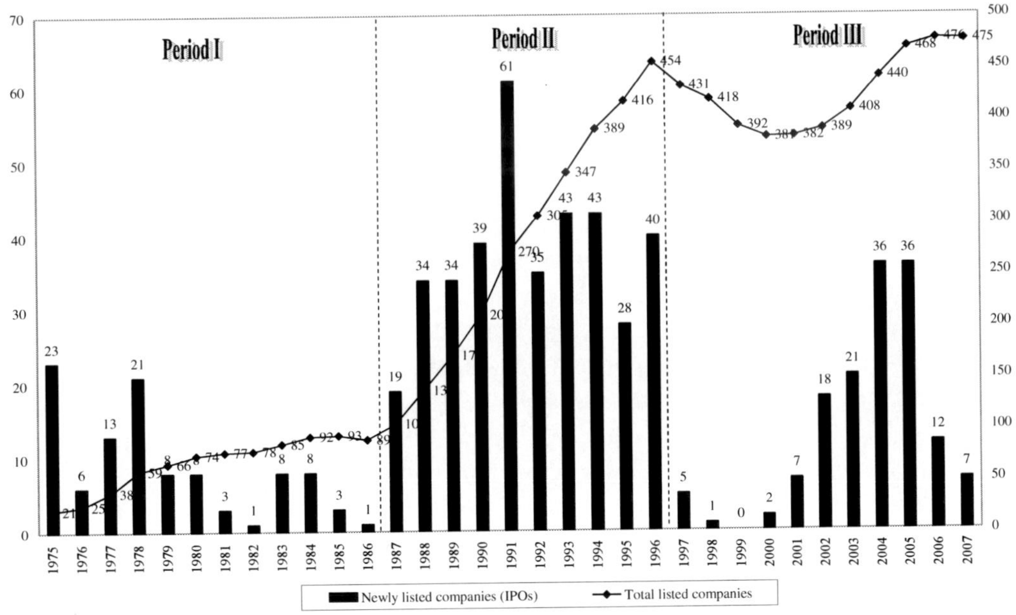

Figure 1. Number of newly listed and existing companies on the SET, 1975–2007.

As shown in Figure 1, past IPO activity in Thailand can be readily divided into three periods: (i) the period from 1975 to 1986; (ii) a period of rapid economic growth from 1987 to 1996; and (iii) a period of 'crisis' and 'post crisis' from 1997 to the present (Lonkani and Firth, 2005). During the first period, few IPOs listed on the market. From 1987 to 1996,

Thailand enjoyed rapid economic growth and many firms used the stock market as a major source for external funding. The third period began with the Asian financial crisis that started in July 1997. The effects of the crisis and its aftermath still linger today and, as a result, the number of IPOs remains below the levels set in the late 1980s and the early and mid-1990s.

During the first period, 103 IPOs were listing at an average rate of nine IPOs per year. However, the number of IPOs began to grow rapidly during the second period with 376 issues (or an average of 38 IPOs per year) by some 280 listed companies (an increase of 251.32 percent). By the third period, the number of total listed companies had increased by approximately 425.09 percent since the SET was established. During this time, only 200 IPOs were listed or just 18 IPOs per year. Nevertheless, since 1975 the total number of listed companies in the SET has on average increased by some 15 companies per year.

3. Review of the Literature

One of the more puzzling phenomena in finance is the underpricing of new stock issues. Various explanations are given, including information asymmetry, signaling relationships, cyclical behavior, and third-party certification. Foremost among these, the information asymmetry hypothesis sees underpricing as an equilibrium occurrence when investors are disproportionately informed. As uninformed investors face the consequences of poor judgment when other investors are better informed, underpricing arises to compensate uninformed investors for the risk of ending up with a less successful IPO.

Underpricing is clearly a concern for entrepreneurs, venture capitalists, and private equity investors, since it reduces the amount received by going public. However, one argument is that the extent of the entrepreneurs' concerns is limited to the influence on their net wealth. Costly action, such as employing reputable underwriters, is undertaken only where advantageous. In general, as the proportion of the company going public escalates, the existing investors in the firm attempt to reduce underpricing at an increasing rate. When informed investors believe an issue is overpriced, they discard the investment opportunity and seek issues elsewhere that are not overpriced.

An alternative rationale for underpricing is that the value of an issue depends on market demand and the underwriter's selling efforts. In general, the underwriter is typically aware of demand levels, more so than the issuer. As such, the issue price is set below its 'true value' to increase interest. Similarly, the issuer is more informed then potential investors. In an attempt to resolve problems with asymmetric information, the underwriter signals the true value of the firm by underpricing the securities and acquires a percentage of the shares. The retention of shares comes as a signaling device to the market—the higher the withholding, the higher the return expected.

Other work draws attention to the signaling relationship between the issuer's fractional holding of the firm's equity and the expected future cash flows. In response to these and other theoretical developments, a body of empirical research has arisen, largely in the US, concluding that IPOs are indeed underpriced [see, most recently, Ibbotson et al. (1994), Megginson and Weiss (1991), Hunt-McCool et al. (1996), Habib and Ljungqvist (1998; 2001), Francis and Hasan (2001), Bradley and Jordan (2002), Loughran and Ritter (1995; 2002)].

Relatively fewer studies concern IPO (under)pricing in Thailand, with all extant work focusing on the pre-1997 Asian financial crisis period [Wethyavivorn and Koo-Smith (1991), Allen et al. (1999), Lonkani (2000) and Lonkani and Firth (2005)]. For example, Wethayavivorn and Koo-Smith (1991) studied 32 IPOs over the period 1988–1989 and found that the average initial return was 56.73%. Similarly, using a sample of 150 IPOs from 1985 to 1992, Allen et al. (1999) reported that the average initial return for Thai IPOs was 63.49 percent, while Lonkani (2000) concluded that the average initial return was 46.70 percent using a sample of 292 IPOs from 1987 to 1997. Generally, and in common with evidence from developed markets, these studies provide evidence that IPOs in Thailand are also substantially underpriced.

However, previous IPO studies in Thailand do suffer from a number of limitations. First, they usually concern the period before the 1997 Asian financial crisis. That is, the period from 1975 to 1986 corresponding to the startup of the SET and/or the period of rapid economic growth from 1987 to 1996. No known study concerns the increasing maturity of the SET IPO market since 1997, as analyzed in this chapter. Second, previous studies employ only a single measure of underpricing, unlike the present analysis that employs five distinct measures that allow for the returns to existing owners, strategic shareholders, and primary and secondary shareholders. Combined together, these measures permit a better understanding of the impact of underpricing upon the parties most involved and affected by the IPO process.

In terms of performance, most of the extant work concurs with work in the US by Moonchul and Ritter (1999) that post-IPO firms generally underperform, as investors are overly optimistic about their potential when listed. However, Loughran and Ritter (1995) counter that underperformance is not a unique trait of IPOs rather a result of IPO firms being small with low book-to-market values. There are just a few recent studies of Thai IPO performance, including Allen et al. (1999) and Kim et al (2004). Allen et al (1999), for instance, studied 150 IPO listed on the SET from 1985 to 1992 and uncovered evidence of poor short-run aftermarket performance: the average market-adjusted cumulative abnormal return at the end of the listing month was –2.9 percent (t-value = 2.18). Nevertheless, they find no evidence for poor long-run performance up to 36 months after the IPO (with the exception of the first two months). Indeed, the average market-adjusted cumulative abnormal return at the end of a 36-month period is 10.02 percent, though not statistically significant.

However, when outliers are removed from cross-sectional analysis, there is still the suggestion that Thai IPOs may underperform on average in the long run. Moreover, aftermarket returns are higher with value-weighted adjustment of the benchmark suggesting that smaller firms have better performance. Once again, the aftermarket performance of Thai IPOs is similar to Wethyavivorn and Koo-Smith (1991) but contrasts with Ritter (1991), Levis (1993), Aggarwal et al. (1993) and Allen and Patrick (1994). Most recently, Kim et al. (2004) suggest evidence of a long-term decline of operating performance for IPO firms in Thailand using a sample of 133 SET IPOs from 1987 to 1993. Once again, existing work on post-listing IPO performance in Thailand suffers from a number of deficiencies. Putting aside the lack of currency in these studies discussed earlier, they invariable employ only one or two measures of stock performance.

In contrast, the present analysis conducts comparisons of post-listing performance of Thai IPOs using three measures: namely, cumulative abnormal returns, buy-and-hold returns, and wealth relatives.

4. METHODOLOGY

A review of the extant literature on the pricing and performance of IPOs suggests two broad hypotheses. First, Thai IPOs are underpriced. Second, Thai IPOs underperform post-listing. In order to test the first set of hypotheses, four complementary measures of underpricing are calculated: headline underpricing, underpricing issuer loss, underpricing loss by market value, and underpricing loss by issue price (Habib and Ljungqvist, 1998; Silva Rosa et al., 2003). To test the second set of hypotheses, monthly average cumulative abnormal returns (CAR), buy-and-hold returns (BHR) and wealth relatives (WR) are calculated. We also employ multivariate regressions to examine aftermarket performance (Ritter 1991; Loughran and Ritter 1995).

4.1. Sample Selection and Data Sources

The sample comprises 136 IPOs listed on the SET from February 1997 to November 2007. This compares favorably with the population of 145 IPOs listed; nine listings were excluded from the sample because of incomplete data. Observations on the issue and first day closing prices are from the SETSMART (SET Market Analysis and Reporting Tool). This web-based application obtained from the SET seamlessly integrates the various sources of Thai listed company data, including historical stock prices, indices, listed company profiles, and news. Details of the distribution of the IPO (number of primary and secondary shares and total shares) are from the official prospectus filing form (Form 69-1) available on the IPO filing database provided by the Capital Market Information Centre at the SEC.

Other information is from the SET Fact Book series 1997–2007. The proportion of free float and strategic shareholders (the proportion of shares retained by the firm) are from the Information and Communication Technology Department at the SEC. For the performance assessment, the sample comprises 142 IPOs of total 145 newly listed on the SET from February 1997 to November 2007; three listing were excluded from the sample because of incomplete data. Data on issue prices, first month closing prices, monthly stock prices, and the SET index are also from SETSMART. We use these to compute the aftermarket performance of Thai IPOs from February 1997 to October 2008.

4.2. Measures of Underpricing

The four underpricing measures used in this study are adapted from Habib and Ljungqvist (1999) and Silva Rosa et al. (2003). First, headline underpricing (*UPH*) is a traditional measure of underpricing:

$$UPH = \frac{(P_c - P_i)}{P_i} \tag{1}$$

where P_c is the closing price on the first day of trading and P_i is the issue price of the company *i*. Second, underpricing issuer loss (*UPIL*) determines the loss to the issuer per share:

$$UPIL = (1 - \text{Strategic Shareholders}) \times \frac{(P_c - P_i)}{P_i} \tag{2}$$

where strategic shareholders is the portion of ownership of the firm retained or the proportion of shares held by the shareholders for the purpose of company management or business strategy and all other variables are as previously defined. Strategic shareholders are equal to 100% minus the percentage in the free float. Free float is the proportion of shares not held by strategic shareholders and not reacquired by the issuing company. This is estimated from the company's shareholder register as of the latest registered book-closing date for the general meeting in each year and is adjusted for subsequent changes in ownership structure.

Third, underpricing loss by market value (*UPLMV*) is the underpricing loss standardized by the firm's market value:

$$UPLMV = \frac{(P_c - P_i) \times (\text{Secondary} + \text{Strategic} \times \text{Primary})}{P_c \times \text{Total shares}} \tag{3}$$

where secondary shares are the number of shares held by pre-IPO shareholders, primary shares are the number of new shares offered in the IPO and total shares are the total shares on issue for the post-IPO firm. Finally, the underpricing loss by issue price (*UPLIP*) shows the loss to the issuer standardized by the value of the firm based on the issue price.

$$UPLIP = \frac{(P_c - P_i) \times (\text{Secondary} + \text{Strategic} \times \text{Primary})}{P_i \times \text{Total shares}} \tag{4}$$

We calculate the four underpricing measures in Equations (1)–(4) for each firm in the sample and compile the mean and median values. Finally, we calculate a value-weighted measure of each underpricing measure using:

$$\sum_i (\text{Total shares}_i \times UP_i) \Big/ \sum_i \text{Total shares}_i \tag{5}$$

where UP_i is *UPSTD*, *UPIL*, *UPLMV* and *UPLIP*, respectively. This measure of underpricing takes into account a firm's size relative to the level of underpricing.

4.3. Measures of Aftermarket Performance

The methodology used to measure IPO performance follows Ritter (1991), Brav and Gromper (1997) and Lyon et al. (1999) in the compilation of monthly (1) cumulative abnormal (CARs) (2) buy-and-hold returns (BHRs) and (3) wealth relatives (WRs). The assumptions and purposes of these alternative measures of performance vary. First, CARs are a traditional performance measure calculated as the accumulated differences between the average initial return and the average benchmark return.

Second, BHRs reflect the returns on a strategy of investing in an average sample company and deducting the return on a corresponding benchmark (market, industry, sector index) over the investment horizon. For instance, Barber and Lyon (1997) and Lyon et al (1999) argue that the investor experience is better captured by compounding short-term returns (for example, at monthly intervals) to obtain the long-term holding period abnormal return. Finally, WRs provide an overall indicator of long-term performance by calculating the ratio of the end-of-period wealth from a portfolio of issuers to the end-of-period wealth from a portfolio of market benchmarks.

The CARs are calculated in the following manner. First, the raw return for company i for event month t is measured as:

$$R_{it} = \frac{(P_c - P_i)}{P_i} \tag{6}$$

where R_{it} is the monthly raw return for company i in event month t where the starting price for each company is its last price for the month of listing, excluding the initial return, P_c is the closing price on the first month of listing, and P_i is the issue price of company i. We first calculate the monthly raw return from months 1 to 36 or until delisting for each company.

The event month is the month following the listing month. Second, benchmark returns for company i is calculated in the same way as the raw return as follows:

$$R_{bencht} = \frac{(P_{c-bench} - P_{i-bench})}{P_{i-bench}} \tag{7}$$

where R_{bencht} is the monthly benchmark return on company i, $P_{c\text{-}bench}$ is the closing price of the benchmark on the first listing month and $P_{i\text{-}bench}$ is the closing price of the benchmark on the previous month. Third, benchmark-adjusted returns are computed as the difference between the raw returns of company i and the return on the benchmark portfolio over the same period.

$$AR_{it} = R_{it} - R_{bencht} \tag{8}$$

Fourth, the average benchmark-adjusted return for month t on a portfolio of n stocks for event month t is the value-weighted arithmetic mean of the benchmark-adjusted returns:

$$\overline{AR_{it}} = \frac{1}{n}\sum_{i=1}^{n} AR_{it} \tag{9}$$

Finally, the cumulative average benchmark-adjusted returns from event month 1 to event month t are defined by $\overline{CAR_{1,t}}$. This is calculated adding the average benchmark adjusted returns ($\overline{AR_{it}}$) over various intervals during the 36-month aftermarket period.

$$\overline{CAR_{1,t}} = \sum_{t=1}^{t} \overline{AR_{it}} \tag{10}$$

To assess whether the cumulative average benchmark-adjusted returns are significantly different from zero, studentised t-tests for cumulative average benchmark adjusted returns are:

$$CAR\_t_{month} = \frac{\overline{CAR_{1,t}}}{\sigma\left(CAR_{1,t}\right)/\sqrt{n}} \tag{11}$$

where σ is the sample standard deviation of abnormal returns and n is the number of IPOs.

The BHRs are from the following series.

First, the buy-and-hold return for company i, denoted as BHR_{it}, excluding the initial return on the first trading day, is defined as:

$$BHR_{it} = \left(\prod_{t=start}^{\min(T,delist)} (1+R_{it}) - 1\right) \tag{12}$$

Second, the benchmark buy-and-hold return, denoted as BHR_{bencht}, is calculated in the same manner:

$$BHR_{bencht} = \left(\prod_{t=start}^{\min(T,delist)} (1+R_{bencht}) - 1\right) \tag{13}$$

Third, the benchmark-adjusted buy-and-hold returns for each company, $BHAR_{it}$, is calculated by deducting the buy-and-hold return for the company i with the return of benchmark portfolio as follows:

$$BHAR_{it} = BHR_{it} - BHR_{bencht} \tag{14}$$

Fourth, the average buy-and-hold return for a period t, denoted as $\overline{BHAR_{it}}$, is the arithmetic mean abnormal return on all IPOs in the sample of size n:

$$\overline{BHAR_{it}} = \frac{1}{n}\sum_{i=1}^{n} BHAR_{it} \tag{15}$$

Finally, the positive (negative) value of *BHAR* indicates that IPOs outperform (underperform) a portfolio of benchmarks. To test whether the average buy-and-hold return is different from zero for the sample of IPO, a *t*-test is calculated:

$$BHAR\_t_{month} = \frac{\overline{BHAR_{it}}}{\sigma\left(BHAR_{it}\right)/\sqrt{n}} \tag{16}$$

where σ is the sample standard deviation of abnormal returns.

The final measure of IPO performance is the wealth relatives from the three-year total buy-and-hold returns. We define these as the ratio of the end-of-period wealth from holding a portfolio of issuers to the end-of-period wealth from holding a portfolio of benchmarks, given by

$$WR_{it} = \frac{1+\overline{BHR_{it}}}{1+\overline{BHR_{bencht}}} \tag{17}$$

We can interpret a wealth relative of greater than unity as meaning that an IPO outperformed a portfolio of benchmarks, whereas a wealth relative of less than unity indicates that the IPO underperformed.

4.4. Regression Analysis

Previous studies also suggest that the initial return and the issue size have a negative effect on long-run performance. For example, Ritter (1991) finds that there is the negative correlation between initial return and aftermarket performance while Allen et al. (1999) suggest that issue size has a negative effect on long-run returns. They also find that market return is likely to have positive relation with 2-year return. However, Ritter (1991) argues that age appears to be a better proxy for ex-ante uncertainty than issue size and concludes that younger IPOs have poorer aftermarket performance. Ritter (1991) also suggests there is a negative relation between volume and aftermarket performance due to the bad luck, overoptimistic forecasts, or fads of investors. Therefore, to test the effects of issue size, initial return, annual volume, market returns, and industry (as a dummy variable to test IPOs performance across industry) on the three-year buy-and-hold return and three-year benchmark-adjusted buy-and-hold return, regression analyses clarify the effect of each factor. Unfortunately, firm age is poorly defined in the sample data and is not included in the analysis. The multiple regressions used are:

$$3BHR_i = \beta_0 + \beta_1 RTN_i + \beta_2 SLE_i + \beta_3 VOL_i + \beta_4 MAR_i + \beta_5 IND_i + \varepsilon_i \tag{18}$$

$$3BHAR_i = \beta_0 + \beta_1 RTN_i + \beta_2 SLE_i + \beta_3 VOL_i + \beta_4 MAR_i + \beta_5 IND_i + \varepsilon_i \tag{19}$$

where the dependent variables are the three-year buy-and-hold return ($3BHR_i$) and the three-year benchmark-adjusted buy-and-hold return ($3BHAR_i$). The explanatory variables are the monthly raw return excluding the initial return (*RTN*), the issue size in millions of baht (*SLE*), the number of IPOs each year (*VOL*), the three-year benchmark buy-and-hold return for the market over the same period as the IPO_i (*MAR*) and various dummy variables (*IND*) for industry in which the IPO_i operates.

5. Empirical Results

5.1. Underpricing

Table 1 presents the headline underpricing (*UPH*), underpricing issuer loss (*UPIL*), underpricing loss by market value (*UPLMV*), and underpricing loss by issue price (*UPLIP*) measures for the sample of 136 IPOs listed on the SET from 1997–2007. Over the full sample period, 17.60% headline underpriced, 6.94% are issuer loss underpriced, 6.68% are issuer price underpriced and 16.10% are market value loss underpriced. These results generally indicate that Thai IPOs are less underpriced than those in most developed markets are. However, there is substantial variability in the magnitude of underpricing over the sample period. For example, the average headline underpricing between 1997 and 2007 is –20.39% (overpriced), –1.44% (overpriced), 36.78%, 14.86%, 50.05%, 14.05%, 10.28%, 1.45%, and 26.42%, respectively.

Table 1. IPO underpricing in percentages by year of issuance

Year(s)	Statistic	UPH	UPIL	UPLMV	UPLIP
1997–2007 (136)	Mean	17.6000	6.9400	6.6800	16.1000
	Median	3.1000	1.4100	2.7500	2.8300
	Std dev.	0.3780	0.1586	0.2556	0.3498
	t-statistic	5.4308	5.1025	3.0466	5.3662
	p-value	0.0000	0.0000	0.0028	0.0000
	Value-weighted	7.1400	3.3100	1.1400	6.4400
1997 (4)	Mean	–20.3900	–11.3300	–58.2800	–18.8000
	Median	–31.5100	–8.7700	–58.2300	–29.1100
	Std dev.	0.4824	0.2101	0.7987	0.4296
	t-statistic	–0.8453	–1.0784	–1.4594	–0.8754
	p-value	0.4601	0.3598	0.2406	0.4458
	Value-weighted	–8.1300	–7.4000	–48.7100	–8.1700
2000 (2)	Mean	–1.4400	–2.7000	–2.7000	–1.5500
	Median	–1.4400	–2.7000	–2.7000	–1.5500
	Std dev.	0.1564	0.0925	0.1425	0.1362
	t-statistic	–0.1304	–0.4126	–0.2684	–0.1610
	p-value	0.9174	0.7509	0.8331	0.8983
	Value-weighted	8.6000	3.2400	6.4400	7.1900
2001 (7)	Mean	36.7800	12.5700	15.3400	33.5300
	Median	21.7100	7.1600	14.7200	17.9200

Table 1. (Continued)

Year(s)	Statistic	UPH	UPIL	UPLMV	UPLIP
	Std dev.	0.6148	0.1811	0.2505	0.5930
	t-statistic	1.5830	1.8367	1.6206	1.4960
	p-value	0.1645	0.1159	0.1562	0.1853
	Value-weighted	6.3600	2.6300	2.9600	5.4800
2002 (16)	Mean	14.8600	6.7100	7.2700	13.2300
	Median	0.7400	0.3900	0.6500	0.6500
	Std dev.	0.3276	0.1640	0.1638	0.2915
	t-statistic	1.8148	1.6367	1.7739	1.8157
	p-value	0.0896	0.1225	0.0964	0.0895
	Value-weighted	9.3600	4.1200	5.3200	8.3900
2003 (19)	Mean	50.0500	19.6100	24.3700	46.3800
	Median	39.2900	14.0600	24.0400	32.0600
	Std dev.	0.4553	0.1917	0.2479	0.4320
	t-statistic	4.7915	4.4599	4.2858	4.6804
	p-value	0.0001	0.0003	0.0004	0.0002
	Value-weighted	60.1200	22.6700	28.9400	110.3200
2004 (36)	Mean	14.0500	5.4500	6.2000	12.9600
	Median	4.6200	1.5700	4.1900	4.4200
	Std dev.	0.3197	0.1253	0.1977	0.2951
	t-statistic	2.6371	2.6082	1.8824	2.6360
	p-value	0.0124	0.0133	0.0681	0.0124
	Value-weighted	9.5000	4.9300	2.4300	8.5300
2005 (34)	Mean	10.2800	3.8200	5.1200	9.3900
	Median	2.6000	0.5800	2.3400	2.3900
	Std dev.	0.2431	0.0946	0.1640	0.2257
	t-statistic	2.4662	2.3562	1.8192	2.4257
	p-value	0.0190	0.0246	0.0780	0.0209
	Value-weighted	7.3200	2.5900	3.2700	6.7200
2006 (11)	Mean	1.4500	1.7800	–0.1500	1.0700
	Median	–1.2500	–0.3200	–1.1900	–1.1700
	Std dev.	0.1352	0.0917	0.1025	0.1177
	t-statistic	0.3552	0.6444	–0.0493	0.3025
	p-value	0.7298	0.5338	0.9617	0.7685
	Value-weighted	–7.7300	–2.3100	–9.0600	–15.3900
2007 (6)	Mean	26.4200	13.4200	10.3400	23.2800
	Median	3.7300	1.1100	3.4500	3.5900
	Std dev.	0.5910	0.3118	0.2089	0.5168
	t-statistic	1.0948	1.0547	1.2127	1.1034
	p-value	0.3235	0.3398	0.2794	0.3201
	Value-weighted	12.8700	6.1900	5.9100	11.5500

Notes: Number of IPOs in year/period in brackets. Statistics only provided where number of IPOs in year are greater than 1. UPH – headline underpricing, UPIL – underpricing issuer loss, UPLMV – underpricing loss by market value, and UPLIP – underpricing loss by issue price. *t*-statistics and *p*-values are tests of null hypothesis that means are equal to zero.

Table 2 provides average headline underpricing (*UPH*), underpricing issuer loss (*UPIL*), underpricing loss by market value (*UPLMV*), and underpricing loss by issue price (*UPLIP*) by industry. The results show that IPOs from the resource and financial industries are the most underpriced (38.09% and 29.74%, respectively) in terms of headline underpricing whereas IPOs in the industrial and consumer product industries are the least underpriced (2.00% and 2.19%, respectively). This contrast with earlier work by Allen et al (1999) that the property and construction industry has the highest initial IPO return of 215.09% among industries while the financial services industry has the lowest (22.37%).

Table 2. IPO underpricing in percentages by industry

Industry	Underpricing	UPH	UPIL	UPLMV	UPLIP
AGRO (4)	Mean	2.9200	0.2400	2.4900	2.8500
	Median	1.4000	0.2400	2.4900	2.6800
	Std dev.	0.0572	0.0103	0.0507	0.0556
	t-statistic	1.0209	0.4550	0.9817	1.0272
	p-value	0.3825	0.6800	0.3986	0.3799
	Value-weighted	3.3800	0.4900	0.5600	0.0000
CONSUMP (2)	Mean	–2.1900	–0.3700	–2.2100	–2.1100
	Median	–2.1900	–0.3700	–2.2100	–2.1100
	Std dev.	0.0219	0.0037	0.0221	0.0211
	t-statistic	–1.4142	–1.4142	–1.4142	–1.4142
	p-value	0.3918	0.3918	0.3918	0.3918
	Value-weighted	–1.8800	–0.3200	–1.8900	–1.8100
FINCIAL (21)	Mean	29.7400	10.2700	14.5700	27.8600
	Median	12.2700	3.0000	10.4000	11.6700
	Std dev.	0.4717	0.1614	0.1985	0.4551
	t-statistic	2.8896	2.9171	3.3640	2.8056
	p-value	0.0091	0.0085	0.0031	0.0109
	Value-weighted	40.5300	15.6400	21.2700	38.0800
INDUS (18)	Mean	2.0000	–0.7800	–9.8200	2.2200
	Median	–0.0100	–0.1500	–0.0400	–0.0200
	Std dev.	0.3238	0.1285	0.4383	0.3002
	t-statistic	0.2626	–0.2560	–0.9502	0.3134
	p-value	0.7960	0.8010	0.3553	0.7578
	Value-weighted	9.4200	2.6800	1.6500	8.9300
PROPCON (39)	Mean	11.9700	4.8100	4.6300	10.6700
	Median	2.2200	0.6000	2.0500	2.0900
	Std dev.	0.2997	0.1108	0.1904	0.2768
	t-statistic	2.4946	2.7120	1.5187	2.4085
	p-value	0.0171	0.0100	0.1371	0.0210
	Value-weighted	–4.4000	–1.2500	–8.1100	–4.4600
RESOURC (11)	Mean	38.0900	16.5700	21.2000	34.4800
	Median	37.5000	11.5400	26.1300	36.6800
	Std dev.	0.3310	0.1561	0.1631	0.2982
	t-statistic	3.8174	3.5212	4.3119	3.8348
	p-value	0.0034	0.0055	0.0015	0.0033
	Value-weighted	18.9200	8.8000	11.7700	17.6600
SERVICE (21)	Mean	17.2400	8.8100	7.5300	15.3600

Table 2. (Continued)

Industry	Underpricing	UPH	UPIL	UPLMV	UPLIP
	Median	3.1300	1.7200	2.7400	2.8200
	Std dev.	0.3861	0.2089	0.1788	0.3396
	t-statistic	2.0467	1.9333	1.9311	2.0721
	p-value	0.0541	0.0675	0.0678	0.0514
	Value-weighted	6.0200	3.5400	1.7800	5.1800
TECH (20)	Mean	23.9100	9.3500	10.0700	21.9500
	Median	14.1300	5.4200	11.1800	12.8100
	Std dev.	0.4063	0.1720	0.2482	0.3755
	t-statistic	2.6313	2.4306	1.8138	2.6144
	p-value	0.0164	0.0251	0.0855	0.0171
	Value-weighted	17.1100	6.5900	8.0400	15.8100

Notes: Number of IPOs in industry in brackets. Statistics only provided where number of IPOs in industry are greater than 1. UPH – headline underpricing, UPIL – underpricing issuer loss, UPLMV – underpricing loss by market value, and UPLIP – underpricing loss by issue price. AGRO – agricultural and food, CONSUMP – consumer products, FINCIAL – financial and banking, INDUS – industrial, PROPCON – property and construction, RESOURC – resources, and TECH – technology. *t*-statistics and *p*-values are tests of null hypothesis that means are equal to zero

5.2. Aftermarket Performance

Figure 2 graphs the monthly average raw return, benchmark-adjusted return and cumulative benchmark-adjusted return for the 142 IPOs included in the sample up to 36 months. Most critically, the cumulative benchmark-adjusted return is above zero up until month 24 and then drops below zero for the remainder of the observation period. This suggests that Thai IPOs at first outperform the market benchmark, but their longer run performance is generally poor.

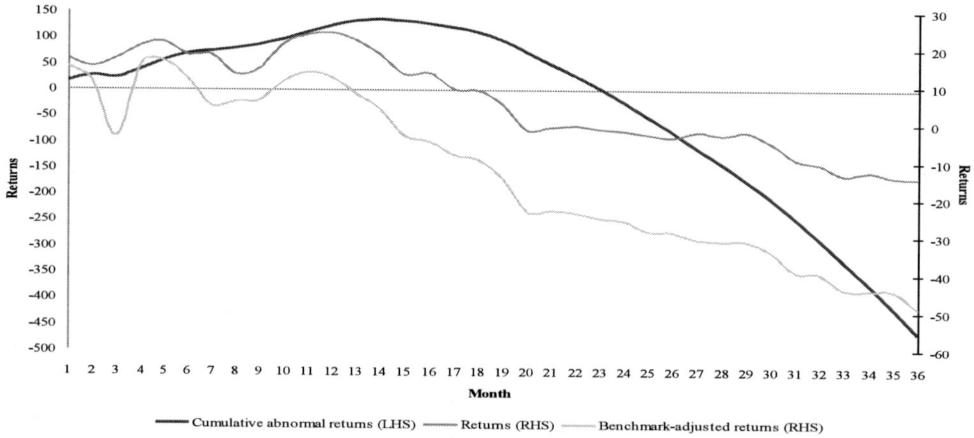

Note: Monthly returns are from the first full month of trading post-IPO to month 36, delisting or end of sample period.

Figure 2. Average and benchmark-adjusted returns and cumulative benchmark-adjusted returns by post-IPO month.

Table 3. Average buy-and-hold returns and wealth relatives excluding initial return

Month	Size	$\overline{BHAR_{it}}$	Std. dev	t-stat	p-value	WR_{it}
1	141	15.4233	0.4699	3.8977	0.0002	6.1368
2	142	12.5950	0.4756	3.1556	0.0020	4.1855
3	142	11.8892	0.4869	2.9098	0.0042	3.4796
4	141	12.6104	0.4966	3.0156	0.0030	3.6130
5	141	12.9219	0.5106	3.0048	0.0031	3.5682
6	140	12.4124	0.5211	2.8181	0.0055	3.2801
7	140	11.7535	0.5323	2.6124	0.0100	3.0596
8	140	10.4675	0.5391	2.2973	0.0231	2.7502
9	141	9.3317	0.5396	2.0534	0.0419	2.4704
10	141	8.8202	0.5514	1.8993	0.0596	2.3155
11	141	8.5515	0.5613	1.8091	0.0726	2.2651
12	140	8.1388	0.5723	1.6828	0.0947	2.1201
13	138	–8.4137	1.2563	–0.7867	0.4328	1.1512
14	138	5.4494	0.5805	1.1028	0.2720	1.6376
15	138	4.1183	0.5831	0.8296	0.4082	1.4569
16	138	2.7027	0.5881	0.5399	0.5902	1.2773
17	136	1.7799	0.5950	0.3488	0.7278	1.1826
18	135	0.6544	0.6005	0.1266	0.8994	1.0639
19	134	–0.5848	0.6050	–0.1119	0.9111	0.9456
20	133	–3.1628	0.6150	–0.5931	0.5541	0.7184
21	131	–3.9676	0.6073	–0.7478	0.4559	0.6561
22	131	–5.3648	0.6064	–1.0126	0.3131	0.5545
23	131	–6.7777	0.6071	–1.2779	0.2036	0.4586
24	131	–8.1023	0.6076	–1.5262	0.1294	0.3746
25	131	–9.2451	0.6084	–1.7392	0.0844	0.3157
26	129	–11.3410	0.6105	–2.1100	0.0368	0.1864
27	125	–12.1316	0.6227	–2.1782	0.0313	0.1833
28	125	–13.6655	0.6245	–2.4465	0.0158	0.0905
29	122	–15.2922	0.6332	–2.6674	0.0087	0.0227
30	123	–15.7789	0.6358	–2.7523	0.0068	0.0204
31	121	–17.3464	0.6378	–2.9918	0.0034	–0.0294
32	121	–18.3996	0.6363	–3.1811	0.0019	–0.0798
33	119	–19.6274	0.6340	–3.3773	0.0010	–0.1116
34	119	–20.9393	0.6279	–3.6381	0.0004	–0.1559
35	119	–21.7356	0.6227	–3.8077	0.0002	–0.1757
36	110	–25.3903	0.6198	–4.2966	0.0000	–0.3037

Table 3 provides additional detail on the benchmark-adjusted returns and cumulative benchmark-adjusted returns. Table 3 reports the average buy-and-hold returns and wealth relatives, exclusive of the initial returns on the first day of trading up to 36 months after listing. The results show that IPO companies begin underperforming in terms of *BHAR* at the end of month 19 (an average of –0.58%), as also evidenced by a wealth relative less than unity (0.95%). The 36-month average buy-and-hold return is –25.39%, with a statistical significant t-statistic of 4.30. This is of considerably greater magnitude than the underperformance of IPOs found in the US by Ritter (1991) and Welch and Ritter (2002) and in Germany by Ljungqvist (1997) and Stehle et al (2000).

5.3. Regression Analysis

Table 4 provides the regression estimates using the three-year buy-and-hold return as the dependent variable. These results suggest that there is a positive effect of monthly returns (RTN), as in Allen et al (1999), on three-year buy-and-hold returns. However, in contrast to Ritter (1991) and Allen and Patrick (1994), there is no significant negative relationship between issue size (SZE) and issue volume (VOL) on three-year buy-and-hold returns.

Table 4. Multiple regression estimates

	Estimated coefficient	Standard error	t-statistic	p-value
Constant	0.0237	0.1639	0.1444	0.8855
RTN	0.5924	0.0610	9.7106	0.0000
SZE	–0.0007	0.0004	–1.6040	0.1119
VOL	–0.0014	0.0041	–0.3284	0.7433
MAR	0.1817	0.1999	0.9088	0.3656
AGRO	–0.1762	0.2471	–0.7132	0.4774
FINCIAL	0.2484	0.1310	1.8963	0.0608
INDUS	–0.0209	0.1382	–0.1512	0.8801
RESOURC	–0.0693	0.1754	–0.3950	0.6937
SERVICE	–0.0667	0.1333	–0.5002	0.6181
TECH	0.0731	0.1356	0.5395	0.5908

Notes: Dependent variable is three-year buy-and-hold returns (3BHR). Industry dummies are agricultural and food (AGRO), financial and banking industry (FINCIAL), industrial (INDUS), resources (RESOURC), services (SERVICE) and technology (TECH). Consumer products (CONSUMP) have only a single IPO and are excluded. Coefficient of property and construction (PROPCON) excluded due to tolerance = 0.000 [tolerance = $1\text{-}R^2$ or (correlation between the predictor and all other predictors)^2].

Table 5 presents the estimated results of a regression analysis using three-year benchmark-adjusted buy-and-hold returns as the dependent variable. The results again suggest the positive effect of monthly returns (*RTN*) on three-year benchmark-adjusted buy-and-hold returns, while issue size (*SZE*), issue volume (*VOL*) and the market benchmark return (*MAR*) are insignificant. Combined together, these findings suggest that the post-listing performance of IPOs, at least in Thailand, relates to initial return (*RTN*), but is not significantly related to either overall IPO activity (*VOL*), the size of the IPO (*SZE*), or the performance of the market (*MAR*).

Of the industry dummy variables in Tables 5 and 6, only the estimated coefficient for the financial services industry is significant and positive. This indicates that only companies in the financial services industry perform consistently better post-listing (excluding the initial return). This finding is similar to Allen et al (1999).

Table 5. Multiple regression estimates

	Estimated coefficient	Standard error	t-statistic	p-value
Constant	0.0237	0.1639	0.1444	0.8855
RTN	0.5924	0.0610	9.7106	0.0000
SZE	–0.0007	0.0004	–1.6040	0.1119
VOL	–0.0014	0.0041	–0.3284	0.7433
MAR	–0.8183	0.1999	–4.0942	0.0001
AGRO	–0.1762	0.2471	–0.7132	0.4774
FINCIAL	0.2484	0.1310	1.8963	0.0608
INDUS	–0.0209	0.1382	–0.1512	0.8801
RESOURC	–0.0693	0.1754	–0.3950	0.6937
SERVICE	–0.0667	0.1333	–0.5002	0.6181
TECH	0.0731	0.1356	0.5395	0.5908

Notes: Dependent variable is three-year benchmark-adjusted buy-and-hold returns (3BHAR). Industry dummies are agricultural and food (AGRO), financial and banking industry (FINCIAL), industrial (INDUS), property and construction (PROPCON), resources (RESOURC), services (SERVICE) and technology (TECH). Consumer products (CONSUMP) have only a single IPO and are excluded. Coefficient of property and construction (PROPCON) excluded due to tolerance = 0.000 [tolerance = 1-R^2 or (correlation between the predictor and all other predictors)^2].

CONCLUSION

This chapter examined the pricing and performance of initial public offerings in the main board of the Thai stock exchange from February 1997 to October 2008. Underpricing is calculated using headline underpricing, underpricing issuer loss, underpricing loss by market value, and underpricing loss by issuer price. Aftermarket performance is calculated using monthly cumulative abnormal returns, buy-and-hold returns and wealth relatives. Regression analysis is also used to control for other impacts on firm performance, including overall IPO activity, market performance, and size effects, and to compare aftermarket performance across industries.

In term of underpricing, the results indicate that Thai IPOs are underpriced, although the magnitude of underpricing is generally smaller than found in many developed markets using similar techniques. However, unlike many of these comparable studies, there is no evidence that IPO underpricing has decreased in the recent years. The measures of underpricing across industry suggest that financial services IPOs are relatively more underpriced whereas industrial IPOs are relatively underpriced. This contrasts strongly with Allen et al (1999) who find that the property and construction industry often has the highest initial return.

In term of performance, monthly cumulative abnormal and buy-and-hold returns and wealth relatives show that Thai IPOs underperform relative to the market at the end of a 36-month post-listing period. However, they generally outperform the market up to 24 months after listing. Regression analysis also provides evidence to support the notion that there is a significant positive relationship between monthly returns and buy-and-hold returns, even after controlling for size, volume, and activity in the IPO market. Further, financial services firms appear to display the best long-run performance in the Thai market.

REFERENCES

Aggarwal, R., Leal, R., and Hernanmdez, L. (1993). The aftermarket performance of initial public offerings in Latin America, *Financial Management*, 22, 42–53.

Aggarwal, R. and Pietra, R. (1990). Fads in the initial public offering market? *Financial Management*, 19, 45–57.

Allen, F. and Faulhaber, G.R. (1989), Signaling by underpricing in the IPO market. *Journal of Financial Economic*, 23, 303–323.

Allen, D.E., Morkel-Kingsbury, N.J. and Piboonthanakiat, W. (1999). The long-run performance of initial public offerings in Thailand. *Applied Financial Economics*, 9, 215–232.

Barber, B. and Lyon, J. (1996). Detecting abnormal operating performance: The empirical power and specification of test statistics. *Journal of Financial Economics*, 41, 359–399.

Bradley D. J. and Jordan, B.D. (2002). Partial Adjustment to public information and IPO underpricing. *Journal of Financial and Quantitative Analysis*, 37, 595–616.

Brav, A. and Gompers, P.A. (1997). Myth or Reality? The long-run underperformance of initial public offerings: Evidence from venture and non-venture capital-backed companies. *Journal of Finance*, 52, 1791–1821.

Brennan, M. and Franks, J. (1997). Underpricing, ownership and control in initial public offerings of equity securities in the United Kingdom. *Journal of Financial Economics*, 45, 391–413.

Brooks, R. and Dimovski, W. (2004). Initial public offerings in Australia 1994 to 1999, Recent evidence of underpricing and underperformance. *Review of Quantitative Finance and Accounting*, 22, 179–198.

Carter, R., Dark, F. and Singh, A. (1998). Underwriter reputation, initial returns, and the long-run performance of IPO stocks. *Journal of Finance*, 53, 285–312.

Ernst & Young (2006). Accelerating growth: Global IPO trends 2006. Available at http://www.ey.com/. Accessed August 2014.

Ernst & Young (2009). Q1's 09 global IPO update. Available at http://www.ey.com/ Accessed August 2014.

Francis, B.B. and Hasan, I. (2001). The underpricing of venture and nonventure capital IPOs: An empirical investigation. *Journal of Financial Services Research*, 19, 99–113.

Habib, M.A. and Ljungqvist, A.P. (1998). Underpricing and IPO proceeds: A note. *Economic Letters*, 61, 381–383.

Habib, M.A. and Ljungqvist, A.P. (2001). Underpricing and entrepreneurial wealth losses in IPOs: Theory and evidence. *Review of Financial Studies*, 14, 433–458.

Hunt-McCool, J., Koh, S.C. and Francis, B.B. (1996). Testing for deliberate underpricing in the IPO premarket: A stochastic frontier approach. *Review of Financial Studies*, 9, 1251–1269.

Ibbotson, R.G., Sindelar, J.L. and Ritter, J.R. (1994). The market's problems with the pricing of initial public offerings. *Journal of Applied Corporate Finance*, 7, 66–74.

Ibbotson, R.G. (1975). Price performance of common stock new issues. *Journal of Financial Economics,* 2, 235–272.

Jain, B. and Kimi, O. (1994). The post-issue operating performance of IPO firms. *Journal of Finance*, 49, 1699–1726.

Kim, K., Kitsabunnarat, P. and Nofsinger, J. (2004). Ownership and operating performance in an emerging market: Evidence from Thai IPO firms. *Journal of Corporate Finance*, 10, 355–381.

Kothari, S.P and Warner, J.B. (1997). Measuring long-horizon security price performance. *Journal of Financial Economics*, 43, 301–340.

Lee, P., Taylor, S. and Walter, T. (1996). Australian IPO pricing in the short and long run. *Journal of Banking and Finance*, 20, 1189–1210.

Lerner, J. (1994). Venture capitalists and the decision to go public. *Journal of Financial Economics*, 35, 293–316.

Ljungqvist, A.P. and Wilhelm, W.J. (2003). IPO pricing in the dot-com bubble. *Journal of Finance*, 58, 723–752.

Lonkani, R. (2000). Information acquisition and dissemination of the initial public offerings: The case of the Thai stock market. Doctoral dissertation, Chulalonkorn University, Bangkok, Thailand.

Lonkani, R. and Firth, M. (2005). The accuracy of IPO earnings forecasts in Thailand and their relationships with stock market valuation. *Accounting and Business Research*, 35, 269–286.

Loughran, T. and Ritter, J. R. (1995). The new issue puzzle. *Journal of Finance*, 50, 23–51.

Loughran, T. and Ritter, J. (2002). Why don't issuers get upset about leaving money on the table in IPOs? *Review of Financial Studies*, 15, 413–444.

Lyon, J.D., Barber, B.M. and Tsai, C-L. (1999). Improved methods for testing of long run abnormal stock returns. *Journal of Finance*, 54, 165–201.

Market for Alternative Investments (2009). Available at http://www.mai.or.th/. Accessed August 2014.

Megginson, W.L. and Weiss, K.A. (1991). Venture capitalist certification in initial public offerings. *Journal of Finance*, 46, 879–903.

Mikkelson, W., Partch, M. and Shah, K. (1997). Ownership and operation performance of companies that go public. *Journal of Financial Economics*, 44, 281–307.

Moonchul, K. and Ritter, J.R. (1999). Valuing IPOs. *Journal of Financial Economics*, 53, 409–437.

Ritter, J. (1991). The long run performance of initial public offerings. *Journal of Finance*, 46, 3–28.

Rosa, R.S., Velayuthen, G. and Walter, T. (2003). The sharemarket performance of Australian venture capital backed and non-venture capital backed IPOs. *Pacific-Basin Finance Journal*, 11, 197–218.

Securities and Exchange Commission (2000). *Re: Application for and Approval of Offer for Sale of Newly Issued Shares (KorChor. 12/2543)*, Bangkok. Available at http://www.set.or.th/. Accessed August 2014.

Stock Exchange of Thailand (2008). Listing manual for common shares in 2008, Available at http://www.sec.or.th/. Accessed May 2008.

Securities Exchange Commission (2009). Available at http://www.sec.or.th/. Accessed May 2009.

Stock Exchange of Thailand (2009a). Available at http://www.set.or.th/. Accessed May 2009.

Stock Exchange of Thailand (2009b). Thailand's capital market in 2008, Accessed May 2009.

Stock Exchange of Thailand (1997–2007). Fact Book, Bangkok. Available at http://www.set.or.th/en/products/publications/fact_book.html/. Accessed October 2008.

Wethayavivorn, K. and Koo-smith, Y. (1991). Initial public offerings in Thailand, 1988–1989: Price and return patterns. in S.G. Rhee and R.P. Chang (ed.), *Pacific-Basin Capital Market Research*, North-Holland, Amsterdam, Vol. 2, 379–394.

World Federation of Exchanges (2007). Annual Report and Statistics, Available at http://www.world-exchanges.org/. Accessed May 2009.

Zingales, L. (1995). Insiders' ownership and the decision to go public. *Review of Economic Studies,* 62, 425–448.

In: Economic and Financial Modeling
Editor: Andrew C. Worthington
ISBN: 978-1-63463-111-2

Chapter 3

TRADING/TRADING-RESTRICTED AND BUSINESS/NONBUSINESS DAYS IN MARKET RETURN MODELS

***Mitesh Mistry*[1], *Andrew C. Worthington*[2*], *Dionigi Gerace*[1] *and Chandra Gulati*[1]**
[1]University of Wollongong, Australia
[2]Griffith University, Australia

ABSTRACT

This chapter provides an empirical analysis of trading-restricted, business days and trading, non-business days on the Australian Securities Exchange (ASX). Seven days are included in the analysis: the Bank Holiday in NSW (non-business), Labour Day in NSW (non-business), Easter Thursday (early close), Labour Day in Victoria (non-business), Melbourne Cup Day in Melbourne (non-business), the last business day before Christmas (early close) and the last business day of the calendar year (early close). Three indexes provide different daily return measures: the All Ordinaries (market), 1958–2007, the Small Ordinaries (small-cap), 1994–2007; and the ASX100 (large-cap), 1992–2007. The findings indicate return abnormalities on three days when trading and/or business activity is restricted: Melbourne Cup Day, the last business day before Christmas and the last business day of the calendar year.

1. INTRODUCTION

The theory of market efficiency proposes that securities prices fully reflect all available information to all market participants. It also assures that the market price mechanism acts accurately and instantaneously to the disclosure of any information. However, many empirical studies have suggested deviations from market efficiency with the presence of

* Corresponding author: Department of Accounting, Finance and Economics, Griffith University, 170 Kessels Road, Nathan QLD 4111, Australia. E-mail. a.worthington@griffith.edu.au.

unexpected or anomalous regularities in the rates of return on individual securities and indices. A number of empirical studies have duly documented anomalies associated with days of the week, days of the month, months of the year, and cultural and festive holidays.

Table 1. 2007 Australian Security Exchange (ASX) financial calendar

Public Holiday	Date	Day and date in 2007	Applies to the following States	Trading Day	Settlement Activity–ASTC (CHESS)	Settlement Activity–ACH (DCS)	Business Day
New Year's Day	1 January	Monday 1 January	ALL	Closed	No Settlement	No Settlement	No
Australia Day	26 January	Friday 26 January	ALL	Closed	No Settlement	No Settlement	No
Labour Day	1st Monday in March	Monday 5 March	WA	Open	Settlement	Settlement	Yes
Labour Day/Eight Hours Day/ Adelaide Cup Day	2nd Monday in March	Monday 12 March	VIC/TAS/ SA	Open	No Settlement	Settlement	No
Easter Thursday	Thursday before Easter Sunday	Thursday 5 April	ALL	Close early	Settlement	Settlement	Yes
Good Friday	Friday before Easter Sunday	Friday 6 April	ALL	Closed	No Settlement	No Settlement	No
Easter Monday	Monday after Easter Sunday	Monday 9 April	ALL	Closed	No Settlement	No Settlement	No
Easter Tuesday	Tuesday after Easter Sunday	Tuesday 10 April	TAS	Open	Settlement	Settlement	Yes
ANZAC Day Holiday	25 April	Wednesday 25 April	ALL	Closed	No Settlement	No Settlement	No
Labour Day	1st Monday in May	Monday 7 May	QLD	Open	Settlement	Settlement	Yes
Queen's Birthday	2nd Monday in June	Monday 11 June	ALL except WA	Closed	No Settlement	No Settlement	No
Bank Holiday	1st Monday in August	Monday 6 August	NSW	Open	No Settlement	Settlement	No
Labour Day/ Queen's Birthday	1st Monday in October	Monday 1 October	NSW, SA, ACT/WA	Open	No Settlement	Settlement	No
Melbourne Cup Day	1st Tuesday in November	Tuesday 6 November	VIC	Open	No Settlement	Settlement	No
Last Business Day before Christmas	Last trading day before Christmas Day	Monday, 24 December	ALL	Close early	Settlement	Settlement	Yes
Christmas Day	25 December	Tuesday 25 December	ALL	Closed	No Settlement	No Settlement	No
Boxing Day	26 December	Wednesday 26 December	ALL	Closed	No Settlement	No Settlement	No
Last Business Day of the Year	Last trading day in December	Monday 31 December	ALL	Close early	Settlement	Settlement	Yes

Notes: Close early – normal trading starts at 10:00 and ends at 14:15 AEST (usually 10:00-16:00 AEST), Business Day is a day other than a Saturday, Sunday, New Year's Day, Good Friday, Easter Monday, Christmas Day, Boxing Day, and any other day which the Exchange shall declare and publish is not a business day, Trading Day is a day other than a Saturday, Sunday, New Year's Day, Good Friday, Easter Monday, Christmas Day, Boxing Day, and any other day which the Exchange declares and publishes is not a trading day.

Together these findings challenge the theory of market efficiency, particularly weak-form efficiency, which suggests that superior returns are not attainable through the analysis of historical data.

One aspect of seasonality that has received rather less attention concerns other systematic patterns in the trading, settlement and clearing of securities on organized exchanges. Consider the Australian Securities Exchange (ASX). As shown in Table 1, a typical trading day on the ASX is a day other than a Saturday, Sunday, New Year's Day, Good Friday, Easter Monday, Christmas Day, Boxing Day, and any other day which the Exchange declares and publishes is not a trading day. On these days, trading takes place 10:00–16:00 Australian Eastern Standard Time (AEST) via the Stock Exchange Automated Trading System (SEATS). A business day is a day other than a Saturday, Sunday, New Year's Day, Good Friday, Easter Monday, Christmas Day, Boxing Day, and any other day which the Exchange shall declare and publish is not a business day. On these days, the ASX Settlement and Transfer Corporation (ASTC) through the Clearing House Electronic Subregister System (CHESS) and the Australian Clearing House (ACH) via the Derivatives Clearing System (DCS) coordinate settlement activities for equities and derivatives, respectively. Outside these days, trading closes and settlement does not place: this applies, of course, to Saturdays and Sundays, along with national public holidays like New Year's Day, Australia Day, Good Friday and Easter Monday, Christmas Day and Boxing Day.

However, two additional categories of days exist on the ASX that encompass restrictions in trading or settlement alone. The first category is where trading is restricted through an early close (10:00–14:15): this arises on trading days before selected public holidays and includes Easter Thursday, the last business day before Christmas and the last business day of the year. Settlement and all other business activities are undertaken normally. In this study, these are denoted 'trading-restricted, business days' as against 'trading, business days'. The second category relates to days where trading proceeds as normal, but the clearing and settlement of securities is not until the next business day. Typically, this arises with public holidays in either New South Wales (Sydney) or Victoria (Melbourne) when trading closes. The presence of trading non-business days results in a market where active trading occurs, though partially restricted by the absence of at least some market participants in these major financial centers, and business activities do not take place. These are 'trading, non-business days'.

The impact of a non-business day is as follows. The current arrangement for the settlement and clearing of transactions is within three trading days of execution. This settlement process is referred to as the T+3 system. This means that if a trade is executed on a Monday, it will be settled on the upcoming Thursday and similarly if a trade is performed on a Wednesday it will be settled on the following Monday. A seller will need to deliver the sold securities on the third business day after the trade date and will receive their funds on the third business day. The buyer will likewise have an obligation to pay for the securities on the third business day after the trade date. However, if within the settlement period a non-business day occurs, the settlements of those securities are postponed a day, resulting in four-day (three-business day plus one non-business day) settlement. Benefits from this fixed system, amongst other things, strengthened market efficiency according to ASX Managing Director Richard Humphry at the time of its adoption in 1999, "The change is part of a global program to minimize counterparty risk and market exposure associated with longer settlement periods. While these risks are less significant in Australia because of the protection offered by

ASX's National Guarantee Fund, it is still important for the Australian market to maintain international parity".

The purpose of this chapter is to consider the impact of trading-restricted, business days and trading, non-business days on Australian market returns. Although some research in this area exists in the United States and elsewhere, Australian studies concerning the impact of these departures from usual transaction and settlement behavior are relatively unknown. Further while trading-restricted, business days approximate pre-holiday trading days in some respects (though with shorter trading days), trading, non-business days represent a novel disjunction between conventional trading and settlement activity.

The remainder of the chapter is structured as follows. Section 2 provides a brief literature review. Section 3 explains the data methodology employed in the analysis. The results are in Section 4. The chapter ends with some concluding remarks in the final section.

2. Literature Review

Three aspects of the literature are relevant to this analysis. These are: (i) the settlement and clearing hypothesis, normally used to explain the day-of-the-week effect; (ii) the holiday effect, typically linked with higher pre-holiday daily returns; and (iii) the individual vs. institutional hypothesis, usually associate with purported differences in the trading behavior of individuals and institutions and the possible impact on the pattern of daily returns.

2.1. Settlement and Clearing Hypothesis

The settlement and clearing hypothesis argues that the day-of-the-week effect can be linked with the differences in time between the purchase of a security and its settlement (Crouchy and Galai 1992). In one of the earlier studies, Gibbon and Hess (1981) considered the impact on the Dow-Jones Industrial Average (DJIA) when the New York Stock Exchange (NYSE) settlement period changed in 1968 from four to five days. While negative returns persisted on the next trading day, Gibbon and Hess (1981) concluded that a small proportion of seasonality (in the form of the weekend effect) is attributable to the settlement regime. More recently, a study of the Kuala Lumpur Stock Exchange by Clare et al. (1998) also found that the settlement and clearing of securities contributed to the weekend effect. Prior to the introduction of a new fixed settlement system, uncertainty had existed around settlement payments as sellers had up until the following Wednesday to deliver their shares. However, after the introduction of the new fixed delivery and settlement system, Clare et al. (1998) concluded that the seasonality effect found in the past had almost vanished.

In terms of cross-institutional analyses, Jaffe and Westerfield (1985) concluded that settlement procedures in the UK, Canada and Japan markets did not cause any seasonality effects, but some aspects of settlement procedure had a role to play in the Australian market. However, while Australian settlement procedures could be linked with abnormally high returns on Friday trading day, this was not possible with the largely negative returns on the following Monday. Conversely, Agrawal and Tandon (1994) suggested that no feasible relationship existed between seasonality effects and the settlement and clearing of securities as many financial markets had differing settlement days "…ranging from one day in France and Hong Kong, to six to fifteen days in the U.K. Thus, it is hard for differences in the settlement periods to explain the consistent negative pattern on Monday or Tuesday that we find in most countries" (Agrawal and Tandon 1994: 92).

For example, Agrawal and Tandon (1994) provided an illustration of the potential behavior of financial markets in the Netherlands, Japan and Sweden, all of which had a settlement period of four days. This meant that if an investor bought a security on Monday and sold the same security on Tuesday, the investor would pay for the security on Friday and receive payment for the security on the following Monday. Agrawal and Tandon (1994) suggested that since the cash payment occurs three days prior to the cash receipt, these markets should realize higher return on the Tuesday trading day to compensate for the loss of interest over the weekend. However, the instead found strong negative returns. These and other results suggest that the settlement and clearing hypothesis provides a feasible explanation for some daily return patterns in some financial markets but not in others.

2.2. Holiday Effects

The holiday effect is where higher expected returns occur on trading days prior to a holiday. Given the volume of work in this area, it is instructive to first consider three early studies by Lakonishok and Smidt (1988), Ariel (1990) and Cadsby and Ratner (1992). To start with, Laskonishok and Smidt (1988) employed approximately ninety years of daily returns data from the DJIA to divide trading days into three distinct categories—pre-holiday, post-holiday and ordinary trading days. They concluded that the average returns of nine hundred and fifteen pre-holiday days was 0.22 percent, compared to a return of only –0.0017 percent on post-holidays and 0.0094 percent on all other trading days. This indicated that pre-holiday returns were more than twenty-three times larger than the ordinary trading day rate of return. Further, while pre-holidays only accounted for 4.2 percent of all trading days, they could be linked with approximately 50 percent of the total advances in the DJIA over the ninety-year period. Analysis of different sub-periods showed that these results appeared to be consistent, with the exception of the most-recent period (1976–1986) where the pre-holidays returns was positive but insignificant.

According to Ariel (1990), pre-holidays displayed abnormal returns nine to fourteen times higher than other days of the week. Using Center for Research in Security Prices (CRSP) equal- and value-weighted indexes, these abnormal returns were found to be independent of the dataset employed and that they did not derive from a small number of very high returns from the period of 1963 to 1982. Ariel (1990) also provided some evidence that the pre-holiday effect was not a manifestation of other calendar anomalies, such as the January or weekend effect, that the pre-holiday volatility in returns are distinctly lower than that for non-holiday returns, and that the holiday effect occurs only on a single trading day prior to the actual holiday. Further, using intraday data, Ariel (1990) concluded that the holiday effect is effectively the result of the last hour of trading.

Finally, Cadsby and Ratner (1992) examined global markets for evidence of the holiday effect. The aim of their study was to investigate firstly whether nine non-US markets exhibited the same pre-holiday effects seen in the US market, and secondly to test for the impact of the US holiday effect on other markets (i.e. a test for independence). The results indicated that eight countries, which shared the same holiday as a US holiday illustrated higher returns than non-holiday trading returns. Moreover, there appeared to be evidence of independencies in some markets, indicating that market integration may partially explain effects unexplained by local holidays. The main findings were that all non-European countries in the study exhibited significant local pre-holiday effects; that no European country showed evidence of a pre-holiday effect; and that Hong Kong was the only market that reflected US holiday effects. On this basis, Cadsby and Ratner (1992) noted that pre-holiday effects could depend solely on local market participation and vary with differences in neighbouring institutions and practices.

More recent work has added additional insights into the holiday effect. In their analysis of the Japanese, UK and US markets, Kim and Park (1994) initially found that it was obvious that there were significantly higher mean returns on trading days before holidays. However, post-holiday effects were found to not exhibit any irregular pattern, leading to the conclusion that holiday effects simply comprise the irregular returns seen on the last pre-holiday trading day. Kim and Park (1994) also found that smaller firms displayed higher mean pre-holiday returns than larger firms did. Most importantly, Kim and Park (1994: 156) concluded:

The persistent of the holiday effect across countries suggest that the holiday effect is not driven by institutional arrangement unique to the stock market of a country. Therefore, institutional factors such as trading methods, clearing mechanism, settlement procedure, and bid-ask spreads cannot be possible explanations for international evidence of the holiday effect because these institutional factors are different across countries.

Using a similar approach, Vergin and McGinnis (1999) found diminishing excess returns in both large and small-sized firms around holidays. Eight US holidays was examined using four different indexes (S&P 500, NYSE Composite Index, NASDAQ and American Stock Exchange Composite Indices) as proxies for differences in firm size. Prior to 1987, strong evidence was found of irregular market behavior around public holidays. However, after 1987 the holiday effect effectively disappeared in large firms, and faded in small firms. Most recently, Keef and Roush (2005) examined pre-holiday returns in the S&P Index from 1930 to 1999. The three main findings include the diminishment of the pre-holiday effect after 1987; no evidence of a weekend effect in pre-holiday returns; and finally that Labor Day returns were significantly greater than returns before other holidays falling on a Monday.

2.3. Individual vs. Institutional Hypothesis

At least some studies have argued that the day-of-the-week effect and other forms of seasonality almost exclusively relate to the differing trading behavior of individual and institutional investors. Much speculation exists as to which particular group is responsible: Lakonishok and Maberly (1990) and Abraham and Ikenberry (1994), for example, directly relate seasonality to the trading behaviour of individual investors while Sias and Starks (1995) suggest that institutional investors' trading patterns are the primary cause.

Arguments supporting individual investors trading behavior as the cause of seasonality could be the result of timely recommendations from stockbrokers (Miller 1988), or the 'inherent psychology' of investors–such as their personal moods, perceptions and emotion (Rystrom and Benson 1989). Other work includes Abraham and Ikenberry's (1994) suggestion that individual investors use Monday trading days to satisfy their liquidity needs flowing from the negative returns seen on the previous Friday and Lakonishok and Maberly's (1990) hypothesis that it is less costly for individuals to gather and process information on weekends than weekdays. Conversely, Sias and Starks (1995) propose that day-of-the-week patterns in volumes and returns are largely the result of institutional investors since securities with larger institutional investor holdings exhibit greater seasonality than comparably sized securities held by individual investors.

More recently, academics have also linked the holiday effect to the behavior and actions of individual investors. Meneu and Pardo (2004) argue that the holiday effect is attributed to increases in the average size bid orders placed by investors prior to holidays. Brockman and Michayluk (1998) and Jacobs and Levy (2000), on the other hand, have suggested that investor's psychology may play a role in the high pre-holiday returns. They argue that investors may look favorably towards the upcoming holiday and react by applying buying pressure, resulting in higher pre-holiday returns.

Brooks and Kim (1997), however, argue that both institutions and individuals are responsible for some seasonal effects as individual investors play a role through their trading patterns and institutional investors via their absence in trading. Using intraday data, Brooks and Kim (1997) found more small-sized transactions linked to individual investors and fewer large-sized orders representing institutional investors' transactions. The absence of institutional investors reduces liquidity in the market and provides evidence that both parties are accountable for the present of seasonality effects.

3. Data and Method

This study examines the impact of three trading-restricted, business days (Easter Thursday, the last business day before Christmas and the last business day of the year) and four trading, non-business days (Labour Day in Victoria, the Bank Holiday in NSW, Labour Day in NSW and Melbourne Cup Day in Victoria) on ASX returns. Additional details are included in Table 1. As discussed, the trading-restricted, business days have the appearance of pre-holiday trading days with the exception that the trading day is 105 minutes shorter. Importantly, the trading, non-business days theoretically associated with normal trading days also involve some restrictions in trading. For instance, Melbourne Cup Day is a public holiday in Melbourne (Australia's second-largest capital city), Labour Day is a holiday in Victoria (Australia's second-largest state), and Labour Day and the Bank Holiday in NSW is a public holiday in NSW (Australia's largest state, with Sydney as Australia's financial capital). Moreover, Victoria shares Labour Day with Tasmania's Eight Hours Day and South Australia's Adelaide Cup Day, while Labour Day in NSW is common with South Australia and the Australian Capital Territory along with the Queens's Birthday in Western Australia. The inference is that trading, non-business days also involve the potential removal of large numbers of market participants.

Returns are measured using three value-weighted indices; the All Ordinaries measures market returns (representing some 92% of total market capitalization), the Small Ordinaries the returns on small-cap stocks (approximately 8% of market capitalization), and the ASX100 the returns on large-cap stocks (the one hundred largest firms by capitalization). The long-term daily data for the first series is from Global Financial Data (2007) while the data for small and large-cap firms is from DataStream (2007). The analysis draws upon the maximum sample length for each index: 6 January 1958–13 August 2007 for the market (n = 12,477), 4 January 1994–31 August 2007 for small-caps (n = 3,463), and 1 June 1992–31 August 2007 for the large-caps (n = 3,869). Following Vergin and McGinnis (1999), Keef and Roush (2005) and Worthington (2007), the market return index is divided into two sub-samples using a Chow breakpoint test: pre-1987 from 6 January 1958 to 19 October 1987 and post-1987 20 October 1987 to 13 of August 2007.

The daily returns for each specified index employ the logarithmic or continuously compounded formula:

$$R_t = \ln(\frac{P_t}{P_{t-1}}) \times 100$$

where R_t is the daily return, P_t is the closing value of the index on day t and P_{t-1} is the closing value of the index on the previous day.

We use two approaches to test for the trading-restricted, business day and trading, non-business day effects. The first employs nonparametric tests of differences in mean returns and the variance of returns. The second is a regression-based approach where:

$$\begin{aligned} R_{it} = \beta_0 &+ \beta_{i1}\text{Labour Day (VIC)} + \beta_{i2}\text{Easter Thursday} + \beta_{i3}\text{Bank Holiday} \\ &+ \beta_{i4}\text{Labour Day (NSW)} + \beta_{i5}\text{Melbourne Cup Day} \\ &+ \beta_{i6}\text{Last Day before Christmas Day} + \beta_{i7}\text{Last Day before End of Year} + \varepsilon_{it} \end{aligned}$$

where R_t is the daily return on index i on day t, Labour Day (VIC), Easter Thursday, Bank Holiday, Labour Day (NSW), Melbourne Cup Day, Last Day before Christmas Day and Last Day before End of Year are binary dummy variables that equal one for the day specified, otherwise zero, and ε is the error term.

4. Empirical Results

The number of observations, means, standard deviations, maximums and minimums of daily market, small-cap and large-cap returns for the trading-restricted business days, trading, non-business days and trading, business days are detailed in Table 2. Also included are distributional statistics for skewness and kurtosis. As shown, there is already some indication that the dispersion and distribution of returns vary across the various categories. For example, the mean market return on a trading business day is 0.028 percent with returns (in brackets) being higher on Easter Thursday (0.088), Labour Day (NSW) (0.058), Melbourne Cup Day (0.179), and the last days before Christmas (0.360) and the end of the year (0.298), and lower on Labour Day (VIC) (-0.047) and the Bank Holiday (0.016). The standard deviations also differ, with higher standard deviations (in brackets) on the Bank Holiday (1.122) and lower standard deviations on Labour Day (VIC) (0.853), Easter Thursday (0.504), Labour Day (NSW) (0.774), Melbourne Cup Day (0.551) and the last days before Christmas (0.392) and the end of the year (0.585) relative to trading business days (0.845). In terms of distribution, daily returns on Labour Day (VIC), Easter Thursday, Labour Day (NSW) and all other days exhibit significant negative skewness or the increasing likelihood of negative values (the remaining days are all positively skewed), while all series show evidence of leptokurtic or fat-tailed distributions with relatively many extreme observations.

Table 2. Descriptive statistics for daily returns

Statistic	Index	Labour Day (VIC)	Easter Thursday	Bank Holiday	Labour Day (NSW)	Melbourne Cup Day	Last day before Christmas	Last day of the year	All other trading days
Observations	Market	50	50	28	27	49	49	43	12180
	Small-cap	14	13	14	13	13	13	13	3370
	Large-cap	15	15	16	15	15	15	15	3763
Mean	Market	–0.047	0.088	0.016	0.058	0.179	0.360	0.298	0.028
	Small-cap	0.049	–0.013	–0.259	0.150	0.221	0.279	0.448	0.021
	Large-cap	0.263	–0.186	–0.150	0.063	0.446	0.346	0.137	0.031
Standard deviation	Market	0.853	0.504	1.122	0.774	0.551	0.392	0.585	0.845
	Small-cap	0.908	0.644	0.920	0.561	0.633	0.260	0.374	0.711
	Large-cap	1.239	0.749	0.842	0.904	0.743	0.345	0.632	0.820
Maximum	Market	1.254	0.875	3.311	1.554	1.891	1.955	2.384	7.016
	Small-cap	0.988	1.344	0.889	0.867	1.299	0.957	1.251	7.848
	Large-cap	1.326	0.739	1.166	1.632	1.898	1.135	1.006	5.592
Minimum	Market	–3.601	–1.896	–2.640	–1.671	–0.825	–0.229	–1.045	–28.761
	Small-cap	–2.807	–1.050	–2.692	–1.154	–0.670	–0.069	–0.044	–9.403
	Large-cap	–3.713	–2.179	–1.577	–1.777	–0.809	–0.215	–1.293	–6.856
Skewness	Market	–1.975	–1.359	0.325	–0.157	1.277	1.466	0.984	–3.633
	Small-cap	–2.360	0.726	–1.353	–0.860	0.384	1.147	0.695	–1.479
	Large-cap	–2.306	–1.151	–0.157	–0.335	0.628	0.448	–0.870	–0.312
Kurtosis	Market	9.569	6.204	4.689	2.534	5.201	6.884	5.822	120.990
	Small-cap	8.272	2.953	4.573	3.221	1.979	4.770	2.711	26.213
	Large-cap	8.245	4.355	2.223	2.717	2.963	3.105	3.226	6.617

Notes: Market (All Ordinaries) 6/01/1958 – 13/08/2007, Small-cap (Small Ordinaries) 4/01/1994 – 31/08/2007, Large-cap (ASX100) 1/06/1992 – 31/08/2007. Mean, median, maximum and minimum expressed as percentages. The critical values for skewness where n = 10, 30, 50 and 1,000 where α = .05 are 1.52, 0.87, 0.68 and 0.15, respectively. The critical values for kurtosis where n = 10, 30, 50 and 1,000 where α = .05 are 3.04, 1.75, 1.36 and 0.30, respectively.

Nonparametric tests for equality of the variances and means are provided in Tables 3 and 4, respectively. The null hypotheses are that the daily variances and means for the respective trading-restricted business days and trading, non-business days are equal to all other (trading business) days. The tests for equality of variance are used to inform whether the tests for equality of means assume equal or unequal variances. To start with, there are significant different variances signifying the volatility of returns for market returns on Easter Thursday, the Bank Holiday, Melbourne Cup day and the last day before Christmas. The pre-1987 market returns show that these differences are relatively consistent for the first sample period, though joined by the last day of the year. However, in the post-1987 sample period only the variance for the last day before Christmas is significantly different from all other days. For small and large cap returns, the variances on the last day before Christmas are again less, but none of the other trading-restricted business days or trading non-business days exhibits any significant differences in variance.

Table 3. Comparison of variances

Day	Statistic	Market	Small cap	Large cap	Market 1958–87	Market 1987–2007
All other days	Variance	0.714	0.505	0.672	0.594	0.893
Labour Day (VIC)	Variance	0.719	0.824	1.535	0.446	1.103
	p-value	0.901	0.807	0.184	0.224	0.679
Easter Thursday	Variance	**0.253**	0.392	0.561	**0.119**	0.411
	p-value	0.044	0.898	0.611	0.018	0.374
Bank Holiday	Variance	**1.260**	0.846	0.709	**0.152**	0.961
	p-value	0.042	0.173	0.766	0.042	0.375
Labour Day (NSW)	Variance	0.599	0.315	0.817	0.578	0.625
	p-value	0.662	0.713	0.751	0.691	0.982
Melbourne Cup Day	Variance	**0.304**	0.401	0.552	**0.192**	0.439
	p-value	0.043	0.823	0.642	0.028	0.332
Last day before Christmas	Variance	**0.154**	**0.068**	**0.119**	**0.112**	**0.223**
	p-value	0.002	0.034	0.011	0.016	0.058
Last day of the year	Variance	0.342	0.140	0.399	**1.713**	0.578
	p-value	0.146	0.186	0.302	0.075	0.683

Notes: p-values are for Levene's equality of variance tests, return variances rounded to three decimal places. Significant differences in variance in bold.

In terms of the daily market returns, the mean return is significantly higher on the last day before Christmas (0.360) and the last day of the year (0.298) when compared with trading, business days (0.028). This also holds for the pre-1987 sample along with lower mean returns on Labour Day (VIC) and higher means returns on Easter Thursday. In the post-1987 sample period, there are higher mean returns on Labour Day (VIC), Melbourne Cup Day and the last days before Christmas and the end of the year. These are generally consistent with the post-1987 sample period except that the difference in mean returns for Easter Thursday are no longer significant, and Melbourne Cup Day is now significantly higher along with Labour Day (VIC).

For small-cap returns, the means are higher on the last day of the year, while for large-cap returns they are higher on Labour Day (VIC), Melbourne Cup Day and the last day before Christmas. One this basis, the firm size effect in trading, business days returns appears inconclusive, in that larger and smaller capitalised stocks appear to show different patterns of significant return differences to the market as a whole and each other in some respects. One basic observation is that the last day before Christmas effect would appear to derive from large-caps, while the last day of the year effect seems to develop from small-caps.

Table 4. Comparison of returns

Day	Statistic	Market	Small-cap	Large-cap	Market 1958–87	Market 1987–2007
All other days	Mean	0.028	0.021	0.031	0.034	0.018
Labour Day (VIC)	Mean	–0.047	0.049	**0.263**	**–0.198**	**0.181**
	p-value	0.631	0.253	0.041	0.029	0.093
Easter Thursday	Mean	0.088	–0.013	–0.186	**0.212**	–0.098
	p-value	0.317	0.405	0.379	0.043	0.496
Bank Holiday	Mean	0.016	–0.259	–0.150	0.594	–0.215
	p-value	0.909	0.361	0.411	0.269	0.409
Labour Day (NSW)	Mean	0.058	0.150	0.063	0.219	–0.010
	p-value	0.744	0.335	0.702	0.401	0.848
Melbourne Cup Day	Mean	0.179	0.221	**0.446**	0.069	**0.339**
	p-value	0.251	0.463	0.057	0.950	0.089
Last day before Christmas	Mean	**0.360**	0.279	**0.346**	**0.351**	**0.376**
	p-value	0.001	0.722	0.047	0.000	0.025
Last day of year	Mean	**0.298**	**0.448**	0.137	**0.259**	**0.342**
	p-value	0.011	0.005	0.412	0.056	0.100

The estimated coefficients and standard errors for the regression equation in (2) are presented in Table 5. The table also includes values for R^2 and adjusted R^2 and the F-statistics and p-values of the null hypotheses that all slope coefficients are zero. Breusch–Godfrey Lagrange multiplier and White's heteroskedasticity tests (not shown) are used initially to test for higher-order serial correlation and heteroskedasticity in the least squares residuals, respectively. To start with, the null hypothesis of no serial correlation is rejected and we may conclude the presence of higher-order serial correlation in the residuals. Then the null hypothesis of no heteroskedasticity in the least squares residuals fails to be rejected and we conclude the presence of heteroskedasticity in the least squares residuals. Accordingly, the standard errors employ corrections for heteroskedasticity and autocorrelation of unknown form (Newey–West).

Consistent with the finding of the non-parametric analysis, there appears to be one trading non-business day and two trading-restricted business days that exert a significant impact at the market level (columns 1 and 2): namely, Melbourne Cup Day, and the last business day of the year and the last business day before Christmas Day, respectively. The magnitude of these impacts appears to be substantial. For example, based on a market capitalization of $1,532 billion in November 2007, the trading, non-business day effects on Melbourne Cup Day adds an additional $2,742 million to market capitalization (six times normal daily returns). The trading-restricted business day effect on the other hand adds $5,515 million on the last day before Christmas (thirteen times normal returns) and $4,565 million on the last day of the year (ten times normal returns). Separate regressions for small-caps (columns 3 and 4) and large caps (columns 5 and 6) again show that the market effect appears to be dominated by small caps for the last day before Christmas and the end of the year, while large caps play a role in the Melbourne Cup Day effect and the last day before Christmas. However, the relative impact of the trading-restricted business days and trading, non-business days appears relatively small, explaining in all instances less than one percent of the variation in returns over the various sample periods.

Table 5. Estimated regression equations

	Market		Small-cap		Large-cap		Market 1958–87		Market 1987–2007	
	Coef.	Std. Error	Coef.	Std. Error	Coef.	Std. Error	Coef.	Std. Error	Coef.	Std. Error
Constant	0.028***	0.009	0.021	0.013	0.031**	0.012	0.034***	0.012	0.018	0.014
Labour Day (VIC)	–0.047	0.088	0.049	0.234	0.263	0.309	–0.198*	0.120	0.181	0.229
Easter Thursday	0.088	0.070	–0.013	0.172	–0.186	0.187	0.212***	0.062	–0.098	0.140
Bank Holiday	0.016	0.191	–0.259	0.237	–0.150	0.204	0.594	0.433	–0.215	0.214
Labour Day (NSW)	0.058	0.076	0.150	0.150	0.063	0.226	0.219	0.252	–0.010	0.177
Melbourne Cup Day	0.179*	0.096	0.221	0.169	0.446**	0.186	0.069	0.080	0.339*	0.145
Last before Christmas	0.360***	0.031	0.279*	0.069	0.346***	0.086	0.351***	0.061	0.376***	0.103
Last day of the year	0.298***	0.074	0.448***	0.100	0.137	0.158	0.259***	0.080	0.342**	0.166
R^2	0.0011	–	0.0029	–	0.0024	–	0.0021	–	0.0019	–
Adjusted R^2	0.0006	–	0.0010	–	0.0007	–	0.0012	–	0.0005	–
F-statistic	2.0030	–	1.4391	–	1.3340	–	2.2905	–	1.3742	–
p-value	0.0473	–	0.1848	–	0.2297	–	0.0249	–	0.2115	–

Notes: All standard errors include Newey–West corrections for serial correlation and/or heteroskedasticity. Asterisks indicate significance at the * – .10, ** – .05 and *** – 0.01 level. F-statistic and p-value is test of the null hypothesis that all slope coefficients are jointly zero.

The regressions results also suggest that these anomalies are inconsistent over time. The pre-1987 sample shows significantly higher returns on Easter Thursday, the last business day before Christmas Day and year-end and significantly lower returns on Labour Day (VIC). However, the regression coefficients in the post-1987 sample period indicate higher returns on Melbourne Cup day and the last day before Christmas and year-end. Moreover, the share of variation accounted for by the trading-restricted, business day and trading, non-business day effects has declined. In fact, the null hypothesis of the joint insignificance of the slope coefficients fails to be rejected for the later sample period.

CONCLUSION

The study investigates posited return anomalies associated with trading-restricted, business days and trading, non-business days on the Australian Stock Exchange. On the former, trading hours are restricted due to the proximity of the public holidays on Easter Thursday and Christmas and on the last business day of the year. On the later, trading proceeds normally, though with the removal of some market participants because of public holidays in some states, while settlement activity is postponed. Potentially, these departures from normal trading, business activity thereby comprise a combination of the pre-holiday effect known in the literature and the various settlement hypotheses. The result show strong evidence of return anomalies associated with Melbourne Cup Day, the last business day of the year and the last business day before Christmas day, and these appear to be consistent across the market, small-cap and large-cap stocks. For this reason, the analysis provides inconclusive evidence of a firm size effect, suggesting that restrictions in trading and/or settlement act almost equally upon firms.

The most puzzling aspect of this analysis is that it has not been possible to identify the underlying cause of the return anomalies. This is important, given there are a number of other hypotheses that could also provide an explanation. Consider Melbourne Cup Day. As a non-business day, market activity may intensity and returns increase with the benefits of a delay in settlement. The results of this analysis provide some indirect support here. However, this could also be result of the market euphoria associated with Australia's premier horse race, as argued by Worthington (2007) with a behavioral finance approach. In either instance, this must be strong enough to offset the reduction in market participation with the public holiday in Victoria. Now consider the last trading days before Christmas and the end of the year. Once again, the evidence found of relatively higher returns on these days, while consistent with a pre-holiday effect lies at odds with a trading day that is nearly thirty percent shorter.

There are a number of possible future directions for research stemming from these and other limitations. One of the more important of these is the extension of the data used to include not only returns but also trading volumes, bid-ask spreads and other market information. For example, trading, non-business days are not only associated with a delay in settlement but also the potential removal of large numbers of market participants and the limited release of price and non-price sensitive company information in some states. As these days are associated with higher returns than normal trading, business days it is not known whether this result truly represents an inconsistency with the lower hypothesized level of market activity or whether broad market activity is entirely unaffected by regional holidays.

Another extension would involve intra-day data. This would allow a more robust analysis of trading-restricted business days in that interest could be focused on the pattern of trades throughout the day and the role of the last few hours of trading on daily returns.

REFERENCES

Abraham, A. and Ikenberry, D.L. (1994). The individual investor and the weekend effect. *Journal of Financial and Quantitative Analysis*, 29(2), 263–277.

Agrawal, A. and Tandon, K. (1994). Anomalies or illusions? Evidence from stock markets in eighteen countries. *Journal of International Money and Finance*, 13(1), 83–106.

Apolinario R.M., Santana, O.M., Sales L.J. and Caro, A.R. (2006). Day of the week effect on European stock markets. *International Research Journal of Finance and Economics*, 2, 53–70.

Brockman, P. and Michayluk, D. (1998). The persistent holiday effect: additional evidence. *Applied Economics Letters*, 5(2), 205–209.

Brooks, M.B. and Kim, H. (1997). The individual investor and the weekend effect: A reexamination with intraday data. *Quarterly Review of Economics and Finance*, 37(3), 725–737.

Cadsby, C.B. and Ratner, M. (1992). Turn-of-the-month and pre-holiday effects on stock returns: Some International evidence. *Journal of Banking and Finance*, 16(3), 497–509.

Chan, M.W.L., Khanthavit, A. and Thomas, H. (1996). Seasonality and cultural influences on four Asian stock markets. *Asia Pacific Journal of Management*, 13(2), 1–24.

Clare, A.D., Ibrahim, M.S.B. and Thomas, S.H. (1998). The impact of settlement procedures on day-of-the-week effects: Evidence from the Kuala Lumpur stock exchange. *Journal of Finance and Accounting,* 25(3/4), 401–418.

Crouhy, M. and Galai, D. (1992). The settlement day effect in the French bourse. *Journal of Financial Services Research,* 6(4), 417–435.

DataStream (2007). Available at http://www.datastream.com/. Accessed August 2014.

Easton, S.A. and Faff, R.W. (1994). An investigation of the robustness of the day-of-the-week effect in Australia. *Applied Financial Economics*, 4(1), 99–110.

Gao, L. and Kling, G. (2005). Calendar effects in the Chinese stock market. *Annals of Economics and Finance*, 6, 75–88.

Gibbons, M. and Hess, P. (1981). Day of the week effects and asset returns. *Journal of Business*, 54(4), 579–596.

Global Financial Data (2007). Available at http://www.globalfindata.com/. Accessed August 2014.

Jaffe, J. and Westerfield, R. (1985). The weekend effect in common stock returns: The international evidence. *Journal of Finance,* 40(2), 433–454.

Keef, S.P. and Roush, M.L. (2005). Day-of-the-week effects in the pre-holiday returns of the Standard & Poor's 500 stock index. *Applied Financial Economics*, 15(1), 107–119.

Kim, C.W. and Park, J. (1994). Holiday effects and stock returns: Further evidence. *Journal of Financial and Quantitative Analysis*, 29(1), 145–157.

Lakonishok, J. and Maberly, E. (1990). The weekend effect: Trading patterns of individual and institutional investors. *Journal of Finance*, 45(1), 231–243.

Lakonishok, J. and Schmidt, S. (1988). Are seasonal anomalies real? A ninety-year perspective. *Review of Financial Studies*, 1(4), 403–425.

Liano, K., Marchand, P.H. and Huang, G.C. (1992). The holiday effect in stock returns: evidence from the OTC market. *Review of Financial Economics*, 2(1), 45–54.

Marquering, W., Nisser, J. and Valla, T. (2006). Disappearing anomalies: A dynamic analysis of the persistence of anomalies. *Applied Financial Economics*, 16(4), 291–302.

Marrett, G. and Worthington, A.C. (2007). An empirical note on the holiday effect in the Australian stock market, 1996-2006. School of Accounting and Finance Working Paper, University of Wollongong.

Meneu, V. and Pardo, A. (2004). Pre-holiday effect, large trades, and small investor behavior. *Journal of Empirical Finance,* 11(2), 231–246.

Miller, E. (1988). Why a weekend effect. *Journal of Portfolio Management*, 14(4), 43–48.

Officer, R.R. (1975). Seasonality in Australian capital markets. *Journal of Financial Economics*, 2(1), 29–51.

Pettengill, G.N. (1989). Holiday closings and security returns. *Journal of Financial Research,* 12(1), 57–67.

Rystrom, D.S. and Benson, E.D. (1989). Investor psychology and the day-of-the-week. *Financial Analysts Journal*, 45(5), 75–78.

Sias, R.W. and Starks, L.T. (1995). The day-of-the-week anomaly: The role of institutional investors. *Financial Analyst Journal*, 51(3), 58–67.

Vergin, R.C. and McGinnis, J. (1999). Revisiting the holiday effect: Is it on holiday? *Applied Financial Economics*, 9(3), 477–482.

Worthington, A.C (2007). National exuberance: A note on the Melbourne Cup effect in Australian stock returns. *Economic Papers*, 26(2), 170-179.

Ziemba, T.W. (1989). Japanese security market regularities: monthly, turn of the month and year, holiday and golden week effects. *Japan and the World Economy,* 3(2), 119–146.

In: Economic and Financial Modeling
Editor: Andrew C. Worthington
ISBN: 978-1-63463-111-2

Chapter 4

THE THEORY AND PRACTICE OF CREDIT RISK MODELING

Mohamed Habara and Andrew C. Worthington*
Griffith University, Australia

ABSTRACT

This chapter reviews models that quantify credit decision making. The first set of models is models of standalone credit risk that attempt to assess credit risk at the firm or individual borrower level. These models include expert and credit rating systems. The second set of models is models of portfolio credit risk that measure credit risk at the portfolio level, including structural models, explicit factor models, and reduced form models. Each model has its own strengths and weaknesses and it is therefore useful to be aware of these in their chosen context.

1. INTRODUCTION

There is a need to develop precise quantitative models to help banks and other financial institutions reduce credit risk associated with lending. The purpose of this chapter is to review those models that quantify credit risk. The first set of models is models of standalone credit risk that attempt to assess credit risk at the firm or individual borrower level. These models include expert and credit rating systems. The second set of models is models of portfolio credit risk that measure credit risk at the portfolio level, including structural models, explicit factor models, and reduced form models. Each set of models have their own strengths and weaknesses and it is therefore useful to be aware of these in their chosen context.

The chapter is divided into seven sections. Section 2 explains the framework for the credit and lending decision. Section 3 examines the concept of credit risk. Section 4 reviews some methods used in analyzing credit risk. Section 5 reviews credit risk models themselves

* Corresponding author: Department of Accounting, Finance and Economics, Griffith University, 170 Kessels Road, Nathan QLD 4111, Australia. Email. a.worthington@griffith.edu.au.

along with credit rating systems and credit portfolio models. Section 6 provides a comparison of the portfolio models with some brief conclusions drawn in Section 7.

2. The Structure of Credit Decisions

Credit and lending decisions may not be easy for banks and other financial institutions because they need to consider the large number of factors that impact on these decisions. Critically, credit decisions do not only involve the analysis of the financial ability of borrowers, they also include other factors (Bierman and Hausman, 1970). Therefore, it is necessary to discuss the framework within which banks and other lenders make such decisions. Figure 1 depicts a sample framework for credit and lending decisions. As shown, the three factor frames have a significant influence on credit decisions and all of these frames relate to each other. What follows is a brief explanation of this general framework.

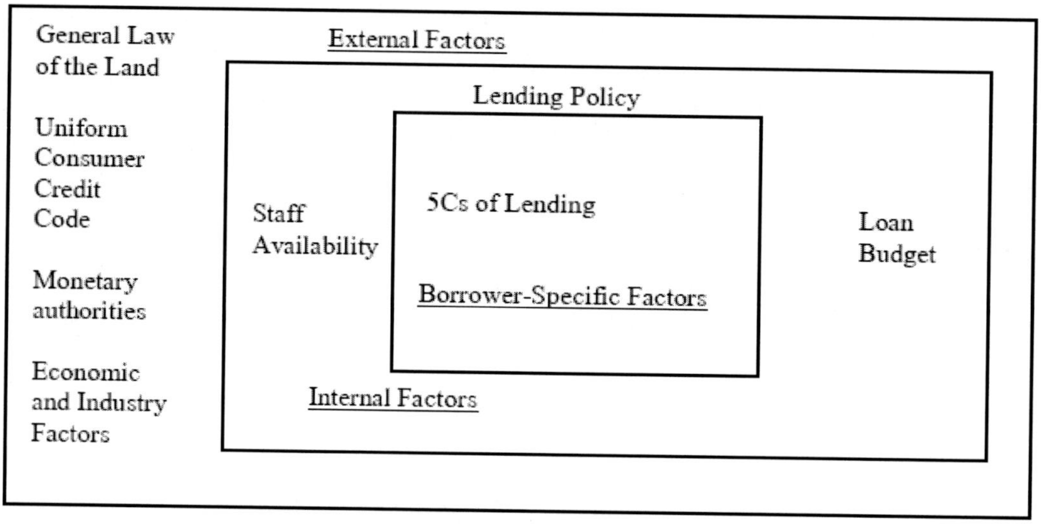

Figure 1. A framework for credit and lending decisions.

2.1. External Factors

Several external factors affect credit decisions (Sathye et al., 2003). First, the *general law of the land*, that is, credit decisions should reflect the laws of a country and ensure compliance with these laws. For example, banks cannot usually grant loans for illegal activities such as drug smuggling. Second, *economic factors* such that lending decisions should take into consideration the state of the economy, including the rate of interest and its relation to the economic cycle. The economic cycle is very important to a bank in its credit and lending decisions. For example, during a recession, banks should pay more attention to companies that sell durable goods rather than nondurable goods companies because the first usually perform badly in times of recession (Saunders and Cornett, 2003, p. 277). Furthermore, the economic cycle has a major impact on interest rates, including when the economy is in a boom or downturn.

There are three impacts on interest rates. First, liquidity refers to the implantation of monetary policy by a central bank in order to influence the money supply and the level of liquidity in the financial system. Second, income has an impact on interest rates. For example, when the central bank desires to reduce the level of expenditure in the economy, it may raise interest rates by introducing government securities. This can lead to reduce liquidity and lower incomes in the all sectors and then slow the rate of economic activity and the demand for loans decreases. Finally, inflation can affect interest rates when the state of economy slows. There is a positive relationship between inflation and interest rates.

Third, *industry-specific factors* in that some industries may not be in a good shape, therefore the bank must think carefully before making decision to grant loans to the firms in those industries. Fourth, *central banking*, the main responsibility of the central bank (sometimes in conjunction with other monetary authorities) is to implement monetary policy to ensure a stable economy, including provision of a stable currency. Central banks can also issue currency, function as bank to the government, regulate the credit system, oversee the behavior of commercial banks, manage exchange reserves, and issue directions about interest rates and other charges. Therefore, banks must be aware of central bank legislation when they decide to grant a loan. Finally, the *uniform consumer credit code* (or equivalent), such that lending decisions must ensure compliance. This code provides protection to consumers who buy goods and services on credit (Sathye et al., 2003).

Moreover, Porter (2004) identified the five forces (first introduced in 1979) which lead to competition on a business. Figure 2 shows these five forces. Porter's five forces analysis deals with factors outside an industry that influence the nature of competition within it and the forces inside the industry (microenvironment) that influence the way in which firms compete. Therefore, Porter's five forces model includes the industry's likely profitability. In addition, banks must realize the behavior of its industries and markets in order to compete successfully in the bank sector.

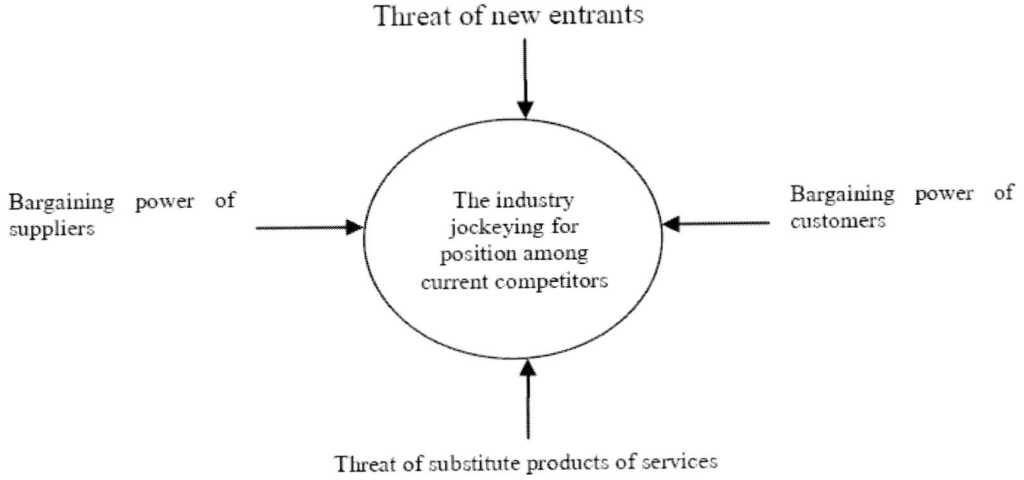

Figure 2. Porter's five forces.

First, the industry jockeying for position among current competitors force, which is located at the center of Figure 2 identifies industry attractiveness and it is the most important force in industries. Second, the threat of new entrants often relies on the market entry difficulties. The most common types of entry difficulties are economies of scale, cost of entry, distribution channels, and cost advantages not associated with the size of the institution, government legislations, and differentiation of product. Third, the threat of substitute products or services relies on the relative price-to-performance ratios of the different kinds of products or services to which customers can turn to satisfy the same essential need. It also requires product-for-product substitution and generic substitution. Fourth, the bargaining power of customers is included in the size and concentration of customers. Finally, bargaining power of suppliers depends on the relative size and concentration of suppliers relative to industry participants and on the degree of differentiation in the inputs supplied. Therefore, banks should clearly understand the nature of their competitive environment if they are to be successful in accomplishing their aims and in building right strategies. Fully understanding the nature of the Porter's five forces can lead to a stronger position to protect a bank against any threats.

2.2. Internal Factors

Internal factors also affect lending decisions. These include *lending policy*, in that the granting of loans needs to comply with the lending policy of the bank. Credit policy is the actions taken by a bank to grant, control, and collect the cash from the outstanding accounts receivables. It also includes *the loan budget*, such that the ability of a bank to grant a loan is limited is arises from the difference between the total numbers of deposits and the part kept by the bank in a liquid form funds to meet the demands of clients. Lending decisions must always comply with the loan budget. Banks also obtain funding from a variety of sources, but it is often useful to differentiate between retail funding, borrowed or wholesale funding, and equity funding. Retail funding generally consists of deposit accounts such as transactions accounts, money market demand retained earnings accounts, savings accounts and short-term deposits. Borrowed funding consists of federal funds purchased, repurchase agreements, Federal Home Loan bank borrowings, and other borrowings. Wholesale funding includes borrowed funds as well as large institutional deposits such as large certificate deposits. Equity funding consists of common and preferred stock, retained earnings, and other equities (Koch and MacDonald, 2006, p. 254).

In addition, securitization is another tool for raising new funds and reducing a bank's risk exposure (Rose, 2002). Banks can decrease their capital requirements and reduce credit risk by selling assets and servicing the payments between borrower and lender, rather than holding the same assets to earn interest (Koch and MacDonald, 2006). The main forms of securitization are the pass- through security, the collateralized mortgage obligation, and the mortgage-backed bond (Saunders and Cornett, 2003). The pass-through security requires accumulating debts in the pool in order to generate cash flow, then sold first to an intermediary who passes them on to the investors as securities. The collateralized mortgage obligation requires accumulating home mortgage loans in the pool and then the government agency guaranteed pass-through securities are issued against the mortgage pool and may be purchased by a bank or other investors.

Finally, these mortgage-backed bonds are issued to reduce credit risk to the investors and these bonds separate the mortgage loans held on balance sheets from other assets and pledge those loans as collateral to support the mortgage-backed bonds (Saunders and Cornett, 2003). Furthermore, credit derivatives are other sources of bank funds (Hogan et al., 2004). They are financial contracts offering protection to the beneficiary in case of loan default. One example of credit derivatives is the credit swap, where two lenders agree to exchange a portion of their customer's loan repayments (Rose, 2002, p. 295). The second type of credit derivatives is the total return swap, where the protection seller pays the protection buyer any losses in market value on the reference loan. Finally, credit options operate as normal options where the strike price is based on credit spreads widening (Sathye et al., 2003, p. 355); (c) *staff availability*; this factor also can impact on credit and lending decision. A shortage of skilled staff that evaluate and control loans for lending institutions may lead to reduction of granting loans. Thus, lending institutions should take into its considerations these and other such internal factors which could have an impact on lending decisions (Sathye et al., 2003).

2.3. Borrower-Specific Factors

In addition to external and internal factors, considered during the lending decision process, there must be attention to borrower-specific factors, often referred to as the five Cs of lending. These factors include (Sathye et al., 2003): (1) *character*; this is the sum total of human qualities of honesty, integrity, and morality and so on. Lenders need to review the character of borrowers to realize whether they have such qualities. Character assessment requires collecting information about the potential applicant, such as credit history, income, occupation, spending habits, reports from credit agencies and so on. This information can help the lender in deciding the character of the expected borrower; (2) *capacity*; capacity is the ability to repay the loan and interest on time. Therefore, lenders investigate the ability of applicants to repay by reviewing borrowers' assets and liabilities and the details of income and expenses; (3) *capital*; capital refers to the capital that is owned by a borrower when he or she applies for a loan. For example, banks often require a set percentage from the applicant as a contribution to total prospective investment; (4) *collateral*; collateral is also known as the secondary source of repayment. The lender should review some qualities in a security, such as the price of the security, and realize that the price is stable. The security can be sold quickly so that the bank can repay the loan, and the collateral should not deteriorate over time; and (5) *conditions*; according to this factor, lenders take into consideration the conditions covering the external and internal factors discussed earlier. Before making credit decision, bank officers also take into consideration credit risk and try to study and analyze all methods that reduce credit default when a credit decision is made and the loan is granted. Therefore, the study of credit risk becomes an importation issue. The following section addresses credit risk.

3. Concept of Credit Risk

Banks face numerous risks affecting profitability throughout their business lines. The management of these risks has always been a major component of bank management (De

Lucia, 2003). The major sources of banking risk can be classified into six main categories (Santomero, 1997): (i) market risk, (ii) operational risk, (iii) liquidity risk, (iv) yield risk, (v) management risk and (vi) credit risk. First, *market risk* is the risk of losses resulting from adverse changes in market asset values from changes in economic factors. Second, according to the Basel committee, *operational risk* is the risk of loss resulting from inadequate or failed internal processes, people, and systems or from external events (Golin, 2001). Third, *liquidity risk* is the risk that an organization may itself fail to meet its obligations when they fall due or encounters difficulty in selling some asset when needed. Fourth, *yield risk* is the risk that the bank's assets may produce less income than the expense produced by its liabilities. Fifth, management *risk* is the risk that investors and managers may be unsuitable for their respective responsibility. Finally, and despite of the importance of these other sources of risks in banks, the biggest risk facing most banks and financial institutions is *credit risk*.

Credit risk has been an important issue for many lenders (Brian and Colleen, 1997). In fact, it is the primary reason for the bankruptcy of most financial institutions in the last century. There has been an explosion of analysis in the past two decades with the development of credit risk techniques. Credit risk is also one of the oldest risks faced by banks as financial institutions and dates back at least as far as 1800 BC (Golin, 2001). The risk of borrower default – on interest and/or principal – may result in capital losses for banks leading to bankruptcy. Managing this type of risk by choosing and screening borrowers and by creating a diversified loan portfolio has always been one of the main challenges in running a bank (Broll et al., 2002). Credit risk is generally found in all fields where success relies on counterparty, issuer, or borrower performance. It arises any time when a bank extends, commits, invests or otherwise exposes it funds through actual or implied contractual agreements, whether on or off the balance sheet (Comptroller of the Currency Administrator of National Banks, 1999).

According to the Basel Committee (2000, p. 1), credit risk can be defined as "... the potential that a bank borrower or counterparty will fail to meet its obligations in accordance with agreed terms". The objective of credit risk management is to increase the bank's rate of return by maintaining credit risk exposure within adequate limits. Credit risk management is also needed to deal with whole portfolios. The relationship between credit risk and other risks should be taken into consideration. The effective management of credit risk is a critical part of a comprehensive approach to risk management and important to the long-term success of any bank.

For most banks, and regardless of whether existing sources of credit risk in many activities at a bank are on or off balance sheet, loans are considered the main source of credit risk although other sources of credit risk exist. Credit risk is increasingly found in a variety of financial instruments other than loans including foreign exchange transactions, financial futures, swaps, bonds, equities, options, and in the extension of commitments and guarantees, and the settlement of transactions (Basel, 2000).

Most researchers refer to credit risk and default risk in similar terms but there is a slight variation in definition. Here, credit risk is "the risk of loss through the default on financial obligations" (Golin, 2001, p. 672) while default risk is "... the risk that the issuer will not fulfil its financial obligations to the investor/creditor in accordance with the terms of the obligation..." (Golin, 2001, p. 675). In these terms, credit risk usually refers to a borrower who may be able to repay a loan with a degree of potential loss, while default risk usually concerns a lender who may miss payments. Thus, it could be said that since there is no major difference between the two types of risks, they could be defined together as the following: credit/default risk is the risk that financial obligations of a borrower within an agreement will not be performed satisfactorily (Sathye et al., 2003, p. 109).

The main components of credit risk can be divided into two main categories (Ong, 2000, p. 63): individual risk and portfolio risk. First, individual risk includes three elements: (i) default probability which is the likelihood that the borrowers will not meet the agreed commitment to repay their loan; (ii) recovery rates which are the extent to which the percentage of the par value of an obligation can be received once in case of default; and (iii) credit migration which is the extent to which the credit risk can change through the life of a loan. The credit migration is usually shown in credit rating tables. Second, portfolio risk includes two main elements: (i) default and credit quality correlation which means the degree to which default or credit quality of borrowers is correlated to other credit quality borrowers; and (ii) the risk contribution and credit concentration which is the extent to which a single asset of a borrower in the portfolio contributes to the total of risk in the whole portfolio (Ong, 2000).

4. Credit Risk Analysis

This section reviews credit risk analysis. Financial institutions use a variety of tools to determine the credit risk of their products. These tools can be divided into four main groups: (i) expert systems; (ii) risk premium analysis; (iii) econometrics; (iv) hybrid systems (Sathye et al., 2003, p. 110).

4.1. Expert Systems

Expert systems (or traditional methods) are a classic form of credit analysis that depends on the subjective judgment of lenders. In these systems, the experience of the senior lender is important for a number of reasons: (i) the senior lender follows the limits of bank's rules; (ii) the senior lender is a source of rules of thumb; (iii) banks rely on their senior lending officers to perform most of the important issues such as interpreting industry trends, assessing a borrower's creditworthiness, or designing the credit structure under which the bank will make the loan (Caouette et al., 1998, p. 83).

A lender receives an application form from the potential borrower and a checklist is provided by bank. After that, the application form is analyzed and assessed by the lender and, if the loan is approved, documentation is completed and the loan is funded. The most common technique of this type is five Cs analyses as discussed (Sathye et al., 2003).

However, expert systems have obvious weaknesses (Caouette et al., 1998). First, they are subjective; decision-making depends on the lending officer who may be subject to external influences such as social relationships and personality. Second, the implement of these systems is uneven, so their success and failure depend on the experience and performance of the lender. For example, some lenders have the talents to analyze credit risk effectively and others do not. In addition, expert systems are quite expensive. For instance, the preparation and implementation of these systems require qualified and experienced staff and these incur high costs. Furthermore, expert systems are related to bureaucratic system of performing business and this can waste time in decision-making. Thus, to overcome these disadvantages, it is generally argued that it is best to apply objective systems that do not depend on the subjective judgment of lenders.

4.2. Risk Premium Analysis

The risk premium in credit analysis is defined as the difference between the interest yield on company debt and government debt. This approach may work well for companies that are rated by a credit rating agency. The calculation of the premium as probability of repayment can be achieved by comparison between the interest rate of the company and the interest rate of government 'risk-free' as follows:

$$P = \frac{1+i}{1+r}$$

where P is the probability of repayment, i is the interest rate on company debt, and r the risk-free rate.

4.3. Econometrics

Econometrics is the branch of economics that studies the mathematical relationship between financial or economic variables to forecast the behavior of economic variables. Econometrics has given credit analysis a scientific base, despite suffering from lack of a creditable theoretical basis. The most important tool of econometrics is regression analysis and discriminant analysis. Principal econometrics techniques involve the modeling of probability of default. This probability is used as a dependent variable whose variance is explained by a set of independent variables. Other econometric techniques include linear and multiple discriminant analysis, multiple regression, logit analysis and probit analysis. These techniques are examined in Chapter 3 as they are the main tools used in this thesis.

4.4. Hybrid Systems

As mentioned previously, econometrics suffers from an unsound theoretical basis for analysis of credit risk because the solutions of econometrics provide only a statistical relationship between the dependent variable (default) and a number of explanatory variables. This relationship results in models that do not include known financial theories such as insurance and option theories (Sathye et al., 2003). Therefore, hybrid systems overcome this deficiency by combining financial theory and economic statistics. In addition, there is a criticism of multivariate models that use historical data from financial reports to calculate the default probability, while hybrid systems use stock prices and credit ratings to forecast default

(Caouette et al., 1998, p. 348). Examples of these systems are expected default frequency and mortality models.

Expected Default Frequency

This model was created by KMV Corporation in 1995 and applies option theory to grant a loan. To determine an expected default frequency for a company, three stages should be followed. The first stage requires that the market value and volatility of the firm are estimated from the market value of its stock, the volatility of its stock, and the book value of liabilities. The second stage is that the firm's default point is calculated from the firm's liabilities. An expected firm value is also determined from the current firm value. Using these two values, plus the firm's volatility, a measure is constructed that is the number of standard deviations from the expected firm value to the default point (the distance to default). Finally, the mapping is determined between the distances to default rate, based on the historical default experience of companies with different distance-to-default values (Caouette et al., 1998, p. 143).

$$\text{Distance of default} = \frac{\text{market value of assets - default point}}{\text{market value of assets (asset volatility)}}$$

The KMV Corporation proportion of firms is the expected default probability:

$$\text{Expected default probability} = \frac{\text{Number of default firms}}{\text{All firms of sample}}$$

Mortality models

These models attempt to derive actuarial-type probabilities of default from historical data on bond defaults, by credit grade and years to maturity. Altman (1989) extended the insurance concept to estimating how many loans default in a year. Altman considers mortalities with respect to survival population and then inputs the defaults to calculate mortality rates. Bonds exit from the original population because of at least four different types of events: default, calls, sinking funds, and maturities. The individual mortality rate for each year (marginal mortality rate, or MMR) is calculated using the equation (Altman, 1989, p. 5).

$$\text{MMR=} \frac{\text{Total value of defaulting debt in the year}}{\text{Total value of bonds at the begining year}}$$

The subsequent issues require consideration in these models: the MMR is calculated for each credit rating and each year, so we would expect the MMR to increase for each year. The MMR can also be converted into a value by which the loan depreciates each year.

5. Credit Risk Modeling

Credit risk modeling can be used as a significant tool for understanding a phenomenon and to aid in decision-making. It also provides several solutions for banks including, for example, identifying the amount of a loan that will be granted, whether the loan will be good or bad, and the accurate degree of the constructed models.

Credit risk model refers to the process of quantifying credit exposure of a financial institution. Some advantages of credit risk models include the following: (Sathye et al., 2003, p. 337): adding objectivity to credit measurement, adding a scientific basis to the credit assessment process, rating loans that have no credit ratings or giving a system of grading and providing a mechanism for controlling loans to ensure they are not potential problem loans.

Models are often built on theories such as financial theories and economic theories. In addition to these theories, models need to the variables in order to produce a more accurate model. Caouette et al. (1998) provides a table containing a range of possible applications of quantitative credit risk models, as shown in Table 1.

Table 1. A range of possible application of quantitative credit risk models

Large corporate borrowers	**Middle market borrowers**	**Middle market and private borrowers**
Publicly traded. Extensive disclosure. Many institutional investors with research capabilities. Low monitoring, (annual cycle). Better scoring models because of better data.	Publicly traded. Moderate disclosure. Little or no publicly traded debt. Low use of credit scoring models. Greater emphasis on management.	Stock not publicly traded. No public debt. More information problems. Reliance on financial statements. Close monitoring. Reliance on collateral and covenants. Limited use of credit scoring models.
Small Business	**Commercial real estate**	**Residential and real estate**
No stock. Even financial statements are unaudited. Information problems. Reliance on individuals. Close monitoring. Collateral. Moderate use of credit scoring models.	No publicly traded stock. Approval based on cash flow, projections and collateral value. Moderate monitoring. More reliance on collateral and covenants.	Reliance on collateral value. Greater use of financial data. Increasing use of credit scoring models.
Consumers		
No financial statements. Fewer information problems because of credit bureaus. Reliance on demographic variables. Collateral only for consumer durables. No covenants. Heavy use of use of credit scoring models.		

Currently, credit risk models are important because they provide the decision maker with insight or knowledge. Credit risk models help bank management to assess the credit risk of individual loans as well as the entire loan portfolio. They also permit a bank to estimate potential credit losses in the future, to determine the risk-based capital requirements, to assess credit concentration limits, and to measure risk-adjusted profitability (Lopez and Saidenberg, 2000). The remainder of this section reviews credit risk models literature. However, the following discussion includes only two models, namely, credit ratings and credit portfolios.

5.1. Credit Ratings

Credit ratings were first introduced by Henry Vernum Poor in 1860 with the issuance of some financial statistics of railroad companies in the United States to attract investors. They were subsequently developed by J. Moody in 1909 by using alphabetical symbols to rate railroad bonds. Currently, there are a large number of credit rating agencies instituted in many countries to provide services to the investors, borrowers and other financial institutions. (Kumar and Haynes, 2003).

Credit ratings have a number of advantages. To start with, they help the investors obtain information at low cost, take a computed risk, and encourage them to invest in securities to obtain high returns. In addition, they can be used as a tool to improve the brand of a company and motivate public investment in the corporate sector. Moreover, internal credit ratings are becoming popular in the assessment of a variety of risks because of the ability in using more data especially for the small to medium–sized business (BIS, 2000).

Credit ratings are a summary indicator of risk for banks' individual credit exposures (Treacy and Carey, 2000; BIS, 2000). The risk components include measures of the borrower's probability of default, the facility's loss given default, the level of exposure at the time of default, the credit's expected loss, effective maturity and unexpected loss associated with these, and possibly other concepts and characteristics relating to borrowers and exposure. Credit ratings rely on a number of variables; quantitative financial ratios and qualitative variables.

The rating methodology covers the assessment of business risks (industry risk, market position of the issuing entity within in industry, operating efficiency of the borrowing entity, legal position) and financial risk (accounting quality, earnings protection, adequacy of cash flows, financial flexibility, interest and tax sensitivity) associated with the issuer/borrowing entity. Treacy and Carey (2000) find that qualitative variables play a major role in identifying the ratings of credit to small and medium-sized firms, with the credit officers essentially responsible for the ratings while, for loans to large firms, the credit officers mainly set the ratings using quantitative methods such as credit scoring models. (Bessis, 2002) shows that credit ratings are a qualitative ordering rather than a quantitative measure of risk. Treacy and Carey (2000, p. 2) conducted a survey of 50 large US banking organizations and BIS and in its survey of 30 financial institutions across the G-10 countries they found significant variety in internal ratings models. While all used similar financial risk variables, there were variations across financial institutions in relation to the relative significance of each of the variables (Allen, 2002).

Credit ratings have different types, with each type depending on the requirements of the rater and the rated. The following are the more common types of credit rating (Kumar and Haynes, 2003): (i) bond rating: issued by a company and government. This concerns the most important industry of credit rating agencies; (ii) short term instruments rating (securities with an initial maturity of up to one year); (iii) commercial paper rating (It is compulsory on the part of a corporate body to obtain the rating of an approved credit rating agency to issue commercial paper); (iv) rating the borrowers (This includes rating a borrower to whom a loan/credit facility may be sanctioned); (v) sovereign/country rating (This shows the risk level of the investing surroundings of a country and is used by investors looking to invest aboard).

Credit ratings may be divided into internal ratings and external ratings. Internal ratings are those constructed for banks for their own use. Internal rating systems were introduced primarily to help credit decision making and control, portfolio monitoring, management reporting, analysis of the adequacy of loan loss reserves or capital and profitability analysis and product pricing models (Treacy and Carey, 2000). Many banks have established internal ratings systems in preparation for the BIS (Bank for International Settlements) New Capital Accord scheduled for implementation in 2006. Basel II (The New Basel Capital Accord) has noted the advantages and disadvantage of using internal rating systems. Internal rating systems should be applied by banks when computing their capital requirements. Basel II also provides the details of regulations for design of an internal rating system such as rating dimension, system structure, rating criteria, assessment horizon, use of models, and documentation of rating system design (Kim, 2005).

In the architecture of an internal rating system, the bank may depend on a one-dimensional model, in which overall rating is assigned only to facility grade and each loan based on the probability of default, or a two-dimensional model, in which the rating system includes both an obligor and facility grade and each borrower's probability of default is assessed independently from loss severity of individual loans. Treacy and Carey (2000) estimated that 60% of the banks in their survey have a one-dimensional rating system, although they recommend two-dimensional systems for banks and regulators. Moreover, the BIS (2000) found that banks have a better ability in assessing their borrower's probability of default than loss given default.

The risk rating process proceeds as follows. First, the banks start by considering risk factors. The financial analysis often includes a formal comparison of the borrower's financial ratios to prevailing industry norms. Raters also appraise the quality of financial statements provided by the borrower. When statement quality is poor or uncertain, financial analysis may produce a distorted view of the borrower's condition, adding substantially to risk. Many banks use external ratings in calibrating their rating systems and in identifying likely mistakes in grade assignments.

A number of banks also use statistical models as an element of the rating process. Statistical models of borrower default probability can be helpful in maintaining the integrity of internal ratings. Most banks formally consider both firm size (sales revenue or total assets) and the book or market dollar value of a firm's equity in assigning ratings. According to the factors considered in rating, rating criteria are identified. Because rating criteria have changed over time at most large institutions, information about borrower and loan characteristics is also required so that the risk implications of different rating criteria can be assessed. Large banks' written definitions of ratings specify risk factors to be used in assigning ratings, but usually the discussion is brief and broadly worded, and gives virtually no guidance regarding the weight to place on each factor. Important informal elements of the rating process, such as negotiation among various organizational units, may lead to a consensus rating or understanding. The human judgment exercised by experienced bank staff is central to the assignment of a rating. Ratings are initially assigned either by relationship managers or credit staff. Relationship managers are lending officers (line staff) responsible for marketing of banking services and then they achieve approval process regarding to ratings.

In turn, the review process is divided into three sub processes; line/credit review, watch processes and loan review. Line/credit review means monitoring by those who assign the primary rating of a transaction; watch processes means regularly scheduled reviews of ratings for groups of exposures; and loan review means occasional reviews of a business unit's rating assignments by a loan review unit (Treacy and Carey, 1998, p. 907). Each process includes a number of procedures. The review process aims to identify and discipline relationship managers who produce inaccurate ratings. Risk ratings are identified by assignment of rating and review processes. Finally, the uses of ratings are important. At most banks, however, the primary demands for quantitative information about the probability of default (PD), loss in the event of default (LIED), and expected loss (EL) (quantitative loss characteristics) have come from those involved in the loan loss reserve process and from credit modeling groups (portfolio risk, capital allocation, profitability, and pricing). In contrast, external ratings denote the rating system independently made outside the bank or creditor such as credit rating agencies, which include, for instance, Standard & Poor's (www2.standardandpoors.com), Moody's (www.moodys.com) and Fitch (www.fitchratings.com).

In general, the categories used by the major ratings agencies, defined in terms of default risk and the probability of payment, are quite similar, although differences of opinion can lead, in some cases, to dissimilar ratings of specific debt obligations (English and Nelson, 1998). The ratings from AAA to BBB (the first level) represent the safest ratings to investors and issuers, while the risk is increasing from the ratings BB to the last rating (second level) in the table which means the level of bankruptcy and inability to repay debts may increase. Some rules in a number of countries prohibit investors from investing in the second level because of the high risk.

The long-term default rates can be calculated by assuming the Markov process for the ratings migration which is explained by a transition matrix. The transition matrix describes the probability of moving to one rating conditional on the rating from one state to another. Calculated transition matrices are obtainable from both Standard & Poor's and Moody's. There are different probabilities in the transition matrices for each state because they use their credit history database with their ratings to calculate the transition matrix. There are differences in default probabilities, which are known as rating transition rate volatilities, because the transition matrices are computed every year. Most of this may be because of the changes in the state of the economy (Haag, 2003). Regardless, .the Markov model is the first and most common way to model the credit rating, Skora (2000) shows that the credit rating process is not a Markov process because it is clearly not accurate.

A large number of studies have considered credit ratings. Udell (1987, 1989) examined the internal rating systems of a sample of US banks regarding loan review and loan department policies. Brady et al. (1998) provide some summary information about the use of loan risk rating scales of a sample of US banks of all sizes and also report both distributions of loans across grades and loan pricing for a stratified random sample of US banks. Robert Morris Associates (1997) surveyed internal rating systems as a part of large study of banks' credit-risk management practices. Machauer and Weber (1998) examined the relationship of bank loan terms to borrower risk defined by the banks' internal credit rating using data from five lending German banks from 1992–1996. Elsas and Krahnen (1998) use bank internal borrower rating data from a sample of borrowers drawn from the credit portfolio of five lending German banks to evaluate borrower quality. Treacy and Carey (2000) provided a detailed analysis of internal credit risk rating systems. Other papers examining credit rating agencies include Cantor and Packer (1994), Ederington and Yawitz (1987), Altman and Saunders (1997).

A number of the criticisms of credit rating agencies result from their mistakes. For example, credit rating agencies have limited abilities in obtaining full information on the rating organizations. They depend on the available information in financial markets, which is sometimes not sufficient to calculate a sound rating. Furthermore, the failure of credit agencies in achieving accuracy ratings has been since the great depression. Sylla (2001, p. 20) shows that Hempel's study showed that the 78% of the defaulted issues were rated Aa or better in 1929. Karacadag and Taylor (2000) show that the credit ratings are poor predictors of default and the rating agencies missed the Asian currency crises before they occurred in 1997-1998. Thus, the credit rating should be taken into consideration as one of the factors that helps in investor and lender decision making.

5.2. Portfolio Models

Harry Markowitz pioneered portfolio theory in 1952 in his Journal of Finance paper titled "Portfolio Selection." The principle idea of portfolio theory is that market risk should be managed at the portfolio level by spreading investments. In 1958, James Tobin developed Markowitz's idea by adding a risk-free asset to the analysis and this resulted in the idea of a super-efficient portfolio and the capital market line. Another important contribution in portfolio theory was by William Sharpe in 1964 in formalizing the capital assets pricing model (CAPM) which simplifies the Markowitz framework by creating a criterion index of the market value weighted portfolio of all potential risk investments. Portfolio theory studies the selection of different mixtures of securities based on their risk-return characteristics as reflected in the portfolio's expected return and the variability of that return under the theory of the efficient market hypothesis (Harrington, 1987, p. 26).

The main aim of portfolio theory, in addition to measuring risk, is to illustrate a method for improving the return and risk characteristics by changing the composition of portfolios (Caouette et al., 1998). Portfolio theory focuses on the expected return per unit of risk. The ratio of return to risk for a portfolio is called the Sharpe ratio, and efficient portfolios are those with the highest achievable Sharpe ratios. Portfolio optimization refers to different types of quantitative techniques for ascertaining efficient portfolios (Geng, 2002). However, portfolio theory faces some problems in its implementation to credit portfolios and these include determination of the return, risk and the correlation measures that are needed as inputs (Caouette et al., 1998).

Caouette et al. (1998) illustrated that there are three key points that emerge from portfolio analysis that have implications for credit risk modeling. These are: (i) the correlation between default risks within a portfolio is an important factor in achieving the diversification in a portfolio; (ii) the amount of risk added by any asset to the portfolio's net diversification relies considerably on how much of the asset is held in the portfolio; (iii) including large numbers of assets, and changing asset holdings, to bring each asset's contribution to the portfolio risk in line with its contribution to the portfolio return, are aimed at comprised of improving portfolio performance.

In a credit context, several portfolio models assess credit risk. Portfolio credit risk is a methodology that estimates the probability of default and credit loss for a loan portfolio over a particular time horizon. It usually combines the probabilities of default for individual loans and estimates the probability level by aggregation (Lopez, 2001). Portfolio credit risk models are financial models that assess portfolio credit risk. Portfolio credit risk modeling is a process to find specific solutions to the two main problems: (1) the modeling of the probability of default for individual loans, and (2) the building of the joint distribution of default by taking into consideration the correlation between defaults in the portfolio (Dietsch and Petey, 2002). Therefore, the main inputs to a portfolio credit risk model are: (1) stand-alone credit risk measure for each loan, (2) its weight in the loan portfolio and (3) the correlation of default between each pair of loans. Smithson (2003) details that there are three types of credit portfolio models in current use: (i) structural models; there are two vendor-supplied credit portfolio models of this type: Moody's-KMV Portfolio Manager and RiskMetrics Group's Credit Manager; (ii) macro factor models; McKinsey and company introduced Credit Portfolio View in 1998 and (iii`) actuarial (reduced form) models; Credit Suisse First Boston first introduced Credit Risk+ in 1997.

Structural Models

Structural models are also referred to as 'asset volatility models' or 'firm value models' or Merton models. Black and Scholes first proposed them in 1973 for option pricing and subsequently developed by Merton in 1974. The idea of structural models depends on the Merton insight that "... debt behaves like a put option on the value of the firm's assets" (Smithson, 2003, p. 110).

In the Merton model, default occurs when the value of the firm's assets drops below some trigger level (Smithson, 2003). When this occurs, bondholders obtain the residual value of the firm and stockholders are given nothing. On the other hand, if the firm survives, bondholders receive the interest and the stockholders obtain the remaining value of the assets (Houweling et al., 2003, p .11). Therefore, default is determined by the structure of the individual firm and its asset volatility, and option-pricing theory can be applied to calculate theoretical credit and stock value. They follow that default correlation must be a function of asset correlation.

An estimation of the market value of the firm's assets and the volatility of that value is required to apply structural model. The reason for this is that asset values and their volatilities are not visible for most firms (Smithson, 2003). Describing how default in reality happens and determines that recovery internally is one of advantages of structural models (Gordy, 2000).

Moreover, structural models may be more suitable for corporate than for sovereign issuers because for countries the 'asset value' concept is not applicable (Houweling et al., 2003). However, it is difficult to estimate the parameters of the structural models because the assets' market value and volatility are hard to observe. The classic structural model has been developed by in number of studies, including Black and Cox (1976), Geske (1977), Geske and Johnson (1984), Shimko, Tejinma and Van Deventer (1993), Longstaff and Schwartz (1995), Leland (1994), Leland and Toft (1996), Mella-Barral and Perraudin (1997), Collin-Dufresne and Goldstein (2001), Zhou (2001), Gordy and Heitfield (2001), Cathcart and El-Jahel, (2004), and Bedendo et al., (2004).

Moody's-KMV Portfolio Manager

Moody's-KMV Portfolio Manager was released in 1993. These models are based on Merton's insights (Lando, 2004). KMV derives the estimated default frequency (EDF) or default probability (the EDF) for each obligor based on the Merton's (1974) option-theoretic, zero-coupon, corporate bond valuation approach (Crouhy et al., 2000). Moody's-KMV Portfolio Manager was the first portfolio credit-risk model developed by KMV in 1993. KMV uses a different approach because it does not determine the default probability directly. It determines a distance to default (DD) measure, which gives how far away the firm is from default. This is accomplished by using both equity market information and from the financial statements. Whitelaw (1997) showed that the model is designed to achieve three objectives: (i) describe the risk and return of credit portfolio; (ii) determine what the optimal trading plan should be for a defined set of trading or origination opportunities; and (iii) optimise portfolios by shifting the view of the existing set of debt assets.

The stochastic variable in KMV Portfolio Manager is the value of the firm's assets. Portfolio Manager is designed to use EDFs obtained from Moody's-KMV Credit Monitor or Private Firm Model (Smithson, 2003). To identify EDF, inputs to the model proceed in four stages (Caouette et al, 1998; Hubal and Meisser, 2000; Crouhy et al., 2000; Altman, 2002a; and Haag, 2003): (i) the market value and volatility of the firm are estimated from the market value of its stock, the volatility of its stock and the book value of its liabilities. The market value and volatility of the firm can be estimated by using the Black and Schole option pricing theory, which assumes that the returns are normally, distributed (Sundaram, 2001). The market value of equity may be expressed as the value of call options, as follows: Market value of equity = *f* (book value of liabilities, market value of assets, volatility of assets, time horizon); (ii) the firm's default point is calculated from the firm's liabilities. Moreover, the current firm value is used to determine the expected firm value. By using these two values and the firm's volatility, a measure is built that represents the number of standard deviations between the mean of the distribution of the asset value and the default point (the distance to default). The distance to default can be calculated as (Crosbie and Bohn, 2003):

$$\text{Distance from default} = \frac{\text{Expected market value of assets - Default point}}{\text{Expected market value of assets} \times \text{Volatility of assets}}$$

(iii) the distance of default measure is used to compare different firms with each other to indicate how many firms are in a similar defaulted situation; and (iv) mapping the distances to default rate to the actual probabilities of default, based on the historical default experience of large sample companies with different distance to default values. The result of mapping is EDF. The starting point of the KMV model is when the market value of the firm's assets drops below a certain point, the firm will default on its obligations (Caouette et al., 1998, p. 144).

To estimate credit risk at portfolio level, Portfolio Manager uses asset return correlations between all couples of obligors as a proxy of asset correlation while taking the effect of portfolio diversification into consideration. This is achieved by deriving a multi-factor structural model to avoid computational problems expected from an enormous correlation matrix in a large loan portfolio. According to the multi-factor model, systematic factors and individual factors generate asset returns and the common systematic factors to all firms explain their correlations between two borrowers. Finally, a default distribution for the loan portfolio is provided by Monte Carlo simulation, and portfolio credit risk is measured by using VaR. (Kim, 2005).

In Moody's KMV model, default correlation is calculated in the Global Correlation Model. This applies the assets-correlation approach by using a factor model that produces correlated asset returns. This requires determination of the return on a unique custom index for a firm in a period.The generation of the simulated portfolio value distributions (custom index) may be summarized in four steps, as follows (Smithson, 2003): (i) simulate the asset value of firm; (ii) valuation of each facility at horizon as a function of the simulated value of the obligor's assets at the horizon; (iii) sum the values of facilities to obtain the value of the portfolio; and (iv) repeating steps 1-3 some number of times (e.g., 1,000,000 times) to obtain a distribution.

The KMV model has a number of advantages. KMV can be applied to any publicly-traded company and is based on stock market data which is timely and contains a forward looking view. On the other hand, the KMV model is difficult for diagnosing a theoretical EDF and the results sensitive to stock market movements.

Risk Metrics Group's Credit Manager

CreditMetrics, a tool of RiskMetrics, is a market-to-market model to measure portfolio credit risk and its value. It was introduced by JP Morgan in April 1997 as a methodology for calculating portfolio value at risk due to changes in obligor credit quality. A data set and software apply its methodology. The idea of this model is that the portfolio value should be viewed not just about the probability of default but also according to the changes in credit quality over time (Caouette et al., 1998). The assumption of this model is that all borrowers can be classified in terms of a rating system, and all borrowers within a similar rating class are credit homogeneous with the same probability of default and the same transition probability (Kim, 2005). CreditMetrics looks for to estimate the full value at risk (VaR) of a loan in portfolio by considering rating credit quality and associated effects of spread changes in the discount rate as a part of the VaR exposure of a credit (Papanyan, 2003).

The important aims of CreditMetrics are to provide a process for estimating the value distribution of any portfolio of assets subject to migrations in credit quality (Caouette et al., 1998) and generate a standard for credit risk measurement to facilitate comparison of different sources and measures of risk (Greg, 1997). CreditMetrics varies slightly from KMV's method, mainly that it relies upon the average historical transition frequencies created by the rating agencies instead of upon the EDF for each issuer. Both models depend on the asset value model introduced by Merton (1974), but the process of the simplifying assumptions that they require to facilitate its application are considerably different (Crouhy et al., 2000).

The CreditMetrics methodology consists of three major building blocks as shown in Figure 3.

The left hand side of the diagram represents the determination of exposures, that is, the amounts actually at risk should a default occur. The middle section represents the determination of stand-alone risks per dollar of exposure. The right hand side of the diagram represents the determination of correlations. The bottom box of the diagram represents the overall portfolio risk calculation, which is arrived at by combining the exposure, stand-alone risk, and correlation values (Caouette et al., 1998).

Exposures are the amount subject to either changes in value upon credit quality upgrade and downgrade or loss in the event of default. To measure the exposures for each credit instrument, the start point is the user's portfolio by analysing all credit instruments in terms of their exposures and by assessing the effect of market volatility on expected exposures on the target data. Building exposures is simply the forward pricing model that applies for each credit rating. The forward pricing model is derived from the present value model using the forward yield curve for the corresponding credit quality (Crouhy et al., 2000). The range of covered instruments includes bonds, loans, swaps, receivable, commitments, and letters of credit.

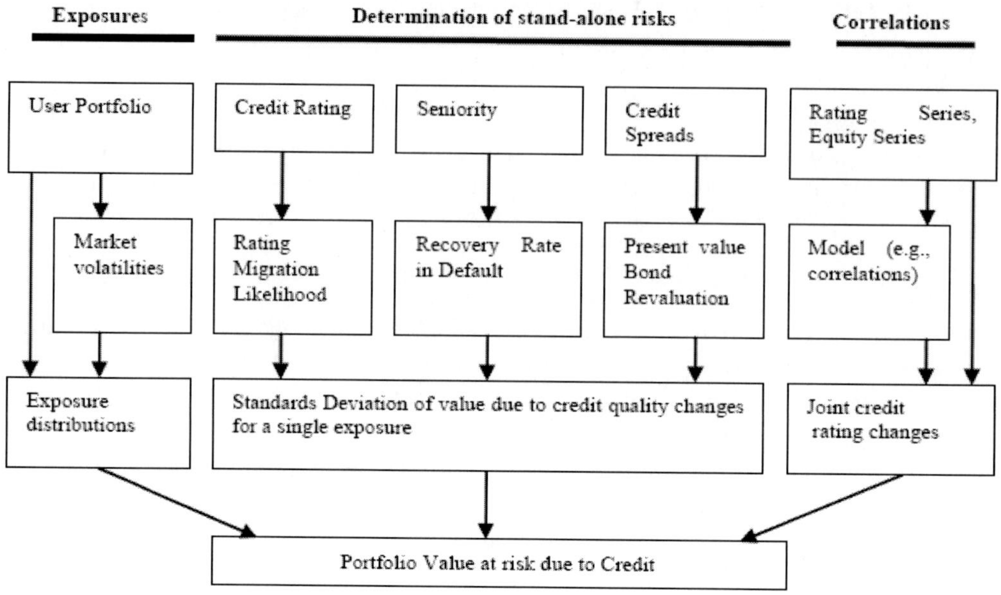

Figure 3. Credit Metrics schematic.

There are three steps to calculating the value volatility in a stand-alone exposure (Masters, 1997; and Gupton et al., 1997): (i) the senior unsecured credit rating of the issuer determines the chance of either defaulting or migrating to any possible credit quality at the risk horizon. In this step, the rating system is specified with rating categories and the probabilities of migrating to any possible credit quality over the risk horizon. This is because the risk occurs from changes in value due to up or down grades not only from default. The transition matrix is derived from rating migration published by credit rating agencies; (ii) revaluation at the risk horizon can take two forms: (a) the seniority of the exposure determines its recovery rate in the case of default, and (b) the forward zero curve for each credit rating category determines the revaluation upon up (down) grade. The mean and standard deviation recovery rates based on the seniority classification of the credit are estimated. The present value of credit is then calculated by obtaining the forward zero curves for each rating and revaluation of the credit's remaining cash flows at risk horizon for each rating category; and (iii) the likelihoods from step 1 and the values from step 2 are then combined to determine volatility of value due to credit quality changes by calculating the standard deviation and the percentile level as the measures of credit risk.

To measure the effect of portfolio diversification we need to estimate the correlations in credit quality changes for all pairs of obligors. Correlations among defaults are concluded from correlations between asset prices. Equity prices for publicly traded firms are used as a proxy to calculate asset correlations because asset values cannot be directly observed from historical data. CreditMetrics then uses simulations of the joint asset values, assuming a multivariate normal distribution. These simulations can be also used to compute a correlation among default events. Because defaults are much less frequent than rating changes, the correlation is typically much less than the correlation between asset values (Jorion, 2003).

CreditMetrics has several advantages. It allows credit risk analysts to identify the nature of the contribution of each asset portfolio risk, the distribution of credit exposures among the rating and overall performance of the portfolio. It also provides the opportunity to restructure the distribution of credit exposures among different ratings in portfolio in order to adjust its risk (Kalapodas and Thomson, 2005). Moreover, CreditMetrics is more suitable for a fixed – income portfolio because considers the probability of changes in credit rating and default events across a portfolio (Papanyan, 2003). CreditMetrics also has several disadvantages. It requires many inputs and complex mathematics techniques. It is difficult to implement to consumer credit because equity cannot measure the obligors (Kalapodas and Thomson, 2006). It also ignores other factors such as the management of a firm. There is no explanation provided by CreditMetrics about using the equity price as a proxy for the asset values of the firm that is not directly observable. This may affect the accuracy of this model (Crouhy et al., 2000). Finally, it relies on a transition matrix in which financial institutions use the traditional methods of evaluating credit risk to conduct these transition matrices (Treacy and Carey, 1998).

Macro Factor Models

According to macro factor models, defaults rely on the level of economic activity, so the probability of default changes as the state of the economy changes. Smithson (2003, p. 134) shows the steps by which the factor models works: (i) simulate the future state of the economy; (ii) adjust the default rate to the simulated state of the economy; (iii) assign probability of default for each obligor, based on the simulated state of the economy; (iv) value individual transactions (facilities) depending on the possibility of default assigned to the obligor in the previous step; (v) compute portfolio loss by totaling results for all transactions; and (vi) repeat steps 1-6 some number of times to map the loss distribution. In factor models, the coefficients on the various factors derive the correlation in default rates. All default rates and transition probabilities are caused by the state of the economy changing together. A high default probability is produced by a low state of economic activity drawn from the simulation of macro variables and this causes correlation in migration risk.

McKinsey's Credit Portfolio View

The Credit Portfolio View is a multi-factor model used to simulate the joint conditional distribution of default and migration probabilities for various rating groups in different industries conditional on the value of macroeconomic factors (Crouhy et al., 2000). The Credit Portfolio View, as the first multi-factor econometric model, was developed by Wilson (1997a, 1997b) who introduced an attempt to evaluate portfolio credit risk through econometrics and Monte Carlo simulation and then it was presented by McKinsey in 1998. Credit Portfolio View is based on the assumption that the default probabilities and migration probabilities are connected to the economy. When the economy improves both upgrades and defaults decrease. The contrary holds when the economy becomes depressed. This means that the credit cycles follow business cycles closely but their behavior is different from that of industries. As the state of the economy is largely driven by macroeconomic variables, the Credit Portfolio View suggests a methodology to connect those macroeconomic variables to the probability of default and migration probabilities (Crouhy et al., 2000).

Credit Portfolio View consists of two model blocks: the default block and the time series block. In the probability of default, default rate for portfolio is formulated as a logit function:

$$Y_{it} = \frac{1}{1+e^{-Z_{it}}}$$

where Y_{it} is the conditional probability of default in period t for obligors in country or industry i, where the index is derived from the multifactor model as follows:

$$Y_{it} = \alpha_{j,0} + \sum_{i=1}^{n} \alpha_i X_{it} + e_t$$

where α are unknown parameters, X_{it} are period t values of the macroeconomics variables and e_t is the error term. The macroeconomics variables are specified for each country. Each macroeconomic variable is supposed to follow a univariate autoregressive process of order 2 (Crouhy et al., 2000; Derviz and Kadlcakova, 2001; Hubner et al., 2005 and Kim, 2005).

$$X_{it} = \gamma_{i0} + \sum_{k=1}^{2} \alpha_{ik} X_{i,t-k} + v_t$$

where each X is normally distributed and independent, γ are coefficients to be estimated, and v is the error term.

When these equations are calibrated, a Monte Carlo method is applied to determine the distribution of the default probabilities conditional on the state of the economy. Credit Portfolio View proposes the use of the following two ratios to adjust the migration probabilities in order to produce a transition matrix conditional on the state of the economy (Crouhy et al., 2000):

$$\frac{SDP_t}{\phi SDP} > 1 \quad \text{(Recession)} \qquad \frac{SDP_t}{\phi SDP} < 1 \quad \text{(Expansion)}$$

where the numerator is the simulated default probability for a speculative grade obligor and the denominator is the unconditional (historical average) probability of default for a speculative grade obligor. If this ratio is greater than one, the unconditional transition matrix is adjusted to give increased probabilities of migration into downgrades and default and decreased probabilities of migration into upgrades, and vice versa (Derviz and Kadlcakova, 2001). This approach can generate multi-period transition matrices:

$$\mathrm{M}_T = \prod_{t=1...T} \mathrm{M}\left(P_{j,i} / \phi SDP\right)$$

The transition matrix produces the distribution of the cumulative conditional default probability for any rating over any period (Crouhy et al., 2000; Kalapodas and Thomson, 2006).

The Credit Portfolio View has some advantages. It takes into account the dependence between the default events and the state of the economy, especially when the portfolio is internationally diversified. It can also be applied to any credit exposure since the creditworthiness of counterparties is described by a number of macroeconomic variables (Kalapodas and Thomson, 2006). Furthermore, the original migration matrix is adjusted according to the widespread macroeconomic condition, resulting in nonconstant ratings. On the other hand, Credit Portfolio View has some limitations. It is a complex method to implement in practice because of the advanced mathematical requirements. Kern and Rudolph (2001) show that the high dependence between the state of economy and default does not affect counterparties. Derviz and Kadlcakova (2001) reported that the most important macroeconomic variables are not referred to the model.

Actuarial Models Including Credit Risk+

Actuarial models were firstly introduced by Jarrow and Turnbull (1992) and subsequently studied by Jarrow and Turnbull (1995), Jarrow et al., (1997), Duffie and Singleton (1999) and Jarrow and Protter (2004). These use a statistical technique common in loss distribution modeling developed in the insurance industry. Actuarial models obtain a closed form expression for joint distribution of loss event. The best known of the actuarial models is CreditRisk+, introduced and developed by the investment bank Credit Suisse Financial Products (1997).

CreditRisk+ is a model of default risk, not migration risk, such as for CreditMetrics and Credit Portfolio View. It does not examine the potential reasons for default and ignores the changes in prices and spreads. It means no assumptions are made about the causes of default. CreditRisk+ is a default mode model instead of a market-to-market model. It assumes that each obligor can be in one of the two states, default or non- default, at the end of the risk period. CreditRisk+ is a purely actuarial model which means that the probabilities of default are based on historical statistical data of default experience by credit class (Crouhy, 2001). CreditRisk+ uses the default as a continuous random variable with a probability distribution. It integrates the volatility of default rates to capture the uncertainty in the level of default rates (Caouette et al., 1998). CreditRisk+ estimates the portfolio's loss variable and assesses the need of economic capital within the Value at Risk framework. It supposes that the probability distribution for the number of defaults over any period of time follows a Poisson distribution. Under this assumption, CreditRisk+ generates the loss distribution of a loan portfolio which depends on the individual default variables of each security and their pair-wise default correlations (Crouhy, 2001).

The inputs of CreditRisk+ are the individual credit exposures, mean default for the obligor, default rate volatilities for the obligor and an estimate of recovery rates (Servigny and Renault, 2004; Smithson, 2003; Derviz and Kadlcakova, 2001; and Kim, 2005). CreditRisk+ firstly assumes that the default rates of individual obligors are fixed over time and for each loan. Default rates are usually estimated by mapping of default rate to its credit rating. Secondly, exposure to a large number of obligors is assumed to be such that each of them has a small probability of default and each loan's probability of default is independent of the default of other loans (Allen et al., 2004; Derviz and Kadlcakova, 2001). This assumption means the probability distribution for the number of defaults during a given period of time can be presented by a Poisson distribution:

$$P(n) = \frac{\mu^n e^{-\mu}}{n!}$$

where n is average number of defaults per year and μ is the expected number of defaults in the portfolio. Finally, the model captures the concentration effect by permitting for differences between sectors. A diversified portfolio means that each exposure is allocated to a different sector whilst a concentrated portfolio means that all exposures are part of a single sector. A sector is a collection of consistent obligors under the influence of a single underlying factor (Derviz and Kadlcakova, 2001).

The second stage of measuring the risk in CreditRisk+ can be divided into two steps (or two degrees of uncertainty) (Allen et al., 2004). The first step requires identification of frequency of default events, estimated by a standard Poisson distribution, and the second step requires identification of the severity of the losses; derived from the exposure for each obligor adjusted with the anticipated recovery rate (Credit Suisse, 1997) and (Hubner et al., 2005). The last stage is to derive the loss distribution of a portfolio (Kadlcakova and Keplinger, 2004). The losses (exposures, net of recovery) are divided into bands, with the level of exposure in each band being approximated by a single number. In CreditRisk+ each band is viewed as an independent portfolio of loans. The derivation of losses for the entire portfolio follows three steps: a probability generating function for each band, a probability generating function for the entire portfolio, and the loss distribution for the entire portfolio (Hubner et al., 2005; Crouhy, 2001).

CreditRisk+ has the advantage that it is rather easy to apply. The method provides a rapid analytical solution to the distribution of credit losses with few data inputs (the probability of default and the individual exposure (Jorion, 2003)) and the computation of the loan loss is easier to perform and is attractive. Conversely, CreditRisk+ has shortcomings. It ignores the relationship with the level of market risk in credit risk assessment. In addition, it does not integrate successfully the correlations between the state of economy and defaults. Furthermore, CreditRisk+ does not estimate the defaults for different time horizons (Kalapodas and Thomson, 2006).

Comparison of Portfolio Models

Table 2 summarises the key characteristics of the portfolio models in terms of definition of risk, credit events, risk drivers, transition probabilities, and correlation of credit events, recovery rates, and the numerical approach. Portfolio credit-risk models have developed under different assumptions; credit risk assessment, data requirements, and mathematical pattern. KMV portfolio manager and CreditMetrics estimate stand-alone credit risk by implementing asset value, but Credit Portfolio View applies an econometric model and CreditRisk+ applies expected default rates. CreditMetrics and Credit Portfolio View are migration and default risk models, while KMV portfolio manager and CreditRisk+ are only default risk models (Kim, 2005). CreditMetrics and CreditPortfolio View are market-to-market, while CreditRisk+ and KMV portfolio manager are the default mode models. In relation to probability distribution for default, Credit Portfolio View estimates the parameters of the default distribution via logistic distribution, while CreditRisk+ applies Poisson distribution for arrival rate and gamma distribution for mean default rate. The default rate distribution in KMV portfolio manager and CreditMetrics derive from a lognormal model of asset value (Smithson, 2003). In relation to methodology, CreditRisk+ is an analytical model, which means the calculation of credit loss distribution can be performed faster. However, CreditMetrics is a simulation model, which means that it saves time, and the input variables need to change (Papanyan, 2003). In spite of these differences, Koyluoglu and Hickman (1998), and Gordy (2000) argue that the underlying mathematical structures are similar.

Several studies deal with comparing credit portfolio models. These generally recognise the mathematical relation between the different types of models and provide some results. Lopez and Saidenberg (2000) discuss the differences between market risk models and credit risk models that make the validation of credit risk models more difficult due to their underlying time horizons. They suggest a "cross-sectional simulation" method to assess credit risk models. Hickman and Koyluoglu (1998) studied three different portfolio models; KMV Credit Manager, CreditRisk+ and Credit Portfolio View. They found similarity of inputs yield outputs. They reported that the actual difference in outputs comes from parameter variance, not the model variance and show that KMV Credit Manager and Credit Risk+ both have a similar underlying probabilistic structure in spite of the surface differences. He demonstrates that KMV Credit Manager and CreditRisk+ can be mathematically measured.

Table 2. Comparison of portfolio models

Model	KMV portfolio manger	CreditMetrics	CreditPortfolioView	CreditRisk+
Definition of risk	Market to market or Default losses	Market to market	Market to market	Default losses
Credit events	Continuous default probabilities	Downgrade/default	Downgrade/default	default
Risk drivers	Asset values	Asset values	Macro factors	Expected default rates
Transition probabilities	Driven by: individual term structure of EDF – asset value process	Constant	Driven by macro factor	Not applicable
Correlation of credit events	Multivariate normal distribution or equity factor model	Multivariate normal distribution or equity factor model	Conditional default probabilities function of macro factors	Conditional default probabilities function of common risk factors
Recovery rates	Random (beta distribution)	Random (beta distribution)	Random(empirical distribution)	Loss given default deterministic
Numerical approach	Analytic/ simulation	Analytic/ simulation	Simulation	Analytic

The question will be; which model is best? In general, there is no overall best model. What is best will depend on the details of problems such as the data requirements and the characteristics used. Some articles tried to answer it but the argument continues without general agreement. Application of models differs between financial institutions and many factors play an important role in identifying the best one; such as the structure and characteristic of its loan portfolio and the size of the financial institution. However, Kim (2005) showed that the final selection criteria rest upon: (1) forecasting accuracy and (2) applicability. There are a few articles in relation to forecasting accuracy of portfolio credit-risk models. Crouhy et al., (2000) and Gordy (2000) show the results of these models are similar. However, Catarianeu-Rabell et al., (2005) and Rosch (2005) reveal that CreditMetrics performs better than does KMV Portfolio Manager. On the other hand, Sobhart et al., (2000) shows that CreditMetrics and CreditRisk+ are superior to KMV Portfolio manager by developing forecasting accuracy indicators to estimate credit risk portfolio models. However, Jarrow and Protter (2004) propose CreditRisk+ if the financial institutions need to reduce credit pricing risk.

Applicability means the ability to apply these models in practice. Kim (2005) explained the applicability of models in three aspects: data availability, manageability, and cost efficiency. Data requirement differs from one model to another; therefore, the financial institutions should have all required data to use the model. CreditMetrics requires a large amount data set such as rating system, historical transition matrix, spread and yield curves, stock price data, loss given default data, correlation, and exposures. KMV also requires historical capital and debt structure data, which means it is difficult to gather from small business or retail loan portfolios. On the other hand, CreditRisk+ requires comparatively small data. It could be said that the CreditPortfolio View is better than other models in respect of data requirements, although it requires time series modeling for the macroeconomic variables. From the above discussion, we conclude there are a number of factors that should be taken into consideration in order to determine the best model, including the structure, loan portfolio, and the size of the financial institution as well as data requirements.

CONCLUSION

This chapter provided an extensive review of the various approaches to credit risk modeling. Section 2 examined a general framework for credit and lending decisions. Internal factors, external factors and the borrower-specific factors were found necessary to know the circumstances of credit decision making in financial institutions and as a foundation for understanding the importance of these factors when credit risk is considered. This section also provided an overview of the traditional models that contribute to assessing credit risk, including the role of the traditional five Cs as an input to most other credit risk models. Section 3 discussed credit risk. First, the types of risks that face banks and other financial institutions were explained and this showed the significance of credit risk to banks as well as the objective of managing and controlling credit risk. We found that the management of credit risk is the main challenge for banks and other financial institutions. In this section, we also clarified the differences between credit and default risk and reviewed the components of credit risk.

Section 4 analyzed the methods of credit risk analysis according to banking theory, including the four principal methods, namely, expert systems, risk premium analysis, econometrics, and hybrid systems. Section 5 reviewed credit risk models. We divided the discussion into that concerning credit rating systems and credit risk portfolios. In the first subsection, we reviewed credit ratings, as one of the most popular methods for modeling credit risk, from the perspective of definition, types, advantages and criticism, internal and external ratings, the process of credit ratings, and credit rating criteria. This is important because many lenders consider credit ratings as an essential factor in building other credit models, such as credit risk portfolios and credit risk scoring. In the second subsection, we reviewed portfolio credit models, most initially developed for commercial use. Finally, we compared the various portfolio models and concluded that a number of factors should be taken into consideration when determining the best model, including loan structure, the loan portfolio, and the size of the financial institution as well as data requirements.

REFERENCES

Allen, L. (2002). *Credit risk modeling of middle markets.* Paper presented to the Wharton Conference on Credit Risk Modeling and Decisioning, 29–30 May, University of Pennsylvania.

Altman, E. (1989). Measuring corporate bond mortality and performance. *Journal of Finance,* 44(4), 909–922.

Altman, E. (2002). *Corporate Distress Prediction models in a Turbulent Economic and Basel II Environment.* Paper presented to the Global Association of Risk Professional Conference, September, Stern School of Business, New York University.

Altman, E. and Saunders, A. (1997). Credit risk measurement: Developments over the last 20 years. *Journal of Banking & Finance,* 21(11), 1721–1742.

Basel Committee on Banking Supervision. (2000). Principles for the Management of Credit Risk, Technical Report, Bank for International Settlement.

Bedendo, M., Cathcart, L. and El-Jahel, L. (2004). The shape of the term structure of credit spreads: an empirical investigation. Tanaka Business School, Working Paper, Imperial College London, South Kensington Campus.

Bierman, H. and Hausman, W. (1970). The credit granting decision. *Management Science,* 16(8), 519–532.

Black, B. and Cox, J. (1976). Valuing corporate securities: some effects of bond indenture provisions. *Journal of Finance*, 31, 351–367.

Brady, T. F., English, W.B. and Nelson, W.R. (1998). Recent changes to the Federal Reserve's survey of terms of bank lending, *Federal Reserve Bulletin,* August, 604–615.

Brian, G. and Colleen, C. (1997). Credit risk in banking. Sydney, Bank Supervision Department. Reserve Bank of Australia.

Broll, U., Pausch, T. and Welzel, P. (2002). *Credit risk and credit derivatives in banking.* Discussion paper No. 228, University of Augsburg.

Cantor, R. and Packer, F. (1994). The credit rating industry. *Federal Reserve Bank of New York Quarterly Review*, Summer, 1–26.

Caouette, J., Altman, E. and Narayanan, P. (1998). *Managing Credit Risk: The Next Great Financial Challenge.* New York: John Wiley & Sons.

Catarineu-Rabell, E., Jackson, P. and Tsomokos, D. (2005). Procyclicality and the new Basel Accord: Banks' choice of loan rating system. *Economic Theory*, 26(3), 537–557.

Cathcart, L. and El-Jahel, L. (2004). *Multiple defaults and Merton's model,* Tanaka Business School, Discussion Paper TBS/DP04/12.

Collin-Dufresne, P. and Goldstein R. (2001). Do credit spreads reflect stationary leverage ratios? *Journal of Finance*, 56(5), 1929–1957.

Comptroller of the Currency Administrator of National Banks. (1999). *Booklet on Internet Banking*.

Credit Suisse Financial Product. (1997). CreditRisk+: A Credit Risk Management Framework, Credit Suisse First Boston International, Retrieved July 9, 2006, from http://www.csfb.com/institutional/research/assets/creditrisk.pdf.

Crosbie, P. and Bohn, J. (2003). *Modeling Default Risk*, Moody's KMV Company, Technical Report, retrieved June 27, 2006, from http://www.moodyskmv.com.

Crouhy, M., Galai, D. and Mark, M. (2000). A comparative analysis of current credit risk models. *Journal of Banking & Finance,* 24(1/2), 59–117.

De Lucia, R. (2003). *Commercial Bank & Financial Institutions Management*. Pyrmont: Thomson.

Derviz, A. and Kadlcakova, N. (2001). Methodological problems of quantitative credit risk modeling in the Czech Economy. Working Paper no. 39, Czech National Bank.

Dietsch, M. and Petey, J. (2002). The credit risk in SME loans portfolios: Modeling issues, pricing, and capital requirements. *Journal of Banking & Finance,* 26(2/3), 303–322.

Duffie, D. and Singleton, K. (1999). Modeling term structure of defaultable bonds. *Review of Financial Studies*, 12, 687–720.

Ederington, L. and Yawitz, J. (1987). The Bond Rating Process. In E. Altman (Ed.), *Handbook of Financial Markets,* New York: John Wiley & Sons.

Elsas, R. and Krahnen, J. (1998). Is relationship lending special? Evidence from credit-file data in Germany. *Journal of Banking & Finance,* 22(10/11), 1283–1316.

Geske, R. (1977). The valuation of corporate liabilities as compound options. *Journal of Financial and Quantitative Analysis*, 12, 541–552.

Geske, R. and Johnson H. (1984). The valuation of corporate liabilities as compound options: A correction, *Journal of Financial and Quantitative Analysis*, 19, 231–232.

Golin, J. L. (2001). *The Bank Credit Analysis Handbook: A Guide for Analysts, Bankers, and Investors*. New York: John Wiley & Sons Ltd.

Gordy, M. (2000). A comparative anatomy of credit risk models. *Journal of Banking & Finance,* 24(1/2), 119–149.

Gordy, M. and Heitfled, E. (2001). *Of Moody's and Merton: A structural model of bond rating transitions*. Working Paper, US Federal Reserve Board.

Gupton, G., Finger, C. and Bhatia, B. (1997). *CreditMetrics: Technical document*. J. P. Morgan, New York.

Haag, M. (2003). Credit risk models: Application to corporate bond portfolios. Masters thesis. Gerhard Beulig, CFA, Austria.

Harrington, D. (1987). *Modern Portfolio Theory, the Capital Asset Pricing Model, and Arbitrage Pricing Theory: A User's Guide*. 2nd ed., New York: Prentice Hall.

Hickman, A., and Koyluoglu, H. (1998). A Generalized framework credit risk models. *Risk*, 11(10), 56–62.

Hogan, W., Katherine, A., Deborah, R. and Christine, B. (2004). *Management of Financial Institution.* 2nd ed., Milton: John Wiley & Sons

Hubal, O. and Meisser, S. (2000). *The Swiss Credit Market.* HEC University of Lausanne.

Hubner, G., Peters, J. and Plunus, S. (2005). *Measuring operational risk in financial institutions: Contribution of credit risk modeling*. Working Paper Series, Social Science Research Network.

Jarrow, R. and Protter, P. (2004). Structural versus reduced form models: A new information based perspective. *Journal of Investment Management,* 2(2), 1–10.

Jarrow, R. and Turnbull, S. (1992). Credit risk: drawing the analogy. *Risk Magazine*, 5, 51–56.

Jarrow, R. and Turnbull, S. (1995). Pricing derivatives on financial securities subject to credit risk. *Journal of Finance*, 50, 53–85.

Jarrow, R., Lando, D., and Turnbull, S. (1997). A Markov model for the term structure of credit risk spreads. Review of Financial Studies 10, 481–523.

Jorion, P. (2003). *Financial Risk Manager Handbook.* 2nd ed., Hoboken, NJ; Chichester: John Wiley & Sons.

Kadlcakova, N. and Keplinger, J. (2004). *Credit risk and bank lending in the Czech Republic.* Working Paper Series 6, Czech National Bank.

Kalapodas, E. and Thomson, M. (2006). Credit risk assessment: A challenge for financial institutions. *IMA Journal of Management Mathematics,* 17(1), 25–46.

Karacadag, C. and Taylor, M. (2000). The new capital adequacy framework: Institutional constraints and incentive structures. Working Papers 00/93, International Monetary Fund.

Kern, M. and Rudolph, B. (2001). Comparative analysis of alternative credit risk models–an application on German middle market loan portfolios. CFC Working Paper no. 2001/3, Centre for Financial Studies, Frankfurt, Germany.

Kim, J. (2005). A credit risk model for agricultural loan portfolios under the new Basel capital accord. PhD thesis, Texas A&M University.

Koch, T. W. and MacDonald, S. S. (2006). *Bank Management.* (6th ed.) Mason, OH: Thomson.

Koyluoglu, H. and Hickman, A., (1998). *A generalized framework for credit risk portfolio models.* Working Paper. Oliver, Wyman & Co, available at: http://www.erisk.com /reference/archive/058_183GeneralizedFrameworkd.pdf.

Kumar, K. and Haynes, J. (2003). The information value of bond ratings. *Journal of Finance,* 55(6), 2879–2902.

Lando, D. (2004). *Credit Risk Modeling: Theory and Applications.* Princeton, NJ: Princeton University Press.

Leland, E. and Toft, K., (1996). Optimal capital structure, endogenous bankruptcy, and the term structure of credit spreads. *Journal of Finance*, 51(3), 987–1019.

Leland, H. (1994). Corporate debt value, bond covenants, and optimal capital structure, *Journal of Finance*, 49, 1213–1252.

Longstaff, F. and Schwartz, E. (1995). A simple approach to valuing risky, fixed, and floating rate debt. *Journal of Finance,* 50, 789–821.

Lopez, J. (2001). Modeling credit risk for commercial loans. *FRBSF Economic Letter* 12, (April 27). Available at http://www.frbsf.org/publications/economics/letter/2001/el2001-12.html.

Lopez, J. and Saidenberg, M. (2000). Evaluating credit risk models. *Journal of Banking & Finance,* 24(1/2), 151–165.

Machauer, A. and Weber, M. (1998). Bank behavior based on internal credit ratings of borrowers. *Journal of Banking and Finance,* 22(4), 1355–1383.

Masters, B. (1997). *Introduction to CreditMetrics™.* J.P. Morgan & Co.

Mella-Barral, P. and Perraudin, W. (1997). Strategic Debt Service. *Journal of Finance*, 52, 531–566.

Ong, K. M. (2000). *Internal Credit Risk Models* .London: Risk Books.

Papanyan, K. (2003). Assessing counterparty risk at private companies in energy industry: A descriptive survey of credit models. Master's thesis, Goteborg University.

Porter, M. (2004). *Competitive Strategy: Techniques for Analyzing Industries and Competitors*. New York: Free Press.

Rosch, D. (2005). An empirical comparison of default risk forecasts from alternative credit rating philosophies, *International Journal of Forecasting*, 21, 37–51.

Rose, P. S. (2002). *Commercial Bank Management*. 5th ed., Boston, MA: Irwin McGraw-Hill.

Santomero , A. (1997). *Commercial Bank Risk Management: an Analysis of the Process*. The Wharton School, Working Paper Series, University of Pennsylvania.

Sathye, M., Bartle, J., Vincent, M and Boffey, R. (2003). *Credit Analysis and Lending Management.* Milton: John Wiley & Sons.

Saunders, A. and Cornett, M. (2003). *Financial Institutions Management: A Risk Management Approach*. Boston, MA: McGraw-Hill/ Irwin.

Servigny, A. d. and Renault, O. (2004). *The Standard & Poor's Guide to Measuring and Managing Credit Risk* .New York: McGraw-Hill.

Sharpe, W. (1994). The Sharpe Ratio. *Journal of Portfolio Management*, 21 (1), Geng, G. (2002). Analysis of portfolio credit risk. PhD thesis, University of Western Ontario.

Shimko, D. Tejima N. and Van Deventer, D. (1993). The pricing of risky debt when interest rates are stochastic. *Journal of Fixed Income*, 3, 58–65.

Skora, R. K. (2000). *Modeling credit risk,* Retrieved June 28, 2006, from http://www.fenews.com/fen16/creditrisk.html.

Smithson, C. (2003). *Credit Portfolio Management.* Hoboken, NJ, John Wiley.

Sobhart, J., Keenan, S. and Stein, R., (2000). *Benchmarking quantitative default risk models: A validation methodology*. Working Paper. Moody's Investors Service, New York.

Sundaram, R. (2001). Merton/KMV approach to pricing credit risk. *Extra Credit*, January/February, 59–68.

Sylla, R. (2001). A Historical Premier on the Business of Credit Ratings. *The Role of Credit Reporting Systems in the International Economy.* Washington DC: World Bank.

Treacy, W. and Carey, M. (2000). Credit risk rating systems at large US banks. *Journal of Banking and Finance,* 24(1/2), 167–201.

Udell, G. (1987). *Designing the optimal loan review policy*. Proceedings, Federal Reserve Bank of Chicago, 507–531.

Udell, G. (1989). Loan quality, commercial loan review and loan officer contracting. *Journal of Banking and Finance,* 13(3), 367–382.

Whitelaw, R. (1997). *Stock market risk and return: An equilibrium approach*. Leonard N. Stern School of Business, Working Paper Series 1998, New York University.

Wilson, T. (1997a). Portfolio credit risk, I. *Risk*, 10(9), 111– 117.

Wilson, T. (1997b). Portfolio credit risk, II. *Risk*, 10(10), 56– 61.

Zhou, C. (2001). The term structure of credit spreads with jump risk", *Journal of Banking and Finance*, 25, 2015–2040.

In: Economic and Financial Modeling
Editor: Andrew C. Worthington
ISBN: 978-1-63463-111-2

Chapter 5

MODELING FIRM-SPECIFIC DETERMINANTS OF INITIAL PUBLIC OFFERINGS

***Jirapun Chorruk*[1] *and Andrew C. Worthington*[2*]**
[1]Mahasarakham University, Thailand
[2]Griffith University, Australia

ABSTRACT

This chapter examines the firm-specific determinants and outcomes of initial public offerings (IPOs) in Thailand using data on 5,228 private and newly publicly listed firms between 2001 and 2007. We use the listing requirements of the Stock Exchange of Thailand (SET) to identify all private firms compulsorily registered with the Department of Business Development, Thai Ministry of Commerce that are potential IPOs. Analysis of the determinants of IPOs reveals that firms that are younger, larger, more leveraged and with lower interest rates from borrowing are more likely to list. Analysis of post-IPO performance suggests that Thai firms going public succeed in lowering their borrowing rates, and that unlike comparable findings elsewhere, profitability does not decline after listing. However, despite these findings, the rate of listing in Thailand remains relatively low, and the paper hypothesizes that relatively high listing costs and the availability of alternative cheaper debt financing sources, the large shares of foreign subsidiary and small and medium-sized business operating in Thailand, along with market and political instability and cultural factors act against Thai IPOs.

1. INTRODUCTION

The decision to 'go public' is an important process in the company lifecycle. By making an initial public offering (IPO) of shares when companies go public, firms can raise external equity finance to fund growth and expansion, provide cash out opportunities for entrepreneurs, and diversify their sources of finance. Concomitantly, through the more

* Corresponding author: Department of Accounting, Finance and Economics, Griffith University, 170 Kessels Road, Nathan QLD 4111, Australia. Email. a.worthington@griffith.edu.au.

efficient allocation and transfer of capital, IPOs enhance financial development and promote economic welfare. Accordingly, the efficiency of the IPO process and the performance of the companies that have gone public have been a long standing focus of academic research and a matter of interest for practitioners and regulators alike.

In this chapter, we attempt to explain the decision of Thai firms to go public and examine their post-IPO performance. We analyze the determinants of IPOs by comparing the pre- and post-IPO characteristics of private firms. Outside the Italian study of Pagano et al. (1998), this paper is only the second to provide evidence on the IPO decision and its motivations while the candidate firms remain private. We also provide further insight into the contention by Singh (1995) that emerging market firms go public to finance future investment and the future growth of assets rather than the more typical argument that firms go public to rebalance their capital structure following periods of high investment and rapid growth.

We employ two samples of 5,118 Thai private firms and 110 IPO firms over the period 2001–2007 in this study. We use the sample of private and IPO firms to obtain predictions about the firm-specific variables that influence the likelihood of an IPO and the sample of IPO firms alone for predictions concerning the likely outcomes of an IPO. The Thai IPO market represents an interesting context for this purpose, especially from an emerging market perspective. Following the 1997 Asian financial crisis, before which mainly mature firms went public in Thailand, the number of IPOs grew steadily from 2001 owing to the increase in the number of young, potential growth firms going public. In part, this was a response to Thai government policy becoming heavily orientated towards exchange equity markets with tax incentives of a corporate tax reduction of 5 percent (from 30 percent) for five consecutive years post-listing.

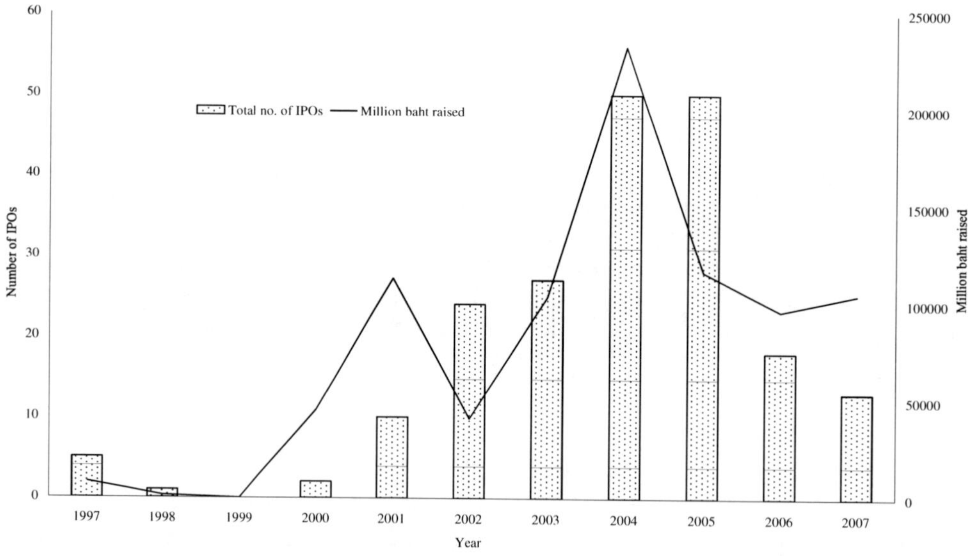

Figure 1. Volume and value of Thai IPOs, 1997–2007.

The Stock Exchange of Thailand (SET) also had a role to play in attempting to make IPOs more attractive, progressively weakening its listing requirements in 2003 and again in 2005. Moreover, the SET more generally adjusted the retained proportion of shareholder distribution to 20 percent of paid-up capital and amended the definition of retail shareholders to include those either who do not have the power of control or who do not exercise administrative power through strategic shareholdings. The expectation was that this amendment would create greater opportunities for retail shareholders to take a role in listed companies and further increase the liquidity of the Thai market (SET, 2001a), thereby enhancing the prospects for successful IPOs.

However, despite these efforts, and as shown in Figure 1, the Thai IPO market peaked in volume and value as early as 2005 and went into decline well before the impact of the current financial crisis became more broadly felt. Even incorporating the peak years for IPOs in 2005 and 2006, the Thai market has lagged behind many comparable Asia-Pacific markets in terms of growth in the number of listed firms. In evidence, while the annual geometric growth rate of listed firms in Thailand (5.19%) over the period 2000–2008 exceeded the Philippines (0.08%), Taiwan (3.31%), Indonesia (3.67%) and Malaysia (2.99%), it lagged well behind other emerging markets, and indeed many developed markets, in Hong Kong (6.49%), Singapore (7.98%), Shenzen (6.52%) and Korea (22.90%). While market factors undoubtedly have a role to play over this long period, if we hold these influences constant by considering firms in Thailand alone, it is of interest what firm-specific factors affect the probability of listing and the outcomes expected and attained. More particularly, what insights may this provide for alternative reasons for the relatively low rate of IPOs in Thailand, despite the apparent best efforts of governments, regulators, and market organizations?

The organization of the chapter is as follows. Section 2 briefly discusses business in Thailand, the process of going public and the SET. Section 3 briefly reviews the theories and empirical evidence on the motivations for and the outcomes of IPOs. Section 4 presents the sample and describes the empirical methodology and Section 6 discusses the empirical results. Section 7 provides some concluding remarks.

2. THAI IPO PROCESS

To establish a business in Thailand, there are a number of required procedures, including submitting the relevant documents and paying registration fees at the Department of Business Development (DBD) of the Thai Ministry of Commerce. As elsewhere, the Thai corporate sector has three common forms of business organization: sole proprietorships, partnerships and limited companies (including private and public limited companies) (DBD 2008a; BOI 2009). A sole proprietorship is a business owned by a single person with unlimited liability, while a partnership includes the liability of the partners.

A private limited company is one whose subscribed shares are at least 25 percent paid up. There is no minimum level of capitalization. In Thailand, the Civil and Commercial Code govern a private limited company whereas a public limited company, or one established for offering the sale of shares to the public, is subject to the Public Limited Company Act of 1992. The Securities and Exchange Act of 1992 under the control of the Securities and Exchange Commission (SEC) determines the rules and regulations concerning the procedures of offering shares for sale. A firm with ordinary shares listed on the SET or its Market for Alternative Investments (mai) is a publicly listed company (hereafter "listed company").

A private limited company with at least 300 million baht (USD/THB35) of paid-up capital seeking to go public and list on the SET has to first register the business as a 'Public Limited Company' at the DBD (SET 2008a). The company is then eligible to apply for approval of the public offering at the SEC and consequently files a listing application with the SET. A company also can also simultaneously submit public offering and listing applications to the SEC and SET, a process known as 'Parallel Listing'. In this paper, we take "going public" (the first process) and "listing" (the second process) as essentially the same, although there are some technical differences (see Figure 2). In practice, most Thai private limited companies apply to go public at the SEC and subsequently list on the SET. Therefore, the SEC and the SET regulate the parallel going public and listing procedures. After all required documents and information has been submitted to the SEC and SET, the consideration of going public and listing applications is normally completed in about 30–45 days. From first application to issue date generally takes two to three months; however, this can be as long as a year (SET 2008a).

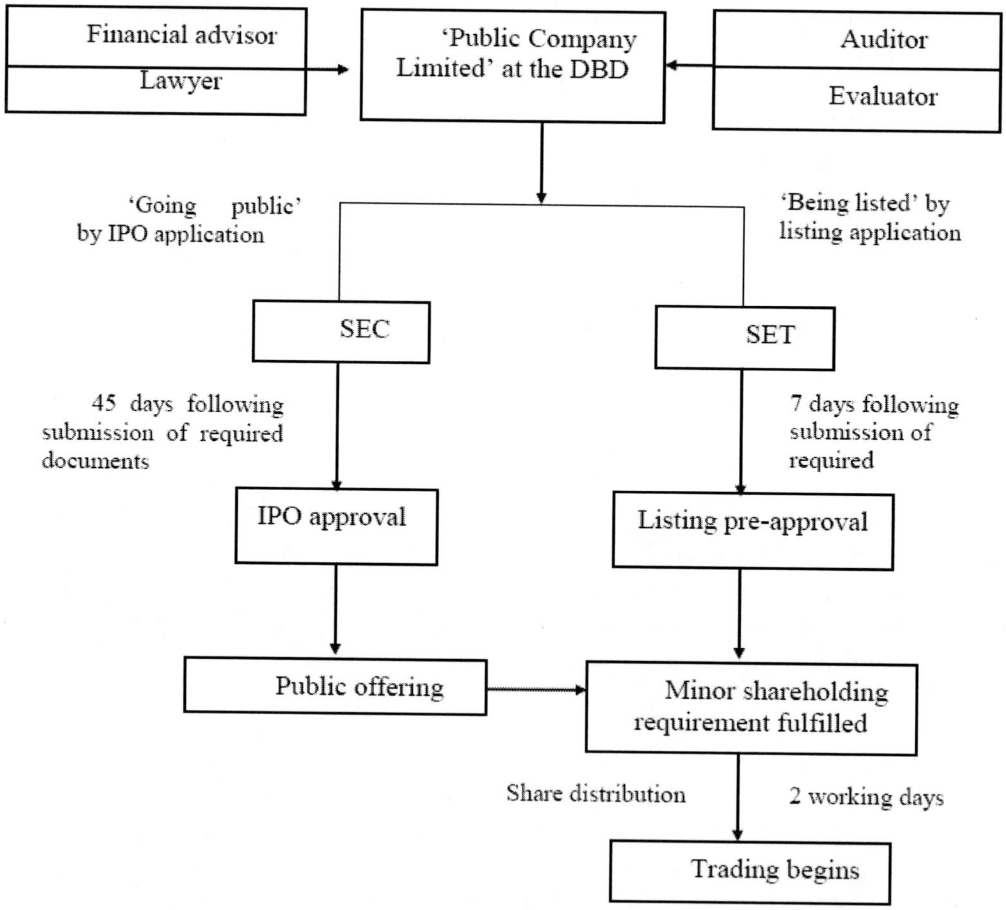

Figure 2. 'Going public' and 'listing' procedures in Thailand.

The SET is the main board for publicly listed companies in Thailand, established in 1961 as an outcome of the Thai government's five-year National Economic and Social

Development plan. The objective of this plan was to support the economic growth and stability of the country and help develop a higher standard of living. The SET officially commenced trading on 30 April 1975. Since then, the SET has grown significantly in size and trading activities, with the total number of listed companies increasing from 21 in 1975 (market capitalization of 153 million baht) to 475 (market capitalization of 784,316.52 million baht) in 2007. Securities currently traded on the SET include common stock and preferred stock, depository receipts, unit trusts, warrants and derivative warrants and transferable subscription rights. Trading of common stocks, however, dominates all other securities. By the end of 2007, the number of common stock issues had grown to 491 alongside 10 issues of preferred stock, 1 depository receipt, 8 unit trusts, and 71 warrants of various types; a total of 581 individual securities. The market value traded reached 6,636,068.73 million baht with a daily average turnover of 17,097.05 million baht over the same period. Currently, the SET is the fourteenth-largest market by capitalization in the Asia-Pacific, and thirteenth largest in terms of the number of listed companies and twelfth fastest by turnover velocity (WFE, 2007).

3. Prior Research

The decision to go public is complex and not easy to incorporate in a single hypothesis, nor discuss comprehensively in a brief review. However, like all other aspects of corporate financial decision-making it involves the relative evaluation of costs and benefits, both from a financial perspective and, more broadly, its influence on firm strategic behavior and corporate governance (Pagano et al., 1998). Starting with costs, the IPO literature discusses both direct costs, including underwriting costs and professional advising fees, and the indirect costs of going public, such as adverse selection costs, increase disclosure requirements, and public scrutiny.

First, the initial and subsequent expenses associated with an IPO can discourage companies from going public (Ritter, 1987; 2003). Going public generally implies considerable direct costs, including underwriting costs, other professional fees and so on. However, as these direct listing expenses does not generally increase proportionally with the size of the IPO, it is generally more cost-effective for larger firms to list. In terms of indirect IPO costs, the two main influences are adverse selection and the loss of confidentiality. First, adverse selection occurs when (some) investors are less informed than the issuers about the true value of the firm going public, and this is argued to cause underpricing (Leland and Pyle, 1976; Rock, 1986; Chemmanur and Fulghieri, 1999). This makes the cost of going public prohibitively high in contexts where information asymmetry prevails, especially small, start-up companies and those firms in emerging markets.

Second, Campbell (1979) first highlighted the loss of confidentiality as a determinant of the firm going public in that the information disclosure entailed harms the competitive advantage of the listed company in terms of future projects and marketing strategy. Moreover, companies that report lower incomes to take advantage of tax minimization schemes prefer to keep this information confidential and therefore they are less likely to go public. Yosha (1995) also suggests that companies with higher information sensitivity more often deter from an IPO as a source of finance as the costs of information disclosure are excessive. R&D may also have a role to play, and Maksimovic and Pichler (2001) provide empirical evidence about the link between technological innovation and IPOs and conclude that the timing and occurrence of IPOs depends critically on the industry.

A large number of factors have also been proposed to account for the benefits of going public. First, Chemmanur and Fulghieri (1999) argue that the firm's choice of going public is about broadening their investor base to raise capital and Ritter and Wealth (2002) suggest that most firms go public primarily to raise new capital for growth. Kim and Weisbach (2008) examine IPOs from 38 countries and find that almost all firms raise a substantial amount of new capital in the IPO, but the new funds raised in the IPO are used for several purposes in addition to financing growth, such rebalancing leverage and increase cash balances. Second, the IPO may serve to help overcoming borrowing constraints. Entrepreneurs with relatively limited personal wealth often establish high-growth firms or they may dislike investing more of their own funds. Simultaneously, when there is a sizeable time lag between investment in new projects and cash generation, debt financing may not be suitable. According to Myers and Majluf's (1984) pecking order theory, firms will first deploy internal equity to meet their financing needs, then external debt and lastly external equity.

Third, the IP process may provide financial flexibility and greater bargaining power with lenders like banks. By gaining stock market access and in the process of disseminating information to investors, firms encourage competition for outside financing and generally receive a lower cost or larger amount of credit (Rajan, 1992). Huyghebaert and Hulle (2006) also suggest that going public is one way of enhancing flexibility in financing. Fourth, Amihud and Mendelson (1986) and others conclude that exchange listing enhances stock liquidity, which in turn increase firm value. Maug (1998) argues that stock liquidity is valuable for managerial incentive schemes and argues for a positive correlation between liquidity and external monitoring. Likewise, Pagano and Röell (1998) suggest that high-investment companies are more likely to go public unlike smaller firms that choose to avoid the diffusion of post-listing stock ownership (Booth and Chua, 1996; Bolton and von Thadden, 1998; Mello and Parsons, 1998).

Fifth, risk sharing and portfolio diversification is another important motivation for going public, see Pagano (1993), Stoughton and Zechner (1998), and Chemmanur and Fulghieri (1999). This line of research suggests that riskier firms are more likely to go public Evidence provided in Meulbroek (2001) supports the argument that owners of high-risk firms will offer a sizable fraction of their shares. However, because risk falls, we expect a reduction in the profitability of firms post-listing, and this phenomenon is consistent with various studies of developed markets, see, for instance, Degeorge and Zeckhauser (1993), Mikkelson et al., (1997), Jain and Kini (1994), Pagano et al., (1998), and Pástor et al., (2009).

A sixth benefit of going public is a lower cost of capital. For example, the trade-off theory implies that firm go public to achieve an optimal capital structure and to lower their cost of capital [see Scott (1976) and Modigiliani and Miller (1963)]. Myers and Majluf (1984) provide the pecking order theory and support the going public theories of increase capital funds, debt and equity. Holmstrom and Tirole (1993) argue that firms can reduce their cost of capital by obtaining cheap financing directly from the capital markets while Diamond (1991) and Holmstrom and Tirole (1997) suggest that a firm with a high fraction of external intermediated finance are more likely to go public. Seventh, Zingales (1995) argues that going public can maximize the total proceeds from eventual sale of the firm. For instance,

Pagano et al (1998) provide empirical evidence from Italy that control turnover increased post-IPO.

An eighth benefit of going public is that an IPO on a stock exchange plays the role of advertising the firm and improves its recognition among a larger set of investors and stakeholders. Merton (1987) explores this aspect in context of the capital asset pricing model with incomplete information and shows that the greater the numbers of investors aware of the company's securities, the higher the stock price. Ninth, Zingales (1995) argues that an IPO is also a first step in the owner's exit strategy. The owner maximizes the total proceeds from the firms' eventual sale by selling part of the cash flow rights in the IPO, and the ownership control rights at the later stage. Black and Gilson (1998) also model the IPO decision as an opportunity for the venture capitalists to cash out their investments.

Tenth, Lyandres et al. (2009) argue that firms go public primarily to pursue an efficient merger and acquisition (M&A) strategy. They assume that a private firm is uncertain about the precise value of its capital. An IPO removes this valuation uncertainty and allows the firm to exercise its restructuring options optimally with cash or stock financing for acquisitions. Consistent with this theory, Celikyurt et al. (2007) find that there is a high incidence of M&A activity among newly public firms in the US, and that the amount post-IPO acquisitions is positively related to the degree of valuation uncertainty and market conditions. Brau et al. (2003) argue that an IPO allows firms to create publicly traded shares that can be used as a currency for growth through M&A. Further, Brau and Fawcett (2006) suggest that the primary motive for going public is to facilitate acquisition.

Eleventh, monitoring is seen as a benefit in some IPO models. Jensen and Meckling (1976) argue that the firm commits to meet the regulations and disclosure requirements of the stock exchanges that increase transparency, lower agency costs between managers, and majority shareholders and facilitates better corporate governance. However, Maksimovic and Pichler (2001) argue enhanced transparency forces the firm to disclosure crucial information that may be an advantage to its competitors. Holmström and Tirole (1993) also construct a model to explain how stock market may provide managerial discipline. Further, the shareholders of public firms can use the information embodied in stock prices to design more efficient compensation schemes for management, for example, by indexing their salaries to the stock price or by offering stock options (Holmström and Tirole, 1993; Schipper and Smith, 1986).

Finally, firms 'recognizing' that listed companies in their industry are overvalued also have an incentive to go public (Ritter, 1984). Merton (1987) predicts that an increase in investor recognition and shareholder base lowers the firm's cost of equity and increases its value. For instance, Bancel and Mittoo (2001) conclude that European CFOs consider enhanced visibility and investor recognization as the most important benefit of listing on foreign exchanges. Maksimovic and Pichler (2001) model going public as the firm's strategic choice to gain the first-mover advantage in the product market. The public trading of stock enhances the firm's visibility, reputation, and credibility, enabling the firm to raise capital for growth but also forcing the firm to disclose sensitive information that may be valuable to its competitors, especially in high-tech industries.

For the most part, it is difficult to incorporate these often-conflicting hypotheses in a single study. The main objective of the current study is to instead take advantage of the limited data available, and use these to proxy most, but not all, of the costs and benefits of an IPO from the firm's perspective.

4. Sample and Method

4.1. Sample

In Thailand, like other emerging markets, it is not easy to obtain financial information on private firms. However, the presence of the DBD's Business Registration System enables us to develop a unique data set for those firms that have qualified for the IPO listing requirements of the SET but may or may not have listed. To analyze the firm-specific determinants and outcomes of IPOs, we categorize the sample into two sample groups: (a) private firms and (b) IPO firms. The selection criteria used for constructing the private and IPO samples are as follows.

We define private firms as non-financial 'Company Limited' registered firms in Thailand registered with the DBD. These firms are in principle eligible to transform to 'Public Company Limited' registered firms in order to raise capital from going public and technically satisfy the IPO listing requirements to list on the SET. The data is extracted from the DBD business registration database. The DBD database contains information on the four forms of business organization in Thailand (sole proprietorships, partnerships, private limited companies and public limited companies), including business registration profiles, financial statements and shareholders by nationality.

The sample comprises those firms that satisfy the IPO listing requirements in each year between 2001 and 2007 (Listed Companies Development Department (2008); Listing and Disclosure Department (2008); SET (2000)). During this time, the SET imposed about 13 listing requirements. These requirements, both quantifiable (e.g. paid-up capital) and non-quantifiable (e.g. audit opinions) were modified several times during the study period. Unfortunately, the only information publicly available in the DBD database is extracts of the financial statements. Therefore, only the quantifiable requirements for listing could be applied for the sampling criteria. However, we did limit the sample to 'Company Limited' registered firms. This is because while 'Partnership Limited' registered firms may satisfy the quantitative criteria their ownership structure precludes listing. The listing requirements for the selection of private firms are in Table 1.

We define the IPO firm sample as 'Public Company Limited' registered firms that were completely approved as going public by the SEC and that subsequently or concurrently listed stocks on the SET. The data is from two main sources: the dates of firm establishment and most financial data are again from the DBD business registration database while the list date and the remaining financial data are from SETSMART (SET Market Analysis and Reporting Tool).

This web-based application provided by the SET seamlessly integrates the various sources of Thai listed company data, including listed company profiles, historical stock prices, indices, and news.

In all, 115 IPOs took place on the SET from 2001 to 2007. However, five listings were removed from the sample because of incomplete financial data. Together, based on these selection criteria, the final sample comprises 5,228 firms operating between 2001 and 2007, including 5,118 private firms and 110 IPO firms. Table 2 provides details of the distribution of the firm samples.

Table 1. Summary SET listing criteria, 2001–2007

Criteria	2001	2002	2003	2004	2005	2006	2007
Years of operation	≥ 3	≥ 3	≥ 2	≥ 2	≥ 3	≥ 3	≥ 3
Paid-up capital, millions of baht	≥ 200	≥ 200	≥ 200	≥ 200	≥ 300	≥ 300	≥ 300
Shareholder's equity, millions of baht	≥ 200	≥ 200	≥ 200	≥ 200	≥ 300	≥ 300	≥ 300
Net profit, millions of baht	≥30 or sales ≥2,000 or market capitalisation ≥1,500	≥30 or sales ≥2,000 or market capitalisatio n ≥1,500	>0	>0	≥30 or ≥50 combined past 2–3 years	≥30 or ≥50 combined past 2–3 years	≥30 or ≥50 combined past 2–3 years

Table 2. Population and sample distribution of private and public firms, 2001–2007

Year	Non-IPO		% included	IPO		% included	Total		% included
	Total	Sample		Total	Sample		Total	Sample	
2001	480	480	100	4	4	100	484	484	100
2002	691	691	100	12	11	92	703	702	99
2003	1,177	1,177	100	19	18	95	1,196	1,195	99
2004	1,288	1,288	100	31	30	97	1,319	1,318	99
2005	672	672	100	31	30	97	703	702	99
2006	693	693	100	11	11	100	704	704	100
2007	117	117	100	7	6	86	124	123	99
Total	5,118	5,118	100	115	110	96	5,233	5,228	99

4.2. Explanatory Variables

Using the available financial statement information and registration profiles of the private and IPO firms we draw on the extant literature to define two sets of explanatory variables to (i) explain the decision to go public, and (ii) the outcomes from going public. First, firm age (AGE) has been used as a proxy for the uncertainty of firms in their future profitability (Pástor and Veronesi, 2003; Boehmer and Ljungqvist, 2004). Generally, these studies propose that younger companies are more uncertain about their future profitability and hence less interested in going public. Our hypothesis is that younger firms are less likely to go public and define the age of firms as the number of year between its founding and the date eligible to list on the market.

Second, the size of the firm (ASS)—as measured by total assets—may both exert an influence on the decision to go public and affected by this decision. The rationale for this relationship is that larger firms are better able to avoid financial distress by using organised equity markets (Goktan, Kieschnick and Moussawi, 2006). Chemmanur and Fulghieri (1999) also suggest that size acts as a proxy for reputation such that a small independent company will find that it is difficult to become known to the investing public, and thus incurs a large adverse selection cost in selling equity. Therefore, we expect that smaller firms are less likely to go public. In terms of the outcomes of the IPO, we hypothesize that firms going public consequently raise capital to fund growth and increase their assets. Therefore, we expect that the total assets of IPO firms will increase and we hypothesize a positive coefficient.

Third, growth (GRW)—measured by the growth rate of sales—may also be a determinant and outcome of an IPO. This is especially true for potentially high growth firms that are often restricted by financing constraints, such as cash flow, and so firms go public to raise capital for growth (Ritter and Welch, 2002). In terms of outcomes, Kim and Weisbach (2008) argue most firms raise new funds in the IPO, and these funds are used for several purposes, including funding growth. Therefore, we hypothesize that firms with high growth are more likely to go public and that growth will increase after going public. Positive coefficients are hypothesized.

Fourth, we use total debt over total assets as a measure of leverage (LEV). In general, we expect that firms with higher leverage are more likely to go public. For example, Kim and Weisbach (2008) suggest that most firms raise new funds in the IPO, and these funds are used for several purposes, including the reduction of leverage. Our hypotheses are that firms with high leverage are more likely to go public and that the leverage of IPO firms decreases after firms go public. We expect positive and negative signs on the estimated coefficients, respectively.

Fifth, the effect of profitability (ROA)—measured by the return on assets—where ROA is earnings before interest, taxes, depreciation and amortization over total assets) on the likelihood of an IPO is ambiguous. On one hand, high cash flows make a company more independent of external investors and relax its financing constraints. According to the pecking order theory, firms refrain from external funding because of excessive agency costs and therefore prefer to fund their investment internally. High cash flows should therefore reduce the likelihood of an IPO. On the other hand, companies with a temporary surge in profitability might use this window of opportunity to sell their shares to stock market investors who mistakenly regard the surge as permanent and overvalue the company.

Alternatively, high profitability could represent a credible signal of a firm's quality, thus allowing it to overcome adverse selection (Diamond, 1991). The expected effect of profitability on the likelihood of listing may then be either positive or negative, depending on the relative strengths of these factors. For the post-IPO effects, we follow the typical observation being a reduction in post-IPO profitability. See, for example, Degeorge and Zeckhauser (1993), Mikkelson et al. (1997), Jain and Kini (1994), Pagano et al. (1998), and Pástor et al. (2009). A negative coefficient is hypothesized.

Sixth, a common observation is that high-investment companies (INV) are more likely to go public (Holmström and Tirole, 1993; Pagano and Röell, 1998). Capital expenditures are normally used to measure current investment and high investment intensity could then make it particularly appealing for a company to tap the stock market for equity finance. Unfortunately, the statement of cash flows for private firms is not available from the DBD database. Thus, we use the growth of investment in property, plant and equipment as a measure of the firm's requirements for direct productive investment funds for fixed assets. This should increase the likelihood of an IPO. In terms of outcomes, Ritter (1991) concludes there is no increase in post-IPO investment, though Mayers (1984) finds higher investment after firms go public. Accordingly, we hypothesize that investment is either unchanged or increases post listing.

Finally, the literature suggests riskier firms are more likely to go public (Pagano, 1993) and that riskier firms generally pay higher rates on existing borrowings. Unfortunately, information on bank credit for private firms in Thailand is unavailable. Therefore, we measure interest (INT) as total interest expenses divided by total debt as a proxy for the actual interest rate for the company. Clearly, companies with relatively high interest costs find equity finance more attractive so we hypothesize that firms with higher borrowing rates are more likely to go public. In terms of outcomes, Rajan (1992) and Pagano et al. (1998) both conclude that there is a decrease in the borrowing rate after firms go public and we hypothesize the interest rate of firms will decrease post-IPO. A negative coefficient is hypothesized.

4.3. Estimation Technique

This study incorporate two separate models, the first estimating the probability of going public and the second estimating the outcomes of going public. The first specification is a probit model:

$$\Pr\left(IPO_{i,t}=1\right)=F\begin{pmatrix}\alpha_1 AGE_{i,t-1}+\alpha_2 ASS_{i,t-1}+\alpha_3 GRW_{i,t-1}+\alpha_4 LEV_{i,t-1}+\alpha_5 ROA_{i,t-1}+\\ \alpha_6 INV_{i,t-1}+\alpha_7 INT_{i,t-1}\end{pmatrix} \tag{1}$$

where $IPO_{i,t}$ is equal to 1 if a firm goes public and 0 otherwise, *AGE* is the difference between the year eligible to list an IPO and the firm's date of incorporation, *ASS* is total assets, *GRW* is the growth rate of total company sales, *LEV* is the ratio of total liabilities to total assets, *ROA* is the value of earnings before interest, taxes, depreciation, and amortization (EBITDA) over total assets, *INV* is the growth rate of the firm's requirements for direct productive investment funds for property, plant and equipment, and *INT* is the ratio of total interest expenses to total liabilities. For this analysis, the full sample of 5,118 private firms and 110 IPO firms are used to estimate the factors influencing the probability of an IPO.

In the second specification, we investigate the consequences of the IPO decision on selected operating and financial variables by estimating a fixed-effects regression as follows:

$$y_{i,t}=\alpha+\sum_{j=0}^{6}\beta_j IPO_{t-n}+\mu_i+\delta_t+\varepsilon_{i,t} \tag{2}$$

where *yit* is the *ith* firm-specific variable in the *tth* period, representing firm operating performance, *IPOt-n* is a dummy variable equal to one if year *t-n* was the year of the IPO and *ui* (*dt*) accounts for firm (calendar year) specific effects. For this analysis, only the sample of 110 IPO firms is used.

5. Empirical Results

5.1. Determinants of IPOs

Table 3 contains summary statistics on the privately held and publicly listed firms. In terms of statistically significant differences in means only, the average age of private firms is 15.5 years whereas the average age of IPO firms is 13.8 years. The average IPO firm is also more than twice as large. Finally, private firms are less leveraged than IPO firms.

Table 3. Descriptive statistics of private and public firms, 2001–2007

Variable	Non-IPO (n = 5,118)		IPO (n = 110)		Equality of variances		Equality of means	
	Mean	Std dev.	Mean	Std dev.	F-statistic	p-value	t-statistic	p-value
AGE	15.498	10.527	13.836	9.113	5.919	0.015	1.885	0.061
ASS	3.188	8.319	7.504	26.904	88.918	<0.001	–1.681	0.095
GRW	1.926	45.467	0.631	2.287	0.388	0.533	0.298	0.765
LEV	0.497	0.328	0.550	0.209	4.404	0.035	–2.569	0.011
ROA	0.106	3.180	0.101	0.151	0.106	0.744	0.016	0.986
INV	4.335	133.244	0.449	1.802	0.377	0.539	0.305	0.759
INT	0.050	0.777	0.028	0.032	0.244	0.621	0.303	0.761

Notes: AGE – years since establishment, ASS – total assets in billions of baht, GRW – sales growth, LEV – leverage, ROA – return on assets, INV – growth of investment in property, plant and equipment, INV – interest. The null hypothesis for the two-sided variance test is equal variances for IPOs and non-IPOs. The null hypothesis of the one-sided means test is non-IPO mean is less than IPO mean. The variance test determines whether the means test assumes equal or unequal variances.

Table 4 provides the estimates of the model of the firm's decision to go public. Of the seven estimated coefficients shown, four are statistically significant at the .01 level or lower. First, the estimated coefficient for firm age is negative, indicating that older firms in Thailand are less likely to go public. This is a similar result to Boehmer and Ljungqvist (2004) who used company age as a proxy for uncertainty in future profitability but contrast with most previous studies in developed countries [see, for example, Leland and Pyle (1977), Rock (1986), Pagano et al. (1998), and Chemmanur and Fulghieri (1999)]. Second, consistent with the results in Pagano et al. (1998) there is a positive relationship between firm size (*ASS*) and the likelihood of going public and this is in agreement with the theories on direct costs, adverse selection costs and stock liquidity as relevant motivating factors for initial owners to go public.

Third, there is a negative relationship between firm leverage (*LEV*) and the cost of borrowing (INT) and the likelihood of going public: that is, firms with more debt and higher borrowing costs are less likely to go public. This is an unusual finding in that the pecking order hypothesis suggests that firms will turn to external equity financing after external debt financing is exhausted and that equity is a relatively cheaper funding source with higher levels of debt. Lastly, the motivations for an IPO differ significantly across industries and the year of issue (now shown). The estimated coefficients for the industry and time controls indicate that Thai firms in manufacturing, electricity, gas and water supply, hotels and restaurants, and real estate, renting and business activities are less likely to go public as are firms operating in 2004, 2005 and 2007.

Table 4. Firm-specific determinants of IPOs

Variable	Est. coef.	Std. error	*p*-value
AGE	–0.076	0.004	<0.001
ASS	0.010	0.002	<0.000
GRW	–0.027	0.025	0.287
LEV	–1.695	0.120	<0.001
ROA	–0.003	0.010	0.762
INV	–0.005	0.012	0.625
INT	–5.877	1.329	<0.001

Notes: Hannan–Quinn criteria = 0.2820, Log likelihood –722.0816.

Unfortunately, despite many of the firm-specific variables being significant in the regression, the ability of the model to predict correctly an IPO using only this information is relatively poor. This is not unexpected as all of the firms included technically satisfy the SET listing requirements (mostly quantitative financial statement information) and so both the very small number of IPOs and the very large number of non-IPOs are homogeneous. Based on a prediction success table, the model correctly identifies 95.36 percent of non-IPOs but only 3.53 percent of IPOs, and incorrectly identifies only 4.64 percent of non-IPOS but 96.47 percent of IPOs. This provides only a marginal increase in predictability over a constant probability model (one including only the sample probabilities) of just 1.46 percent. Of course, the ability of firm-specific financial variables to predict the probability of an IPO would be much higher if the sample was drawn across, say, all Thai firms. However, once the threshold set by the SET is attained, it is very difficult to separate firms into those more or less likely to pursue an IPO, suggesting that other factors are at play.

5.2. The Outcomes of IPOs

Tables 5 and 6 respectively summarize the year and industry effects following an IPO. In terms of significant differences in means, IPOs in 2004 have a higher ROA post-IPO while IPOs in 2005 have higher growth than other IPOs. However, the post-IPO growth of IPOs in both 2006 and 2007 is lower, while leverage in 2007 is higher. There is also some variation in the post-IPO effects by industry. For example, ROA is lower post-IPO in the services (SER) industry but significantly higher in resources (RES) and agricultural and food (AGR). In terms of assets, pots-IPO firms are larger in resources (RES) but smaller in industrial (IND), consumer products (CNS) and agricultural and food (AGR). Finally, leverage is lower in agricultural and food (AGR) firms post-IPO, but higher in consumer products (CNS).

Table 7 uses regression models to estimate the effects of the decision to go public. As shown, firm size (*ASS*) increases slowly and is statistically significant for 4 to 6 years post-IPO. We also find a reduction in sales growth (*GRW*) after listing, but this is only significant two years after the IPO. Unlike previous work that indicates that leverage (*LEV*) declines after an IPO (Kim and Weisbach 2008; Mayers 1984; Sah and Stiglitz 1986; Allen and Gale

1999) our results indicate that leverage slowly increases and is statistically significant at the 1% level for years 2, 3, 5 and 6 after the IPO.

Table 5. Descriptive statistics by year

Year	Variable	Mean	Std. dev.	Mean	Std. dev.	Equality of variances		Equality of means	
						F-statistic	*p*-value	*t*-statistic	*p*-value
2001 (4, 417)	ASS	22.885	0.003	21.721	0.001	4.957	0.027	–0.9215	0.425
	GRW	–0.027	0.445	0.218	0.622	0.030	0.864	0.788	0.431
	LEV	0.549	0.270	0.413	0.223	0.102	0.750	–1.2104	0.227
	ROA	0.048	0.046	0.065	0.145	0.326	0.569	0.233	0.816
	INV	0.108	0.388	0.491	5.777	0.032	0.857	0.132	0.895
	INT	0.014	0.012	0.148	2.481	0.036	0.850	0.107	0.915
2002 (15, 406)	ASS	21.675	0.001	21.734	0.001	0.013	0.908	0.174	0.862
	GRW	0.675	1.257	0.199	0.580	15.683	0.000	–1.4616	0.166
	LEV	0.361	0.172	0.417	0.225	0.693	0.406	0.934	0.351
	ROA	0.102	0.110	0.064	0.145	0.003	0.959	–1.0348	0.301
	INV	0.215	0.623	0.497	5.854	0.078	0.781	0.186	0.853
	INT	0.020	0.018	0.151	2.514	0.131	0.717	0.200	0.841
2003 (33, 388)	ASS	21.574	0.001	21.745	0.001	0.574	0.449	0.733	0.464
	GRW	0.450	0.912	0.196	0.587	3.213	0.074	–1.5764	0.124
	LEV	0.362	0.170	0.419	0.227	0.801	0.371	1.387	0.166
	ROA	0.097	0.092	0.062	0.148	0.291	0.590	–1.3281	0.185
	INV	0.363	1.532	0.497	5.974	0.042	0.839	0.129	0.898
	INT	0.021	0.022	0.157	2.572	0.299	0.585	0.303	0.762
2004 (63, 358)	ASS	21.716	0.001	21.735	0.001	0.303	0.583	0.102	0.919
	GRW	0.344	0.619	0.193	0.619	0.353	0.553	–1.7928	0.074
	LEV	0.388	0.200	0.419	0.228	0.008	0.929	1.011	0.313
	ROA	0.098	0.071	0.059	0.153	1.543	0.215	–1.9985	0.046
	INV	0.235	0.317	0.531	6.234	0.703	0.402	0.376	0.707
	INT	0.023	0.031	0.168	2.678	0.623	0.430	0.429	0.668
2005 (93, 328)	ASS	21.683	0.001	21.746	0.001	0.495	0.482	0.410	0.682
	GRW	0.372	0.743	0.171	0.575	2.191	0.140	–2.7822	0.006
	LEV	0.400	0.185	0.419	0.234	0.960	0.328	0.701	0.484
	ROA	0.079	0.074	0.061	0.158	2.628	0.106	–1.0977	0.273
	INV	0.298	0.857	0.540	6.500	0.573	0.450	0.357	0.721
	INT	0.022	0.017	0.182	2.797	1.043	0.308	0.550	0.583
2006 (104, 317)	ASS	21.799	0.001	21.710	0.001	0.080	0.778	–0.6180	0.537
	GRW	0.089	0.317	0.257	0.687	7.457	0.007	3.395	0.001
	LEV	0.417	0.193	0.414	0.233	0.234	0.629	–0.1459	0.884
	ROA	0.052	0.110	0.069	0.154	0.001	0.976	1.011	0.313
	INV	1.389	11.491	0.191	0.741	11.055	0.001	–1.0634	0.290
	INT	0.031	0.022	0.184	2.846	1.169	0.280	0.548	0.584
2007 (109, 312)	ASS	21.730	0.001	21.733	0.001	0.543	0.461	0.014	0.989
	GRW	0.003	0.339	0.290	0.678	5.575	0.019	5.717	0.000
	LEV	0.457	0.297	0.400	0.190	3.861	0.050	–1.8975	0.060
	ROA	0.031	0.234	0.077	0.092	6.545	0.011	1.997	0.048
	INV	0.020	0.351	0.650	6.671	1.574	0.210	0.984	0.326
	INT	0.493	4.852	0.025	0.023	11.291	0.001	–1.0082	0.316

Notes: Number of IPO and non-IPO firms in brackets after industry.

Table 6. Descriptive statistics by industry

Year	Variable	Mean	Std. dev.	Mean	Std. dev.	Equality of variances		Equality of means	
						F-statistic	*p*-value	*t*-statistic	*p*-value
TECH (86, 335)	ASS	21.355	0.001	21.829	0.001	2.716	0.100	3.085	0.002
	GRW	0.195	0.587	0.221	0.630	0.250	0.617	0.346	0.730
	LEV	0.406	0.182	0.417	0.234	1.625	0.203	0.417	0.677
	ROA	0.076	0.096	0.062	0.154	1.413	0.235	–0.7870	0.432
	INV	0.080	0.347	0.591	6.441	1.049	0.306	0.736	0.462
	INT	0.021	0.019	0.179	2.768	0.931	0.335	0.530	0.596
SER (85, 336)	ASS	21.928	0.001	21.682	0.001	0.806	0.370	–1.5843	0.114
	GRW	0.265	0.818	0.203	0.561	2.631	0.106	–0.8144	0.416
	LEV	0.439	0.339	0.408	0.184	19.687	0.000	–0.8053	0.423
	ROA	0.010	0.263	0.079	0.088	19.229	0.000	2.385	0.019
	INV	0.463	1.597	0.493	6.388	0.011	0.918	0.043	0.966
	INT	0.024	0.023	0.178	2.764	0.897	0.344	0.512	0.609
RES (39, 382)	ASS	23.245	0.002	21.577	0.001	90.375	0.000	–4.8128	0.000
	GRW	0.205	0.583	0.217	0.625	1.295	0.256	0.115	0.909
	LEV	0.437	0.205	0.412	0.226	0.001	0.972	–0.6625	0.508
	ROA	0.107	0.056	0.061	0.150	2.008	0.157	–1.8964	0.059
	INV	0.086	0.257	0.528	6.035	0.479	0.490	0.456	0.648
	INT	0.029	0.017	0.159	2.592	0.368	0.545	0.313	0.755
PRP (137, 284)	ASS	21.628	0.001	21.782	0.001	10.390	0.001	1.285	0.200
	GRW	0.249	0.661	0.200	0.601	2.739	0.099	–0.7468	0.456
	LEV	0.435	0.173	0.405	0.244	8.118	0.005	–1.2959	0.196
	ROA	0.057	0.077	0.069	0.167	3.137	0.077	0.962	0.337
	INV	1.066	9.992	0.208	0.921	5.771	0.017	–1.0031	0.318
	INT	0.399	4.328	0.025	0.020	8.057	0.005	–1.0136	0.313
IND (52, 369)	ASS	21.345	0.001	21.786	0.001	6.818	0.009	3.463	0.001
	GRW	0.118	0.221	0.230	0.657	7.282	0.007	2.443	0.015
	LEV	0.410	0.176	0.415	0.230	1.245	0.265	0.159	0.874
	ROA	0.077	0.064	0.063	0.152	1.484	0.224	–0.6223	0.534
	INV	0.147	0.294	0.535	6.140	0.624	0.430	0.455	0.650
	INT	0.032	0.018	0.163	2.637	0.510	0.476	0.358	0.721
CNS (4, 417)	ASS	20.893	0.000	21.740	0.001	3.370	0.067	10.741	0.000
	GRW	0.110	0.044	0.217	0.624	1.346	0.247	0.343	0.732
	LEV	0.178	0.095	0.417	0.224	1.525	0.218	2.131	0.034
	ROA	0.119	0.047	0.065	0.145	0.242	0.623	–0.7509	0.453
	INV	0.002	0.080	0.492	5.777	0.066	0.797	0.169	0.866
	INT	0.032	0.031	0.148	2.481	0.032	0.859	0.093	0.926
AGR (18, 403)	ASS	21.422	0.001	21.746	0.001	4.549	0.034	2.076	0.048
	GRW	0.158	0.170	0.218	0.633	3.452	0.064	1.181	0.244
	LEV	0.204	0.094	0.424	0.223	6.103	0.014	8.854	0.000
	ROA	0.196	0.142	0.059	0.142	2.279	0.132	–3.9967	0.000
	INV	0.097	0.189	0.504	5.877	0.243	0.622	0.294	0.769
	INT	0.016	0.016	0.152	2.524	0.162	0.688	0.229	0.819

Notes: Industries (post-IPO) are technology (TCH), services (SER), resources (RES), property and construction (PRP), industrial (IND), consumer products (CNS) and agricultural and food (AGR). Number of IPO and non-IPO firms in brackets after industry.

Table 7. Firm-specific post-IPO outcomes

Variable		≤YR 1	IND	TME	≤YR 2	IND	TME	All	IND	TME
ASS	Coef.	0.840	–	–	2.631	–	–	9.755	–	–
	F–stat.	–	8.106	1.805	–	10.895	3.719	–	–	–
	Std. dev.	4.153	–	–	2.985	–	–	4.361	–	–
	p–value	0.839	<0.001	0.180	0.378	<0.001	0.054	0.025	–	–
GRW	Coef.	–0.047	–	–	–0.124	–	–	–0.040	–	–
	F–stat.	–	3.170	2.586	–	4.633	4.279	–	–	–
	Std. dev.	0.137	–	–	0.059	–	–	0.027	–	–
	p–value	0.727	0.003	0.109	0.037	<0.001	0.039	0.135	–	–
LEV	Coef.	0.024	–	–	0.024	–	–	0.022	–	–
	F–stat.	–	11.875	0.285	–	15.035	0.261	–	–	–
	Std. dev.	0.026	–	–	0.014	–	–	0.011	–	–
	p–value	0.353	<0.001	0.593	0.088	<0.001	0.609	0.039	–	–
ROA	Coef.	–0.013	–	–	–0.017	–	–	–0.010	–	–
	F–stat.	–	9.768	1.068	–	11.456	4.280	–	–	–
	Std. dev.	0.010	–	–	0.006	–	–	0.0082	–	–
	p–value	0.211	<0.001	0.302	0.005	<0.001	0.039	0.199	–	–
INV	Coef.	0.969	–	–	–0.138	–	–	–0.238	–	–
	F–stat.	–	0.265	0.313	–	0.259	0.381	–	–	–
	Std. dev.	0.978	–	–	0.152	–	–	0.181	–	–
	p–value	0.322	0.966	0.575	0.366	0.968	0.537	0.189	–	–
INT	Coef.	–0.012	–	–	–0.006	–	–	0.233	–	–
	F–stat.	–	1.414	9.005	–	1.540	14.121	–	–	–
	Std. dev.	0.003	–	–	0.001	–	–	0.234	–	–
	p–value	<0.001	0.201	0.003	<0.001	0.153	<0.001	0.319	–	–
Variable		≤YR 3	IND	TME	≤YR 4	IND	TME	All	IND	TME
ASS	Coef.	3.845	–	–	5.149	–	–	9.755	–	–
	F–stat.	–	12.506	5.427	–	13.565	7.480	–	–	–
	Std. dev.	2.843	–	–	3.212	–	–	4.361	–	–
	p–value	0.177	<0.001	0.020	0.109	<0.001	0.006	0.025	–	–
GRW	Coef.	0.0628	–	–	–0.046	–	–	–0.040	–	–
	F–stat.	–	5.913	9.073	–	6.331	10.883	–	–	–
	Std. dev.	0.042	–	–	0.032	–	–	0.027	–	–
	p–value	0.135	<0.001	0.002	0.155	<0.001	0.001	0.135	–	–
LEV	Coef.	0.018	–	–	–0.046	–	–	0.022	–	–
	F–stat.	–	16.616	0.180	–	6.331	10.883	–	–	–
	Std. dev.	0.011	–	–	0.032	–	–	0.011	–	–
	p–value	0.095	<0.001	0.671	0.155	<0.001	0.001	0.039	–	–
ROA	Coef.	–0.008	–	–	–0.006	–	–	–0.010	–	–
	F–stat.	–	13.761	5.362	–	15.475	5.773	–	–	–
	Std. dev.	0.004	–	–	0.003	–	–	0.0082	–	–
	p–value	0.069	<0.001	0.021	0.101	<0.001	0.016	0.199	–	–
INV	Coef.	–0.274	–	–	–0.251	–	–	–0.238	–	–
	F–stat.	–	0.261	0.451	–	0.285	0.437	–	–	–
	Std. dev.	0.214	–	–	0.203	–	–	0.181	–	–
	p–value	0.202	0.968	0.502	0.216	0.959	0.508	0.189	–	–
INT	Coef.	–0.004	–	–	–0.002	–	–	0.233	–	–
	F–stat.	–	2.086	13.494	–	2.157	12.931	–	–	–
	Std. dev.	0.001	–	–	0.001	–	–	0.234	–	–
	p–value	0.001	0.044	<0.001	0.007	0.037	<0.001	0.319	–	–

Variable		≤YR 5	IND	TME	≤YR 6	IND	TME	All	IND	TME
ASS	Coef.	6.956	–	–	9.755	–	–	9.755	–	–
	F-stat.	–	14.034	7.880	–	14.678	7.427	–	14.678	7.427
	Std. dev.	3.669	–	–	4.361	–	–	4.361	–	–
	p-value	0.058	<0.001	0.005	0.025	<0.001	0.006	0.025	<0.001	0.006
GRW	Coef.	–0.045	–	–	–0.040	–	–	–0.040	–	–
	F-stat.	–	6.483	11.480	–	6.524	11.896	–	6.524	11.896
	Std. dev.	0.028	–	–	0.027	–	–	0.027	–	–
	p-value	0.110	<0.001	<0.001	0.135	<0.001	<0.001	0.135	<0.001	<0.001
LEV	Coef.	0.022	–	–	0.022	–	–	0.022	–	–
	F-stat.	–	13.836	0.157	–	13.944	0.158	–	13.944	89.515
	Std. dev.	0.011	–	–	0.011	–	–	0.011	–	–
	p-value	0.054	<0.001	0.691	0.039	<0.001	0.690	0.039	<0.001	<0.001
ROA	Coef.	–0.011	–	–	–0.010	–	–	–0.010	–	–
	F-stat.	–	8.818	2.849	–	8.867	3.045	–	8.867	3.045
	Std. dev.	0.009	–	–	0.008	–	–	0.0082	–	–
	p-value	0.191	<0.001	0.092	0.199	<0.001	0.081	0.199	<0.001	0.081
INV	Coef.	–0.250	–	–	–0.238	–	–	–0.238	–	–
	F-stat.	–	0.280	0.452	–	0.280	0.444	–	0.280	0.444
	Std. dev.	0.191	–	–	0.181	–	–	0.181	–	–
	p-value	0.191	0.961	0.501	0.189	0.961	0.505	0.189	0.961	0.505
INT	Coef.	0.254	–	–	0.233	–	–	0.233	–	–
	F-stat.	–	0.429	0.280	–	0.446	0.241	–	0.446	0.241
	Std. dev.	0.254	–	–	0.234	–	–	0.234	–	–
	p-value	0.318	0.883	0.596	0.319	0.872	0.623	0.319	0.872	0.623

Notes: YR# – year after IP0, ALL – all years, IND – test of joint significance of industry dummies, TME – test of joint significance of time dummies.

In terms of profitability, we find a statistically significant increase at the 1% level for each year after the second year. These results contrast with the findings in Jain and Kini (1994), Mikkelson et al. (1997), and Pagano et al. (1998). However, the decision to go public has no impact on investment (*INV*) as in Ritter (1991). One of the more interesting findings is that interest rates (INT) decrease post-IPO from the first to the fourth year. The decline in borrowing costs is a common observation for firms post-IPO because: (i) companies become safer borrowers when they reduce their leverage with the IPO; (ii) more information becomes publicly available so lenders have more information about creditworthiness; and (iii) being listed on the stock market offers a company an outside financing option that improves firm bargaining power with banks (Rajan, 1992; Pagano et al. (1998).

Conclusion

In this chapter, we first seek to explain why Thai firms decide to go public. Using a large database of eligible private firms in Thailand, we empirically study the determinants of initial public offerings (IPOs) by comparing the pre- and post-IPO characteristics of private firms. The results suggest that the likelihood of an IPO is increasing with firm size and leverage. However, contrary to most previous studies, Thai firms that are generally younger and with lower borrowing rates are more likely to go public. The post-IPO results show that IPO firms went public to reduce borrowing rates not to fund future investment and growth, which is similar to the results in Pagano et al. (1998) but contrasts with Singh (1995). Furthermore, we find that the profitability of Thai firms increases strongly during the post-listing period for a period of two years. Combined together, we find strong support for financial flexibility and greater bargaining with banks, the exploitation of mispricing, and a lower cost of capital as a motivation for IPO and moderate support for theories emphasizing risk sharing and portfolio diversification. However, we find rather less support for indirect costs (loss of confidentiality), raising capital for funds growth and the reduction of leverage and overcoming financing (borrowing) constraints as a motivation for IPOs in Thailand.

As discussed earlier, the firm-specific financial variables, industry and calendar effects examined in this study provide only a partial insight into the motivations for or against an IPO in Thailand. Clearly, IPOs are infrequent events in Thailand with only 110 firms conducting an IPO in the sample period 2001 to 2007, just a fraction of the 5,118 private firms technically eligible. The question is why Thai firms prefer to remain private rather than pursuing the putative benefits of going public. This has important implications for the SET's future business model and for the expectations and hopes of the Thai government for a strong equity market sustained by IPOs. Of course, the necessarily short sample period in this study coincided with a period when debt capital was relatively cheap and easily available, so the focus here is on longer-term conditions.

First, one of the most defining features of the corporate sector in Thailand is the dominance of family controlled businesses. In many respects, the situation in Thailand is very similar to China, Hong Kong and Singapore where the commercial class is mainly of Thai-Chinese origin (Ch'ng 1993)]. Thai firms are closely held and managed by these majority family interests, and so if they decide to go public, the ownership structure may need to change substantially to meet government regulations. This effectively precludes many Thai firms from seeking an IPO.

Second, the costs of an IPO can be prohibitive for many Thai firms. One aspect of this concerns the additional reporting burdens associated with a publicly listed firm. For instance, public companies listed on the SET are required to submit both periodic and non-periodic reports (describing the acquisitions or disposal of assets, connected transactions, agreement to form or discontinue a joint venture, increase or decrease in capital, initial public offerings, repurchases of stock, dividend payments or non-payment, etc.) to the SET (Listed Company Handbook 2009). They are also required to submit forms enclosing a balance sheet and income statement to the DBD. This contrasts with the relatively low level (and costs) of reporting found in Thailand for private firms. The actual costs of launching an IPO are also considerable for Thai entrepreneurs in both direct and indirect terms. For example, Chorruk and Worthington (2009) found that IPOs listing on the SET between 1997 and 2007 were about 17.6 percent underpriced.

Third, the number of firms registered in Thailand may actually overstate those firms able to convert to a publicly listed form, even though they satisfy the technical requirements. Since the Foreign Business Act 1999, many multinational companies have set up representative officers, joint ventures, branches or locally incorporated subsidiaries in Thailand. As at 30 September 2009, there are 2,312 foreign companies across 37 industry sectors in Thailand (some 90.63% of all private limited companies) (Business Registration Office 2009; Foreign Business Office 2009) and these businesses are often involved in significant cross-border related-party transactions. In some cases, their primary purpose actually is to advise their overseas affiliates on investment or business opportunities in Thailand. Even at the more autonomous end of the spectrum, where a business is established to serve domestic retail or corporate customers, its overseas related-party transactions may be so insignificant in global terms in that it can rely on its overseas affiliates for funding, oversight, support and execution. These firms would then prefer to raise funds from their own savings or by borrowing from their overseas parent company.

Fourth, the strong Thai culture imposes the setting of a particular 'moral' code on companies listing on the Thai market. A recent example is the popular protests surrounding the listing of Thai Beverage, the country's largest alcoholic brewer and distiller. These protests caused the company to delay listing after it failed to set the offer price at the appropriate deadline. The protesters surrounded the SET's headquarters to pressure the exchange into rejecting the listing on moral grounds, a repeat of the widespread protests seen in 2005 when the company first sought listing. The protesters including Buddhist monks, students and social activities who claimed that their religion prohibited the consumption of alcohol (about 95 percent of Thais are Buddhist). Ultimately, Thai Beverage listed its shares on the Singapore Stock Exchange in 2006 after the first attempt to list on the SET failed.

Finally, Thailand is frequently wracked by social unrest aggravated by domestic and global economic ills. These serve to dull the interest in Thai IPOs of investors and entrepreneurs alike. For instance, since the 1997 Asian Financial Crisis alone, the 2004 Indian Ocean tsunami, the September 2006 military coup that led to Thaksin Shinawatra's self-imposed exile and the effects of the global financial crisis in 2007 have all impacted heavily on the Thai economy and its markets, with Thailand continuing to have political problems at the present time.

REFERENCES

Allen, F. and Gale, D. (1999). Diversity of opinion and financing of new technologies. *Journal of Financial Intermediation*, 8, 68–89.

Amihud, Y. and Mendelson, H. (1986) Asset pricing and the bid-ask spread. *Journal of Financial Economics*, 17, 223–249.

Atje, R. and Javanovic, B. (1993) Stock markets and development. *European Economic Review*, 37, 632–640.

Bancel, F. and Mittoo, R.U. (2009). Why do European firms go public? *European Financial Management*, 15, 844–884.

Black, B.S. and Gilson, R.J. (1998). Venture capital and the structure of capital markets: Banks versus stock markets. *Journal of Financial Economics*, 47, 243–247.

Board of Investment (2009). Establishing a Business in Thailand. Retrieved October 2009, Available at http://www.boi.go.th.

Boehmer, E. and Ljungqvist, A. (2004). On the decision to go public: Evidence from privately-held firms. Working Paper No. 16/2004, New York University.

Bolton, P. and von Thadden, E-L. (1998). Blocks, liquidity, and corporate control. *Journal of Finance*, 53, 1–25.

Booth, J. and Chua, L. (1996). Ownership dispersion, costly information, and IPO underpricing. *Journal of Financial Economics*, 41, 291–310.

Bradley, D., Jordan, B., and Ritter, J.R. (2003). The quiet period goes out with a bang. *Journal of Finance*, 58, 1–36.

Brau, J. and Fawcett, S. (2006). Initial public offerings: An analysis of theory and practice. *Journal of Finance,* 61, 399–436.

Brau, C. J., Francis. B, and Kohers, N. (2003). The choice of IPO versus takeover: Empirical evidence. *Journal of Business*, 76, 583–612.

Business Registration Office, Department of Business Development (2009). Business Registrations Statistics in Thailand, Retrieved October 2009, Available at http://www.dbd.go.th.

Campbell, T.S. (1979). Optimal investment financing decisions and the value of confidentiality. *Journal of Financial and Quantitative Analysis*, 14, 913–24.

Celikyurt, U., Sevilir, M. and Shivdasani, A. L. (2007). Going public to acquire? The acquisition motive in IPOs. Working Paper, North Carolina University, Available at http://ssrn.com/abstract=1153508.

Chemmanur, T, He, S. and Nandy, D. (2008). The going public decision and product market. Working Paper, Center for Economic Studies, U.S. Census Bureau.

Chemmanur, T. and Fulghieri, P. (1999). A theory of the going-public decision. *Review of Financial Studies*, 12, 249–279.

Chen, H. C. and Ritter, J.R. (2000). The seven percent solution. *Journal of Finance*, 55, 1105–31.

Chorruk J. and Worthington, A. C. (2009). New evidence on the pricing and performance of initial public offerings in Thailand: 1997–2008. Working Paper No. 13, Department of Accounting, Finance and Economics, Griffith University.

Ch'ng, D. (1993). The Overseas Chinese Entrepreneurs in East Asia: Background, Business Practices and International Networks. No. 100, Committee for Economic Development of Australia, Sydney, Australia.

Degeorge, F. and Zeckhauser, R. (1993). The reverse LBO decision and firm performance: Theory and evidence. *Journal of Finance*, 48, 1323–48.

Department of Business Development (2008a). Type of Business Organization in Thailand, Retrieved November 2008, Available at http://www.dbd.go.th.

Department of Business Development (2008b). Registered business database, Retrieved November 2008, Available at http://www.dbd.go.th.

Diamond, D. W. (1991). Monitoring and reputation: The choice between bank loans and directly placed debt. *Journal of Political Economy*, 99, 689–721.

Draho, J. (2004). The IPO decision: Why and How Companies Go Public. Edward Elgar, Cheltenham, UK.

Foreign Business Office of Department of Business Development (2009). Statistics of foreign business certificate classified by nationality and business sector, Retrieved October 2009, Available at http://www.dbd.go.th.

Goergen, M., Khurshed, A. and Mudambi, R. (2006). The strategy of going public: How UK firms choose their listing contracts. *Journal of Business Finance and Accounting*, 33, 79–101.

Gomes, A. (2000). Going public without governance: Managerial reputation effects. *Journal of Finance*, 55, 615–646.

Gompers, P. (1995). Optimal investment, monitoring, and the staging of venture capital. *Journal of Finance*, 50,1461–1489.

Habib, M.A. and Ljungqvist, A.P. (2001). Underpricing and entrepreneurial wealth losses in IPOs: Theory and evidence. *Review of Financial Studies*, 14, 433–458.

Helwege, J. and Packer, F. (2003). The decision to go public: Evidence from mandatory SEC filings of private firms. Working Paper, Ohio State University.

Holmstrom, B. and Tirole, J. (1993). Market liquidity and performance monitoring. *Journal of Political Economy*, 101, 678–709.

Holmstrom, B. and Tirole, J. (1997). Financial intermediation, loanable funds, and the real sector. *Quarterly Journal of Economics*, 112, 663–91.

Huyghebaert, N. and Hulle, C.V. (2006). Structuring the IPO: Empirical evidence on the portions of primary and secondary shares. *Journal of Corporate Finance*, 12, 296–320.

Jenkinson, T. and Ljungqvist, A. (1996). Going Public: The Theory and Evidence on How Companies raise Equity Finance, Clarendon Press, Oxford.

Jain, B. and Kini, O. (1994). The post-issue operating performance of IPO firms. *Journal of Finance*, 49, 1699–1726.

Jensen, M.C. and Meckling, W.H. (1976). Theory of the firm: Managerial behavior, agency costs and ownership structure. *Journal of Financial Economics*, 3, 305–60.

Kim, W. and Weisbach, M.S. (2008). Motivations for public equity offers: An international perspective. *Journal of Financial Economics,* 87, 281–307.

Leland, H. E. and Pyle, D. H. (1977). Informational asymmetries, financial structure, and financial intermediation. *Journal of Finance*, 32, 371–87.

Levine, R. And Zervos, S. (1998). Stock markets, banks, and economic growth. *American Economic Review*, 88, 537–558.

Listed Companies Development Department (2008). Listing Requirements in Thailand, Retrieved November 2008, Available at http://www.set.or.th.

Listing and Disclosure Department (2008). Circular Letters of Listing and Disclosure Department, Retrieved November 2008, Available at http://www.sec.or.th.

Lyandres, E., Zhdanov, A., and Hsieh, J. (2009). A theory of merger-driven IPOs. Working Paper, Available at http://ssrn.com/abstract=932117.

Maksimovic, V. and Pichler, P. (2001). Technological innovation and initial public offerings. *Review of Financial Studies,* 14, 459–494.

Maug, E. (1998). Large shareholders as monitors: Is there a trade-off between liquidity and control? *Journal of Finance*, 53, 65–98.

Mello, S.A. and Parsons, E.J. (1998). Going public and the ownership structure of the firm. *Journal of Financial Economics*, 49, 79–109.

Merton, R. (1987). Presidential address: A simple model of capital market equilibrium. *Journal of Finance,* 42, 483–510.

Meulbroek, L. K. (2001). The efficiency of equity-linked compensation: understanding the full cost of awarding executive stock options. *Financial Management*, 30, 5–24.

Mikkelson, W. H., Partch, M.M., and Shah, K. (1997). Ownership and operating performance of companies that go public. *Journal of Financial Economics*, 44, 281–307.

Modigliani, F. and Miller, M.H. (1963). Corporate income taxes and the cost of capital: A correction. *The American Economic Review*, 53, 433–43.

Myers, S.C. (1984). The capital structure puzzle. *Journal of Finance*, 39, 575–592.

Myers, S.C. and Majiluf, N.S. (1984). Corporate financing and investment decisions when firms have information that investors do not have. *Journal of Financial Economics*, 13, 187–221.

Pagano, M. (1993). The flotation of companies on the stock market: A coordination failure model. *European Economic Review,* 37, 1101–1125.

Pagano, M., Panetta F., and Zingales L. (1998). Why do companies go public?: An empirical analysis. *Journal of Finance*, 53, 27–64.

Pagano, M. and Röell, A. (1998). The choice of stock ownership structure: Agency costs, monitoring, and the decision to go public. *Quarterly Journal of Economics*, 113, 187–225.

Pástor, L., Taylor, L.A., and Veronesi, P. (2009). Entrepreneurial learning, the IPO decision, and the post-IPO drop in firm profitability. *Review of Financial Studies*, 22, 3005–3046.

Pástor, L. and Veronesi, P. (2003). Stock valuation and learning about profitability. *Journal of Finance*, 58, 1749–90.

Phagaphasvivat, S. (1995). Vision for Thailand for the Year 2000, Competitive Strategies, and Strategic Planning and Management. Bangkok: Matichon.

Rajan, R.G. (1992). Insiders and outsiders: The choice between informed and arm's-length debt. *Journal of Finance*, 47, 1367–1400.

Revenue Department (2007). Royal Decree no. 467 B.E. 2550: Issued under the revenue code governing reduction of taxation. Bangkok, Thailand: RD. Retrieved October 2008, Available at http://www.rd.go.th.

Ravasi, D. and Marchisio, G. (2003). Going public and the enrichment of a supportive network: Some evidence from Italian initial public offerings. *Small Business Economics*, 21, 381–395.

Ritter, J.R. (1987). The costs of going public. *Journal of Financial Economics*, 19, 269–281.

Ritter, J.R. (1991). The long run performance of initial public offerings. *Journal of Finance*, 46, 3–28.

Ritter, J.R. (2003). Differences between European and American IPO markets. *European Financial Management*, 9, 421–34.

Ritter, J.R. and Welch, I. (2002). A review of activity, pricing, and allocations. *Journal of Finance*, 57, 1795–1828.

Rock, K. (1986). Why new issues are underpriced? *Journal of Financial Economics*, 15, 187–212.

Rosen, J.R., Smart, B.C. and Zutter, J.C. (2005). Why do firms go public? Evidence from banking industry. Working Paper No. WP 2005-17, Federal Reserve Bank of Chicago, Chicago.

Sah, R.K. and Stiglitz, J.E. (1986). The architecture of economic systems: Hierarchies and polyarchies. *American Economic Review*, 76, 716–727.

Schipper, K and Smith, A. (1986). A comparison of equity carve-outs and seasoned equity offerings: Share price effects and corporate restructuring. *Journal of Financial Economics*, 15, 153–86.

Scott, J. H. (1976). A Theory of optimal capital structure. *Bell Journal of Economics*, 7, 33–54.

Securities Exchange Commission (2008). Retrieved November 2008, Available at http://www.sec.or.th.

Singh, A. (1995). Corporate financial pattern in industrializing economies: A comparative international study. International Financial Corporation Technical Paper No. 2, World Bank, Washington, DC.

Singh, A. and Hamis, J. (1992). Corporate financial structure in developing countries', International Financial Corporation Technical Paper No. 1, World Bank, Washington, DC.

Stock Exchange of Thailand (2000). Notification of the Securities and Exchange Commission Re: Application for and Approval of Offer for Sale of Newly Issued Shares (KorChor. 12/2543), Retrieved May 2009, Available at http://www.set.or.th.

Stock Exchange of Thailand (2001a). New SET Listing Requirements Adopted: Tax Incentives to Lure in Companies (No. 102/2001), Retrieved May 2009, Available at http://www.set.or.th.

Stock Exchange of Thailand (2001b). Listing of Ordinary Shares of Preferred Shares as Listed Securities (Bor. Jor./Ror. 01-00), Retrieved May 2009, Available at http://www.set.or.th.

Stock Exchange of Thailand (2008a). Listing Manual for Common Shares in 2008, Retrieved May 2009, Available at http://www.set.or.th.

Stock Exchange of Thailand (2008b). Thailand's capital market in 2008, Retrieved May 2009, Available at http://www.set.or.th.

Stock Exchange of Thailand (2008c). Benefits of being listed on the Thai stock exchange, Retrieved October 2009, Available at http://www.set.or.th.

Stoughton, M. N. and Zechner, J. (1998). IPO-mechanisms, monitoring, and ownership structure. *Journal of Financial Economics*, 49, 45–77.

Subrahmanyam, A. and Titman, S. (1999). The going-public decision and the development of financial markets. *Journal of Finance*, 54, 1045–82.

UNCTAD (1993). Portfolio Equity Investment and New Financing Mechanisms: Foreign Portfolio Equity Investment in Developing Countries, Current Issues and Prospects, New York: UNCTAD Secretariat.

World Federation of Exchanges (2009). Annual Report and Statistics, Retrieved May 2009, Available at http://www.world-exchanges.org.

Yosha, O. (1995). Information disclosure costs and the choice of financing source. *Journal of Financial Intermediation*, 4, 3–20.

Zingales, L. (1995). Insiders' ownership and the decision to go public. *Review of Economic Studies,* 62, 425–448.

In: Economic and Financial Modeling
Editor: Andrew C. Worthington
ISBN: 978-1-63463-111-2

Chapter 6

MODELS OF POLITICAL CYCLES AND MARKET RISK AND RETURN

Andrew C. Worthington*
Griffith University, Australia

ABSTRACT

This chapter examines the presence of a political cycle in Australian daily stock returns over the 47 years from 6 January 1958 to 30 December 2005. The period selected includes 19 federal elections, 25 ministries and 5 terms of Liberal–National or Labor government. We define the political cycle in terms of the party in power, the time since the last election and election information effects. We define the market variables in terms of nominal and real returns and nominal and real return volatility. The results indicate returns are highest during the ministries of Holt–McEwen and Hawke and lowest during Whitlam and Fraser, while risk is highest during Whitlam and Hawke and lowest during Menzies and Holt–McEwen. However, regression analysis shows that Liberal–National and Labor governments more generally differ in the volatility of returns where political cycle-sourced return volatility increases at a decreasing rate with the time in power. Such risk differences potentially arise from the different parties' economic and social policies, uncertainty among investors about these policies, or doubt among voters concerning future election outcomes.

1. INTRODUCTION

Anecdotal evidence abounds of the link between securities markets and politics. In the financial media, most economic and social policy is analyzed concerning possible market reactions, and industry and consumer groups comment on anticipated and hoped for changes in policy. At election time, politicians are frequently accused of pork barreling, with firms and investors alike anticipating the heady mix of tax breaks, consumption and production

* Department of Accounting, Finance and Economics, Griffith University, 170 Kessels Road, Nathan QLD 4111, Australia. Email. a.worthington@griffith.edu.au.

subsidies and fiscal and monetary stimulation that accompanies changes in the political party in power. At the same time, parties are routinely pigeonholed as pro- or anti-business and pro- or anti-investor, reflected in some way in the flow and source of political donations.

At least three empirical questions arise from such observations. First, does market behavior differ when governments are drawn from different political parties? That is, is stated ideology reflected in actual policy, and does this systematically vary in its influence on market participants. Second, is this political influence constant or changing with the ebb and flow of mandated terms in office and efforts to secure re-election? Put differently, is ideology or any form implemented in a different way in business and investor policy at the beginning of terms of an office that at the end? Finally, if the differences in markets are taken as given, do markets react suddenly with the announcement of elections results, or are expectations developed more gradually with the benefit of political comment and opinion polls?

The purpose of this chapter is to add to this intriguing body of work the results of an analysis of the Australian federal political cycle and its impact on the Australian equity market. The chapter itself is divided into five main areas. Section 2 briefly reviews the relevant literature. Section 3 provides a snapshot of recent Australian political history. Section 4 explains the empirical methodology and data collection employed in the analysis. Section 5 presents the results. The chapter ends with a brief conclusion.

2. Literature Review

The analysis of political cycles in stock market returns has been almost exclusively conducted in the United States, and therein the context of presidential elections. Part is generic, to the extent that institutional rigidities in the political cycle – mandated terms in office for example – impose structure upon market returns. Herbst and Slinkman (1984), for example, examined the period from 1926 to 1977 and found a 48-month cycle during which returns were higher than average, peaking in November during presidential elections. Likewise, Huang (1985) used data from 1832 to 1979 and discovered that stock returns were systematically higher in the last half of a political term than in the first, as did Hensel and Ziemba (1995), though with small and large-caps only. On this basis, Hensel and Ziemba (1995) suggested "…these findings are consistent with the hypothesis that political re-election campaigns create policies that stimulate the economy and are positive for stock returns".

However, the larger part of this research focuses on differences in political ideology and the differential impact of the political cycle on stock returns. Herein the focus of interest is on the apparent preference of the market for right-of-center presidents (i.e. Republicans). Niederhoffer et al. (1970), for instance, showed that US stock market movements around election dates were consistent with a pro-Republican bias on Wall Street, though evidence was not forthcoming on any longer-term relationship between Republican presidents and stock returns. Similarly, Riley and Luksetich (1980) concluded that the market prefers Republicans, and the market tends to rise following presidential elections. Dobson and Dufrene (1993) extended this analysis outside of the United States, concluding that in equity market terms US presidential elections invoke significant structural changes, with international markets becoming more highly correlated. Other studies concerning the posited positive market effect of Republican presidencies have been undertaken by Allvine and

O'Neil (1980), Hobbs and Riley (1984), Foerster and Schmitz (1997), Johnson and Chittenden (1999), Booth and Booth (2003) and Bohl and Gottschalk (2005), while Nordhaus (1975), MacCrae (1977), McCallum (1978), Hibbs (1977), Beck (1982a; 1982b), Havrilesky (1987), Alesina and Sachs (1988) and Haynes (1989) address business cycles more broadly.

Most recently, Santa-Clara and Valkanov (2003) have re-examined the 'presidential puzzle' sometimes arising in this research: that is, real returns are higher under Democratic presidents, contradicting the conventional wisdom that Republicans are good for markets in a manner unexplained by considerations of risk. Using data since 1927, Santa-Clara and Valkanov (2003) found average excess returns for value-weighted market indexes over three-month Treasury bills of about 2 percent under Republicans and 11 percent under Democrats. Further, a decomposition of returns revealed that the difference was due to real market returns being 5 percent higher under Democrats and real interest rates almost 4 percent lower. Responding to the question of whether the difference in average returns was due to a difference in expected (a Democratic risk premium) or unexpected (surprises in the economic policies of the party in the presidency) returns, Santa-Clara and Valkanov (2003) concluded that presidential parties capture variations in returns that are largely uncorrelated to what is explained by business cycle fluctuations, and hence must be associated with systematic differences in political policies.

Outside of the United States, the United Kingdom and New Zealand are the only other national contexts known for the analysis of political cycles in stock returns. These are interesting in that while these have a two-party system in common with the United States (Labor and Conservative (Tory), Labor and Nationals, respectively), unlike the United States, the prime minister (leader of the Executive) is always controls the dominant party in the elected house (House of Commons, House of Representatives). For this reason, and as in Australia, there is a clearer connection between the political ideology of the elected party and the implementation of economic policy. In New Zealand, Cahan et al. (2005) concluded that the presidential puzzle was reversed, and that New Zealand market returns were lower under left-leaning Labor governments than under National party governments. This lay at odds with parallel analysis that suggested that market risk was actually higher under the former.

In the United Kingdom, Manning (1989) showed that British Telecom shares, though not the market as a whole, reacted to opinion polls surrounding the 1987 General Election in the face of impending nationalization, while Peel and Pope (1983), Gwilym and Buckle (1984) and Thompson and Ioannidis (1987) examined the connection between the stock market and business support for Tory (Conservative) governments. But most recently, Hudson et al. (1998) found that while short-term price movements reacted to opinion polls in the run-up to and including elections, there was no statistically significant evidence of a difference in nominal or real returns between Tory and Labor governments.

3. Recent Australian Political History

Two groups dominate the Australian political spectrum at the federal level. The first is a conservative coalition of parties made up of the Liberal Party and the Nationals (including the Country Liberal Party), collectively referred to as the Coalition. The second comprises a single social democratic party, the Australian Labor Party.

Table 1. Australian federal elections, governments, and oppositions, 1958–2005

Election date	Elected party or coalition	Prime Minister	Start of term	End of term	Opposition party	Opposition leader	Start of term	End of term
22 Nov 58	Liberal–Country Party	Menzies, Robert	19 Dec 49	26 Jan 66	Australian Labor Party	Evatt, Herbert	20 Jun 51	9 Feb 60
9 Dec 61						Calwell, Arthur	7 Mar 60	8 Feb 67
30 Nov 63								
26 Nov 66		Holt, Harold	26 Jan 66	19 Dec 67				
		McEwen, John	19 Dec 67	10 Jan 68				
25 Oct 69		Gorton, John	10 Jan 68	10 Mar 71		Whitlam, Gough	8 Feb 67	5 Dec 72
		McMahon, William	10 Mar 71	5 Dec 72				
2 Dec 72	Australian Labor Party	Whitlam, Gough	5 Dec 72	11 Nov 75	Liberal–Country Party	Snedden, William	20 Dec 72	21 Mar 75
18 May 74						Fraser, Malcolm	21 Mar 75	11 Nov 75
13 Dec 75	Liberal–Country Party	Fraser, Malcolm	11 Nov 75	11 Mar 83	Australian Labor Party	Whitlam, Gough	27 Jan 76	22 Dec 77
10 Dec 77								
18 Oct 80						Hayden, William	22 Dec 77	3 Feb 83
						Hawke, Robert	3 Feb 83	11 Mar 83
5 Mar 83	Australian Labor Party	Hawke, Robert	11 Mar 83	20 Dec 91	Liberal–Country Party	Peacock, Andrew	11 Mar 83	5 Sep 85
1 Dec 84								
11 Jul 87						Howard, John	5 Sep 85	9 May 89
24 Mar 90						Peacock, Andrew	9 May 89	3 Apr 90
13 Mar 93		Keating, Paul	20 Dec 91	11 Mar 96		Hewson, John	3 Apr 90	23 May 94
						Downer, Alexander	23 May 94	30 Jan 95

Election date	Elected party or coalition	Prime Minister	Start of term	End of term	Opposition party	Opposition leader	Start of term	End of term
						Howard, John	30 Jan 95	11 Mar 96
2 Mar 96	Liberal–National Party of Australia	Howard, John	11 Mar 96	–	Australian Labor Party	Beazley, Kim	19 Mar 96	22 Nov 01
3 Oct 98								
10 Nov 01						Crean, Simon	22 Nov 01	2 Dec 03
						Latham, Mark	2 Dec 03	18 Jan 05
9 Oct 04	Liberal–Nationals					Beazley, Kim	28 Jan 05	–

Source: Australian Electoral Commission (2006a; 2006b). Notes: The Australian Parliament consists of two houses, the Senate – selected by voters within a state - and the House of Representatives – selected by voters within an electorate. The party or coalition of parties that has a majority in the House of Representatives (of which the Prime Minister and Leader of the Opposition are normally part) forms the Government. Voting is compulsory with elections always held on a Saturday. The maximum length until a House of Representatives election is held is three years from the first sitting day of the current Parliament plus up to sixty-eight days of adjustments for the issuance of writs, close of nominations, etc. Senators are elected for six year terms on a rotating basis with half of the Senators retiring every three years. If there is a 'double dissolution' all Senators and Members of the House of Representatives face election as in 1973, 1975, 1983 and 1987. Vote is the two-party preferred vote for the Liberal-Country/National Party coalition. The Country Party changed its name to the National Country Party in the 1970s, then to National Party in the 1980s, and finally to the Nationals in 2003.

There have been 59 ministries since Federation in 1901, with the Coalition and its antecedents accounting for 38 (64 percent) and the Labor Party 21 (36 percent). Originally formed by the merger of the Protectionist and Free Trade parties in 1910, the Liberal Party has undergone several reformations—including as the Nationalist Party in the late 1910s and 1920s and the United

Australian Party in the 1930s and early 1940s—culminating in its present-day incarnation founded by Sir Robert Menzies in 1944.

The Liberal Party is a center-right party and broadly represents the interests of business, the suburban middle classes, and urbanized regions. Since the October 2004 election, the Liberals account for 74 of the 150 House of Representatives seats (47 percent), and from July 2005, 321 of the 76 seats in the Senae (42 percent).

The Nationals are a conservative party that traditionally represents rural and regional interests. Originally known as the Country Party, it has held seats in the federal parliament since 1919.

While the party has witnessed the steady erosion of its rural support base in recent years, it still holds the balance of power for the Coalition with 12 seats in the House of Representatives (16 percent) and 6 in the Senate (8 percent). It is joined by the Country Liberal Party, which is the representative of both parties in the Northern Territory, holding a single seat in both House of Representatives and the Senate.

The opposing party active at the federal level is the Australian Labor Party, a center-left party founded by the trade union movement in 1890 [by providing for the direct affiliation of trade unions, the Australian Labor Party is most like labor parties in the UK and New Zealand, and less like progressive parties such as the Democrats in the United States (ALP 2006)].

Historically, support for either the Coalition or the Labor Party was viewed as class based, with the middle class supporting the Coalition and the working class supporting Labor. In recent years, this has been a less important factor: in the 1970s and 1980s Labor gained a significant bloc of middle class support and the Coalition enjoyed some working class support. Indeed, part of the current electoral success of the Coalition is attributed to its appeal to disaffected working class Labor voters.

The Labor Party has endured a number of debilitating splits in its long history, most notably with Prime Minister Billy Hughes and the conscription debate during WWI leading to the creation of Nationalist Labor in 1917, and the formation of the anti-communist Democratic Labor Party in 1955. It currently accounts for 60 seats in the House of Representatives (40 percent) and 28 in the Senate (37 percent). Parties other than these have enjoyed limited success in Australia.

These currently include the Australian Greens, a left-wing environmental party, and the Australian Democrats, middle-class centrists—both with four seats in the Senate—and Family First, a Christian-influenced party appealing to social conservatives with one Senate seat. In the past, the minor parties have also included the centrist Democratic Labor Party from the mid-1950s until the mid-1970s and the rightist One Nation party during the 1990s. The proportional representation system often allows minor parties to win seats in the Senate and, on occasion, the balance of power, but they have usually been unable to win seats in the House of Representatives given its electorate-based preferential voting system, along with the nationwide dominance and broad based appeal of the Coalition and Labor parties.

4. Research Method and Data

Table 1 provides details of the 19 federal elections held since 6 January 1958. All information is from the Australian Electoral Commission (2006a; 2006b). Five distinct political periods are noted, with the Coalition in power from 1958 to 1972 (five prime ministers and five winning elections), 1975 to 1983 (one prime minister and three elections) and 1996 to 2005 (one prime minister and four elections) and the Labor Party in power from 1972 to 1974 (one prime minister and two winning elections) and again from 1983 to 1996 (two prime ministers and five elections). This information is used to define the political cycle variables in this analysis. The first political variable specified in this analysis is a dummy variable that takes a value of one on days the Coalition is in power and zero otherwise (C_t) while the second takes a value of one if the Labor Party is in power and zero otherwise (L_t).

Within this broad division, different samples are defined representing the 25 prime ministerial terms. In most cases, the starting and ending dates for these terms are defined by two of the 19 elections during the period (with allowance for a transition period of a few days) with the following exceptions: Menzies was re-elected out-of-sample in 1955 and resigned in 1966, replaced by Holt; Holt disappeared while swimming, presumed dead, in 1967 and replaced by McEwen; Gorton was overturned in a party room vote in 1971 and replaced by McMahon; Whitlam was sacked by Governor-General Sir John Kerr in 1975 with Fraser taking a caretaker role until an election was held one month later; Hawke was overturned by Keating in a party room vote in 1991; and Howard is the serving prime minister at the end of the sample. The separate prime ministerial terms are then aggregated by prime minister with Menzies, Hawke and Howard serving four terms; Holt, Gorton, Whitlam and Keating two terms; and McEwen and McMahon one term. Because McEwen governed for just twenty-three days and McMahon never successfully contested an election, they are included with Holt and Gorton, respectively.

The next two political variables are included to take account of whether the return on equities varies across the term in office. Rather than using dummy variables to identify whether a day falls in, say, the first or second half of the period in office as in Hudson et al. (1998), a continuous variable is specified as a simple linear trend (T_t) taking a value of one on the first trading day in office, two on the second day, and so on. This variable is reset at the beginning of the next government's term in office. The square of this variable (S_t) is also included to take account of any non-linear relationships between the political cycle and market returns. Two additional dummy variables take account of election effects on market returns. The first of these takes a value of one for each day of the trading week (Monday to Friday) before the election date (Saturday) (B_t), and zero otherwise, while the second takes a value of one for each day of the trading week following the election (A_t) and zero otherwise.

The market data employed in the study are closing prices from the Australian Stock Exchange (ASX) over the period Monday 6 January 1958 to Friday 30 December 2005. This sample encompasses 12,067 trading days and represents the longest period for which daily data is available. The capitalization-weighted All Ordinaries Price Index is used. The index includes the top ASX-listed stocks by capitalization, covering about 92 percent of domestic companies by market value. To be included in the index, stocks must have an aggregate market value of at least 0.02 percent of all domestic equities, and maintain an average turnover in excess of 0.5 percent of quoted shares each month. The long-term index includes base recalculations by Global Financial Data (2006).

A series of daily nominal returns are calculated where:

$$R_t^n = 100 \ln(P_t / P_{t-1})$$

where P_t is the index level on day t. The daily real return is also calculated:

$$R_t^r = 100 \ln(P_t / P_{t-1}.i_t)$$

where i_t is the daily rate of increase in the consumer price index as defined by the Australian Bureau of Statistics' (2006) retail/consumer price index (1945 = 100) and all other variables are as previously defined. Finally, a simple measure of the daily volatility of both the nominal and real return series is calculated using the standard deviation of rolling one-month period returns. Santa-Clara and Valkanov (2003) suggest that differences in risk may arise across presidential terms (Democrats and Republicans) because of differences in economic policies, or from varying levels of uncertainty among investors about these policies. In this manner, "…it would be reasonable to argue that it [higher realised returns] should command a risk premium to compensate investors for the greater risks incurred in those periods" (Santa-Clara and Valkanov 2003: 1867). The method used in this analysis to calculate volatility is identical to Santa-Clara and Valkanov (2003). As an alternative, Cahan et al. (2005) estimated return volatility with the absolute value of returns.

Two approaches are used to test the political cycle hypotheses. The first involves a descriptive analysis of the mean daily returns and tests of equality of means using parametric analysis. As a rule, the mean return for Coalition governments is expected to be higher than the mean return for Labor governments. Further, it is hypothesized that returns one week before and after elections may be higher or lower than returns during the same political term, but the direction may be dependent upon whether the election comprises a shock. Santa-Clara and Valkanov (2003: 1863), for example, argued that "…if the observed difference in returns is due to a difference in expected returns, the change in the level of the market at the time that the information is revealed should be quite large".

The second approach used is a regression-based approach where the 12,067 daily nominal and real returns are regressed separately against the political cycle variables:

$$R_t = \beta_1 C_t + \beta_2 L_t + \beta_3 T_t + \beta_4 S_t + \beta_5 B_t + \beta_6 A_t + \varepsilon_t$$

where R_t is the nominal or real Monday to Friday market return at time t, C_t is a dummy variable that equals one for a Coalition government and zero otherwise, L_t is a dummy variable that equals one for a Labor government and zero otherwise, T_t and St are political cycle time trends, B_t and A_t are election effects, β_i are coefficients to be estimated and ε is the error term. Following the hypotheses presented, the sign on the coefficient for C_t is expected to be positive and larger in magnitude than Lt, the sign on T_t is expected to be negative. The hypothesised sign of S_t may be positive or negative, depending upon whether the political cycle trend in returns and volatility increases at an increasing or decreasing rate. Two additional regressions are also specified for risk where:

$$V_t = \beta_1 C_t + \beta_2 L_t + \beta_3 T_t + \beta_4 S_t + \beta_5 B_t + \beta_6 A_t + \varepsilon_t$$

where V_t is the nominal or real return volatility and all other variables are as previously defined. The first null hypothesis tested is:

$$H_0 : \beta_1 = \beta_2 = \beta_3 = \beta_4 = \beta_5 = \beta_6 = 0$$

against the alternative that at least some $\beta \neq 0$. The second null hypothesis tested is:

$$H_0 : \beta_1 = \beta_2$$

against the alternative $\beta_1 \neq \beta_2$. If the first null hypothesis is rejected, then the market returns and/or risk exhibit a form of political cycle, related to either the party in power and/or the tenure of power and/or election effects. If the second is rejected, then the parties have a differential impact upon market returns and/or risk.

5. Empirical Results

Figure 1 plots the daily nominal market returns and return volatility. Mean nominal returns are highest during Holt–McEwen (0.0651) and Hawke (0.0509) and lowest during (Whitlam (–0.0556) and Menzies (0.0245), while real returns are highest during Holt–McEwen (0.0562) and Hawke (0.0323) and lowest during Whitlam (–0.0889) and Fraser (0.0066). The nominal and real volatility of returns (as measured by standard deviation) is highest during Whitlam (1.1632 to 1.1629) and Hawke (1.1376 to 1.1375) and lowest during Menzies (0.4553 to 0.4556) and Holt–McEwen (0.5308 to 0.5307).

Figure 2 plots the annualized nominal return for each of the 25 prime ministerial terms since 1958. Clearly, there is again much variation in the annual returns experienced under the various prime ministers, ranging between –11 percent for Whitlam II and +53 percent for McEwen (albeit with a very short sample period). Augmented Dickey–Fuller and Phillips–Peron tests (with allowance for autocorrelation) (not shown) for the nominal and real return and nominal and real return volatility series all reject the null hypotheses of a unit root at the .01 level and we conclude that the return series are stationary and suitable for regression-based analysis.

5.1. Parametric Tests of Mean Return Differences

At first impression, there appears to be some evidence of a political cycle effect in the Australian stock market. Certainly, returns appear to vary across the various prime ministries, whether aggregated by prime minister or by individual ministry. Returns and risk also appear to differ by political affiliation.

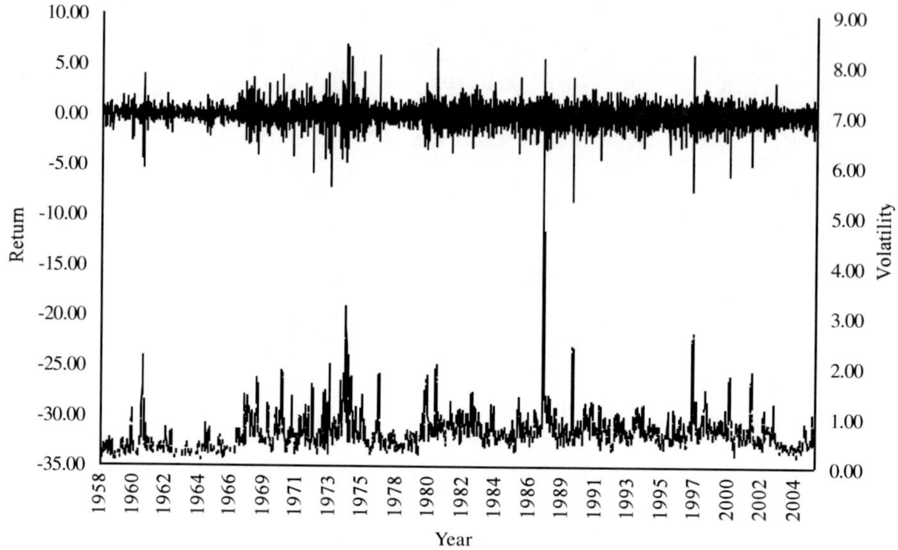

Notes: Figures show daily returns (left-hand side axis) and daily return volatility (right-hand side axis). Volatility is measured as the rolling one-month standard deviation of returns.

Figure 1. Daily nominal returns and return volatility.

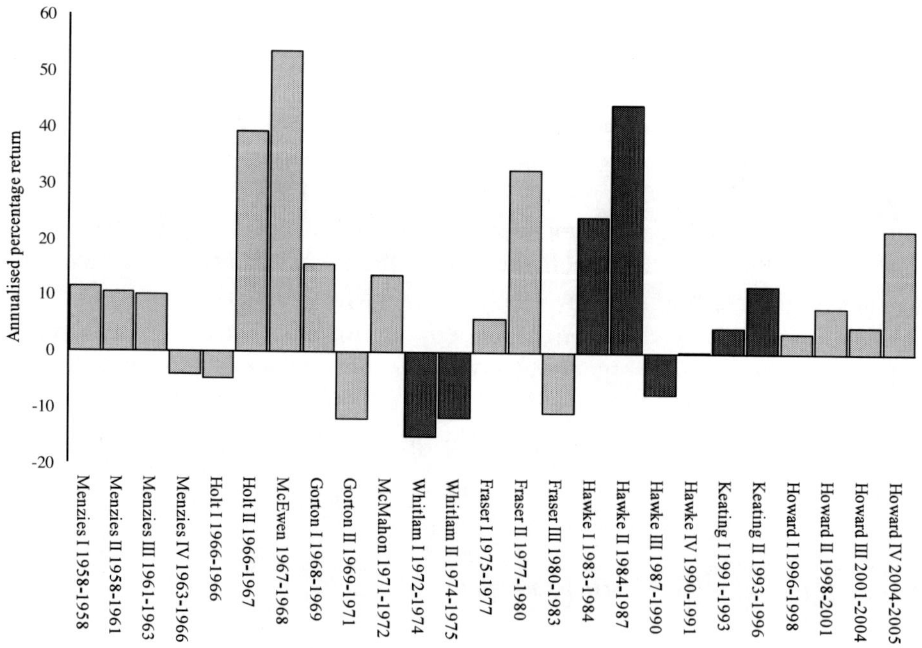

Figure 2. Annual nominal returns by prime ministerial term.

As shown in Table 2, the mean daily nominal (real) return for Liberal–National governments is 0.0307 (0.0187) compared to 0.0269 (0.0089) for Labor governments. Risk appears higher during Labor governments with a nominal (real) standard deviation of returns of 1.0542 (1.0543) for Labor governments compared to 0.7115 (0.7117) for Liberal–national governments. However, while Levene's test of equality of variances is rejected for nominal (statistic = 225.293, p-value = 0.0000) and real (statistic = 224.293, p-value = 0.0000) returns, indicating unequal risk, it fails to be reject the null hypothesis of the equality of means assuming unequal variances. This indicates that risk (standard deviation) is significantly higher for Labor governments in Australia, but there is no significant difference in returns between Liberal–National and Labor governments in the last 47 years. However, returns are significantly lower during the (Labor) prime ministry of Whitlam (1972–1975).

Table 2. Comparison of daily returns by government

	Government	In-government returns			Out-of-government returns			Tests of equality of means	
		Days	Mean	Std. dev	Days	Mean	Std. dev	t-statistic	p-value
Nominal returns	Menzies	2003	0.0245	0.4553	10064	0.0305	0.8986	0.4422	0.6584
	Holt–McEwen	488	0.0651	0.5308	11579	0.0280	0.8519	−1.4674	0.1428
	Gorton–McMahon	1231	0.0247	0.8284	10836	0.0300	0.8428	0.2143	0.8304
	Whitlam	733	−0.0556	1.1632	11334	0.0350	0.8159	2.0763	0.0382
	Fraser	1846	0.0342	0.8198	10221	0.0286	0.8452	−0.2700	0.7872
	Hawke	2220	0.0509	1.1376	9847	0.0246	0.7587	−1.0353	0.3006
	Keating	1068	0.0337	0.7495	10999	0.0290	0.8498	−0.1742	0.8617
	Howard	2478	0.0295	0.7614	9589	0.0295	0.8608	−0.0015	0.9988
	Liberal–National	8046	0.0307	0.7115	4021	0.0269	1.0542	−0.2088	0.8346
Real returns	Menzies	2003	0.0191	0.4556	10064	0.0148	0.8987	−0.3166	0.7516
	Holt–McEwen	488	0.0562	0.5307	11579	0.0138	0.8520	−1.6773	0.0940
	Gorton–McMahon	1231	0.0133	0.8285	10836	0.0157	0.8430	0.0955	0.9240
	Whitlam	733	−0.0889	1.1629	11334	0.0222	0.8159	2.5465	0.0111
	Fraser	1846	0.0066	0.8198	10221	0.0171	0.8453	0.5034	0.6147
	Hawke	2220	0.0323	1.1375	9847	0.0117	0.7590	−0.8158	0.4147
	Keating	1068	0.0274	0.7494	10999	0.0143	0.8499	−0.4844	0.6281
	Howard	2478	0.0229	0.7615	9589	0.0136	0.8609	−0.4913	0.6232
	Liberal–National	8046	0.0187	0.7117	4021	0.0089	1.0543	−0.5335	0.5937

Notes: Days is the number of trading days.

Table 3 presents the means and tests of equality of means for the trading week before and after the election during each ministry. The purpose is to test for the presence of an election effect. However, only during Keating are returns (both nominal and real) significantly higher in the week before the election and only during Whitlam are returns significantly lower in the week following an election. The latter appears consistent with the (negative) information effects associated with Whitlam outside of the immediate election period. With the former, Keating contested just two elections: the first (winning) election in 1993 ("the sweetest victory of all"), was a surprise with a Coalition victory widely predicted; the second (losing) election was associated with the highest Liberal–National two–party preferred vote since 1977. In both cases, there was a general perception of a change in government with the defeat of a deeply unpopular (at least from the business perspective) incumbent.

Table 3. Comparison of daily returns before and after elections

	Government	Returns and tests of equality of means one week before election				Returns and tests of equality of means one week after election			
		Mean	Std. dev	*t*-statistic	*p*-value	Mean	Std. dev	*t*-statistic	*p*-value
Nominal returns	Menzies	0.1103	0.3501	–0.7331	0.4636	0.0199	0.4954	0.0387	0.9691
	Holt–McEwen	0.0019	0.2009	0.2672	0.7894	0.2024	0.1683	–0.5811	0.5614
	Gorton–McMahon	–0.1146	0.8176	0.5337	0.5936	–0.1146	0.8176	0.5337	0.5936
	Whitlam	–0.1349	0.4471	0.1528	0.8786	–0.8886	1.5077	2.1670	0.0306
	Fraser	0.2702	1.1465	–0.9513	0.3527	0.2040	1.8738	–0.3986	0.6948
	Hawke	0.0396	0.9432	0.0383	0.9695	–0.0821	0.7606	0.4692	0.6390
	Keating	0.5058	0.5014	–2.0038	0.0453	–0.1048	1.1753	0.3755	0.7159
	Howard	0.0602	0.8359	–0.1569	0.8754	0.0272	0.8748	0.0115	0.9908
	Liberal–National	0.1075	0.8330	–0.7268	0.4700	0.1165	1.1526	–0.5647	0.5744
Real returns	Menzies	0.1058	0.3503	–0.7404	0.4592	0.0154	0.4964	0.0311	0.9752
	Holt–McEwen	–0.0061	0.2010	0.2637	0.7921	0.1944	0.1683	–0.5848	0.5590
	Gorton–McMahon	–0.1268	0.8182	0.5369	0.5915	–0.1268	0.8182	0.5369	0.5915
	Whitlam	–0.1734	0.4471	0.1629	0.8707	–0.9170	1.5170	2.1550	0.0315
	Fraser	0.2396	1.1470	–0.9391	0.3588	0.1729	1.8748	–0.3904	0.7008
	Hawke	0.0222	0.9403	0.0347	0.9723	–0.1001	0.7571	0.4675	0.6402
	Keating	0.4998	0.5016	–2.0057	0.0451	–0.1108	1.1756	0.3744	0.7167
	Howard	0.0535	0.8349	–0.1562	0.8759	0.0205	0.8738	0.0121	0.9903
	Liberal–National	0.0928	0.8319	–0.7527	0.4543	0.1023	1.1524	–0.5800	0.5641

Notes: Levene's test of equality of variances determines whether the test for equality of means assumes equal or unequal variances. Tests of equality of means one week before and after election are against all other days during that government. Mc–Ewen is with Holt, McMahon is with Gorton. Howard remains in government at the end of the sample period. Liberal–National refers to the Menzies, Holt–McEwen, Gorton–McMahon, Fraser and Howard governments.

5.2. Regression-Based Analysis of the Political Cycle and Election Effects

The estimated coefficients and standard errors of the parameters are presented in Table 4. Four separate regressions with four different regressands are included: nominal returns and nominal return volatility, real returns and real return volatility. The regressors for the four regressions are common. The independent variables are dummy variables for Liberal–National and Labor governments, a political term trend and its square, and dummy variables for the week before and after a federal election. Breusch–Godfrey Lagrange multiplier and White's heteroskedasticity tests (not shown) are initially used to test for higher-order serial correlation and heteroskedasticity in the least squares residuals, respectively. The null hypothesis of no serial correlation is rejected in all cases and we may conclude the presence of higher-order serial correlation in the residuals.

Table 4. Estimated coefficients of political cycle models

Dependent variable	Variable	Liberal–National	Labor	Trend	Trend squared	Before election	After election	Joint test	Equality test
Nominal returns	Coef./stat.	0.0533	0.0477	–4.22E-05	1.32E-08	0.0970	–0.0656	2.7267	0.0582
	Std. error	0.0251	0.0272	5.44E-05	2.30E-08	0.0830	0.1283	–	–
	p-value	0.0334	0.0800	0.4377	0.5649	0.2429	0.6091	0.0120	0.8094
Nominal return volatility	Coef./stat.	0.5289	0.7749	2.34E-04	–1.09E-07	0.0024	0.0570	637.7383	55.5420
	Std. error	0.0346	0.0282	7.50E-05	3.10E-08	0.0804	0.0939	–	–
	p-value	0.0000	0.0000	0.0018	0.0005	0.9760	0.5439	0.0000	0.0000
Real returns	Coef./stat.	0.0432	0.0316	–4.88E-05	1.66E-08	0.0954	–0.0669	1.3136	0.2431
	Std. error	0.0251	0.0272	5.43E-05	2.30E-08	0.0829	0.1288	–	–
	p-value	0.0852	0.2464	0.3693	0.4689	0.2501	0.6035	0.2470	0.6220
Real return volatility	Coef./stat.	0.5288	0.7748	2.34E-04	–1.09E-07	0.0024	0.0570	637.6852	55.5350
	Std. error	0.0346	0.0282	7.50E-05	3.10E-08	0.0804	0.0939	–	–
	p-value	0.0000	0.0000	0.0018	0.0004	0.9759	0.5438	0.0000	0.0000

Notes: All standard errors and *p*-values incorporate Newey–West corrections for heteroskedasticity and autocorrelation of unknown form. Joint test – *F*-statistic and significance of null hypothesis that all coefficients are zero. Equality test – Wald statistic and significance of null hypothesis that estimated coefficients for Liberal–National minus Labor equals zero.

The null hypothesis of no heteroskedasticity in the least squares residuals is also rejected. All standard errors and p-values in Table 4 incorporate Newey–West corrections for heteroskedasticity and autocorrelation of unknown form.

Once again, the signs on the estimated coefficients initially appear to offer some support for the posited influence of political cycles on market returns. In terms of returns, the coefficient on Liberal–National is always positive and higher than Labor. However, only for nominal returns are the estimated coefficients both significantly different from zero; with real returns, only the coefficient for Liberal–National is significant. But in either case, the Wald tests (column 12) fail to reject the null hypotheses that the coefficients are equal. The trend and the trend square term and the before and after election terms offer fleeting support for a political cycle and election effect in that their coefficients are of the hypothesized sign, but in no case are they significant. That said, the null hypotheses of the joint insignificance of the coefficients for both return regressions are rejected (column 11) and we confirm that the political cycle and effect variables jointly influence mean returns.

However, the regressions for nominal and real return volatility (risk) present quite different results. As before, there is no evidence of a market effect immediately before or after an election: the information content of elections themselves appears limited. But return volatility is always significantly higher for Labor governments than Liberal–National governments, by about a quarter of one percent on any day. This is a similar result to Cahan et al. (2005), who also found that market risk was higher under the left-leaning Labor government in New Zealand. At the same time, return volatility is seen to increase, though at a decreasing rate, over the time in office. The magnitude of the increase in return volatility is very small, however, increasing by only about one-fifth of a percent during the typical parliamentary term of three years. Importantly, this increase in volatility with the political term in office is common to both Liberal–National and Labor governments. As before, the null hypothesis of the joint insignificance of the coefficients is rejected and we may conclude that the political cycle jointly influences return volatility (risk) in the Australian stock market.

CONCLUSION

The present study employs parametric analysis to test for a political cycle in the Australian stock market. A comparison of mean returns provides some empirical evidence to support the conjecture that returns depend upon the government in power. There is limited support for an election effect where returns are systematically higher or lower in the period leading up to ot immediately following an election. Any apparent differences are lessened when returns are expressed in real rather than nominal terms. Similar results are obtained with a regression-based analysis.

However, return volatility is significantly higher under Labor governments than Liberal–National governments. This is problematic in that with any difference in the riskiness of the market across political parties, it is reasonable to argue that the market should command a risk premium to compensate investors for the greater risks incurred. Certainly, abundant evidence exists elsewhere of a positive relation between the expected risk premium and the predictable level of volatility. Why then do investors appear to require no such compensation under Labor governments in Australia?

One possibility is that a large and persistent difference in risk unmatched in return cannot exist in an efficient market, but can in an inefficient one. Investors may perceive the Labor Party in power as a noisy signal of economic and social policy. Given the relatively small number of Labor ministries during the sample, investors may never really systematically understand the influence on stock prices. And in many cases, past experience offers little guidance. For example, compare the radical social non-market reforms of Whitlam with the pro-market deregulation and microeconomic reform undertaken during the Hawke–Keating period. In this general setting, stock volatility reflects diffuse and easily changed beliefs about future political behavior, but on balance, these views are never systematically 'bad' or 'good' over extended periods of time.

Another possibility follows suggestions by Beaulieu (2005) that investors may not simply require a premium for domestic political risk. This suggests the presence of some form of diversification on the part of domestic investors or the exercise of real options by businesses. For example, firms may bring forward or delay investment projects given current policies: only a marginal net effect on future expected cash differs. This may in be aided, in part, by the fact that political horizons are short and investment horizons can be long.

REFERENCES

Alesina, A. and Sachs, J. (1988). Political parties and the business cycle in the United States, 1948–1984. *Journal of Money, Credit and Banking*, 20(1), 63–82.

Allvine, P. and D. E. O'Neil, (1980). Stock market returns and the presidential election cycle. *Financial Analysts Journal*, 36, 49–56.

Australian Bureau of Statistics (2006). *Retail/Consumer Price Index Numbers*, available at http://www.abs.gov.au/. Accessed April 2006.

Australian Electoral Commission (2006a). *Federal, State and Territory Election Dates 1946–Present*, available at http://www.aec.gov.au/. Accessed April 2006.

Australian Electoral Commission (2006b). Electoral Pocketbook 2005, available at http://www.aec.gov.au/. Accessed April 2006.

Australian Labor Party (2006) http://www.alp.org.au/. Accessed April 2006.

Beaulieu, M.C. Cosset, J.C. Essaddam, N. (2005). The impact of political risk on the volatility of stock returns: The case of Canada. *Journal of International Business Studies*, 36(6), 701–18.

Beck, N. (1982a). Domestic political sources of American monetary policy: 1955–82. *Journal of Politics*, 46, 786–817.

Beck, N. (1982b). Parties, administrations and American macroeconomic outcomes. *American Political Science Review*, 26, 83–94.

Bohl, M.T. and Gottschalk, K. (2005). International evidence on the Democratic premium and presidential cycle effect, Paper presented at the 8th Conference of the Swiss Society for Financial Market Research, 8 April, Zurich.

Booth, J.R. and Booth, L.C. (2003). Is the presidential cycle in security returns merely a reflection of business conditions? *Review of Financial Economics*, 12(1), 131–159.

Cahan, J. Malone, C.B. Powell, J.G. and Choti, U.W. (2005). Stock market political cycles in a small, two-party democracy. *Applied Economics Letters*, 12, 735–740.

Dobson, J. and Dufrene, U. B. (1993). The impacts of U.S. presidential elections on international security-markets. *Global Finance Journal*, 4(1), 39–47.

Foerster, S. R. and Schmitz, J. J. (1997). The transmission of US election cycles to international stock returns. *Journal of International Business*, 28, 1–27.

Global Financial Data (2006). http://www.globfindata.com, Accessed February 2006.

Gwilym, O. A. P. and Buckle, M. (1994). The efficiency of stock and options markets: Tests based on 1992 UK election opinion polls. *Applied Financial Economics*, 4, 345–54.

Havrilesky, T. (1987). A partisanship theory of fiscal and monetary regimes. *Journal of Money, Credit and Banking*, 19, 308–25.

Haynes, S. E. and Stone, J. A. (1989). An integrated test for electoral cycles in the US economy. *Review of Economics and Statistics*, 71, 426–34.

Hebst, A.F. and Slinkman, C.W. (1984). Political-economic cycles in the US stock market. *Financial Analysts Journal*, 40(2), 38–44.

Hensel,C.R. and Ziemba, W.T. (1995). United States investment returns during Democratic and Republican Administrations, 1928–1993. *Financial Analysts Journal*, 51(2), 61–69.

Hibbs, D. A., (1977). Political parties and macroeconomic policy. *American Political Science Review*, 71, 1467–87.

Hobbs, G.R. and Riley, W.B. (1984). Profiting from a presidential election. *Financial Analysts Journal*, 40(2). 46–52.

Huang, R.D. (1985). Common stock returns and presidential elections. *Financial Analysts Journal*, 41(2), 58–65.

Hudson, R. Keasey, K. and Dempsey, M. (1998). Share prices under Tory and Labour governments in the UK since 1945. *Applied Financial Economics*, 8, 389–400.

Johnson, R. R., and Chittenden, W. (1999). Presidential politics, stocks, bonds, bills, and inflation. *Journal of Portfolio Management*, 26, 27–31.

MacRae, D. (1977). A political model of the business cycle. *Journal of Political Economy*, 85, 239–63.

Manning, D. N. (1989). The effect of political uncertainty on the stock market: The case of British Telecom. *Applied Economics*, 21, 881–9.

McCallum, B. (1978). The political business cycle: An empirical test. *Southern Journal of Economics*, 44, 504–15.

Niederhoffer, V., Gibbs, S. and Bullock, J. (1970). Presidential elections and the stock market. *Financial Analysts Journa*l, Mar/Apr, 111–13.

Nordhaus, W. D. (1975). The political business cycle. *Review of Economic Studies*, 42, 169–90.

Peel, D. A. and Pope, P. F. (1983). General elections in the U.K. in the post 1950 period and the behaviour of the stock market. *Investment Analyst*, 67, 4–10.

Riley, W. B. and Luksetich W. A. (1980). The market prefers Republicans: Myth or reality. *Journal of Financial and Quantitative Analysis*, 15(3), 541–560.

Santa-Clara, P. and Valkanov, R. (2003). The presidential puzzle: Political cycles and the stock market. *Journal of Finance*, 58(5), 1841–1872

Thompson, R. S. and Ioannidis, C. (1987). The stock market response to voter opinion polls. *Investment Analyst*, 83, 19–22.

In: Economic and Financial Modeling
Editor: Andrew C. Worthington
ISBN: 978-1-63463-111-2

Chapter 7

A Combined Conceptual, Theoretical and Empirical Review of Credit-Scoring Models

Mohamed Habara and Andrew C. Worthington* [*]
Griffith University, Australia

Abstract

This chapter reviews credit-scoring models as quantitative tools used by lenders to evaluate credit risk. It provides a wide-ranging review of existing and novel parametric and nonparametric techniques used in credit score modeling. It also contains a comprehensive survey of empirical work in the literature on credit-scoring models from 1992 to 2006. The main purpose of the chapter is to facilitate the selection of the variables and techniques used in constructing credit-scoring models by industry practitioners and academic researchers.

1. Introduction

The purpose of this chapter is to review credit-scoring models as a quantitative tool used to evaluate credit risk. These models provide a scientific basis for assessing an applicant to help in making the decision about whether to grant credit. Credit scoring is generally regarded as one of the more successful practical applications of statistical and operations research modeling in finance and banking. This is because lenders use credit scoring to estimate the possible risk that results from lending money to consumers and helps to reduce losses from bad loans. The initial steps in credit scoring are to identify the predictor's variables extracted from application forms and other credit information and then to apply statistical and nonstatistical techniques to produce a score that contributes to estimating credit risk.

---

[*] Corresponding author: Department of Accounting, Finance and Economics, Griffith University, 170 Kessels Road, Nathan QLD 4111, Australia. Email. a.worthington@griffith.edu.au.

The remainder of the chapter comprises four sections. Section 2 provides a brief conceptual overview of credit scoring. Section 3 examines and evaluates the various parametric, nonparametric, and newer methods of credit scoring from a theoretical perspective. Section 4 reviews recent empirical applications of credit-scoring models in the academic literature. Section 5 concludes the chapter.

2. An Overview of Credit Scoring

2.1. Definition

Credit scoring is one of several of credit measurement methods (DeVaney and Lytton 1995). According to The New Basel Capital Accord Glossary of Terms (BIS, 2000: 6), credit scoring is "…a method of evaluating the credit risk of loan applicant using historical data and statistical techniques. It is the process of assigning a single quantitative measure, the score, to represent the borrower's probable the future loan performance". While credit-scoring models are statistical techniques and mathematical systems used to assist credit decisions, the objective of these models is to maximize measurable risk (Papanyan, 2003). Nonetheless, Thomas et al. (2002) argue that credit-scoring models do not actually assess the creditworthiness of applicants because this is not an attribute of the applicant, rather an assessment by the lender, and therefore reflects the circumstances of the borrower and the lender's view of expected future economic situations.

There are two main kinds of credit-scoring techniques. The first is 'application credit scoring' used to evaluate new applicants. The second is 'behavioral scoring' used to assess existing applicants (Banasik and Crook, 2005). Regardless of the form used, a large sample of historical data is usually collected to identify those characteristics that discriminate between 'good' and 'bad' credit risks.

2.2. Development of Credit Scoring

Credit scoring is a statistical method based on the idea of discriminating between groups in a population (Caire and Kossmann, 2003). Fisher (1936) introduced the basic statistical techniques when aiming to discriminate between populations of irises through measurement of the physical size of the plants. Durand (1941) was the first study published that recognized that similar statistical techniques could help identify good loans and bad loans (Thomas, 2000). However, credit scoring itself originated during World War II with Henry Wells, an executive of Spiegel Inc. During that time, credit management was experiencing many difficulties associated with finance houses and mail order companies. At the time, credit analysts usually made credit decisions on a judgmental basis, with the dominance of rules of thumb (from the shortage of experts during the war) by inexperienced workers to help making credit decisions.

At the time, credit-scoring systems did not employ the sophisticated technology we know today when first implemented in a finance company (the American Investment Company) by Fair Isaac in 1959. Fair Isaac Corporation (FICO) was established in 1956 by Bill Fair, an engineer, and Earl Isaac, a mathematician as a provider of decision management solutions using credit scoring. Their system spread rapidly through financial institutions in the US because it was cheaper, faster, more objective, and more predictive than traditional approaches (Komorad, 2002). At that time, Fair and Isaac identified a small sample of bad and good loans in the American Investment Company and applied the discriminant analysis approach to identify variables that helped differentiate the 'good' sample from the 'bad' sample.

By 1960, credit cards as a form of consumer of credit were introduced and used for making purchases on borrowed money [see for example, Kaynak et al., (1995), Dunn and Kim (1999), and Lucas (2001)]. At the same time, financial institutions recognized the advantages of credit scoring. In addition, the 1960s saw the introduction of statistical tools for credit scoring like logistic regression and linear programming, with estimates that default rates could drop by half following the introduction of scoring systems (Thomas, 2000). Because of the success of statistical scoring techniques for credit cards, the development of computer technology and an increasing rate of credit applications, banks started implementing credit scoring for other loans, such as personal, home, and small business loans.

In addition, credit-scoring models provide valuable contributions in microfinance area. A number of studies show that scoring models does reduce arrears and so reduces time spent on collections, and this greater efficiency improves both outreach and sustainability. See for example, Kimenyi et al., (1998), Schreiner, (2000; 2003b), and Dellien and Schreiner (2005). However, the widespread use of credit scoring was not easy because some practitioners and researchers opposed the using of statistical techniques in scoring. For example, Capon (1982: 90) argues "...the brute force empiricism of credit scoring offends against the traditions of our society". He felt that there should be more dependence on credit history, and it should be possible to explain why a scoring system needs certain variables and not others (Sathye et al., 2003, p. 90). Despite these critiques, all loans products, including individual, small business and corporate loans, currently use credit-scoring systems and they have become a standard tool in loan pricing.

2.3. Credit Scoring and Judgmental Systems

The judgmental system is a traditional method based on the human assessment of credit risk. This was widely employed before credit-scoring methods emerged during the 1950s. Currently, the introduction of many statistical and mathematical techniques provides better validity and results, especially in relation to classification accuracy. It is important, however, to compare credit scoring and judgmental system to ensure that the credit-scoring models provide a proper scientific basis and measurable advantage to financial institutions.

Chandler and Coffman (1979) provide a good comparison between the two systems in respect of their respective strengths and weaknesses. First, in credit scoring, a large sample of good and bad loans is selected to develop the scoring model. In contrast, judgmental systems based on the credit officer's own experience ignore sample selection or trend to focus too deeply on bad loans. Second, credit-scoring models require less information, which may include a mixture of continuous and categorical variables, and they are better able to remove redundant information. Third, credit-scoring models are based on multivariate statistical analysis that assigns the appropriate weights given the impact of other characteristics to compensate for weakness in other models. With judgmental credit, however, it is impossible for the credit analyst to consider all relevant information that may be related to creditworthiness at the same time. Fourth, credit-scoring models are generally argued to be time and cost effective (Ely and Robinson, 200; Fishelson-Holstine, 2004 and Huang et al., 2006). Mester (1997), for example, refers to a study by the Washington Business Banking Board that found that the judgmental credit systems in small business took more than twelve hours to approve a loan, whereas credit scoring could reduce the time taken to about one hour. Finally, credit-scoring models represent an objective approach to the loan granting decision. For instance, two banks with the same characteristics and the same applicant should obtain a similar score, whereas in judgmental credit systems, the decision may differ from lender to lender.

Sathye et al., (2003) have identified two categories of scoring based on a comparison between credit scoring and judgmental systems. First in accounting-based systems, the credit analyst compares various key accounting ratios of the applicant with industry standards and the credit analyst then determines whether a particular ratio for an applicant varies markedly from the industry standard. Second, quantitative credit screening models depend on statistical analysis and can be divided into one of types: credit-scoring applications are used for granting credit to a new borrower, and behavioral scoring deals with existing borrowers and the decision to extend credit or improve profitability.

2.4. Consumer and Small Business Credit Scoring

Consumer credit is sources of short- or intermediate-term credit that individuals require to finance personal needs for non-business purposes (Hand, 2001). Auto loans, home loans, secured and unsecured revolving loans, and credit cards are the most common forms of consumer credit. The growth of consumer credit over the last 60 years has seen spectacular. For example, according to the US Federal Reserve, total consumer credit in the United States grew from US$5.7 billion in 1943 to US$2,100 billion in 2005. On the negative side, and according to the American Bankruptcy Institute, the number of consumer bankruptcy filings per year in the United States increased from 331,264 filings in 1980 to more than 2,000,000 filings in 2005 (Thomas et al., 2005). Therefore, credit-scoring models are developed to use statistical and mathematical techniques to produce a score for each applicant and compare it with a predetermined cut-off to measure credit risk. The process of these models requires the use of personal, economic, and financial variables including age, the number of dependents, occupation and the loan amount. Small business credit, on the other hand, is defined as the amount of money granted to small business to finance its business activities. In small business, financial ratios and even some personal variables, are used to evaluate credit risk (Immergluck and Smith, 2003) but Fair and Isaac Corporation originally argued that they found that the same variables determining the owner's probability of loan repayment also determined a large part of credit scoring.

Over the last decade, however, banks have increasingly changed to credit-scoring systems. This is one of the more dramatic changes in small business lending. The reason is that these loans are less homogeneous than credit card loans and other types of personal loans, and also because the amount of this kind of lending is smaller, so the scoring models generally require less information (Longenecker et al., 1997). Mester (1997) and Agarwal et al., (2007), for instance, found that information on the business owner is a more important indicator of small business loan evaluation than the business itself. Alternatively, Thomas et al., (2002) showed that information about the owner might not be an important indicator because other persons may run the business. Therefore, extraneous information about the business and the business environment should also be considered.

Several credit-scoring studies in small business have illustrated significant advantages. According to Feldman (1997), credit scoring may change small business lending regarding the interaction between applicants and underwriters, loan pricing, and credit availability. For example: (i) credit scoring can allow lenders to extend loans without any contact; (ii) credit scoring can reduce cost of borrowing, documentation requirements and loan losses especially when it provides an accurate credit assessment; (iii) credit scoring can allow a lender to increase the size of loans and this leads to profitability. Moreover, Frame et al., (2001) and Padhi et al., (2001) found that when banks changed to small business credit scoring of loans, they were able to increase small business lending by US$4 billion. Finally, Frame et al., (2001) showed that the use of credit scoring has a positive impact on the level of small business loans made by large banks in low and moderate-income census tracts, as well as increasing profitability.

Caouette et al. (1998) explained the reasons for the effectiveness of scoring models in consumer lending over business lending as follows. First, at an institutional level, business lenders believe that the process of business lending is complex and requires judgmental systems rather than quantitative methods. Consumer lenders, on the other hand, accept quantitative methods because they may focus on commercial terms instead of lending terms. Second, at an analytic level, building consumer models is easier because of the availability of applicant information and quantitative methods to test and improve credit models. Finally, at the economic level, losses in consumer lending tend to be relatively large in number, but small. Losses from business lending, however, are relatively uncommon, but of greater magnitude.

2.5. Credit Scoring and Credit Ratings

Credit rating is the assessment of the credit risk of companies and individuals (Coyle, 2000). It also measures the ability of borrower to repay a loan by classifying credit risk into rates. The process of rating is generally achieved by agencies including the four major US rating agencies, namely, Moody's, Standard Poor's, Fitch, and Duff Phelps. The result of this process is a gradation of groups represent their evaluation of companies starting with the highest rating and terminating with the lowest rating (AAA, AA, A, BBB, etc.). Table 1 from Liu (2001: 6) summarizes the essentially differences between credit scoring and credit rating in terms of producers, objects of evaluation, results, users, main purpose, methods, and approach.

First, credit-scoring models can be built by the lender or external institutions for evaluating consumer and small business loans. Credit scoring models usually produce a score that is used by lenders for identifying the credit risk of borrowers. The main purpose of credit-scoring models is to help make routine decisions relating to grant loans. Credit-scoring models use statistical and mathematical techniques, which produce a score used in evaluating the creditworthiness of borrowers, so objectivity is a main feature.

On the other hand, credit rating systems are similar to credit-scoring models in terms of the producers, but generally produce ratings only for business loans, not for consumer loans. Credit rating systems produce grades, which are used in making credit decisions but not on routine base. The ratings are usually issued by credit agencies and they can be used as an independent variable in credit-scoring models. Credit rating systems use both statistical techniques and expert system to produce grades so the approach is divided into two branches: objective and subjective.

Table 1. Credit scoring vs. credit rating

	Credit scoring	Credit rating
Producers	Internally by banks and financial intuitions or externally by vendors of scoring systems	Internally by banks and financial intuitions or externally by rating agency
Objects of evaluation	Consumer credit and small business credit	Corporate loans and loans within institutions and international companies
Results	Scores	Grades
Users	Institution itself	Banks and financial intuitions lenders, investor, regulator
Purpose	Routine credit decision	Credit risk management and control General reference for various purposes in business, industry and finance
Methods	Statistical and mathematical techniques	Expert systems and credit risk models
Approach	Objective	Subjective

3. Credit-Scoring Approaches

When implementing a credit-scoring system, a financial institution must clearly define and understand the outcome. In this section, we review the methods of scoring models used in practice. Figure 1 provides a summary of the important approaches and models of credit scoring.

3.1. Parametric Statistical Approaches

In a credit-scoring context, parametric statistical approaches require the use of regression analysis to discriminate between good loans and bad loans using a sample of applicants (Bramma, 1999). These approaches were the first used in building credit-scoring systems and are still considered to be one of the more successful approaches. These approaches can also recognize and eliminate trivial variables and ensure that all the important variables remain in the scoring system (Thomas et al., 2002). In turn, parametric statistical approaches can be divided into four models frequently employed: the linear probability model; probit models; logit models and discriminant models. These models all attempt to estimate the probability of default based on the past data (i.e. good and bad credit risk) of the applicants and classify them into two different groups. Each of these models is reviewed in the following subsections.

Linear Probability Model

By far the most common empirical model form used is the linear regression model; mainly because it is generally easy to use and understand.

The linear probability model is an econometric model in which the dependent variable takes a value of zero or one.

It assumes a linear relationship between the probability of default and the independent variables and employs historical data as inputs to explain the repayment experience on past loans. Ordinary least squares or weighted least squares is employed to regress Z (the dependent variable) on X_n (the independent variables) to find the parameter(s) β_j which gives the estimated importance of the j th variable in explaining past repayment experiences (Turvey, 1991). The structural model takes the form:

$$Z = \alpha + \sum_{n=1}^{N} \beta_j X_n + u \tag{1}$$

where Z is the dependent variable or the probability of default ($Z=1$ if the event is default; $Z=0$ otherwise), β are parameters to be estimated, X are independent variables of the value for i th the observation, $n = 1,....N$ and u is the unobserved error term assumed to be a random variable.

The major disadvantage of the linear probability model is the chance that some estimated values may lie outside the zero-one interval (known as the linearity problem). This is problematic in several respects (Altman et al., 1981, p. 8).

First, there is no economic meaning if the probability is a negative or takes a value of one. Second, a value greater than one or less than zero means the violation of the assumption of zero-expectation errors necessary for least squares estimation. Another problem caused by estimated probabilities outside the zero-one interval is the possibility of inadmissible weights for the adjustment of heteroskedasticity.

Probit Model

A probit model is an econometric model where the dependent variable Z can only be zero or one, and the continuous independent variables X_{ij} are estimated:

$$prob(Z = 1) = F\left(\beta_{ij} X_{ij}\right) \tag{2}$$

where β is a parameter to be estimated, and F is the normal cumulative distribution function (CDF). The probit models are generalized linear models with a probit link:

$$Z = \Phi^{-1}\left(\mu\right) \tag{3}$$

where Φ^{-1} is the inverse of the standard normal cumulative distribution function, and

$$\mu = \sum_{j=1}^{n} \beta_j X_{ij} \tag{4}$$

This may be expressed as a probit model in probability,

$$prob(Z=1) = 1 - F\left(-\sum_{j=1}^{n} \beta_j X_{ij}\right) = F\left(\sum_{j=1}^{n} \beta_j X_{ij}\right) = \Phi\left(\sum_{j=1}^{n} \beta_j X_{ij}\right) \tag{5}$$

where the more general form of cumulative distribution function, F, is substituted by the standard normal cumulative distribution, Φ.

The probit model takes only one naturally significant form because a probit model expressed in η is a linear regression of the Z-score of the event probability. The equation for the probability of non-event is then:

$$prob(Z=0) = 1 - \Phi\left(\sum_{j=1}^{n} \beta_j X_{ij}\right) \tag{6}$$

This equation can be derived from equation (5), because the response is a binary outcome (Liao, 1994, p. 21). Probit models are a major alternative to the linear probability model and overcome its major deficiency by finding the appropriate transformation that such probability estimates fall within the[0,1] interval.

Grablowsky and Talley (1981) suggested this analysis by comparing the assumptions and results of this method and multi discriminant analysis in predicting retail credit applications and found that probit analysis performs better, as well as having better predictive power. Bovenzi et al., (1983) also used a probit model to predict bank default but similar results to multiple discriminant analysis were found.

Gessner et al., (1988) compared the probit model with OLS, logit, linear discriminant and quadratic discriminant analysis and they found that the probit and logit models were superior. Later, Boyes et al., (1989) used probit models to estimate the failure probability of credit card loans.

They found that the probit model occurs in a way that is not consistent with the minimization of default risk. Greene (1992) and Jacobson and Roszbach's results (2003) were similar to the results reached by Boyes et al., (1989).

Feelders (2000; 2003) and Chen and Asterbro (2003) also used the model for reject inference in credit scoring and found that probit model performs significantly better than the other two comparative models, while Banasik et al., (2003) found a small improvement when using the probit model to examine the predictive accuracy.

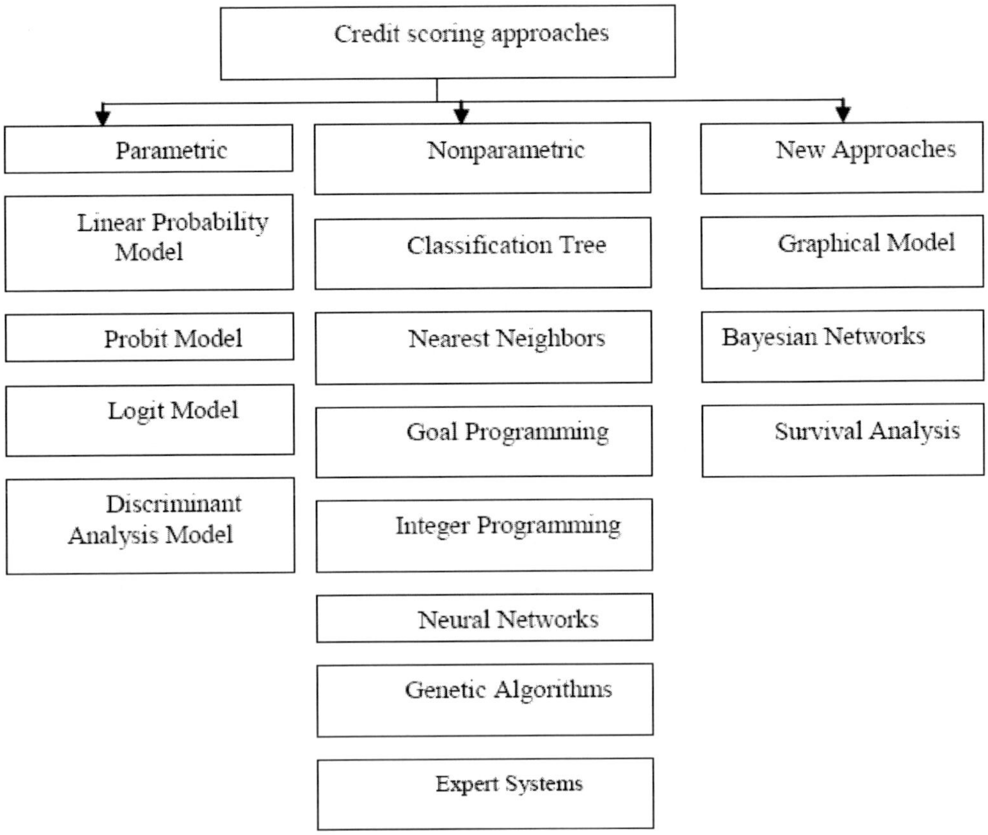

Figure 1. Approaches to credit scoring.

Logit Model

The logit model is a natural complement of the regression model where the dependent variable is a qualitative variable. The dependent variable in the logit model (also known as the logistic model) also takes a value only of 0 and 1 but differs from the probit model by assuming that the probability of default has a logistic distribution instead of a normal distribution. The equation form of the logistic model is:

$$F(Z) = \frac{1}{1+\ell^{-Z}} \tag{7}$$

where ℓ is the exponential and $F(Z)$ is the cumulative probability of default.

In brief, there could be transferred into a logit model by replacing the general CDF, F, with a specific CDF, L, representing the logistic distribution:

$$prob(\mathrm{Z}=1) = 1 - L\left(-\sum_{j=1}^{n} \beta_j \mathrm{X}_{ij}\right) = L\left(-\sum_{j=1}^{n} \beta_j \mathrm{X}_{ij}\right) \tag{8}$$

The previous equation represents the probability of an event occurring. For a non-event, the probability is equal to zero as follows:

$$prob(Z=0)=L\left(-\sum_{j=1}^{n}\beta_j X_{ij}\right)=\frac{\ell^{-\sum_{j=1}^{n}\beta_j X_{ij}}}{1+\ell^{-\sum_{j=1}^{n}\beta_k X_{ij}}}=\frac{1}{1+\ell^{\sum_{j=1}^{n}\beta_j X_{ij}}} \tag{9}$$

Both probit and logit parameters are estimated using Maximum Likelihood Estimation (MLE) unlike the linear probability models estimated using Least Squares (LS) Estimation. The difference between LS and MLE is that LS identifies decrease in the parameter estimates that yield the smallest sum of squared errors in the fit between model and data, while MLE is considered by selecting parameter estimates that imply the highest probability or probability of having obtained the observed sample Z.

In a credit-scoring context, Wiginton (1980) was the first study applied logistic regression by comparing it with discriminant analysis on consumer credit scoring but he found only a small advantage in logistic regression in relation to classification accuracy. Srinivasan and Kim (1987), Davis et al., (1992) and Martin (1997) found similar result, though Desai et al., (1997) and Hua and Ansell (2007) concluded that the logistic regression was superior to other methods. On the other hand, Henley (1995) found that the performance of logistic regression was less than for the other method. The same conclusions arise from Salchnberger et al., (1992). Andreeva (2006) compared logistic regression with survival analysis and found that it is competitive with survival analysis. Gana and Rossi (1997, p. 8) found that ridge regression estimated probit model may compete successfully with the logit model in relation to splitting the distribution of the dependent variable.

Discriminant Analysis Model

Discriminant analysis is the most common statistical technique used for credit scoring. The purpose of discriminant analysis is to classify firm into one of two possible groups (financially non-distressed and financially distressed) based on one or more variables. In generally, it is used mainly to classify or make forecasts in problems where the dependent variable is qualitative in choice. Hence, the first step is to create clear group classifications and then collect data for the objects in the groups. This technique attempts to derive a linear combination of a number of independent variables that discriminate clearly between the groups. The technique originated in psychology and biology and first was suggested by Fisher (1936) who used it in taxonomic problems and was used by Durand (1941) to discriminate between good and bad loans. The outcome of this technique is the discriminant score that take the following form:

$$Z=\beta_1 X_1+\beta_2 X_2+\ldots+\beta_j X_j \tag{10}$$

where Z is the discriminant score (Z=1 if the event is default; Z=0 otherwise), β_j are the coefficients to be estimated and X_j are the independent variables.

The most common forms of discriminant modeling in credit scoring are the Z-score and the ZETA model. The Z-score was developed by Altman (1968) as a multivariate approach built on a set of five financial ratios, producing the following equation:

$$Z = 1.2X_1 + 1.4X_2 + 3.3X_3 + 0.6X_4 + 0.99X_5 \quad (11)$$

where Z is the discriminant score, X_1 is working capital/total assets, X_2 is retained earnings/total assets, X_3 is EBIT/total assets, X_4 is market value of equity/book value of liabilities, and X_5 is sales/total assets.

Discriminant analysis has a number of advantages as a credit-scoring model: (i) it can identify complex models for the set of predictor characteristics and considers the interaction of these characteristics; (ii) it does not involve complicated mathematics; (iii) it is based on a specific normal distribution and it is more powerful in interpreting between group-differences; (iv) it achieves a reduction in error rates; and (v) it is a good technique for classification accuracy.

On the other hand, discriminant analysis is also suspected of a number of concerns: (i) discriminant analysis assumes normally distributed variables of the members of the groups and this violates the classic linear regression assumptions; (ii) it employs linear discriminant rather than quadratic functions, which may be problematic especially when the group dispersion is unequal; (iii) it is dependent on a relatively equal distribution of group membership. If one group of the population is larger than the other, discriminant analysis will ordinarily classify all observations in this group.

Discriminant analysis was the first technique used in a credit-scoring context. Many analysts applied this method to classify loans or to predict bankruptcy in corporate loans, including Altman (1968), Orgler (1970), Apilado et al., (1974), Altman et al., (1977), Altman and Narayanan (1997), Altman (1980), Galitz (1983), Altman and Izan (1984), Pantalone and Platt (1987), Betts and Belhoul (1987), Turvey (1991), Crook et al., (1992b), Eisenbeis (1996), Altman (2000; 2002b), Crook et al., (2002), and Chang (2005). In addition, several comparative studies of discriminant analysis techniques with other credit-scoring models, both parametric and nonparametric, were applied by studies such Myers and Forgy (1963), Srinivasan and Kim (1987), Coffman (1986), Bardos (1998), Ariyo et al., (1992), Crook et al., (1992a), King et al., (1994), Altman et al., (1994), Avery et al., (1996; 2000), Henley and Hand (1996), Desai et al. (1996, 1997), Bardos and Zhu (1998), Yobas et al., (2000), Hamilton and Khan (2001), Zhu et al., (2002), Baesens et al., (2003), and Yang (2005).

In spite of these comparisons with discriminant methods, the conclusions of these studies are often in conflict. For instance; King et al., (1994) and Desia et al., (1997), in studies to investigate the predictive power of new techniques in comparison to traditional techniques, found that discriminant analysis did not perform as well as other methods in terms of accuracy. To the contrary, Boyle et al., (1992), Yobas et al., (2000) discussed and compared various statistical methods on credit-scoring models and found that discriminant analysis was superior to the other methods.

Although successful in credit-scoring field, it has some criticisms. Eisenbeis (1977) discussed the problems of application of discriminant analysis techniques such as the distribution and the interpretation of the significance of individual variables and showed that discriminant analysis suffers from statistical deficiencies as mentioned earlier. Capon (1982) provided a critical analysis of credit-scoring models and showed that the bias of sample, the size of sample, overriding, and multicollinearity could change the score by several points. However, Hand et al., (1998) compared the error rate of linear discriminant analysis with that of the optimal classification rule under certain conditions and showed that discriminant analysis leads to a similar decision to the decision of the optimal rule and that two rules can lead to very different error rates.

3.2. Nonparametric Approaches

The aforementioned parametric approaches assume the distributions of the variables being assessed belong to known parameterized families of probability distributions. Non-parametric approaches, however, do not rely on the stringent assumption of the shape of the population distribution. These approaches are also called distribution-free approaches. The non-parametric approaches can deal with missing values and multicollinearity among variables compared with parametric approaches. Nonparametric approach can be classified into two categories for building credit-scoring methods, comprising simultaneous and sequential methods. Simultaneous classification methods are usually used goal programming and integer programming. Sequential methods commonly partition borrower data with the purpose of achieving separation of data into good and bad loans. These methods include the recursive partitioning algorithm, the nearest-neighbors method, neural networks, genetic algorithms, and expert systems.

Recursive Partitioning Algorithm Approach

The recursive partitioning algorithm (RPA) or classification tree is a non-parametric, complex and computerized intensive sorting algorithm. The basic idea is to split the sample responses into the two new sub-samples that are as homogeneous as possible and as different from each other, and then repeatedly split the subsample into subgroups until it generates the possibility for decision-making. The entire sample is the root node, while the sub-samples are called nodes. Each terminal node is classified as either of 'Good' or 'Bad'. Figure 2 illustrates a typical RPA.

In this figure, terminal subsets are represented by rectangular text boxes while non-terminal subsets are represented by circle text boxes. The tree classifier predicts a class for the measurement vector Z, which goes into Z2, Z3. If Z goes to Z3, then from the definition of split 3, it determines whether Z goes into Z6 or Z7. The process stops when the subsets meet the requirements to be a terminal node of the tree.

The objective of RPA in respect to credit scoring is to develop a sequence of questions or rules which either approve or disapprove to classify loans data into good loans and bad loans. The RPA itself looks for defining cut-off values for default risk. The best splitting rule is defined as one that allows the decrease in the total impurities of the resulting sub samples compared with the impurity of the root node. The RPA is completed when terminal nodes are assigned to all possible default risks and all loans data is finally classified. The outcome of the RPA is a set of terminal nodes representing the minimization of the observed expected cost of misclassification of each assignment.

There are many methods of splitting used in RPA, including the Kolmogorov-Sminov statistic, the basic impurity index, the Gini index, the entropy index, and the maximize half-sum of squares. In the credit-scoring context, applications of this technique suggested by Makowski (1985), Frydman, Altman and Kao (1985) applied in corporate distress. Coffman (1986), Carter and Catlett (1987) compared sophisticated decision tree methods with discriminant analysis for assessing credit applications. Srinivasan and Kim (1987) applied it to a sample of corporate credit data as did Boyle et al., (1992) and Hu and Ansell (2006). All these studies have generally shown that the RPA provides better classification precision than many of the other techniques examined.

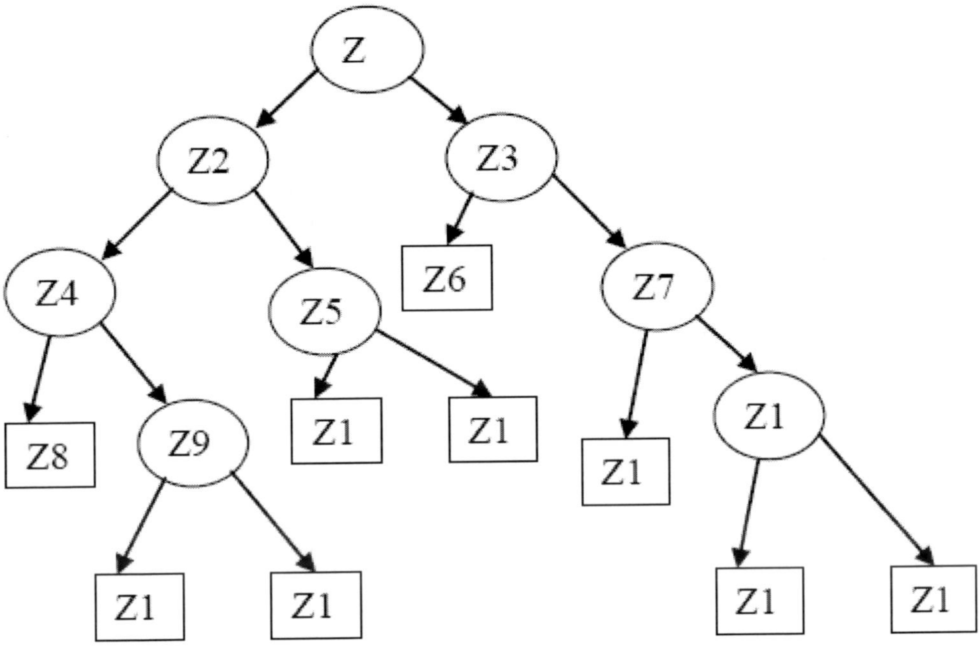

Figure 2. Example of a classification tree.

Nearest-Neighbors Approach

The nearest-neighbors method (also called pattern recognition) is a nonparametric approach for classifying. "The idea of this method is to select a metric on the space of application data to measure how far apart any two applicants are" (Thomas et al., 2002, p. 60). In the nearest methods, credit risk is assessed for an applicant from a sample of past applicants as a representative standard and then classified by the proportions of 'goods' and 'bads' among the κ nearest applicant 'most similar' points in a training sample. The similarity of points is assessed using an appropriate distance metric. The selection of a suitable distance measure is an important part of the κ nearest-neighbor method. The purpose of selecting a metric is to improve classification accuracy by comparing with some specific criterion. Therefore, an applicant is classified as good, if a majority of its neighbors are good; if not, the applicant is classified as bad.

Henley and Hand (1996) suggested a metric of the form:

$$d(X,Y)=\{(X-Y)^{T}(I+Dww^{T})(X-Y)\}^{1/2} \tag{12}$$

where X and Y are points in the feature space, I is the identity matrix, D is a distance parameter, and w is a particular direction in the measurement space.

The nearest-neighbor method has some advantages in credit scoring (Henley and Hand, 1996): (i) this method can build a model of irregularities in the risk function over the feature space because of the nonparametric nature; (ii) the performance of this method is superior to other nonparametric techniques, such as Kernel methods, when the data are multidimensional; (iii) it is straightforward to update dynamically by adding applicants to the design set when their true class becomes known and by dropping older cases.

A simple nearest-neighbor was applied to credit-scoring data by Chatterjee and Barcun (1970) on personal loan applications. Chatterjee and Barcun (1970) found that the method was quicker and far less subjective than many numerical credit-scoring methods. Hand (1986) also compared a variety of credit-scoring models, including nearest neighbor for home loans. Forgarty and Ireson (1993) compared the performance of some credit-scoring models, including nearest-neighbor method and the result showed a good performance for the nearest-neighbor method. Henley and Hand (1996) used nearest-neighbor method for loan applications compared with scoring methods and found that the performance of the nearest-neighbors method achieved the lowest expected bad risk rate but it had the advantage over the other methods in relation to classification. However, Baesens et al., (2003) found the nearest-neighbor method was worse than other methods such as neural networks, discriminant analysis, and logistic regression when they applied it to loan data from different countries.

Goal Programming

Goal programming is a branch of mathematical programming that is concerned with the optimal allocation of limited resources to achieve a desired goal by maximizing and minimizing values as well as an efficient part of operations research to solve many practical problems. Mangasarian (1965) was the first to study suggested goal programming in classifying problems where there are two groups and there is a separating hyperplane, which can separate the two groups accurately. Freed and Glover (1981) proposed that goal programming can be applied for discriminant problem when the two groups are not necessarily separable by using objectives such as minimization of the sum of absolute errors or minimizing the maximum error (Thomas et al., 2002).

In a credit-scoring context, goal programming aims to determine a relationship between weights or scores associated with explanatory variables and a scalar that defines a cut-off point between good and bad loans. To solve the problem by linear programming, a popular formulation is as follows:

$$\begin{aligned}
&\text{Minimize } a_1+a_2+\ldots+a_{n_G+n_B}\\
&\text{Subject to: } w_1x_{i1}+w_2x_{i2}+\ldots+w_px_{ip}\geq c-a_i,\ 1\leq i\leq n_G\\
&w_1x_{i1}+w_2x_{i2}+\ldots+w_px_{ip}\leq c+a_i,\ n_G+1\leq i\leq n_G+n_B,\\
&a_i\geq 0,\ 1\leq i\leq n_G+n_B,
\end{aligned} \tag{13}$$

where $a_1 + a_2 + ... + a_{n_G+n_B}$ is the objective function that includes the possible errors (all are positive or zero), $w_1, w_2, ..., w_p$ the weights that minimize the sum of the absolute values of errors, $x_{i1}, x_{i2}, ..., x_{ip}$ the predictive variables of a borrower i, and c the cut-off.

If an applicant in the sample is good, we would require $w_1x_{i1} + w_2x_{i2} + ... + w_px_{ip} \geq c - a_i$. However, if an applicant in the sample is bad, we require $w_1x_{i1} + w_2x_{i2} + ... + w_px_{ip} \leq c + a_i$

Hardy and Adrian (1985) showed that while mathematical programming could be used in loan classification, it performs the same as the conventional models based on discriminant analysis. Chhikara (1989) showed that the linear programming method may be further developed to consider more complex problems, including multi-group classifications. On the other hand, Joachimsthaler and Stam (1990) undertook comparative studies of the mathematical programming technique with statistical techniques to estimate expected rates of their misclassification. They found the later classified marginally better. Nath et al., (1992) also found that statistical methods were superior to goal programming. Baesens et al., (2003) also concluded that linear programming performed worse than most scoring methods.

However, goal programming has some advantages over statistical methods. To start with, it can easily include the bias into the scorecard development by including additional constraints (Thomas et al., 2002: 65) and it can often deal with large numbers.

Integer Programming

Any decision problem (with an objective to be maximized or minimized) in which the (quantifiable) decision variables must assume non-fractional or discrete values may be classified as an integer optimization problem. If only some of unknown variables are required to be integers, then the problem is called mixed integer programming, which prevents a trivial solution. This method overcomes the limitations of linear programming resulting from minimization and maximization of deviation.

In this technique, at least some of the variables will have to be integer (0, 1, 2, etc.), as in the following model:

$$\text{Minimize } L\left(d_1 + ... + d_{n_G}\right) + D\left(d_{n_{G+1}} + ... + d_{n_{G+B}}\right)$$
$$\text{Subject to: } w_1x_{i1} + ... + w_px_{ip} \geq c - Md_i, \quad 1 \leq i \leq n_G,$$
$$w_1x_{i1} + ... + w_px_{ip} \leq c + Md_i, \quad 0 \leq d_i \leq 1, \quad d_i \text{ integer.} \tag{14}$$

where L is the cost of misclassifying a good as a bad, D the cost of misclassifying a bad as a good, M is a positive number, and d_i is a variable that is 1 if a customer in the sample is misclassifying a good and 0 otherwise.

Joachimsthaler and Stam (1988, 1990) and Koehler and Erenguc (1990) found that the integer model is a better classification model than the goal programming model. Glen (1997) suggested a mixed integer programming for classification and showed that it can be expanded to allow variables to be chosen in a stepwise way. However, it has two major disadvantages (Thomas et al., 2002). First, it takes much longer than goal programming to solve and hence can deal with only very small sample sets with the number of cases in the hundreds. Second, there are often a number of optimal solutions with the same number of misclassifications on the training set but with quite different performances on the holdout sample.

Neural Networks

Neural networks, which can be considered as a form of nonlinear regression (Thomas, 2000), consist of layers of interconnected nodes, each node producing a non-linear function of its inputs. These nodes may come from other nodes or directly from the data. This method is based on computer systems that develop artificial intelligence and try to imitate the functioning of the human brain. This method involves a number of similar units consisting of a large number of interconnected processing elements which are called neurons. The process of this method include three layers; the input, hidden and output layers. More specifically, each neuron in these layers has its own activation or transfer function to the output layer. The input and hidden layers send signals to the output layer. Figure 3 represents the general scheme of a single-layer neural networks. It can be represented in the following equations

$$Y = f\left(w_{i0}x_0 + w_{i1}x_1 + \ldots + w_{in}x_n\right) \tag{15}$$

$$Y = \sum_{p=0}^{n} w_{ip}x_p \tag{16}$$

where w is the weight connecting input n and neuron I (=1 because there is only one neuron), p indicates the integer input, and x is a variable represented in a characteristic of a borrower.

However, multilayer perceptrons are more commonly used than the single-layer. Multilayer consist of three layers of neuron: input, hidden, and output of interconnected neurons and each neuron has a set of weights. A three-layer network is shown in Figure 3. From Figure 3, the equation of multilayer perceptron will be as follows

$$y_k = F_1\left(\sum_{q=0}^{p} w_{kq}x_q\right) \tag{17}$$

where the subscript 1 on F_1 indicates it is the first layer after the input layer. The y_k, $k = 1, \ldots, r$, are the outputs from the first hidden layer. From the Figure 4 below, the equation of multilayer perceptron will be as follows

$$y_k = F_1\left(\sum_{q=0}^{p} w_{kq}x_q\right) \tag{18}$$

where the subscript 1 on F_1 indicates it is the first layer after the input layer. The y_k, $k = 1, \ldots, r$, are the outputs from the first hidden layer.

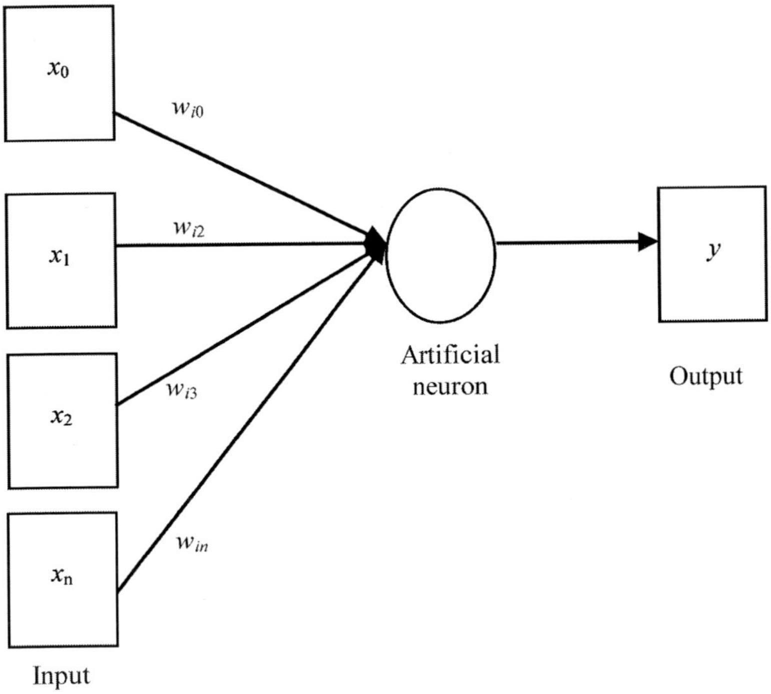

Figure 3. A simple single-layer neural network.

The computation of the vector of weights is known as training (Liu, 2002). There are several such methods but the most commonly used method is the back-propagation algorithm. Training pairs, comprising a value for each of the input variables for a case and the known classification of the case, are frequently introduced to the network and the weights are adjusted to minimize some error function (Thomas et al., 2002).

The earliest work in neural networks date to the 1940s when McCulloch and Pitts introduced the first neural computing model. In the 1950s, Rosenbaltt's work resulted in a two layer network, the perceptron, which was capable of learning certain classifications by adjusting connection weights.

In the credit-scoring context, the kind of neural network that is generally implemented to credit fields can be seen as a statistical model requiring linear combinations of nested sequences of non-linear transformations of linear combinations of variables (Hand and Henley, 1997: 534). The input layers are represented by the application characteristics such as financial ratios or applicant characteristics and the output is the credit performance of borrower then the procedures at network repeated with various weights until the weighting system with the least error appears and the weights are adjusted to minimize some error function (Thomas et al., 2002).

There are many studies that used the neural networks in the credit arena. One of the first studies to apply neural networks was published by Odom and Sharda (1990) who used the variables of the Altman model (Z-score) as inputs to the neural networks for predicting the bankruptcy problem. Carter and Catlet (1987) used them in accepting consumers of credit cards. Vellido et al., (1999) reviewed the use of neural network in business applications in relation to bankruptcy prediction. Wong et al., (1997) also conducted a survey of this method to examine the historical trends in business applications including some references on the bankruptcy prediction problem to investigate the potential neural network research fields in the future.

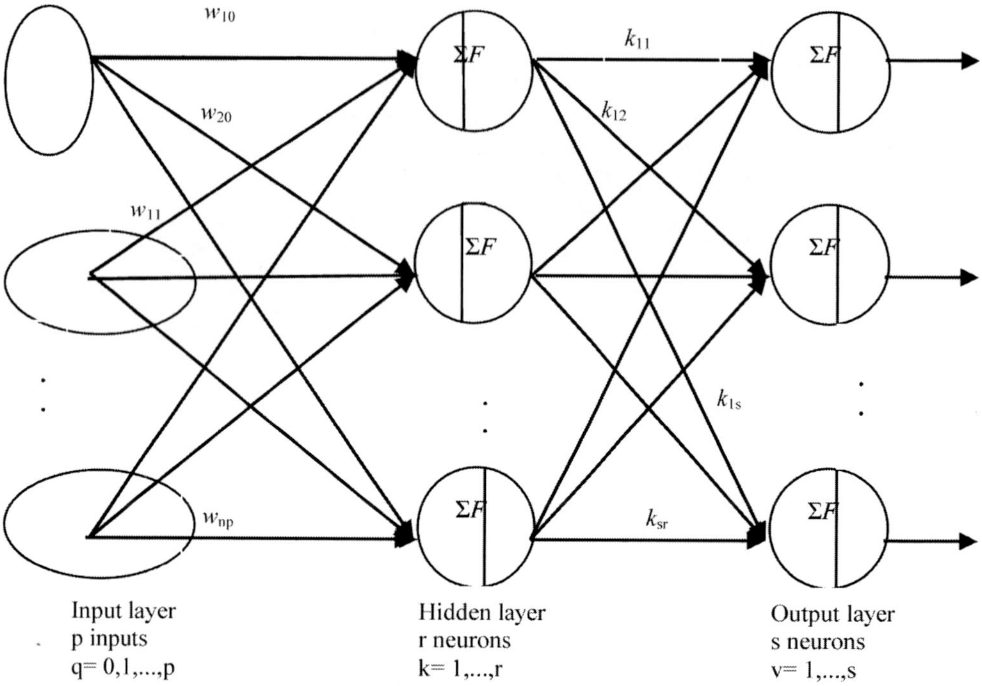

Figure 4. Example of a multilayer perceptron.

where q, k and v are neurons for the input layer, hidden layer and output layer respectively.

Kim and Scott (1991) found good accuracy and performance for this method. They used an artificial neural network for a sample of a 190 Compustat firms to predict bankruptcy. Tam and Kiang (1992), and Min and Lee (2004) applied neural networks to identify banking bankruptcy cases and compared several methods including multiple discriminant analysis, logistic regression, k-nearest neighbors and decision tree. They found that the multilayer network was the best. Salchenberger et al., (1992) compared neural networks with logit regression for predicting thrift failures and found it outperformed the logit regression. Coats and Fant (1993), Jost (1993), Wilson and Sharda (1994), Alici (1999), and West (2000) all found the same result in applying neural networks. However, Altman et al., (1994) analyzed the comparison between discriminant models and neural networks to identify corporate bankruptcy in Italy and found that neural networks performed had similar accuracy to other scoring models but they suggested using both types of methods in certain applications, especially in complex ones in which the flexibility of neural networks would be particularly valuable.

On the other hand, Desai et al., (1997) investigated the predictive power of feed forward neural networks, which are an artificial network where connections between the units do not form directed cycles, and genetic algorithms in comparison to traditional techniques using the good and bad loans data and they found neural networks were inferior to logistic regression.

Yobas et al., (2000) and Yang et al., (1999) ensured the same result when compared with discriminant analysis.

In other kinds of applications, neural networks were used in hybrid approaches with other scoring techniques. Mangasarian (1993) used linear programming and training neural networks. Lee et al., (1996) also applied hybrid models, which included multiple discriminant analysis, classification tree, self-organizing maps and neural networks. Iginzio and Soltys (1996) used genetic algorithms to train and design neural networks.

Neural networks have many advantages when applied in the credit field. Kalapodas and Thomson (2006) showed that neural networks can built a complex model with non-linear relationships, they can represent any function, and they can deal with many characteristics. Allen et al., (2004) also showed that they are more flexible than other methods since there are no assumptions about the probability distribution of the predictor variables. Limosbunchai et al., (2005) added that neural networks can detect Type I errors better than other methods because the costs of classifying loans into bad and good (Type I) are greater than the costs of misclassifying loans into bad and good (Type II). They used artificial neural network to construct the credit-scoring models and to predict credit risk for the agricultural loans in Thailand. On the other hand, Allen et al., (2004) reported that neural networks are costly to apply and maintain.

Genetic Algorithms

Genetic (or evolutionary) algorithms are one of the artificial intelligence methods used in credit scoring. Genetic algorithms were pioneered by Holland (1975) who took the same ideas of the general principles of evolutionary natural selection suggested by Charles Darwin and used them on unconstrained optimization problems. The idea of this method is to attempt to simulate the survival of the fitness rule of genetic mutation to develop optimization algorithms (Thomas et al., 2004). A basic genetic algorithm represents selecting a population of candidate solutions (called individuals) to a problem. Solutions are represented as strings of genes (called chromosomes). Genetic algorithms assess the performance (called fitness) of each possible solution in each generation and then calculate the fitness of each string to achieve a given objective. From the initial population of chromosomes, a new population (children replaced their parents within the population) is generated using three genetic operators: reproduction, crossover and mutation.

The next stages are then repeated a chosen numbers of times. The algorithm ends when either a fixed number of generations have occurred, or when the improvement from one generation to the next satisfies a minimum predetermined threshold value (Finaly, 2006). Generic algorithms operate in four steps: (i) establishment of a set of initial individuals, (ii) assessment of individual, (iii) selection of good individuals, and (iv) manipulation to produce a new set of individuals

In the credit-scoring context, the solutions are potential scorecards. There are two methods to represent a scorecard. The first one suggested by Albright (1994) is to estimate the coefficients and parameters of a polynomial scoring equation where each chromosome consisted of estimated parameters. The classification is identified according to whether or not the value of a function exceeded a predetermined value. According to the second approach, the ranges of values are estimated for each characteristic and an exchanging value that indicates whether a characteristic is to enter the classification or not.

Fogarty and Ireson (1993) found that the genetic algorithms performed better compared to many methods but did not perform better than a simple decision rule to classify all cases as good. The result of Albright's research (1994) showed a good classification of the sample. On the other hand, Desai et al., (1997) reported that genetic algorithms did not perform better than other methods, especially in classifying bad loans. Yobas et al., (2000) found the genetic algorithms were inferior to linear discriminant analysis but superior to neural networks and the decision tree. Finlay (2006) showed that genetic algorithms can perform as well as other methods which included OLS regression stepwise and non-stepwise, logistic regression stepwise and non-stepwise, and neural networks.

Desai et al., (1997) showed the advantages of this method; the evaluation function does not require being linear, differentiable, or even continuous and genetic algorithms are less susceptible to optimal solution than traditional optimization methods. On the contrary, Walker et al., (1995) also found some disadvantages of this method: (i) compared to statistical methods, genetic algorithms do not have a theoretical framework for the evolutionary process, and (ii) it is very hard to predict the time for the solution of serious problems.

Expert Systems

Expert systems (called artificial intelligence) are processes of decision making that are performed by a computer program that contains stored knowledge and solves problems in a specific field of human expertise. Expert systems consist of three main parts: (i) a knowledge base which consists of stored rules, (ii) an inference engine that applies the knowledge to the problem, and (iii) a user interface that presents information and questions to the operator and supplies the operator's response to the inference engine.

In a credit-scoring context, however, expert systems have few examples. Thomas et al., (2002) showed that the reason for this is because the details of such systems are not usually generic. None has been published to give exact details. However, Pearson (1994) applied it to small business loans and Tamai and Fujita (1989) to commercial loans.

3.3. Other Methods in Credit Scoring

In Sections 3.1 and 3.2, the parametric and non-parametric, approaches to credit scoring were discussed. Traditional methods such as discriminant analysis and linear programming were reviewed as well as the recent methods such as neural networks and nearest-neighbor methods which have been used in credit scoring in the last decade. In this section, new methods under research in credit scoring are discussed. These approaches attempt to improve the accuracy of credit scoring and include graphical models, Bayesian networks, and survival analysis.

Graphical Models

Graphical models are statistical models to study the relationship among variables of multivariate data by graphs containing nodes and edges. In the graph, the nodes represent continuous or discrete variables and these nodes are connected by edges, which show dependence relationships between the variables.

In a credit-scoring context, graphical models can be applied three ways (Thomas et al., 2002, p. 197): (i) they illuminate the relationship between the factors that affect the behavior of borrowers, so subpopulations can be identified with certain behavioral characteristics, (ii) they can be used to forecast risk or profit for each individual in the same way as statistical credit-scoring models, and (iii) they ensure that the credit granting process is well designed.

Graphical models have grown in the credit-scoring field during the last decade. Hand et al., (1997) and Chang et al., (2000) reported that graphical models are useful for building models in the credit-scoring arena. hey give a description of the credit-scoring selection process in term of influence diagrams and assess the effect of selection bias and stratification on interdependency of variables.

Bayesian Networks

Bayesian networks are a form of directed graphical model. A Bayesian network is a directed acyclic graph of nodes representing variables and arcs representing dependence relationships among these variables. If there is an arc from node A to another node B, then we say that A is a parent of B. If a node has a known value, it is said to be an evidence node. A node can represent any kind of variable be it an observed measurement, a parameter, a latent variable, or a hypothesis. Nodes are not restricted to representing random variables; this is the 'Bayesian' part of Bayesian networks.

Chang et al., (2000) used the notion of this model in a credit-scoring context, showing that the objective of Bayesian networks is to determine the independent relationships that exist between variables in data sets and precisely embody these conditional independent relationships in a directed graph. They reported that Bayesian networks may be able to construct credit-scoring models to classify the subsets of variables in a database. They suggested that much investigative work needs to be done in developing this method. Baesens et al., (2002) used a Markov Chain Monte Carlo search to learn unrestricted Bayesian network classifiers and Markov-Blanket They found powerful models for credit scoring resulted.

Survival Analysis

Survival analysis is a class of statistical methods for studying the occurrence and timing of events. These methods are most often applied to the study of deaths. Survival analysis is called different things in different fields such as history analysis, reliability analysis, failure time analysis, duration analysis and transition analysis. For the application of survival analysis we need to know the time of event. This time is termed survival times or lifetimes.

The aim of survival analysis is to estimate predictive models in which the risk of an event depends on the independent variables of retrospective data.

There are many methods in survival analysis such as life table, Kaplan-Meier estimators, exponential regression, log-normal regression, proportional hazards regression, competing risk models, and discrete-time methods (Morrison, 2004). There are also three different ways to describe the probability distributions in survival analysis: (i) cumulative distribution function: $S(t) = prob\{T > t\} = 1 - F(t)$ where S is survival function, t is time, T is the time of default and $F(t)$ represents the cumulative distribution function, (ii) probability density function: $f(t) = \frac{dF}{dt} = -\frac{dS}{dt}$, and (iii) Hazard function: $h(t) = \lim_{\Delta t \to 0} \frac{\Pr\{t \le T < t + \Delta t \mid T \ge t\}}{\Delta t}$.

In a credit-scoring context, survival analysis has several advantages (Thomas et al., 2001): (i) survival analysis handles censored data easily, (ii) when choosing a fixed term to measure the performance of loans, survival analysis avoids the instability that results from this selection (iii) estimating when there is a default is a main factor toward calculating the profitability of an applicant, and (iv) this approach facilitates the incorporation of the effect of changes in the economic environment over the life of the loan into the scoring system.

Narain (1992) was the first to use survival analysis for credit scoring. Narain applied the Kaplan-Meier method by fitting exponential regression models to data sets of loans and the results showed that survival analysis gives a reasonable estimation of the time until default. A scorecard was then built using multiple regression and it showed that it can significantly improve the credit granting decisions by likely survival times. Kelly and Hand (1999) describe the use of survival analysis for a rather different application to credit data. They used survival analysis to compare the distribution of the probability of default of 3861 unsecured personal loans with a loan term of 24 months for different independent variables. Banasik et al., (1999) developed the idea of survival analysis by comparison with logistic regression and other approaches of survival analysis including Cox non-parametric, proportional hazards exponential and proportional hazards Weibull baseline. They showed that survival analysis methods are competitive with logistic regression and may be superior for looking at the customers who pay-off early in the first year. Stepanova and Thomas (2001) tried to develop survival analysis approaches to behavioral scoring by using Cox's proportional hazards model and found that the scores resulting from the model are competitive with logistic regression, especially after two years into the loan. They also found that survival analysis can estimate the profit from the loan. Hand and Kelly (2001, p. 990) showed that none of the previous papers describe survival models over time. They only focused on the survival model with fixed time. Therefore, they provided a new model called look ahead, which assumes that all customers' loans will go bad at some time during the product's term and they concluded that the new model of survival analysis performs better than logistic regression. Stepanova and Thomas (2002) also used survival analysis to build credit-scoring models that estimate the default of loan as well as profits by using a new approach of coarse-classify suggested by authors but the findings were the same as reported by the former article. Baesens et al., (2005) suggested neural network methods for survival analysis methods. They were compared with traditional logistic regression and the authors found that the neural network methods did not significantly outperform the survival analysis method. Andreeva (2006) found that survival analysis is suitable for building generic models and is competitive with logistic regression using data from retail cards from three European countries.

3.4. Choice of Approach

In previous sections, the many techniques for credit scoring were reviewed. The question remains; which is the better technique? There are studies that have searched this question but the answer has not yet been determined. Hand and Henley (1997), for example, showed that there is no overall best method and the best one depends on the data, the variables, and the objective of the classification. Yobas et al., (2000) concluded that there are a number of different things which cause the different results; such as differences in type and size of sample, difference in the ranges of controllable parameters and differences in the transformation applied to the data. Thomas et al., (2005) showed that when the comparison applies, the sophistication and subtlety of the version of each technique used should be taken into consideration.

Thomas et al., (2002) provides a summary of the important results of articles that compared credit-scoring methods, as shown in Table 2. It should be noted that there are significant differences among the techniques in relation to classification accuracy and these studies show different results in respect of the best method. For example, Srinivisan et al., (1987) suggested the classification tree is best, Boyle et al. (1992) and Yobas et al., (2000) found that linear regression classified better while Henley and Hand (1996) reported that neural networks have an advantage over other methods considering bad risk and Desai et al., (1997) suggested logistic regression is best.

Over more than a decade plenty of papers have been published about combining the result of different techniques in relation to classification. Zhu et al., (2001, p. 974) presented strategies which combine these techniques into three categories; static-parallel, multistage, or dynamic. The static-parallel considers the classification in parallel with the combination rule built only once and then applied to each technique. Multistage assumes that the classification techniques have different stages that can be applied to reduce the set of possible classes. Dynamic evaluates the efficiency of each classification techniques over the attribute space and uses accuracy estimates to choose the best techniques.

Table 2. Comparison of credit-scoring approaches for classification accuracy

Study	Linear regression	Logistic regression	Classification tree	Linear programming	Neural networks	Genetic algorithms
Srinivisan et al.,(1987)	87.5	89.3	93.2	86.1	–	–
Boyle et al.,(1992)	77.5	–	75.0	74.7	–	–
Henley and Hand (1996)	43.4	43.3	43.8	–	43.1	–
Yobas et al., (1997)	68.4	–	62.3	–	62.0	64.5
Desai et al., (1997)	66.5	67.3	–	–	66.4	–

Table 3.3 summarises the main advantages and disadvantages of the credit-scoring methods. Credit-scoring models have been applied to three categories; consumer loans, small business loans and corporate loans. In consumer loans, models of scoring are applied to several products such as mortgage, home loans, car loans, farm loans and credit cards.

When the sample is selected in credit-scoring models it is categorized into groups; loans defined as good or bad. Asch (1995) defines a good loan as one had not been 30 days delinquent more than twice during the first four years while a bad loan as one had been delinquent at least once during 60 days or more. However, the definition of bad can be related to other events such as bankruptcy. In addition, the definition of bad and good loan differs according to the type of loan. For example overdraft accounts with no fixed expected monthly repayment cannot be in arrears. Therefore, it is important to identify a sound definition of good and bad loans because the different definitions may create different results when the credit-scoring model is built.

Table 3. Advantages and disadvantages of credit-scoring methods

Technique	Advantages	Disadvantages
Linear probability	Understandable and easy to use Deals with large sample	Estimated probabilities lie outside the 0,1 interval
Logistic	Restrict the probability to the 0,1 interval Does not require restrictive hypotheses of variables	Interpreting parameters is not easy Does not consider the correlation between independent variables
Probit	Restrict the probability to the 0,1 interval Overcome sample selection bias	Interpreting parameters is not easy
Discriminant	Does not involve complicated mathematics Has good performance	It is dependent on a relatively equal distribution of group membership It includes restrictive statistical requirements
Classification tree	Considers more complex problems Deals with many variables	Difficult to understand
Nearest neighbors	The residues are assigned a value in each class rather than binary decision Good performance	Very sensitive to the presence of irrelevant parameters Slow performance
Linear programming	Easy to score problems with large variables Easy to include bias	Low prediction accuracy Difficult to understand
Neural networks	Deals with problem containing many parameters Detects Type I error better than other methods	Slow performance Difficult to determine how this method is making its decision
Genetic algorithms	Less susceptible to optimal solution Evaluation function does not require linearity	Does not have theoretical framework for the evolutionary process It is very hard to use for predictors
Survival	Deals easily with censored data It allows the probability at a point in time to differ from the probability at different point in time.	The relative ranking among applicants of the risk does not vary over time.

Once the definition of loans has been identified, statistical and mathematical techniques such as those in Table 3 are usually proposed to distinguish between the groups. Most of the techniques used in this survey have meaningful results, good performance in classifying loans and an ability to build credit scoring.

Furthermore, some of these studies compared the results of these techniques and show that there are only small differences in the classifying accuracy and others show that discriminant analysis was superior to the other techniques in predictive performance. On the other hand, some studies show that survival analysis offers a number of benefits that make it more attractive if compared to logistic regression.

4. EMPIRICAL CONSIDERATIONS

4.1. Independent Variables in Credit Scoring

Table 4 provides details of selected recent credit-scoring analyses. As shown, independent variables play an important role in building credit-scoring models. Independent variables can be extracted from the application forms and credit bureaus. They may differ from country to country. For example, in Germany the applicant is asked if he has yet completed his military obligation. In Italy, lenders ask for province of birth and the marital contract. In France and Belgium, lenders ask for country of origin, language and the duration of time the applicant has been in the country. Some of variables are prohibited for legal reasons. The US and UK, for example, have legislation that prohibits the discrimination in the granting of credit on the basis of race, color, national origin, sex, marital status, religion, age, or receipt of public assistance. Andreeva et al., (2004b) showed that the previous empirical research suggested that forbiddance of variables may not only have an effect on the ability to discriminate between good and bad loans, but may also have a negative impact on the groups the legislation is supposed to protect. However, Johnson (1998) argues that all of the prohibited variables should be included for statistical purposes.

Independent variables types rely on the loan types. In case of a loan grant to a company, a number of financial ratios of an applicant are recorded including profitability, solvency, leverage and liquidity. Most of these financial ratios take from the financial statements prepared by the borrower. However, decisions about consumer loans are made by evaluating the applicant's creditworthiness including home ownership, income, occupation, number of dependents and so on. Vojtek and Kocenda (2006) divided independent variables into four categories: demographic indicators, financial indicators, employment indicators and behavioral indicators. Demographic indicators contain characteristics such as age, marital status, gender, number of children and residential status. Crook et al., (1992b) showed that demographic indicators may be expected to enter both the utility function and scoring functions of lenders. For instance, Coval et al., (2000) found that women default less frequently on loans possibly because they are more risk averse. Thanh and Kleimeier (2006) showed that older borrowers are more risk averse and will therefore be less likely to default. Vojtek and Kocenda (2006) showed that home owners are less risky because they can provide their houses as collateral.

Financial indicators contain characteristics such as income and expenditures of an applicant. The importance of these indicators is evident (Vojtek and Kocenda, 2006). The third set of indictors is employment status, which includes characteristics such as type of occupation and time with employer. Vojtek and Kocenda (2006) shows that self-employed frequently receives a lower score in the evaluation of loan applications than employed persons because of lack of stability of employment. In addition, Thanh and Kleimeier (2006) mentioned that Crook et al., (1992) found more stable employment means higher ability to repay loans. The last set of characteristics is the behavioral indicators which relate to the type of an applicant's account, the average balance of account, loans outstanding, number of payment per year and the collateral. In the view of lenders, collateral is considered one of the most important variables used in determining a bank's lending decision because it is the source of repayment the debt.

Table 4. Credit-scoring survey

Author(s)	Sample	Explanatory variables	Analytical technique	Main findings
Herbert (1992)	125 loan applications, United States.	Residence status, years with employer, whether a credit card held, whether a store account held, type of bank account, occupation, previous account status, credit bureau report.	Neural networks.	Building s neural network has ability to analyze the credit risk of loan applications; quite practical and can be performed quite easily.
Lawrence and Smith (1992)	42,000 loans 1980s United States.	Payment history of borrower, loan amount, initial loan to value ratio, initial annual percentage rate, original maturity, current loan characteristics, residence status, monthly income, occupation, number of dependents, current age of borrower, unemployment rate in state , retail sales per household in state, effective buying income per household in state, average mobile home price by state in year, average number of months to complete foreclosure, number of months borrower has to redeem property after foreclosure.	Logit models.	Loans which are several years old, the borrower payment history is paramount in estimating default risk.
Crook, Hamilton and Thomas (1992a)	1,001 credit card applicants 1986-1987 United Kingdom..	Postcode, age of applicant, number of children, number of dependents, whether an applicant has a home phone, spouse's income, applicant's employment status, applicant's employment category, years at present employment, applicant's income, residential status, years at present address, estimated value of home, mortgage balance outstanding, years at bank, whether a current account is held, whether a deposit account is held, whether a loan account is held, whether a check guarantee card is held, whether a major credit card is held, whether a charge card is held, whether a store card is held, whether a building society card is held, value of outgoings.	Discriminant analysis.	Using discriminant analysis can discriminate between those who miss one or more payments and those who do not, and between those who miss three consecutive payments and those who do not.
Narain (1992)	1242 loan applicants 1986 – 1988.	Marital status, % deposit, whether an applicant has a home phone, residential status, time at address, time with bank, time with employer.	Multiple regression-Survival analysis.	Survival analysis adds an additional dimension to that provided by standard scorecard.

Author(s)	Sample	Explanatory variables	Analytical technique	Main findings
Boyle, Crook, Hamilton and Thomas (1992)	1,001 credit card applicants 1986-1987 United Kingdom.	Postcode, age, number of children, number of dependents, whether an applicant has a home phone, spouse's income, applicant's employment status, applicant's employment category, years at present employment, applicant's income, residential status, years at present address, estimated value of home, mortgage balance outstanding, years at bank, whether a current account is held, whether a deposit account is held, whether a loan account is held, whether a check guarantee card is held, whether a major credit card is held, whether a charge card is held, whether a store card is held, whether a building society card is held, value of outgoings.	Linear discriminant analysis- Recursive Partitioning Algorithm.	Linear discriminant analysis seems marginally more satisfactorily and uses all the data in all scoring weightings.
Ziari, Leatham and Turvey (1995)	1,199 loans Province 1981-1983 Canada.	Liquidity ratio, rate of return on assets, debt-to-asset ratio, loan-to-security ratio, contribution, margin, repayment ratio, refinancing status.	Discriminant analysis, logit analysis, mathematical programming	There are only small differences in the classifying accuracy of statistical and mathematical programming.
Dionne, Artfs and Guilldn (1996)	4,691 loans 1989 Spain.	Date of birth, marital status, number of non-payments, number of months from the beginning of the contract at the sampling date, level of education, if the client receives the salary through the bank, net monthly income, amount of income, housing ownership, geographical location, monthly instalment, availability of credit card, requested amount, interest rate, date of loan contract.	Logit model.	The methodology increases the degree of flexibility in comparison with standard count models.
Novak and LaDue (1994)	70 New York State dairy farms 1985-1993 United States.	Solvency ratios, liquidity ratios, debt/assets ratio, coverage ratios, credit evaluation model.	Logistic regression-OLS.	The average models' creditworthiness prediction rates are more accurate than the annual models' creditworthiness prediction rates.
Glen (1997)	21 firms before bankruptcy and 25 firms not bankrupt.	Cash flow to total debt, net income to total assets, current assets to current liabilities, current assets to net sales.	Mixed integer programming	The result of mixed integer programming overcomes the limitations of standard linear programming and it can be extended to allow variables to be selected in a stepwise manner.

Table 4. (Continued)

Author(s)	Sample	Explanatory variables	Analytical technique	Main findings
Desai, Conway, Jonathan, Crook and Overstreet (1996)	Three samples 962 – 918 - 856 loan files credit unions 1988- 1991 United States.	Number of major credit cards, residential status, salary plus other income, rating of credit bureau reports, number of years on current job, number of dependents, number of inquiries in past 7 months, number of months since trade lines (different loan accounts)opened, monthly payments as a proportion of income, age of borrower, number of year at the current address, number of open accounts on credit bureau reports, number of active accounts on credit bureau reports, number of previous loans with credit union, information based upon 01-09 ratings on credit bureau reports.	Linear discriminant analysis-Logistic regression, Genetic algorithm- Neural networks.	Neural networks performed somewhat better than the other methods for classifying the most difficult group (bad loans).
Stewart and Whittaker (1998)	7,702 credit card applicants 1992 United Kingdom.	Bank account type, own check guarantee card, number of children, employment status, whether an applicant has a home phone, income band, marital status, residential status, time at address, time at employment, age of applicant.	Graphical models.	Display and interpretation of multivariate interactions between variables. Useful in building models in credit scoring.
Schreiner and Nagagajan (1998)	7,16 loans 1993 Gambia.	Number in family, gender, age of applicant, education of applicant, household size, informal borrowing, loan size, the size of instalments, the number of instalments.	Bivariate probit model.	Some publicly observable characteristics help predict creditworthiness.
Banasik, Crook and Thomas (1999)	50,000 loans 1994 - 1997 United Kingdom.	Age of applicant, marital status, employment status, residency type, the purpose of loan, terms of loan whether an applicant has a home phone, monthly income.	Logistic regression - Survival analysis.	Using survival analysis in credit scoring has meaningful results.
Kelly and Hand (1999)	3,861 unsecured loans United Kingdom.	Average balance for the month, credit turnover during the month, balance at the end of the month, minimum balance attained during the month, maximum balance attained during the month, current overdraft excess.	Global models.	Global models perform at least as well as purpose –built scorecards by constructing separate scorecards for each new definition of 'good'.
Yobas, Crook and Ross (2000)	1,001 credit card applicants 1986-1987 United Kingdom.	Applicant's employment status, years at bank home, mortgage value, number of children, years at present employment, residential status, types of account, other cards held, outgoings, estimated value of home, home phone, applicant income, major credit cards held, spouse's income.	Linear discriminant analysis- neural networks, decision trees, genetic algorithms.	Linear discriminant analysis was superior to those other three techniques in predictive performance.

Author(s)	Sample	Explanatory variables	Analytical technique	Main findings
Chen and Astebro (2001)	4,589 observations in 1993 and 2,805 observations in1998 United States.	Delinquency, trade type, owned other assets, has any account payable, ratio of sales/total expense, ratio of sales/total liability, ratio of profit/total liability, age of principal owner, years at work experience, age of firm, location of main office and sales area, sales national or international, line of credit, capital lease from financial insinuations, other loans, if the firm owned any other assets.	Reject inference model-logit model- Heckman's bivariate two stage probit model-augmentation model, logit model with the proposed maximum likelihood reject inference technique.	Reject inference technique would improve the classification power for credit scoring when samples suffer from a selection bias caused by credit applicants being rejected. It is an efficient reject inference technique when logit regression is used for credit scoring.
Frame, Srinivasan and Woosley (2001)	99 banks 1993-1997 United States.	Total equity capital/ total domestic banking assets, net commercial loan charge-offs/ total commercial and industrial loans, total loans/ total domestic banking assets, number of subsidiary banks, number of branches, total domestic banking assets acquired in previous two years/ total domestic banking assets, the natural logarithm of total domestic banking assets, scoring (dummy variables), small business ratios.	OLS and probit model.	Credit scoring increased the portfolio share of small business loans by 8.4% for sample organization. Credit-scoring models lowers information cost between borrowers and lenders.
Collins, Harvey and Nigro (2002)	2,266 unsecured home loan applications United States.	Applicant income, credit bureau score, customer address, number of bank trade lines, number of finance company inquiries, number of overall inquires, number of times 30-60 days late, revolving credit limit, number of satisfactory trade lines, age of trade file in months.	Logistic regression.	Low-to-moderate income applicants' fare significantly worse in a customized scoring environment when compared to machine-replicated judgmental regression model. Financial regulators should focus more resources on the evaluation and study of customized scoring models.
Stepanova and Thomas (2002)	50,000 loans 1994-1997 United Kingdom.	Customer age, amount of loan, account closing date, years at current address, years with current employer, customer gender, number of dependent children, frequency paid, home phone, insurance premium, loan type, marital status, account opening date, term of loan, home ownership, purpose of loan.	Survival analysis.	Using survival analysis from reliability and maintenance modeling allows one to build credit-scoring models that assess aspects of profit as well as default.
Bugera, Konno and Uryasev (2002)	150 credit card applications 1995-1996 Greece.	Family status, profession, business telephone number, residence, bank account for credit card payments, age, years at business.	Mathematical programming algorithms.	The approach used leads to quite robust classification techniques. The including constraints based on expert judgments and improve the performance of the algorithm.

Table 4. (Continued)

Author(s)	Sample	Explanatory variables	Analytical technique	Main findings
Jacobson and Rozbach (2003)	13,338 loan applications 1994 -1995 Sweden.	Age of applicant, gender, marital status, house (own or rent), big city, number of requests for information on the applicant that the credit agency received during the last 36 months, taxable income, change in annual income, taxable income from capital, ratio of total collateral, free credit facilities actually utilized and income, collateral, free loans outstanding, amount of credit granted, applicant has a guarantor.	Bivariate probit model.	Value-at-risk calculations indicate that an efficient selection of loan applicants can reduce credit risk by up to 80%.
Schall (2003)	7,50 loans 1990- 1999 United States.	Loan decision variables (32 variables) (management capacity, business financial condition personal financial condition, personal credit history, collateral/co-borrower factors), loan performance factors (5 variable) (loan delinquency data, loan loss data), loan descriptors (6 variables)(loan number, original and outstanding loan amount, data of loan origination), (demography variables) (5 variables) race and gender of primary borrowers, household income of primary borrowers, year business started.	Regression analysis.	Credit scoring will never entirely replace judgmental-based underwriting at CDFIs, but it can be used to select the best and worst loan applications.
Roszbach (2004)	13,338 loan applications 1994 -1995 Sweden.	Gender, age of applicant, marital status, months since migration, months since change in marital status, nationality, zip code, owns company, pieces of real estate that are owned, assessed value of real estate, information requests credit agency received in past 3 years, annual income before taxes, business income, capital income, capital costs, general, deductions, individual's share of the family's assets, family total assets, prepaid income tax, number of loans registered, collateral, product type, status of an account, amount of credit granted, amount of credit utilized, applicant has guarantor.	Bivariate and univariate Tobit Bivariate and univariate Logit.	Tobit model is shown to be a useful tool to predict the expected survival time on a loan for any kind of applicant and increases the portfolio's average survival time.
Till and Hand (2003)	88,577 delinquency accounts 1995- 1996 United Kingdom.	whether an applicant has a home phone, time in job, number of dependents, time at address, time at bank, income, values of balance, number of cash advances, value of cash advances, value of sales vouchers.	Markov chain models – the logistic discriminant.	These models can be used to predict likely future behaviour, and can also serve as the basis of predictions of what one might expect when economic circumstances change.

Author(s)	Sample	Explanatory variables	Analytical technique	Main findings
Baesens, Van Gestel, Viaene, Stepanova, Suykens and Vanthienen (2003)	39,003 loan data Belgium- The Netherlands- Luxembourg, UK- Germany- Australia.	N/A	Logistic regression- Linear and quadratic discriminant analysis- Linear programming- Least squares support vector machines- Neural networks- Naïve Bayes -Nearest-neighbor.	The RBF least squares support vector machines and nearest-neighbor classifiers yield a good performance in terms of both PCC and AUC. Linear classifiers also gave very good performances.
Astebro and Bernhadt (2003)	738 loan applicants 1982- 1992 United States.	Education level of applicant, occupation, former owner, if any owner in the firm had a start-up commercial bank loan, if any owner financed the start-up with a loan from either friends, family, spouse, former owner, or home mortgage, experience of owner, number of owners, firm capital, time as owner.	Probit regression model.	There is a negative correlation between having a bank loan and business survival and positive correlation between having a non-bank loan and survival.
Jung, Thomas and Thomas (2003)	331 loan applicants United Kingdom.	whether an applicant has a home phone, gender, marital status, number of children, number of credit card, some income from loan, some income from wage, some income parental contribution, interest in travel, interest in music, interest in cars, interest in cinema, interest in sport, interest in clubbing, interest in beer, interest in gardening, overdraft limit, credit card including with account, no fees in ordering foreign currency for travel, discounts on insurance, interest paid when account in surplus, introductory, free gift.	Logistic regression model- linear programming- accelerated life model.	It is possible to build acceptance probability models using such data and makes a preliminary investigation of three different approaches. All three approaches can result in real time decisions in order to maximize profit.
Chen and Astebro (2003)	7,394 loans 1993 - 1998 United States.	Delinquency of loan, trade type, owned other assets, has any account payable, ratio of sales/total expense, ratio of sales/total liability, ratio of profit/total liability, age of principal owner, years at work experience, age of firm, location of main office and sales area, sales national or international, line of credit, capital lease from financial insinuations, other loans, if the firm owned any other assets.	Two stage probit model- reject inference model.	The model will improve classification power when there is sample selection bias caused by data missing not at random. Under missing at random or models may not be superior to simply dropping missing data.

Table 4. (Continued)

Author(s)	Sample	Explanatory variables	Analytical technique	Main findings
Schreiner (2003a)	39,956 loans 1988-1996 10555 loans 1997 Bolivia.	Previous loans, months since first loans, longest spell in days, number of spells, gender, sector, amount disbursed, guarantee branch experience of loan officer in months.	Logit Regression.	A scoring model for arrears suggested that it can help microfinance. Microloan scorecard will give an accurate estimate of the risk of the poor. Scoring will not replace loan officer, but it can flag high-risk cases and act to cross-check on loan officer's judgment.
Verstraeten and Van Den Poel (2003a)	41,510 loans 2000- 2000 Belgian.	Home status, occupation, bank account type, debt amount, delinquency, black list, credit history.	Logistic regression.	The sample bias does not appear to have a negative influence on credit-scoring performance and profitability.
Chye, Chin and Peng (2004)	4,117 credit card one year.	Age of applicant, annual income, gender, marital status, number of children, number of other credit card cards held, whether the applicant has an outstanding mortgage loan.	Data mining techniques, logistic regression, neural network, decision tree.	The decision tree model is the best prediction model and it is easy to interpret. Credit scoring will continue to be a major tool in predicting credit risk in consumer lending.
Crook, Thomas and Hamilton (2004)	26,043 credit card applicants 1989-1990 United Kingdom.	Age of applicant in 1990, number of children, number of dependents, whether an applicant has a home phone, spouse's income, spouse's employment category, applicant's employment status, applicant's employment category, years at present employment, applicant's income, residential status, years at present address, estimated value of home, mortgage balance outstanding, years at same bank, whether a current account is held, whether a deposit account is held, whether a loan account is held, whether a check guarantee card is held, whether a major credit card is held, whether a charge card is held, whether a store card is held, whether a building society card is held, value of outgoings.	Linear discriminant analysis.	Changing the cut-off scores to maintain the same reject rate will not restore the decision for each applicant.
Crook and Banasik (2004)	8,139 loan applicants 1997 United Kingdom.	Time at present address, weeks since last county court judgment, television area code, age of applicant, number of children under 16, whether an applicant has a home phone, type of bank/building society accounts, occupation code, current electoral role category, years on electoral role at current address, number of searches in last 6 months, and other bureau variables.	Logistic regression.	Measures of predictive performance of accepted applicants are liable to be misleadingly optimistic. Useful implementation of reject inference depends on accurate estimation of the potential good-bad ratio for the population of all applicants.

Author(s)	Sample	Explanatory variables	Analytical technique	Main findings
Schreiner (2004)	37,982 loans 1996 Bolivia.	Loan size, gender, sector, experience of the borrower, arrears, loan officer, experience of the loan officer, branch.	The logit model.	Credit scoring may help microfinance lenders to detect segments of their clients who are at risk of drop-out. Credit scoring may become common among the largest micro lenders in low-income countries.
Avery, Calem and Canner (2004)	90,357 Credit accounts 1997 – 1999 United States.	Average unemployment rate, married (new, recent, other), divorced (new, other), never married, period of deliquesces (one month, half year, one year, disappeared), kind of loans (revolving, instalment, mortgages, line-of –credit accounts), account age, age of individual.	OLS.	Generic credit history scoring models of consumer credit do not factor in local economic circumstances.
Andreeva, Ansell and Crook (2004b)	75,848 store card 1998- 1999 Germany.	whether an applicant has a home phone, residential status, marital status, occupation, applicant's age, time at address, time in employment, type of business, employer's phone, number of dependents, spouse's age, card insurance, credit insurance, product, type, product price, payment date, contract type.	Survival analysis.	Using survival probability of default and the survival probability of second purchase rather than a logistic regression improves profit.
Frame, Padhi and Woosley (2004)	99 banks 1993-1997 United States.	The banking organization use of credit scoring, the natural logarithm of total domestic banking assets, ratio of small business loans to total domestic banking assets, leverage ratios (total equity to total assets), rural(dummy variable), median household income, total small business revenues, the percent of individuals identified as Asian, the percent of individuals identified as Black, whether the banking organization has a bank branch located in the census tract, whether the banking organization has a bank branch located in the relevant geographic banking market.	Regression analysis, Tobit procedure.	Credit scoring increases small business lending in LMI census tracts by $ 16.4 million.
Cramer (2004)	20,862 loans The Netherlands.	The ratio of own capital to the balance-sheet total, the ratio of gross returns to the balance-sheet total, the ratio of working capital to the balance-sheet total, the ratio of cash flow to the interest and repayments due, dummy variable for the presence of material stocks.	Plain logit, logit - Nearest-neighbor analysis.	The performance of these methods is nearly same.

Table 4. (Continued)

Author(s)	Sample	Explanatory variables	Analytical technique	Main findings
Andreeva, Ansell and Crook (2005)	(44,256- 13,1190- 137,136card applicants) Belgium, The Netherlands and Germany 1998-2000.	whether an applicant has a home phone, residential status, marital status, occupation, age of applicant, time at address since 18 years old, time in employment, type of business, employer's phone, card insurance, credit insurance, number of dependents, spouse age, goods code, goods price, payment data.	Logistic regression generic model.	The generic model showed an adequate predictive performance comparable to that of its national counterparts. Generic models are less costly in terms of development and maintenance.
Akhavein, Frame and White (2005)	99 banks 1993-1997 United States.	the natural logarithm of total domestic banking assets, the ratio of small loans to businesses to total domestic banking assets, number of subsidiary banks, number of branches, net income as percent of total equity capital (profitability), the ratio of noninterest income to net operation revenue, the length of time that an executive has been with an organization.	Hazard model and Tobit model.	The likelihood of adopting small business credit scoring was positive. Various chief executive officer characteristics did not have significant explanatory power in statistical tests.
Berger, Frame and Miller (2005)	99 banks 1995-1997 United States.	Whether a bank had adopted small business credit scoring, number of years since the bank opened, whether the bank purchased credit scores from a vendor, whether the bank used small business scoring to set loan terms, whether the bank used small business scoring to automatically approve or reject loan application, the natural logarithm of gross total assets, ratio of nonperforming loans to total loans, the ratio of net income to equity, the ratio of equity to gross total assets, weighted average of Herfindal indices of local markets in which the bank has deposits, weighted average of local market nonperforming loans, weighted average of local market ROE, weighted average of local market equity ratio, proportion of bank loans that are collateralized, proportion of bank loans drawn under commitment, the weighted average scheduled time until the principal and interest on the bank's average loan is repaid , proportion of bank loans with a floating rate of interest, average size of loans measured by the maximum of the loan amount and the amount commitment if any, small business loans/ total assets, the loan rate premium, risk-rating.	OLS- Logit	Small business credit scoring is associated with expanding quantities of small business credit at rising average prices and increasing credit risk. Small business credit scoring is associated with no significant change in credit availability, lower prices and diminished loan credit risk for slightly larger credit.

Author(s)	Sample	Explanatory variables	Analytical technique	Main findings
Finlay (2006)	88,792 credit applications 2002 United Kingdom.	Age of applicant, accommodation status, council tax banding, employment type, employment status, gross annual income, home phone indicator, marital status, mortgage indicator, number of credit cards, number of dependents, time at address, time with bank, time in current employment, in addition to 37 variable from UK credit bureaus.	OLS regression (stepwise and non-stepwise), logistic regression (stepwise and non-stepwise), neural network, Genetic Algorithm.	Genetic Algorithm derived models can perform as well as other approaches to model development when measured in terms of GINI and misclassification rates for a range of cut-off scenarios, but in other cases the performance can be marginally worse.
Andreeva (2006)	(26,290-82,237-75,848) credit card applicants 1998-2000 Belgium, The Netherlands and Germany.	whether an applicant has a home phone , residential status, marital status, occupation, age, time at address since 18 years old, time in employment, type of business, employer's phone, card insurance, credit insurance, number of dependents, spouse age, goods code, goods price, payment data.	Survival analysis, logistic regression, non-parametric Cox PH model.	The predictive accuracy is not affected by using the approaches. The survival analysis offers a number of benefits that make it more attractive if compared to Logistic regression.
Baesens, Van Gestel, Sepanova and Van de Poel (2005)	50,000 loans 1994-1997 United Kingdom.	Customer age, amount of loan years at current address, years with current employer, customer gender, number of dependent children, frequency paid, home phone number given, insurance premium, loan type, marital status, term of loan, home ownership, purpose of loan.	The statistical and neural network survival analysis techniques, logistic regression model.	These models suffer from a number of drawbacks. The neural network approach did not significantly outperform survival analysis.
De Waal, Toit and Rey (2005)	59,60 home equity loans South Africa.	Reason of loan, job type, loan amount, amount due to existing mortgage, value of current property, debt to income ratio, years at present job, number of derogatory reports, number of trade lines, number of delinquent trade lines, age of the oldest trade line in months, number of credit inquires.	Logistic regression, Generalized additive neural networks model.	The pre-processing step exploits generalized additive models to achieve significant reductions in marginal and cumulative bad rates.

Table 4. (Continued)

Author(s)	Sample	Explanatory variables	Analytical technique	Main findings
Sarlija, Bensic and Bohacek (2005)	44,089 customer accounts 2004 Croatia.	Client's age, client's gender, working status, living in town or city, has a second job, has a credit card, age of the client's account, has saving account, contracted overdraft, cash payments to the account, payments to the account from other accounts, irregular, payments to the account, regular payments(salaries), interests paid to the client, withdrawals with standing order, withdrawals with cheques, withdrawals with credit and debit card, cash withdrawals from the account, interests paid from the client, total payment to the account, total payment to the account/ contracted overdraft, balance, balance plus contracted overdraft, total payments to the account/ total withdrawals from the account, percentage of usage of contracted overdraft, how many times client's overdraft exceeded contracted overdraft.	Logistic regression- Cox's regression.	Logistic regression and Cox's regression identify a group of the same variables being important in consumer behavior with the difference that in logistic regression scoring model some additional variables were extracted.
Holmes, Isham, Petersen and Sommers (2005)	609 car loan applications 1998- 2002 United States.	Age of applicant, resident in bank's town, years at present address, relationship, monthly income, missing monthly income, declared bankruptcy, co-applicant, credit score, missing credit score, car value, loan-to-value ratio, mark up, missing mark up	Probit regression.	Financial information, particularly credit score, is the primary determinant of loan approval at the community bank
Glennon and Nigro (2005)	29,577 small businesses loans 1984- 2001.	Percentage of outstanding loan balance guaranteed by SBA, straight-line distance in miles between borrower and lending office of the lending institution, natural log of distance, whether lender used credit-scoring models to evaluate at least some of its small business loans, loan interest rate/ prime rate at the time of the loan, loan period, loan age, number of full-time employees at borrowing firm, deposit-based Herfindahl index in local market of the borrower, if borrower is located in a Metropolitan Statistical Area, lender assets, ratio of lender's loan charge-offs to assets, ratio of lender's loan reserves to assets.	Discrete –time hazard model- stacked-logit model.	Borrower lender distance is positively associated with loan default, and that adoption of credit scoring dampens this relationship. Credit-scoring lenders experience higher default rates on average.

Author(s)	Sample	Explanatory variables	Analytical technique	Main findings
Andreeva, Ansell and Crook (2005)	18,040 retail cards Belgium.	whether an applicant has a home phone, residential status, marital status, occupation age, time at address since 18 years old, time in employment, type of business, employer's phone, spouse age, number of dependents, product code, product price, payment date, card insurance, credit insurance, agreement type, difference between the outstanding balance and credit limit at period, delinquency status at period, percent of outstanding balance repaid at period.	Survival analysis.	The results obtained are similar in a large part to those seen when using survival techniques for credit scoring. There are differences that reflect the need for certain customers to use the card to enhance their spending power.
Ziemba (2005)	9,787 customers Poland.	Customer's age when filling application form, customer's gender, level of bad payers in the region of customer's residence, concentration of entrepreneurs in the region of customer's residence, population in the region of customer's residence, information gathered during a verification process, information about customer's choice concerning the offer and product.	Linear and Logistic regression models, classification trees.	It is computationally possible to update scoring models in the form of logistic regression by finding posterior distribution of its parameters based on Markov chains simulation for real data problems encountered in credit-scoring area.
Andreeva, Ansell and Crook (2007)	25,792 credit card applicants 1990s Belgium.	whether an applicant has a home phone, residential status, occupation, spouse age, applicant age, time at address since 18 years old, product code, product price, payment date, difference between the outstanding balance and credit limit at period, percent of outstanding balance repaid at period, delinquency status at period, time in employment, type of business, employer's phone, number of dependents, credit insurance, contract type, card insurance.	Hazard models.	It is important that a lender builds subsequent models after the application model because the incorporation of subsequent data would enhance the predictive performance of the model. There seems to be differentiation between models for the good and for the bad.

The most important independent variables that have been used in evaluating consumer credit risk ranked according to number of usages in studies (Table 3.4) are: age, months at current job, residential status, occupation, marital status, number of dependents, whether an applicant has a home phone, months at current address, monthly income, loan amount, gender, credit card, delinquency, mortgage value, number of children, time with bank, types of bank account, other loans, original maturity, spouse's income, spouse's age, estimated value of home, purpose of loan, credit bureau reports, educational level, rating of credit bureau reports and postcode.

Sample Size Considerations

Credit-scoring models involve a sample of the history of previous borrowers. This sample should be representative of the entire population and it could be applied to credit granting in the future. It should also include the good and bad loans to identify which characteristics reflect this behavior.

The size of samples is a questionable issue (Parnitzke, 2005). However, there is no certain number of samples to be used in credit-scoring models but some studies give opinions related to sample size. Lewis (1992) suggested that there is no certain number of samples but the scoring will perform effectively if the sample consists of 1,500 good, 1,500 bad and 1,000 rejected applications in building credit-scoring models. Nevertheless, it could be said that Lewis' suggestion would be applied when scoring models are established for implementation in real life rather than for research purposes. Lucas and Powell (1997, p. 21) showed that it can use very small samples to construct scoring models. Makuch (1999) showed that a large number of both good and bad applications should be involved to maximize the power of credit-scoring models.

Nevertheless, in Table 3.4, it could be noted that there is no certain number of samples; the size of sample differs from one research to another. Table 3.4 shows many studies that use credit-scoring models with different sample sizes, which differ from one study to another. The biggest sample is 254,630 loans and the smallest one is 125 loans.

When the sample is identified, then it is randomly split into two samples. One is used for estimating credit-scoring model and the other is used as a holdout sample to test it (Thomas et al., 2002).

Hair et al., (1995) show that there are no guidelines for determining the relative sizes of the analysis sample and holdout sub-samples but the most popular approach is to divide the total sample into equal sub-samples.

Thomas et al., (2002) argue that there are two reasons for splitting samples into subpopulations. First, policy reasons which are considered by the lender when building scoring models such as distinguishing between new customers and long existing customers because some variables are available for the new customers but not for the existing customers. Second, the statistical reason that considers the interactions between one variable and the others means that it is rational to build a separate scoring model for the different attributes of that variable.

Another consideration of sampling is the ratio of sample size to the number of independent variables. Hair et al., (2006) show that the minimum size recommended is five observations per independent variable. In addition, the smallest group size of a category must exceed the number of independent variables, at minimum

CONCLUSION

Section 2 of this chapter provided a brief conceptual overview of credit scoring, comprising an explicit definition of credit scoring and the difference between application scoring and behavior scoring. The history of credit-scoring development that occurred over the past century was reviewed. To state the importance of credit scoring, comparisons with judgmental systems, consumer versus business scoring and credit scoring versus credit rating were explained. Section 3 presented credit-scoring approaches used in empirical research. The linear probability model, probit model, logit model and discriminant analysis were reviewed as parametric approaches while recursive partitioning algorithm, nearest-neighbors, linear programming, integer programming, neural networks, genetic algorithms and expert systems were provided as nonparametric approaches. In addition, survival analysis, Bayesian networks and graphical model were introduced as new approaches.

Section 3 also provided a comparison of scoring methods. The main findings of this section are that it could be said that there is no best method in credit scoring to evaluate loan applications. Each method has advantages and disadvantages. Section 4 reviewed credit-scoring models used in empirical studies. It gave a summary of the important variables, techniques, and main findings of studies surveyed over the last decade. The main findings of this section were to examine the extent of applying credit-scoring approaches application in financial institutions. This can help in building the methodology for this research. This section also examined the explanatory variables used in credit-scoring models. It shows the nature of these variables and focuses on a discussion of demographic and financial independent variables. Finally, the section discussed sample considerations for credit-scoring models. It examines the sample size and the reasons for splitting samples into holdout samples and analysis samples. The main contribution of this chapter is to facilitate the selection of variables and techniques used in building credit-scoring models. Clearly, despite some limitations, credit-scoring models will continue to be a major tool in predicting credit risk in consumer lending.

REFERENCES

Agarwal, S. Chomsisengphet, S., and Liu, C. (2007). Determinants of small business default. In G. Christodoulakis and S. Satchell (Eds.), *The analytics of risk model validation* (pp. 1–12). Basingstoke, Palgrave-Macmillan Publishing.

Akhavein, J., Frame, S., and White, L. (2005). The diffusion of financial Innovations: An examination of the adoption of small business credit scoring by large banking organizations. *Journal of Business,* 78(2), 577–596.

Albright H. (1994). *Construction of a polynomial classifier for consumer loan applications using genetic algorithms*, Department of Systems Engineering, Working Paper, University of Virginia.

Alici, Y. (1999). *Neural networks in corporate failure prediction: The UK experience*. In Proc. Third International Conference Neural Networks in the Capital Markets, A. N. Refenes, Y. Abu Mostafa, J. Moody, and A. Weigend. (Eds), London, UK, 393–406.

Allen, L., DeLong, G., and Saunders, A. (2004). Issues in the credit risk modeling of retail markets. *Journal of Banking and Finance,* 28(4), 727–752.

Altman, E. (1968). The prediction of corporate bankruptcy: A discriminant analysis. *Journal of Finance,* 23(1), 193–194.

Altman, E. (1980). Commercial bank lending: Process, credit scoring, and costs of the errors in lending. *The Journal of Financial and Quantitative Analysis,* 15(4), 813–832.

Altman, E., and Izan, H. (1984). Identifying corporate distress in Australia: An industry relative analysis, Working Paper, New York University.

Altman, E., and Narayanan, P. (1997). An international survey of business failure classification models. *Financial Markets, Institutions and Instruments,* 6(2), 1–57.

Altman, E., Avery, R., Eisenbeis, R., and Sinkey, J. (1981). *Application of Classification Techniques in Business, Banking, and Finance.* Greenwich, Conn., Jai Press.

Altman, E., Haldeman, R., and Narayanan, P. (1977). ZETA analysis: A new model to identify bankruptcy risk of corporations. *Journal of Banking and Finance,* 1(1), 129–54.

Andreeva, G. (2006). European generic scoring models using survival analysis. *Journal of Operational Research Society,* 57(10), 1180–1187.

Andreeva, G. Ansell, J., and Crook, J. (2004a). Impact of anti-discrimination laws on credit scoring. *Journal of Financial Services Marketing,* 9(1), 22–33.

Andreeva, G., Ansell, J., and Crook, J. (2004b). *Credit scoring in the context of the European integration: Assessing the performance of the generic models.* Credit Research Centre, School of Management. Working Papers 2004, University of Edinburgh.

Andreeva, G., Ansell, J., and Crook, J. (2005). Modeling the purchase propensity: Analysis of a revolving store card, *Journal of the Operational Research Society,* 56(9), 1041–1050.

Andreeva, G., Ansell, J., and Crook, J. (2007). Modeling profitability using survival combination scores, *European Journal of Operational Research*, 183(3), 1537–1549.

Apilado, V. Warner, D., and Dauten, J. (1974). Evaluating techniques in consumer finance–experiment results and policy implications for financial institutions. *The Journal of Financial and Quantitative Analysis,* 9(2), 275–283.

Ariyo, A., and Abegunde, E. (1992). Predictive accuracy of judgmental vs. statistical approaches to bank loan appraisal: Empirical evidence from Nigeria. *Managerial Finance,* 18(6), 4–14.

Avery, R., Bostic, R., Calem, B., and Canner, G. (1996). Credit risk, credit scoring, and the performance of home mortgages. *Federal Reserve Bulletin*, 82(7), 621–648.

Avery, R., Bostic, R., Calem, B., and Canner, G. (2000). Credit scoring: Statistical issues and evidence from credit-bureau files. *Real Estate Economics,* 28(3), 523–547.

Avery, R., Calem, P., and Canner, G. (2004). Consumer credit scoring: Do situational circumstances matter? *Journal of Banking and Finance,* 28(4), 835–856.

Baesens, B., Emgont-Petersen, M., Castelo, R., and Vanthienen, J. (2002). Learning Bayesian Network Classifiers for Credit Scoring using Markov Chain Monte Carlo Search, Technical report, No. UU-CS-2001-58, Institute of Computer and Information Sciences, Utrecht University.

Baesens, B., Van Gestel, T., Stepanova, M., Suyken, J., and Vanthienen, J. (2003). Benchmarking state-of-the-art classification algorithms for credit scoring. *Journal of the Operational Research Society,* 54(6), 627–635.

Banasik, J., and Crook, J. (2005). *Explaining aggregate consumer delinquency behavior over time.* Credit Research Centre, Working Paper Series No 05/03, University of Edinburgh.

Bank for International Settlements (BIS). (2000). *Range of practice in banks' internal ratings systems.* A discussion paper, the Basel Committee on Banking Supervision, retrieved September 22, 2006, from http://www.bis.org.

Bardos, M. (1998). Detecting the risk of company failure at the Banque de France. *Journal of Banking and Finance,* 22(10), 1405–1419.

Bardos, M., and Zhu, W.(1998). Comparison of linear discriminant analysis and neutral networks, application for the detection of company failures. *Bio-mimetic Approaches in Management Science*, Kluwer Academic Publishers 1998, 77–100.

Berger, A., Frame, S., and Miller, N. (2005). Credit scoring and the availability, price, and risk of small business credit. *Journal of Money, Credit, and Banking,* 37(2), 191–222.

Betts, J. and Belhoul, D. (1987). The effectiveness of incorporating stability measures in company failure models. *Journal of Business Finance and Accounting*, 14(3), 323–334.

Bovenzi, J., Marino, J., and McFadden, F. (1983). Commercial bank failure prediction models, *Economic Review*, Federal Reserve Bank Atlanta, November 1983, 14–26.

Boyes, W., Hoffman, D., and Low, S. (1989). An econometric analysis of the bank credit-scoring problem. *Journal of Econometrics,* 40(1), 3–14.

Boyle, M., Crook, J., Hamilton, R., and Thomas, L. (1992) *Methods for credit scoring applied to slow payers*. In: Thomas, L., Crook, J., and Edelman, D. (Eds), Credit scoring and credit control, Oxford University Press, Oxford, 75-90.

Bramma, K. (1999). An evaluation of bank credit policies for farm loan portfolios using the simulation approach. PhD thesis, University of Sydney.

Bugera, V., Konno, H., and Uryasev, S. (2002). Credit Cards Scoring with Quadratic Utility Functions. *Journal of Multi-Criteria Decision Analysis,* 11, 197–211.

Caire, D., and Kossmann, R. (2003). *Credit Scoring: Is It Right for Your Bank?*, Bannock Consulting. Working Paper, Retrieved June 23, 2006, from http://www.microfinance.com/English/Papers/Scoring_For_Your_Bank.pdf.

Caouette, J., Altman, E., and Narayanan, P. (1998). *Managing Credit Risk: The Next Great Financial Challenge.* New York: John Wiley and Sons.

Capon, N. (1982). Credit scoring systems: A critical analysis. *Journal of Marketing (pre-1986),* 46(2), 82–91.

Carter, C., and Catlett, J. (1987). Assessing credit card applications using machine learning. *IEEE Expert* 2, 71–79.

Chandler, G., and.Coffman, J. (1979). A comparative analysis of empirical versus judgemental credit evaluation, Journal *of Retail Banking*, 1, 15–26.

Chang, E. (2005). *Developing and validating credit scoring model for Taiwan's enterprises.* Paper presented to the 13th Annual Conference on Pacific Basin Finance, Economics, and Accounting, Livingston Student Centre and Janice H. Levin Building Livingston Campus Rutgers University at New Brunswick, New Jersey.

Chang, K., Fung, R., Olveri, R., Lucas, A., and Shikaloff, N. (2000). Bayesian networks applied to credit scoring. *IMA Journal of Mathematics Applied in Business and Industry,* 11(1), 1–18.

Chatterjee, S., and Barcun, S. (1970). A nonparametric approach to credit screening. *Journal of the American Statistical Association,* 65(320), 150–154.

Chen, G., and Astebro, T. (2003). Bound and Collapse Bayesian reject inference When Data are Missing not at Random. When Data are Missing not at Random," in T. Astebro, P. Beling, D. Hand, B. Oliver and L. Thomas (Eds.), *Mathematical approaches to credit risk management* (pp. 11–16). Conference Proceedings, Banff International Research Station for Mathematical Innovation and Discovery.

Chhikara, R. (1989). The state of the art in credit evaluation. *American Journal of Agricultural Economics,* 71(5), 1138–1144.

Chye, K., Chin, T., and Peng, G. (2004). Credit scoring using data mining techniques. *Singapore Management Review,* 26(2), 25–47.

Coats, P., and Fant, F. (1993). Recognizing financial distress patterns using a neural network tool. *Financial Management,* 22(3), 142–155.

Coffman, J. Y. (1986). The proper role of tree analysis in forecasting the risk behaviour of borrowers, Management Decision Systems, Atlanta, MDS Reports 3,4,7, and 9.

Collins, C., Harvey, K., and Nigro, P. (2002). The influence of bureau scores, customized scores, and judgemental Review on the bank underwriting decision-making process. *The Journal of Real Estate Research,* 24(2), 103–120.

Coval, J., Shumway, T. (2000). Do behavioral biases affect prices? Working Paper, University of Michigan.

Crook, J., Hamilton, R., and Thomas, L. (1992a). Credit card holders: Characteristics of users and non-users. *The Service Industries Journal,* 12(2), 251–262.

Crook, J. Hamilton, R. and Thomas, L. (1992b). A comparison of a credit scoring model with a credit performance model. *The Service Industries Journal,* 12(4), 558–579.

Davis, R., Edelman, D., and Gammerman, A. (1992). Machine learning algorithms for credit card applications. *Journal of Mathematics Applied in Business and Industry, 4*, 43–5.

De Wall, D., Toit, J., and Ray, D. (2005). *An investigation into the use of generalized additive neural networks in credit scoring*, Paper presented to the International Conference on Credit Scoring and Credit Control IX, Edinburgh, University of Edinburgh, Scotland.

Dellien, H., and Schreiner, M. (2005). Credit scoring, banks, and microfinance: Balancing high-tech with high-touch. *Microcenterprise Development Review,* 8(2), 1–5.

Desai, V., Conway, D., Crook, J., and Overstreet, J. (1997). Credit scoring models in the credit-union environment using neural networks and genetic algorithms. *IMA Journal of Mathematics Applied in Business and Industry,* 8(4), 323–346.

DeVaney, S., and Lytton, R. (1995). Household insolvency: A review of household debt repayment, delinquency, and bankruptcy. *Financial Services Review,* 4(2), 137–156.

Dionne, G., Artfs, M., and Guillden, M. (1996). Count data models for a credit scoring system. *Journal of Empirical Finance,* 3(3), 303–325.

Dunn, L., and Kim, T. (1999). *An empirical investigation of credit card default.* department of Economics. Working Paper no. 99-13, the Ohio State University.

Durand, D. (1941). Risk elements in consumer installment lending. *Studies in Consumer Installment Financing*, vol. 8, National Bureau of Economic Research, New York.

Eisenbeis, R. (1977). Pitfalls in the application of discriminant analysis in business, finance, and economics. *The Journal of Finance,* 32(3), 875–900.

Ely, D., and Robinson, K. (2001). Consolidation, technology, and the changing structure of banks' small business lending. *Economic and Financial Review,* First Quarter, 23–32.

Feelders, A. (2000). Credit scoring and reject inference with mixture models. *International Journal of Intelligent Systems in Accounting, Finance and Management,* 9(1), 1–8.

Feelders, A. (2003). *An Overview of Model Based Reject Inference for Credit Scoring.* Paper presented to the Banff Credit Risk Conference, 11–16 October, Banff, AB, Canada.

Feldman, R. (1997). Small business loans, small banks and a big change in technology called credit scoring. *The Region,* 11(3), 18–25.

Finlay, S. (2006). *Using genetic algorithms to develop scoring models for alternative measures of performance.* The Department of Management Science, Working Paper 2006/022, Lancaster University Management School.

Fishelson-Holstine, H. (2004). *The role of credit scoring in increasing homeownership for underserved populations.* Joint Centre of Housing Studies, Working Paper BABC 04-12, Harvard University.

Fisher, R. A. (1936). The use of multiple measurements in taxonomic problems. *Annals Engenics,* 7, 179–188.

Frame, S., Srinivasan, A., and Woosley, L. (2001). The effect of credit scoring on small-business lending. *Journal of Money, Credit, and Banking,* 33(3), 813–825.

Freed, N., and Glover, F. (1981). Simple but powerful goal programming models for discriminant problems. *European Journal of Operational Research,* 7, 44–60.

Frydman, H., Altman, E., and Kao, D. (1985). Introducing recursive partitioning for financial classification: The case of financial distress. *The Journal of Finance,* 40(1), 269–291.

Galitz, L. (1983). Interbank: A bank management simulation exercise. *Journal of Banking and Finance,* 7, 355–82.

Gana, R., and Rossi, C. (1997). *An empirical comparison of linear probability and logit models of mortgage default.* Paper presented to the International Conference on Credit Scoring and Credit Control, V, Edinburgh University, Scotland.

Gessner G., Kamakura, W., Malhotra, N., and Zmijewski M. (1988). Estimating models with binary dependent variables: Some theoretical and empirical observations. *Journal of Business Research,* 16(1), 49–65.

Glen, J. J. (1997). Integer programming methods for normalization and variable selection in Mathematical programming models for discriminant analysis. Credit Research Centre, Department of Business Studies. Working Paper Series No. 97/3, University of Edinburgh, UK. .

Glennon, D., and Nigro, P. (2005). An analysis of SBA loan defaults by maturity structure. *Journal of Financial Services Research,* 28, 77–111.

Hamilton, R., and Khan, M. (2001). Revolving credit cardholders: Who are they and how can they be identified? *The Service Industries Journal,* 21(3), 37–48.

Hand, D. (2001). Modeling consumer credit risk. *IMA Journal of Management Mathematics,* 12(2), 139–155.

Hand, D., Oliver, J., and Lunn, D. (1998). Discriminant analysis when the classes arise from a continuum. *Pattern Recognition,* 31(5), 641–650.

Henley, W. (1995). Statistical aspects of credit scoring. PhD thesis, Milton Keynes, United Kingdom.

Henley, W., and Hand, D. (1996). k-nearest- neighbor classifier for assessing consumer credit risk. *The Statistician,* 45(1), 77–95.

Herbert, J. (1992). Using neural networks for verdict scoring. *Managerial Finance,* 18(6), 15–26.

Holmes, J., Isham, J., Petersen, R., and Sommers, P. (2005). Does relationship lending still matter in the consumer banking sector? Evidence from two financial service organizations in Vermont. Department of Economics, Working Paper Series, Middlebury College.

Hu, Y. C., and Ansell, J. (2006). *Developing financial distress prediction models: A study of US, Europe and Japan retail performance.* Management School and Economics, Working Paper, University of Edinburgh.

Huang, J., Tzeng, G., and Ong, C. (2006). Two-stage genetic programming (2SGP) for the credit-scoring model. *Applied Mathematics and Computation,* 174(2), 1039–1053.

Immergluck, D., and Smith, G. (2003). How changes in small business lending affect firms in low- and moderate-income neighborhood. *Journal of Developmental Entrepreneurship,* 8(2), 153–175.

Jacobson, T., and Roszbach, K. (2003). Bank lending policy, credit scoring and value-at-risk. *Journal of Banking and Finance,* 27(4), 615–633.

Joachimsthaler, E. and Stam, A. (1990). Mathematical programming approaches for the classification problem in two-group discriminant analysis. *Multivariate Behavioral Research,* 25, 427–454.

Joachimsthaler, E., and Stam, A. (1988). Four approaches to the classification problem in discriminant analysis: An Experimental Study. *Decision Sciences,* 19(2), 322–333.

Jost, A. (1993). Neural networks. *Credit World,* 81(4), 26–33.

Kalapodas, E., and Thomson, M. (2006). Credit risk assessment: A challenge for financial institutions. *IMA Journal of Management Mathematics,* 17(1), 25–46.

Kaynak, E., Kucukemiroglu, O., and Ozmen, A. (1995). Correlates of credit card acceptance and usage in an advanced developing Middle Eastern country. *Journal of Services Marketing,* 9(4), 52–63.

Kelly, M., and Hand, D. (1999). Credit scoring with uncertain class definitions. *IMA Journal of Mathematics Applied in Business and Industry,* 10(4), 331–345.

Kim, K., and Scott, J. (1991). Prediction of corporate failure: An artificial neural network approach. Southwest Missouri State University, Working Paper, September.

Kimenyi, M., Wieland, R., and Pischke, J. (1998). *Strategic Issues in Microfinance*. England: Ashgate Publishing.

King, R., Henery, R., Feng, C., and Sutherland, A. (1994). *A comparative study of classification algorithms: statistical machine learning and neural network.* In Machine Intelligence (Eds). K. Furukwa. D. Michie, and S Muddleton. 13, Oxford University Press, Oxford.

Koehler, G., and Erenguc, S. (1990). Minimizing misclassifications in linear discriminant analysis. *Decision Sciences,* 21(1), 63–85.

Komorad, K. (2002). On credit scoring estimation. Master thesis, Humboldt University.

Lawrence, E., and Smith, D. (1992). An analysis home credit of default risk in mobile. *Journal of Banking and Finance,* 16(2), 299–312.

Lewis, E. M. (1992). *An Introduction to Credit Scoring.* San Rafael, CA: Fair, Isaac and Co. California, USA: Athena Publishing

Liao, T. F. (1994). Interpreting probability models: Logit, probit, and other generalized linear models. Thousand Oaks, Calif., Sage.

Liu, Y. (2001). *New issues in credit scoring application.* Institute of Information Systems, Working paper, University of Gottingen.

Longenecker, J., Moore, C., and Petty, J. (1997). *Credit Scoring and the Small Business: A Review and the Need for Research.* Texas, USA: Baylor University.

Lucas, A. (2001). Statistical challenges in credit card issuing. *Applied Stochastic Models in Business and Industry,* 17(1), 83–92.

Makowski, P. (1985). Credit scoring branches out. *Credit World*, 75, 30–37.

Makuch, W. (1999). The basics of a better application score, in *Credit Risk Modeling, Design and Applications*, E. Mays, ed., Fitzroy Dearborn Publishers, Chicago, 59-80

Mangasarian O. (1965). Linear and nonlinear separation of patterns by linear programming, Operations Research 13, pp. 444–452.

Martin, D. (1977). Early warning of bank failure: A logit regression approach. *Journal of Banking and Finance,* 1(3), 249–276.

Mester, L. (1997). What's the point of credit scoring? *Business Review - Federal Reserve Bank of Philadelphia*, issue September, 3–16.

Min, J., and Lee, Y. (2004). Business Failure Prediction with Support Vector Machines and Neural Networks: A Comparative Study. Brain Korea 21 Project.

Myers, J., and Forgy, E. (1963). The Development of numerical credit evaluation systems. *Journal of the American Statistical Association,* 58(303)**,** 799–806.

Narain, B. (1992). *Survival analysis and the credit granting decision*, In: Thomas, L., Crook, J., and Edelman, D. (Eds), Credit scoring and credit control, Oxford University Press, Oxford, 109 –122.

Nath, R., Jackson, W. and Jones, T. (1992). A comparison of the classical and the linear programming approaches to the classification problem in discriminant analysis. *Journal of Statistical Computation and Simulation*, 41, 73–93.

Novak, M., and LaDue E. (1994). An analysis of multi-period agricultural credit evaluation models for New York dairy farms. *Agricultural Finance Review,* 54, 55–65.

Odom, M., and Sharda R. (1990). A neural network model for bankruptcy prediction. In Proceedings of the second IEEE international joint conference on neural networks (Vol. II, pp. 163-168).

Orgler, Y. (1970). A credit scoring for commercial loan. *Journal of Money, Credit, and Banking,* 2(4)**,** 435–445.

Pantalone, C., and Platt, M. (1987). Predicting commercial bank failure since deregulation. *New England Economic Review*, Jul/Aug, 37–47.

Papanyan, K. (2003). Assessing counterparty risk at private companies in energy industry: A descriptive survey of credit models. Master thesis, Goteborg University.

Parnitzke, T. (2005). *Credit scoring and the sample selection bias.* Institute of Insurance Economics, Working Paper, University of St. Gallen.

Pearson, V. (1994). Designing a Prescreening Scorecard for Small Business Customers. *Journal of Commercial Lending*, 77(4), 39–44.

Salchenberger, L., Cinar, E., and Lash, N. (1992). Neural networks: A new tool for predicting thrift failures. *Decision Sciences,* 23(4)**,** 899–916.

Sarlija, N., Bensic, M., and Bohacek, Z. (2005). *Customer revolving credit – how the economic conditions make a difference.* Presented to the International Conference on Credit Scoring and Credit Control, IX, Edinburgh University, Scotland.

Sathye, M., Bartle, J., Vincent, M, and Boffey, R. (2003). *Credit Analysis and Lending Management.* Milton, Qld: John Wiley and Sons Australia.

Schall, R. (2003). Raising the bar: Achieving scale and sustainability in microlending in the United States, Terry Sanford Institute for Public Policy, Working Paper, Duke University, Durham, NC.

Schreiner, M. (2000). Credit scoring for microfinance: Can it work? *Journal of Microfinance,* 2(2)**,** 105–118.

Schreiner, M. (2003b). *Scoring: The Next Breakthrough in Microcredit?* CGAP Occasional Paper series, no. 7 (January 2003), The World Bank.

Srinivasan, V., and Kim, Y. (1987). Credit granting: A comparative analysis of classification procedures. *The Journal of Finance,* 42(3), 665–681.

Stepanova, M., and Thomas, L., (2001). PHAB scores: Proportional hazards analysis behavioral scores. *Journal of the Operational Research Society,* 52(9), 1007–1016.

Tam, K., and Kiang, M. (1992). Managerial applications of neural networks: The case of bank failure predictions. *Management Science,* 38(7), 926–947.

Tamai, T., and Fujita, M., (1989). Development of an expert system for credit card application assessment. *International Journal of Computer Applications in Technology,* 2(4), 234–240.

Thanh, D., and Kleimeie, S. (2006). Credit scoring for Vietnam's retail banking market: Implementation and implications for transactional versus relationship lending, Working Paper series, Maastricht Research School of Economics of Technology and Organization, Maastricht University.

Thomas, L. (2000). A survey of credit and behavioral scoring: Forecasting financial risk of lending to consumers. *International Journal of Forecasting,* 16(2), 149–172.

Thomas, L., Edelman, B., and Crook, N. (2002). *Credit Scoring and its Applications.* Philadelphia, PA, Society for Industrial and Applied Mathematics.

Thomas, L., Oliver, R., and Hand, D. (2005). Survey of the issues in consumer credit modeling research. *Journal of the Operational Research Society,* 56(9), 1006–1015.

Turvey, C. (1991). Credit scoring for agricultural loans: a review with application. *Agricultural Finance Review*, 51, 43–54.

Vellido, A., Lisboaa, P., and Vaughan, J. (1999). Neural networks in business: A survey of applications (1992–1998). *Expert Systems with Applications,* 17(1), 51–70.

Verstraeten, G., and Van den Poel D. (2003). *Quantifying credit scoring performance.* Department of Marketing, Faculty of Economics and Business Administration, Working Paper, Ghent University, Belgium.

Walker, R., Haasdijk, J., and Gerrets, M. (1995). Credit Evaluation Using a Genetic Algorithm. In G. Suran and P. Treleaven (Eds.), *Intelligent Systems for Finance and Business.* New York: John Wiley and Sons.

West, D. (2000). Neural network credit scoring models. *Computers and Operations Research,* 27(11/12), 1131–1152.

Wiginton, J. (1980). A note on comparison of logit and discriminant models of consumer credit behaviour. *The Journal of Financial and Quantitative Analysis,* 15(3), 757–770.

Wilson, R., and Sharda, R. (1994). Bankruptcy prediction using neural networks. *Decision Support System*, 11(5), 545–557.

Wong, B., Bodnovich, T., and Selvi, Y. (1997). Neural network applications in business: A review and analysis of the literature (1988-95). *Decision Support Systems,* 19(4), 301–320.

Yang, Y. (2005). *Adaptive credit scoring with Kernel learning methods.* Paper presented to the International Conference on Credit Scoring and Credit Control, IX, Edinburgh University, Scotland.

Yobas, M., Crook, J., and Ross, P. (2000). Credit scoring using neural and evolutionary techniques. *IMA Journal of Mathematics Applied in Business and Industry,* 11(2), 111–125.

Ziari, H., Leatham, D., and Turvey, C. (1995). Application of mathematical programming techniques in credit scoring of agricultural loans. *Agricultural Finance Review,* 55, 74–88.

Ziemba, A. (2005). *Bayesian updating of generic scoring models.* Paper presented to the International Conference on Credit Scoring and Credit Control, IX, Edinburgh University, Scotland.

In: Economic and Financial Modeling
Editor: Andrew C. Worthington

ISBN: 978-1-63463-111-2

Chapter 8

Contextual Factors in Social and Environmental Accounting Disclosure Models

Omer Elsakit and Andrew C. Worthington*
Griffith University, Australia

Abstract

There are many studies on social and environmental accounting disclosure practice throughout the world. A range of determinants affects the motivation of firms to provide social and environmental information, and the adequacy and suitability of this type of information to assist decision makers. These include the impact on corporate governance and firm characteristics on differences in social and environmental disclosure practices by firms operating in similar or different sectors in terms of the level and quality of disclosure. Moreover, contextual factors are of significance when it comes to justifying these differences in disclosure practices by firms in different countries acting in similar and dissimilar sectors. The importance of contextual factors is evident by their impact on the expected influence of corporate governance and firm characteristics, which has prevented researchers generalizing the results of studies in countries not included in their samples and, thus, creating the need to conduct more research in different countries to consolidate these results. This chapter casts light on these important factors suitable for modeling, including include political, economic and cultural factors.

1. Introduction

In an attempt to gain a better understanding of social and environmental practices and what affects its quality, many prior studies have focused attention on particular factors. These are external factors or so-called general contextual factors. External factors are those elements that are out of a firm's control, but at the same time could potentially affect its performance

* Corresponding author: Department of Accounting, Finance and Economics, Griffith University, 170 Kessels Road, Nathan QLD 4111, Australia. Email. a.worthington@griffith.edu.au.

and sustainability. These represent many factors derived from the firm's political, economic, and cultural context. Hence, we also assume that the practice of social and environmental accounting disclosure as a medium for disseminating information about the interaction of economic entities with society and the environment are also subject to influence. In turn, social and environmental disclosure is simply a communication tool between interested groups and in order to evaluate the effectiveness of such a tool, we should include general contextual factors in the evaluation of a firm's performance, especially in communication with its several stakeholders.

In terms of background, Belal (2001) concluded that social disclosure by public and private Bangladeshi companies was generally positive, descriptive, and very poor in volume. Belal (2001) provided a list of factors that caused companies to produce such weak disclosure, including political problems, the ineffectiveness of the regulatory framework implemented, and the weakness of the law and punishment system. The reasons also included the intervention of the social elite, the prevalence of corruption, a lack of social awareness and organized social groups, the newness of the stock market, weakness of corporate culture, and the nonexistence of independent verification. We can note from this result that some factors mentioned as reasons for weak levels of disclosure relate to political, economic and social context of the country in which firms operate. On this basis, Belal (2001) argued that researchers should consider the social, political, regulatory, and economic contexts to gain a better understanding of social disclosure practices.

However, globalized stock markets may also downplay the effect of differences between countries on disclosure matters (Cormier and Magnan, 2003b). For example, Branco and Rodrigues (2008) pointed to this as justification for the similarity in the results of their study and those conducted in other countries. This may in turn question the importance of general contextual factors in affecting the disclosures made by listed companies. Branco and Rodrigues (2008, p. 699) stated that "…there is no reason to expect that companies in the less developed capital markets will behave in a significantly different manner than companies in more developed capital markets". Despite this, both Branco and Rodrigues (2008) and Cormier and Magnan (2003b) recommend further study as a means of providing some validation.

In contrast, Sobhani et al. (2009) rejected these claims, and ascertained that the level of development in the country in which firms conducted their activities has an influence on disclosure practices. Their study suggested that companies operating in developing countries (such as Bangladesh and Malaysia) appear to have some similarities in their focus on disclosing more information regarding their employees, while there is disagreement regarding the importance of consumers between Bangladeshi companies (which deemed it less important) and their counterparts in developed countries such as the UK and the US. It is obvious that such differences will result in differences in social disclosures, at least in the content of reports.

Differences are also evident among developed countries. Golob and Bartlett (2007) alluded to some studies (Owen, 2003; Van der Molen, 2005) which indicated that information regarding employees, environment and services are more prevalent in social reporting in European countries, while Australian companies are more focused on products, management and financial performance. They interpreted these differences as a reflection of the social and economic circumstances prevalent in those countries. This then confirmed the argument by Deegan (2002) and Guthrie and Parker (1990) that the country context is one of the key factors influencing reporting practices. Similarly, Simnett et al. (2009) analyzed sustainability reports (published voluntarily) of a sample of 2,113 companies across 31 countries and found that taking into consideration country-specific factors is not just an important assurance issue, but an accounting issue more generally.

The meaning of 'country' includes a vast range of circumstances that discriminate a group of people from others. This involves factors such as history, geography, natural environment, language, culture, economic and political systems that, together directly or indirectly affect any kind of activity in which people are engaged. As a result, each country is at least unique in its own way. For this reason, and as a micro example, there are still difficulties in implementing unified standards in accounting practices worldwide. As such, it is difficult to believe that social and environmental disclosure practices are unaffected by the circumstances of countries where such practices are implemented. In supporting such a claim, this paper discusses some general contextual factors in terms of their effect on the practices of social and environmental accounting disclosure, grouped according to law and regulation, monetary authorities, professional bodies, politics, economics, culture, and education.

2. Law and Regulation

There is no doubt that law has an effect on economic relations. Contracts, transactions, and every economic action are controlled by rules in order to be considered legal. As such, as relations between firms and their stakeholders, including society as a whole, is seen as economic action, it can be argued that laws and regulations have a role to play in the process of releasing information regarding such relations. In evidence, Inchausti (1997, p. 62) stated that: 'Legislation appears to produce a strong increase in disclosure'.

Tsang (1998) considered social disclosure of Singaporean companies (including banks), and found that this kind of disclosure was found to have increased during the period from the late 1980s to 1993, then remained at a stable level until 1995. Tsang (1998) justified the increased level by describing—inter alia—steps taken by the Singaporean government, including training workers, launching campaigns regularly to save energy and water, and implementing further legislation relating to environmental issues. The impact of government efforts has also been highlighted in a study of Amran and Devi (2008) who found that the social and environmental disclosure practice of firms that were dependent on governments or significantly government owned, as well as those seeking governmental contracts was influenced by the perception of the Malaysian government on social and environmental matters. This confirmed the result in Baskin (2006), which considered the case of 1,827 companies around the world. This international study demonstrated that firms are strongly affected by laws implemented where they operate, and government does have the power to promote corporate responsibility.

Notwithstanding regulations, which are normally the main tool governments use to prevent some actions and to prompt others, there are some arguments as to whether social and environmental disclosure should be mandatory or voluntary. Accordingly, in investigating the determinants of corporate disclosure, many studies have focused on mandatory disclosure, while others concentrated on voluntary disclosure (Barako and Brown, 2008). It is especially important to recognize the differences between mandatory and voluntary disclosure; in the latter, some factors such as attitudes and perceptions of managers should be given more attention and focus in order to have a better understanding of social and environmental disclosure practices. Yet, this assumed importance may not be found at the same level in the case of developing countries, where the effect of laws, regulations, and enforcement mechanisms might be questionable due to the influence of other dominant factors such as the political situation or levels of corruption.

However, many companies make disclosures in response to formal regulations issued by governmental bodies (Boden, 1999; Jacobs and Kemp, 2002). Moreover, the absence of these regulations is more likely to result in the absence of disclosure or weak disclosures. Jacobs and Kemp (2002) support this argument. In responding to the question 'Why do we need accounting information?' they offered many possible answers, and the 'absence of governmental bodies' in the demand for accounting information' was found to be the potential cause for the lack of such information. A study by Belal (2001) demonstrated that weaknesses in the law and punishment system and ineffective regulations generally contributed to the weak levels of disclosure by Bangladeshi companies. This lends support to the findings of Imam's (2000) study, which established that the relevant laws—inter alia—are a possible factor for the low level of social and environmental disclosure made by Bangladeshi companies in the period 1996–97. Similar results emerged from Belal and Cooper (2007), where the lack of legal requirements was one of the main reasons for not disclosing information on some social responsibility issues, namely, child labor, equal opportunities, and poverty alleviation.

Voluntary social and environmental disclosures practices also tend to be influenced by orientation. For example, in the absence of related regulations, companies are more inclined to disclose positive information (Belal and Cooper, 2007) as demonstrated by Deegan and Gordon (1996) who concluded that managerial objectivity is questionable where regulations are absent. This particular study revealed that the environmental information disclosed in annual reports of Australian companies was generally self-laudatory. Investors may also deem such information as too self-serving and lacking credibility (Cormier and Magnan, 2003a). On contrast, in the presence of unfavorable information, companies may choose not to disclose, as releasing such information could damage their value in the stock market (Cormier and Magnan, 2003b). As an example, Wiseman (1982) evaluated the voluntary environmental disclosures of 26 companies and demonstrated that these were either incomplete or inaccurate. Moreover, voluntary disclosure motivate managers to apply cost–benefit measures (Cormier and Magnan, 2003a). That is, in the case of voluntary disclosure, decisions on disclosing information may be based on the evaluation of the costs and benefits of such action. As such, decisions are more likely to not be taken according to the interests of society and the environment; rather, priority will be given only to the interests of management and the company. Such actions take firms many steps backwards by restoring the traditional objective of company, which is no more than maximizing profits. Another point to be made in respect to voluntary disclosure is that it may not encourage firms to go further when they reach a certain level of disclosure, due to imitation behavior found in the conduct of some firms. Tsang (1998, p. 630), for example, justified the stability of the level of social disclosure made by Singaporean firms during the period 1993–95 by stating that: "One reason may be due to the voluntary nature of CSR. Once the companies attained a certain level of disclosure, they were not motivated to go further".

Based on the above, a considerable number of studies have generally come out in favor of mandatory disclosure, and their results underscore the importance of making disclosure mandatory to ensure company practice in a proper way. Potential conflicting interests between managers and investors, imitation behavior conducted by many firms, and the trust of investors in disclosures made in accordance to mandatory rules are all matters creating a need for implementing legislation regarding disclosures (Cormier and Magnan, 2003a). Legislators and policymakers of environmental information and the users of such information—who disagree with each other on many points in the study of Deegan and Rankin (1999)—both agree that legal obligations are the most influential element in disclosure decisions.

It is argued that legislation pertaining to social and environmental disclosures is one of the factors causing an increase in such kinds of disclosure in some developed countries (Haniffa and Cooke, 2005). For instance, the percentage of French firms which disclosed environmental information increased dramatically from 4% in 1999 to 21% in 2002, possibly because of the trend in making environmental disclosure mandatory and imitating policies (regarding environmental issues) implemented in some European countries such as Denmark, Norway, Sweden and the Netherlands (Owen, 2003). Not only did the level of reporting increase, but also the quality of reporting, because of the introduction of more regulations regarding social reporting. A study by Crawford and Williams (2010) compared the case of French banks and that of US banks in respect to country context and its impact on the quality of social reporting in an attempt to answer the following question: Should corporate social reporting be voluntary or mandatory? The findings demonstrated that quality disclosure (on average) was higher in France, which represented a case of countries with higher regulative pressures, i.e. the more regulation implemented, the higher the quality of disclosure. This result confirmed the claim of Cormier and Magnan (2003a) (which resulted from evaluation of environmental disclosure made by Canadian firms) that implementing tough regulations regarding environmental disclosure leads to the quality of such disclosure being enhanced. From another angle, as firms want to add credibility to this high quality information, they require auditing services provided by auditors and Simnett et al. (2009) found that the demand for auditing services is typically higher in countries with a strong legal system.

However, the impact of legislation and regulations on the level and quality of social and environmental disclosure is not as strong as it should be. Belal (2001) found that more than half the firms investigated in his study did not disseminate mandatory information such as that required for foreign currency transactions. Belal (2001) pointed to the weakness of regulatory frameworks as the cause, and also mentioned the negative impact of social and economic factors such as corruption or an unstable political situation. This study shows that the effect of some factors, such as law, can be undermined by political and social situations. In this sense, more legislation per se, especially in developing countries, may not necessarily improve social and environmental disclosure practices.

3. Monetary Authorities

In the case of investigating social and environmental disclosure made by banks, it is necessary to discuss, even briefly, the role of monetary authorities, especially central banks, as these have the highest authority and are the dominant players in banking systems. Due to regulatory and supervision authority, the central bank activities are directly influenced by policies and regulations issued and imposed. As such, central banks can improve the process of considering social and environmental issues in the daily work of banks, and disclosing information about the impact of banks on society and environment. After investigating the case of social and environmental disclosure by 100 Bangladeshi listed companies (operating in 19 different industries), Sobhani et al. (2009) found that banks were the most disclosing firms, achieving the highest level of consumer, social and environmental disclosure (CSED) in all aspects, even environmental. Sobhani et al. (2009) justified this finding by highlighting the important role of the Bangladeshi Central Bank in implementing strong monitoring and control procedures on Bangladeshi banks, leading to a good corporate culture in the banking sector and, as a result, an increased awareness of banks regarding social and environmental issues. Studies y Khan (2010) and Khan et al. (2010), which focused exclusively on Bangladeshi banks, also confirmed the results of this study and the explanation provided earlier.

Having a good culture with regard to the impact of banks' activities on environment and society, and being aware of factors positively influencing social and environmental disclosures made by banks, the central bank is more likely to encourage steps in improving and consolidating the performances and disclosures of banks. Barako and Brown (2008) studied corporate social disclosure of Kenyan banks, and investigated some factors that might influence this kind of disclosure. Their findings revealed that a high level of nonexecutive directors on a bank board enhances bank disclosure. The researchers indicated that this was a result of a long-standing central bank policy of encouraging Kenyan banks to increase the number of independent directors on their boards.

The relationship between the central bank and other international financial organizations also has a positive impact on the direction of improving social and environmental disclosure practices. Khan *et al.* (2010) examined the sustainability reports of major Bangladeshi commercial banks by using the indicators included in the Global Reporting Initiative (GRI). The finding was that social disclosures practices of these banks could be improved by being more holistic, and this improvement is conditioned by the participation of the central bank as a regulatory agency. The researchers mentioned that the Bangladeshi Central Bank has a partnership relationship with some global partners such as the IFC, a member of the World Bank Group, and such relationship affects—through the process of monitoring or encouragement—the way Bangladeshi banks conduct their activities. It encourages them to become more positive in terms of their effect on society and the environment, and to release information beyond their financial performance. Khan et al. (2010) argued that the regulatory requirements of the central bank and its financial partners are the main motivation for Bangladeshi banks to discharge their responsibilities towards the environment and society.

4. Professional Bodies

Pressure from both market and regulatory bodies are influential factors in accounting information (Inchausti, 1997). Regulatory bodies, in terms of their impact on the process of disclosing information, can be divided into two categories: governmental agencies and nongovernmental agencies (Belal and Cooper, 2007). The accounting profession is included in the last group (nongovernmental bodies). For instance, Deegan and Rankin (1999) demonstrated that information users such as shareholders, academics and reviewers of organizations were more likely (compared to information producers) to consider the accounting profession (in addition to government) as an appropriate body to issue guidelines for environmental reporting. Along with standards, this includes the development of accounting objectives and practices, which are both influenced by the accounting profession (Radebaugh, 1975). Furthermore, Deegan and Rankin (1999), whose study proved the existence of a gap between environmental reporting policymakers and users, recommended professional bodies (beside institutions of higher education) as a tool to remedy the problem.

The accounting profession is believed to have an important role to play in social and environmental disclosure. This role can be performed by accounting associations in many ways. Firstly, accounting associations can issue particular regulations regarding what kind of information should be published in company reports, and what means should be used in the disclosure process. In addition, a continuous revision should be applied to current practices in order to ensure their suitability for social and environmental issues. Cormier and Magnan (2003a, p. 45) argued that financial statements have a weakness in terms of environmental information and liabilities, and suggest some ideas to address this weakness such as 'a revision of accounting recognition and measurement in order to restrict the freedom of management and auditors to refrain from reporting environmental liabilities due to the uncertainty about their magnitude'. Secondly, some methods can be adopted such as introducing social and environmental awards. Such initiatives should encourage companies to act in a positive way regarding social and environmental issues related to their activities, and to publish their social and environmental information at an acceptable level. Thompson (2002) mentioned the positive impact of the ACCA's UK Awards Scheme in promoting environmental disclosure practices—which stimulated other countries such as Singapore and Malaysia to adopt similar initiatives. Thirdly, the accounting association has a responsibility to enhance the abilities of its members via, for example, the use of training programs pertaining to understanding and applying new perspectives, methods and approaches to improve the process of decision making by providing high quality information. Finally, suitable methods should be developed and implemented to raise awareness in society with respect to the required role of banks on social and environmental issues.

5. Politics

In many ways, corporate social and environmental disclosure is simply a tool of communication between firm managers and a range of information users. Thus, as interactions between people are likely to be influenced by the environment in which they live in, it is reasonable to assume that this environment also affects communication processes. The political environment, represented by political rights, civil liberties and the type of political system, is argued to be influential in disclosure issues. Political rights (such as voting rights) and civil liberties (being free from the control of the state) are likely to have an impact on the communication process between individuals and organizations alike (Belkaoui, 1983). Belkaoui (1983, p. 209) proposed that 'violations of political rights and civil liberties associated with various forms of political structure may restrict political freedom in general and may act as a hindrance to tradition of a full and fair disclosure'. This study was conducted to examine the validity of this proposition and other assumptions related to the economic and demographic environment in more than fifty countries.

Archambault and Archambault (2003, p. 192), who investigated the case of a large number of firms (more than 500 firms in some 31 countries) regarding the financial disclosure of corporations, found disclosure was affected by many systems, including political ones. The researchers found that 'disclosure is influenced by factors from a broad range of social systems: cultural, political, economic, and corporate'. More explanation of the association between disclosure and political system can be found in the study of Deese (1998) who demonstrated the existence of a relationship between political freedom and economic freedom which is, in turn, likely to influence the process of disclosing information by firms. Regarding social and environmental disclosure, Williams (1999) considered the case of 356 listed firms operating in Australia, Singapore, Indonesia, Malaysia, the Philippines, Thailand and Hong Kong and confirmed that the quantity of social and environmental disclosure made by those firms is significantly influenced by political and civil systems. Haniffa and Cooke (2005) also mentioned politics as one of the many factors behind the increased level of social disclosure.

Even though a significant relationship between political system and accounting groups was proven (Goodrich, 1986), the reciprocal relationship between firms, individuals, accounting system and political environment which affect the disclosure process can be seen from different angles. The respondents to the questionnaire distributed by Al-Khater and Naser (2003) believe that corporate social disclosure should be encouraged instead of being enforced by authorities. Those researchers see such disclosure as a reflection of 'the government's participative style of leadership that encourages public freedom and ensures openness and transparency' (Al-Khater and Naser (2003, p. 547). They assumed that such opinion 'may reflect the nature of the Qatari society, which is moving towards democracy'. On the other hand, Matten and Crane (2005) highlighted the significant role of corporations in affecting and shaping social, economic, and political situations in countries and the rights of their citizens. Regardless of who has an impact upon the other, what can be understood is that the political situation affects social (and environmental) disclosure.

Amran and Devi (2008) established the significant influence of the Malaysian government on the level of corporate social reporting (provided by companies operating in seven sectors including a financial one). The explanation for the positive impact of government on social disclosure issue was that the ruling party is using the issue to enhance its position and image, locally and internationally, and to be distinguished favorably against its competitor parties. This justification shows that the practices of social and environmental disclosure can benefit under some political systems. In line with this kind of reasoning, one can presume that in countries where there is just one ruling party, or one person controls political life, there is no need for some tools to enhance the position of the ruling individual or party. Hence, social and environmental disclosure practices are likely to be negatively affected in countries with particular kinds of political systems such as dictatorial systems. From another angle, there is a belief that social accounting might encourage democratic practices, if not in a general meaning at least for information users, such as stakeholders—as discussed by O'Dwyer (2005). Thus, a correlation may emerge between the existence (or absence), and the level of democracy in a country from one side, and social and environmental disclosures made by firms operating in that country from the other side. In other words, levels of oppression or freedom or political instability in a country formulate communication tools including firms' reports, which comprise social and environmental information.

Belal and Cooper (2007) indicated instability in political situations and military coups as a reason—inter alia—for low and unsatisfactory levels of social and environmental disclosures. Such political situations create—among other factors—corruption, described by the World Bank as a situation that 'increases wealth for the few at the expense of society as a whole' (Neu and Gomez, 2006, p. 5). Corruption in Bangladesh was described by Belal and Owen (2007) as being widespread and reaching Bangladeshi companies, resulting in illegal actions such as bribery, tax evasion, loan defaults, and share scandals. As such, the 'few' mentioned in the statement of the World Bank can be firms which do anything, legally or illegally, to make profits at the expense of society and the environment. In such cases, companies are not interested in producing social and environmental information voluntarily or even mandatorily. Belal (2001) indicated that half of the Bangladeshi companies he surveyed did not disclose the required information. As a result, it can be presumed that the low level of social and environmental disclosure of Bangladeshi firms can partly be seen as a natural result of the political situation.

Political repression has also been highlighted by many researchers as negatively influential in disclosure practices. Companies operating in repressed countries where civil rights and freedom as a whole are absent or at low levels are more likely to be conservative, or not active, in regard to communicating information pertaining to their effects on the environment and society. In such societies, some specific trends can be noted concerning the press and societal interest groups. The press, as a tool for disseminating all kinds of information (citizens might be interested in) and as a means of highlighting the importance of some issues which touch the daily lives of people (such as social and environmental issues), seems to lose its capacity to be influential. This is because the activities of the press are more likely to be restricted by repressive governments (Farook *et al.*, 2011). Consequently, the assumed role of the press in raising awareness of social and environmental matters in society and putting pressure on companies to be socially and environmentally responsible is more likely to be questionable. This situation could also apply to societal interest groups. In repressed environments, societal organizations and groups (such as environmental groups) appear unable to criticize the harmful conduct of some companies (Farook et al., 2011), which results in negative consequences on society and the environment. This confirms the arguments of Gastil (1990) in that the impact of societal interest groups and human resources organizations (such as trade unions) is likely to be downplayed when repression and political and civil violations increase. Thus, the weak role of both the press and societal groups results in a low level of social expectations and pressure on companies in countries controlled by repressive governments (Williams, 1999) and, as a result, a low level of social and environmental disclosure practices.

In a study conducted in another African country, Wiig and Kolstad (2010) investigated the interaction between multinational corporations (oil companies) and host country institutions represented in Angola during the year 2004. It was intended to establish whether social and environmental responsibility issues play a role in the competitive process to acquire licenses and contracts, and the impact of that on CSR activities of multinational companies. Results of the study indicated a relative insignificance of social and environmental responsibility in the issue mentioned. The researchers found that democratic accountability in Angola is very limited, and argued that this is the main cause of the poor social and economic situation in the country. Many factors were presented as contributors, including the lack of transparency (an inheritance from the civil war), the weak role of civil society (governmental policies discouraging civil movements in adopting and practicing more responsibility in social and environmental issues), and the wide authority concentrated in the Angolan president's hands (which reflects limited freedom practices, even at the organizational level). Wiig and Kolstad (2010) argued that this is the case in some African oil countries. Ite (2004, p. 8) confirmed such arguments by stating that underdevelopment in the Niger Delta region is because of 'corruption, poor governance (political and corporate) and lack of accountability on the part of the Nigerian government, its leaders and statutory agencies'.

In the case of the banking sector, Farook *et al.* (2011) studied the case of Islamic banking by analyzing the annual reports of 47 Islamic banks in 14 countries in order to gauge the level of social disclosure and determine the factors influencing levels of disclosure. One of the hypotheses of the study presented a prediction that the level of social disclosure by Islamic banks is affected negatively by the level of political and civil repression existing in the countries where these banks are operating. The result of the study confirmed this prediction. More confirmation of the influence of the political environment on disclosure practices, and social and environmental disclosure in particular, came from another country with more freedom. Tagesson et al. (2009), considered the case of Swedish companies, and found that government owned companies disclosed more social and environmental information on their websites than did privately owned companies. The researchers attributed this finding to the scrutiny and pressure of the Swedish government and the Swedish media regarding the effect of companies' activities on the environment and society. National culture in Swedish was highlighted as the main cause of the improvement of social and environmental disclosure made by public companies, 'In Sweden there is a long tradition of transparency in the public sector, which is also legally regulated in the principle of public access to official records. This principle gives all Swedish citizens the right to inspect State documents' (Tagesson *et al.*, 2009, p. 361). Having the right to investigate state documents by Swedish citizens reflects the political environment and the atmosphere of freedom Swedish people live in.

In addition to social and environmental disclosure practices, the extent of democracy also affects social and environmental disclosure policies. Welford (2005) investigated the case of companies operating in 15 nations across three continents (Europe, North America and Asia) by considering the written policies of those companies in regard to corporate social responsibility and concluded as follow. We find CSR policies more common in countries with a social democratic tradition such as Germany, Norway and Canada' (Welford, 2005, p. 52).This lends support to the argument in Williams (1999) that companies operating in more open societies with greater levels of freedom may need to prove their eligibility and competence to continue doing their business. One way is by providing more information about their interaction with the environment and society. Farook (2011) agreed with Williams's argument and emphasized the case of Islamic banks, which are assumed to provide more social and environmental information because of operating in such open societies.

From the above discussion, we conclude that the political environment likely influences social and environmental disclosure practices made by companies. Thus, the level of social and environmental disclosure may vary from country to country depending on the level of freedom. This conclusion obviously contradicts the result of Belkaoui's (1983) study, which hypothesized the existence of a relationship between freedom and corporate disclosure, but revealed no significant relationship between the two. Belkaoui (1983, p. 216) justified this insignificance by providing some possible causes 'such as misspecification of the disclosure adequacy scores, and the economic, political and civil indicators, and misrepresentation of the countries included in the sample'. More explanation for that finding rests in the limitations of his study, which included possible bias in regard to a notion of accounting adequacy (used in the study) which were more appropriate to developed countries than developing countries, and confining the indicators of political, civil and economic factors to Gastil-type indices rather than other alternative indicators. Lastly, it may be worth mentioning that his study considered only financial statements, not social and environmental information.

6. Economics

Although some studies failed to prove a connection between economic environment and accounting reporting (such as the study of Belkaoui 1983 who hypothesized that economic environment—inter alia—is likely to have an impact on reporting and disclosure adequacy , but did not find an association between the respective variables), many have argued and demonstrated the opposite. For instance, Belal (2001) argued that economic context—besides some other contexts—should be taken into consideration to have a better understanding of social disclosure matters. Adams (2002) also stated that an association does exist between such context and the nature of reporting since economic factors—inter alia—can influence other factors such as firms' characteristics and corporate governance. In line with that, Archambault and Archambault (2003), who studied the determinants of corporate disclosure made by more than 500 firms in more than 31 countries, underscored the effects of economic systems on the relation between firms, investors, and information disclosed.

A number of conceptual studies (Choi and Mueller, 1984; Arpan and Radebaugh, 1985) have discussed economic factors as influential factors on the development of both accounting and disclosure. Regarding the latter, many factors have been investigated in order to prove the correlation between the economy and disclosure practices. For instance, Adhikari and Tondkar (1992) focused on the degree of economic development, type of economy, size of equity market, activity on the equity market, and dispersion of stock ownership; while Archambault and Archambault (2003) choose economic development, capital markets and inflation as representatives of economic factors to investigate. As an example, more explanation is provided regarding one of these factors.

One topic here is economic development. Economic development is 'a country's ability to increase its per capita income or production—i.e. a transitional process between economic stagnation and economic progress; and the ability to execute a series of structural, social and economic changes and developments—a transformation process, e.g. more equitable income distribution, improved medical services and housing, enhanced education and training, and greater employment' (Nobes and Parker, 1991, p. 255). Based on this conception, it is reasonable to conceive how much the role accounting can play in this process. Similarly, accounting development in a country is also affected by the stage of development in that country (Adhikari and Tondkar, 1992), because the priorities of each country differ from those of other countries (Rock, 2002). Elijido-Ten (2004) stated, 'We cannot generalize the findings from one country to another especially if the countries are of different culture and of different stages of economic development'. The root of such argument can be found in many studies (Cooke and Wallace, 1990; Adhikari and Tondkar, 1992; Ahmed, 1995; Salter, 1998; Williams, 1999; Archambault and Archambault, 2003) which have paid attention to the impact of the stage of economic development on disclosure practices.

One explanation to justify the relationship in question is that in countries with high levels of economic development there is a diversity of economic activities (Haniffa and Cooke, 2005) and, as Archambault and Archambault (2003) mentioned, a trend of the companies to raise more capital. As such, there is a great need to report the results of these activities to many interested groups such as investors. Furthermore, the resources owned by developed countries leverages the opportunity that such tasks are more likely to be achieved successfully (Adhikari and Tondkar, 1992). Belal and Cooper (2007) named the lack of resources as one of the main reasons for not disclosing some social information. From another angle, development of the economy in a country results in an increase in the demand for improved living standards and work conditions (Gordon, 1990). This, in turn, creates more pressure by some groups such as labour unions and consumer bodies on companies to consider environmental and social issues in their activities, and to show their commitment in their reports (Williams, 1999).

The case of many developing countries adds support to this discussion. Jordan, Abu-Baker and Naser (2000) argued that moving the economy to rely more on heavy industries (which have a more obvious impact on the environment) will make social disclosure more relevant to the information users. This confirms the marginal assurance found in Adhikari and Tondkar's (1992) study that disclosure of agricultural economics is low. In Nigeria, Ite (2004) found that the social efforts of multinational companies in their commitment to their social responsibility are affected negatively by many factors such as lack of macro-economic planning. This deficiency was also documented by Belal and Owen (2007) who found that lack of a sustainability development plan is one of the reasons for the low level of social disclosure in Bangladesh. Many programs have been implemented to change this situation. For instance, Amran and Devi (2008) mentioned that the Malaysian government started to rely economically on foreign affiliates (from developed countries), and follow international business orientations (in developed countries), including those pertaining to social disclosure. Privatization programs and developing private sectors are also some examples of reforms steps taken by governments in developing countries to improve their economies and affect positively disclosure practices as a result, and social and environmental practices in particular (Sobhani et al., 2009).

Nevertheless, some studies provided reserve results. Adhikari and Tondkar (1992) investigated the association between stock exchange disclosure requirements of 35 stock exchanges operating in different countries and five environmental factors including the degree of economic development. They hypothesized that in states with higher per capita GNP, stock markets may have rigorous levels of disclosure requirements, but the result of their investigation did not offer support for such expectation. However, the researchers justified the result by arguing that this might be attributed to the fact that the sample of their study encompassed countries that have stock exchanges, which reflects a certain level of economic development in all the countries investigated. The researchers suggested that considering other factors such as cultural and regulatory environments may offer better explanations in such cases. From this justification, it can be assumed that the existence of exchange markets in all countries investigated may spoil the possibility of having a more accurate result concerning the impact of economic development level on disclosure requirements in such comparative studies. This impact may be found more clearly, as the researchers mentioned, in comparative studies where the sample is chosen from all countries with or without stock exchanges. The last note on this study is that what have been investigated are disclosure requirements of stock exchange rather than the actual disclosure made by companies themselves. In this case, it is worth mentioning that many studies, such as Welford (2005), emphasize the fact that the existence of codes does not always mean implementing them and, at the same time, some social and environmental activities might be conducted in a responsible manner even though they are not stated in policy documents. Thus, the result of Adhikari and Tondkar's (1992) study should be interpreted with caution.

In another study, Williams (1999) investigated the case of seven countries and found that the level of economic development was insignificant in explaining the differences in the quantity of social and environmental disclosure (which is voluntary in nature). The researcher justified this result by mentioning the opinion of Patten (1991a; 1992) that social pressure, not economic pressure, is the cause of releasing social and environmental information voluntarily. Williams (1999) proceeded to justify the difference in his study from that of Salter (1998) by arguing that the focus of the latter was exclusively on financial disclosure rather than social and environmental disclosure. However, what can be noted from the results of Williams's (1999) study is that all of the 356 companies investigated in his study were listed companies. This may render the result of this study less accurate as Adhikari and Tondkar (1992) suggested beforehand. Furthermore, another assumption can be provided here to justify these findings is that some other factors not investigated in these two studies may have an effect on the results. Cooke and Wallace (1990, p. 79) pointed to the arguments of some researchers that 'accounting practice is a function of inherent national characteristics: the interaction between the levels of political, economic, educational, and technological development of each country'.

In line with common beliefs in respect to the impact of economic development, many studies have supported the idea that the stage of economic development is an influential factor in the issue of disclosure practices. In the study of Frank (1979), the sample included thirty-five countries, and the results demonstrated that economic environment of a country is found to be influential in regard to accounting principles and reporting practices implemented in that country. Confirming such results, the study of Cooke and Wallace (1990), which investigated the relationship between the level of corporate financial disclosure regulation and some national and international factors, demonstrated a difference between developed and developing countries. It revealed that some factors, including the stage of economic development, are more likely to affect the level of corporate financial disclosure regulation in developed nations. The authors concluded that 'It is probably true that a nation's accounting profile is a function of both internal and external environmental factors, which may be cultural/anthropological as much as political/economic' (Cooke and Wallace, 1990, p. 103). This study, along with those of Doupnik and Salter (1995) and Salter (1998), have been mentioned by Williams (1999) as studies emphasising the importance of the level of economic development in accounting practices. In the study of Salter (1998), the first research question was about whether there is a difference in the levels of disclosure made by companies in emerging market economies compared to the disclosure of companies acting in developed markets. The result of the study revealed that in the period of the study (1989, 1991 and 1993), the higher mean level of corporate financial disclosure was achieved by companies operating in developed market economies, and the difference compared to companies in emerging market economies was significant.

The importance of the degree of economic development in disclosure issues is also proved in respect to social disclosure. Written policies of firms in 15 nations in three continents (Europe, North America and Asia) were investigated by Welford (2005) in relation to the issue of corporate social responsibility. In this study, this responsibility was found to be partly linked to the economic development of countries investigated. Welford (2005, p. 52) stated, 'Generally the more developed the country the higher the incidence of policies in the area of CSR'. Moving from written policies to actual disclosure, a comparative study between companies (including banks) in Hong Kong and UK was carried out by Xiao et al. (2005) and established that social and environmental disclosure made by U.K. companies was significantly more than that of their counterparts in Hong Kong during the whole period investigated, which was five years. The researchers concluded that the findings of their study underpin social and economic development being an important reason for the differences in social and environmental disclosure practices between companies in the two countries. In another study, the result also lent support to the argument that the stage of economic development is a significant issue in non-financial disclosure, not just in the international context but also between different parts of the same country. Liu and Anbumozhi (2009) analyzed annual reports, separate environmental reports and the websites of 100 companies operating in industrial sectors in the year 2006. One of the findings of this study was that companies acting in regions where the economy is more developed (eastern coastal regions) were found to be the most disclosed companies concerning emissions, compared to those operating in other regions.

7. Culture

Many definitions have been provided for the term *culture*. Hofstede (1980, p. 26) defined it as 'the collective programming of the mind which distinguishes the members of one human group from another'.. In more detail, Harris's (1987, p. 6) definition describes it as 'the learned, socially acquired traditions and life style of the members of a society, including their patterned, repetitious way of thinking, feeling and acting'. From both definitions, it can be noted that the behavior of humans and organizations is, at least partly, a function of culture. Archambault and Archambault (2003) argue that culture impacts the way of perceiving and evaluating situations which people encounter in their lives and businesses. Regarding the case of companies, since accounting is a social activity involving human thought and work, companies' activities (including disclosure activity) are affected by culture (Mathews, 1993; Tsang, 1998; Haniffa and Cooke, 2002). As a result, findings of studies conducted in a country cannot be generalized to other countries which have—inter alia—a different culture (Elijido-Ten, 2004).

Based on this, researchers in the accounting field tend to pay more attention to the influences of culture on both groups: managers' decisions pertaining to financial disclosure, and information users with regard to their reaction to such disclosure (Hope, 2003). Adams

(2002), who argued that a relationship does exist between culture and reporting, presented an explanation of how the first group is affected by culture. He argued that as moral values are influenced by culture, the decision on which kind of information should be released will be influenced as well. An empirical confirmation of such claims can be found in the study of Welford (2005), who investigated corporate social responsibility in three continents. His study indicated that, in Asia, national culture is likely to influence firms which often consider needs of stakeholders in their own nation. Another confirmation can be also found in the study of Lau and Caby (2010) which verified the impact of national culture on managers' attitudes.

In the literature, many studies have provided support to culture as an influential factor in disclosure issue. In the study of Williams (1999), which covered the case of seven Asia-Pacific countries, culture was found to be significant in determining the quantity of corporate social and environmental disclosure. The researcher pointed out that his study not only lends support for the theoretical framework developed by Gray (1988), but also proved its validity in social and environmental disclosure. The same result was found in Hope (2003) who considered the case of financial disclosure made by companies in 39 countries. The researcher demonstrated that it is a mistake to ignore the impact of culture on firms' disclosure choices. He concluded that cultural factors should be taken into consideration in accounting research. As his study was confined to the first half of 1990s, the researcher suggested investigating whether cultural factor still has important role. This importance has been emphasized in many other studies.

In the study of Archambault and Archambault (2003) the influence of a wide range of factors (including political, economic, financial and operating systems, and national culture) on the financial disclosure practices in 37 countries was tested. In this study, culture—inter alia—was also found to be an influential factor in disclosure matters. This result did not differ when it comes to written policies (in regard to corporate social responsibility) of companies operating in 15 countries in Europe, North America and Asia. The study of Welford (2005) indicated that many corporate social responsibility policies were influenced by cultural traditions. Moving from policies to practices, the study of Haniffa and Cooke (2005), which was carried out in Malaysia, proved the existence of an association between culture and corporate social disclosure, and contended that the latter cannot be culture free. This was the case also in Egypt, where the result of Dahawy and Conover's (2007) study showed a low level of disclosure practices conducted by firms listed on the Egyptian stock exchange. Thirty-nine percent of the disclosure requirements of the Egyptian capital market authority, which is based on international accounting standards, were not met by companies. The researchers attributed that to cultural reasons, and indicated that inconsistency does exist between such standards and Egyptian culture. In line with this result, Mwaura and Nyaboga (2011, p. 37), in discussing the case of Middle Eastern and North African countries, describe these countries as having a unique culture and stated, 'Due to the diversity of the region and its individuality when compared to the rest of the world, there are many obstacles that stand in the way of total IFRS (International Financial Reporting Standards) integration. Culture, legal systems, tax, and the business practices of the companies themselves all need to be addressed'.

Returning attention to some comparative studies, the study of Golob and Bartlett (2007) investigated the issues of corporate social responsibility reporting in Australia and Slovenia and proved the existence of differences in national culture which, in turn, led to differences in social expectations and differences in kinds of information released in firms' reports. In another study, René (2010) investigated the case of 600 large firms in 22 countries and across 10 sectors in order to establish whether corporate social disclosure and national culture are correlated. Findings of the study indicated that national culture is likely to have an influence on corporate social disclosure. René (2010) concluded that such results can be useful to managers of multinational companies, who should take the national culture into account when preparing the corporate social disclosure of their companies.

In the same vein, it can be said that researchers should also take cultural factors into consideration when investigating the factors influencing social and environmental disclosure practices. In doing so, many factors can be used as proxies of culture such as ethnic background (of directors, shareholders, etc.), religious values and cultural dimensions (Haniffa and Cooke, 2005), and education (Archambault and Archambault, 2003). The following is an extended explanation regarding the last suggested factor.

8. EDUCATION

As individuals are the operators of the companies they work for, it seems a plausible assumption that changing individuals' attitudes and behaviors positively towards environmental and social issues is an important and necessary step to change companies' attitude to be more responsive towards the environment and society at large. In changing personnel's attitude and then behavior, education is likely to be proposed as a key tool. Babcock (2009) emphasized the need for norms in order to modify people's behavior to be environmentally more responsive, and he mentioned an effective public education campaign—inter alia—as a necessary mean for the effectiveness of the suggested norms. He stated, 'One thing by now should be apparent, and that is that public education must be a central part of any effort to change behavior' (Babcock, 2009, p. 175). Notwithstanding he was addressing the action of individuals in their daily life, there is no reason to not generalize his argument on the case of companies.

The level of education one might have reflects a person's knowledge and skills (Hambrick and Mason, 1984) and, as such, the quality of accounting work is likely to be influenced by the level of accounting (and finance, as well as business) education the accountants and managers have. Education is one of the institutional consequences influencing accounting systems (Gray, 1988) and, as a result, disclosure practices can be affected. A study by Behn et al. (2010) documented that even in non-profit organizations, the most disclosed organizations are those distinguished—inter alia—as higher education. They willingly disclose their audited financial information. By the same token, managers with an academic background are assumed to play a positive role in disclosure issues, as Hambrick and Mason (1984 , p. 200) suggested: 'The amount, but not the type, of formal education of a management team will be positively associated with innovation'. As such, there is no reason for not assuming that the same case applies to those who are responsible for preparing the reports (in financial departments or other departments) and releasing the information required. The lack of necessary competence is likely to have a negative consequence on accounting practices, such as that found in Lodhia (2003). In this study, environmental accounting practices (including reporting) in Fiji were found to be weak. The author attributes this finding to the voluntary nature of such practices and the lack of qualified staff to master this kind of accounting. The solutions suggested by the author to improve this situation included, as expected, educating accountants in environmental accounting.

The study by Deegan and Rankin (1999) which proved the existence of a gap between environmental reporting and users also recommended education as a remediation for the problem. It suggested modifying teaching programs (by professional bodies and institutions of higher education such as universities), not just for both accountants and responsible managers, but also for commerce students to enhance awareness of environmental (and social) issues in relation to firms' activities. What can be added to this suggestion is that education (or training) abroad for those in developing countries can be more effective in improving corporate disclosure practices (Ahmed and Nicholls, 1994) since issues of corporate disclosure are more advanced in developed countries. Baskin (2006) found no significant difference (in reporting corporate responsibility) between emerging- market companies and companies in developed economies, and noted that the first group is likely to give importance to the continuous training of their employees.

Despite the above argument, some studies presented contradictory findings. Haniffa and Cooke (2002) examined the impact of many factors relating to corporate governance and culture on the extent of voluntary disclosure and education (in addition to race) was chosen as a proxy of culture. Two hypotheses were stated expecting a positive relationship between the extent of voluntary disclosure and trained (and educated) directors on the board (in business and/or accounting) and finance director (in accounting or finance). The results did not identify those two variables. This lent support to the study of Parry and Groves (1990) who did not find a significant association between employing qualified accountants and the quality of financial reporting. A possible explanation is that high quality information is unlikely to be provided in the case of not implementing laws and regulations regarding information provision and (more importantly) in light of the absence of the demand for such information (Haniffa and Cooke, 2002). This was clearly stated by one of the interviewees in the study of Belal and Owen (2007), who regards social disclosure as superfluous and irrelevant due to the absence of some necessary factors. He stated, 'Until awareness increases, literacy levels rise and the agenda is thrust from the government level, I don't see any point in it (social disclosure)' (Belal and Owen, 2007, p. 481).

Apart from the possibility that some other factors which might affect the result of investigating the case of voluntary disclosure, the disclosure process is simply an interaction between sender and receiver, and judging the effectiveness of any factors which influence this process by focusing solely on their impact on one of them (sender or receiver) might lead to flawed results. The impact of education is more likely to be captured if the educational level of both information preparers and information users were evaluated alike. The study of Haniffa and Cooke (2002) investigated the impact of educational level of those who are responsible for producing the information, but did not consider the educational level of information users. Low level of education, and awareness as a result, among the expected information users and society at large will lead to both a lack of demand for social (and environmental) information and low level of corporate disclosure in regard to such information (Belal, 2001; Al-Khater and Naser, 2003). As such, considering both sides can cast more light on the real impact of education upon disclosure issues. Deegan et al. (2002 , p. 335), in the conclusion to his study, stated: '...higher levels of disclosure will only occur when community concerns are aroused, or alternatively, until such time that specific regulation is introduced to eliminate managements' disclosure discretion'. In line with this, it is reasonable to conclude that education is an effective way to achieve the first possibility and facilitate the second.

The impact of the awareness of society pertaining to social and environmental issues (raised mainly by educational programs) can be felt in its influence on corporate social and environmental disclosure practices. Deegan and Gordon (1996), in analyzing the case of some Australian companies (operating in 16 industries), found that there was a significant increase in environmental disclosure, and such increase can be seen as a result of an increase of awareness of society pertaining to environmental issues. Haniffa and Cooke (2005) also pointed to societal awareness as one of the reasons explaining the increased level of corporate social disclosure.

This argument gained confirmation at international level in the study of Baskin (2006) who did not find a significant difference between social and environmental disclosure made by companies in developed economies and that provided by leading emerging-market companies.

Baskin (2006) listed some conditions that exist in countries where the last group of companies is operating, and one of those conditions mentioned was the interest of civil society and activity in social and environmental issues. Among many possible explanations of such relationships between improvement of social and environmental disclosure practices and the awareness of society regarding such issues can be attributed to the impact of the awareness on the effectiveness of stakeholders' role.

Van der Laan Smith et al. (2005, p. 132) stated that if 'a society concerned with social issues, we argue stakeholder groups will have more power, possess greater legitimacy, and have their claims viewed with greater urgency'. They added, 'Managers in countries that exhibit strong concern with social issues would be more cognizant of and attach greater importance to stakeholder claims'.

CONCLUSION

Social and environmental disclosure is simply a communication process. As such, like other types of communication, the political, economic, and cultural atmosphere influences where and how disclosure takes place.

Desire, will, need, and ability in preparing and disseminating information on the impact of firm activities upon society and the environment cannot be evaluated properly without considering political, economic, and cultural contexts existing in the country where the firm operates. Legal factors and regulations, in addition to the political environment, affect a firm's desire and will pertaining to releasing social and environmental information. In terms of the need for such information, level of economic development of a country determines whether social and environmental information has a role to play in the decision making process. Finally, the desire, will, and need to produce social and environmental information are not enough to guarantee adequacy and quality of this type of information where the ability of doing so is absent or questionable. Education is a vital factor in creating and underpinning the ability to provide high quality social and environmental information.

REFERENCES

Abu-Baker, N. and Naser, K. (2000). Empirical evidence on corporate social disclosure (CSD) practices in Jordan. *International Journal of Commerce and Management*, 10, 18–34.

Adams, C.A. (2002). Internal organizational factors influencing corporate social and ethical reporting: Beyond current theorizing. *Accounting, Auditing and Accountability Journal,* 15, 223–250.

Adhikari, A. and Tondkar, R.H. (1992). Environmental factors influencing accounting disclosure requirements of global stock exchanges. *Journal of International Financial Management and Accounting*, 4, 75–105.

Ahmed, K. 1995. The impact of environment on disclosure practices: An empirical study. *Asian Review of Accounting*, 3, 90–104.

Ahmed, K. and Nicholls, D. (1994). The impact of non-financial company characteristics on mandatory compliance in developing countries: The case of Bangladesh. *International Journal of Accounting*, 29, 60–77.

Al-Khater, K. and Naser, K. (2003). Users' perceptions of corporate social responsibility and accountability: evidence from an emerging economy. *Managerial Auditing Journal*, 18, 538–548.

Amran, A. and Devi, S.S. (2008). The impact of government and foreign affiliate influence on corporate social reporting: The case of Malaysia. *Managerial Auditing Journal*, 23, 386–404.

Archambault, J.J. and Archambault, M.E. (2003). A multinational test of determinants of corporate disclosure. *International Journal of Accounting*, 38, 173–194.

Arpan, J.S. and Radebaugh, L.H. (1985). *International Accounting and Multinational Enterprises*. New York, Wiley.

Babcock, H.M. (2009). Assuming personal responsibility for improving the environment: Moving toward a new environmental norm. *Harvard Environmental Law Review,* 33, 117–175.

Barako, D.G. and Brown, A.M. (2008). Corporate social reporting and board representation: Evidence from the Kenyan banking sector. Journal of Management and Governance, 12, 309–324.

Baskin, J. (2006). Corporate responsibility in emerging markets. *Journal of Corporate Citizenship*, 24, 29–47.

Behn, B. K., Devries, D.D. and Lin, J. (2010). The determinants of transparency in nonprofit organizations: An exploratory study. *Advances in Accounting*, 26, 6–12.

Belal, A.R. (2001). A study of corporate social disclosures in Bangladesh. *Managerial Auditing Journal,* 16, 274–289.

Belal, A.R. and Cooper, S. (2007). Absence of corporate social reporting (CSR) in Bangladesh: a research note. In: Paper presented at European Critical Accounting Conference. Available at www.st-andrews.ac.uk/business/ecas/7/papers/ECAS-Belal.pdf (accessed September 2011).

Belal, A.R. and Owen, D.L. (2007). The views of corporate managers on the current state of, and future prospects for, social reporting in Bangladesh: An engagement-based study. *Accounting, Auditing and Accountability Journal,* 20, 472–494.

Belkaoui, A. (1983). Economic, political, and civil indicators and reporting and disclosure adequacy: Empirical investigation. *Journal of Accounting and Public Policy*, 2, 207–219.

Boden, R. (1999). Figure it out yourself: Financial reporting, accountability and the self-employed. *Critical Perspectives on Accounting*, 10, 37–62.

Branco, M. and Rodrigues, L. (2008). Factors influencing social responsibility disclosure by Portuguese companies. *Journal of Business Ethics*, 83, 685–701.

Choi, F.D.S. and Mueller, G.G. (1984). *International Accounting*. Englewood Cliffs, N.J, Prentice-Hall.

Cooke, T.E. and Wallace, R.S.O. (1990). Financial disclosure regulation and its environment: A review and further analysis. *Journal of Accounting and Public Policy*, 9, 79–110.

Cormier, D. and Magnan, M. (2003a). Does disclosure matter? *CA Magazine,* 136, 43.

Cormier, D. and Magnan, M. (2003b). Environmental reporting management: a continental European perspective. *Journal of Accounting and Public Policy*, 22, 43–62.

Crawford, E.P. and Williams, C.C. (2010). Should corporate social reporting be voluntary or mandatory? Evidence from the banking sector in France and the United States. *Corporate Governance*, 10, 512–526.

Dahawy, K. and Conover, T. (2007). Accounting disclosure in companies listed on the Egyptian Stock Exchange. *Middle Eastern Finance and Economics*, 1, 5–20.

Deegan, C. (2002). The legitimizing effect of social and environmental disclosures—A theoretical foundation. *Accounting, Auditing and Accountability Journal*, 15, 282–311.

Deegan, C. and Gordon, B. (1996). A study of the environmental disclosure practices of Australian corporations. *Accounting and Business Research,* 26, 187–199.

Deegan, C. and Rankin, M. (1999). The environment reporting expectations GAP: Australian evidence. *British Accounting Review,* 31, 313–346.

Deegan, C.M., Rankin, M. and Tobin, J. (2002). An examination of the corporate social and environmental disclosures of BHP from 1983–1997: A test of legitimacy theory. *Accounting, Auditing and Accountability Journal,* 15, 312–343.

Deese, D.A. (1998). Why political and civil freedom are fundamental to economic freedom, reform, and restructuring. *Journal of Private Enterprise*, 14, 45–67.

Doupniko, T.S. and Salter, S.B. (1995). External environment and accounting practice: A preliminary test of a general model of international accounting development. *International Journal of Accounting, Education and Research*, 30, 189–207.

Elijido-Ten, E. (2004). Determinants of environmental disclosures in a developing country: an application of the stakeholder theory. Paper presented at 4th Asia Pacific Interdisciplinary Research in Accounting Conference, Singapore.

Farook, S.Z., Lanis, R. and Hassan, K.M. (2011). Determinants of corporate social responsibility disclosure: The case of Islamic banks. *SSRN eLibrary* [Online]. http://dx.doi.org/10.2139/ssrn.1828624.

Frank, W.G. (1979). An empirical analysis of International accounting principles. *Journal of Accounting Research*, 17, 593–605.

Gastil, R.D. (1990). The comparative survey of freedom: Experiences and suggestions. *Studies in Comparative International Development*, 25, 25–50.

Golob, U. and Bartlett, J.L. (2007). Communicating about corporate social responsibility: A comparative study of CSR reporting in Australia and Slovenia. *Public Relations Review*, 33, 1–9.

Goodrich, P.S. (1986). Cross-national financial accounting linkages: An empirical political analysis. *British Accounting Review*, 18, 42–60.

Gordon, W C. (1990). *Institutional Economics*. Austin TX, University of Texas Press.

Gray, S.J. (1988). Towards a theory of cultural influence on the development of accounting systems internationally. *Abacus*, 24, 1–15.

Guthrie, J.E. and Parker, L.D. (1990). Corporate social disclosure practice: A comparative international analysis *Advances in Public Interest Accounting,* 3, 159–176.

Hambrick, D.C. and Mason, P.A. (1984). Upper echelons: The organization as a reflection of its top managers. *Academy of Management Review*, 9, 193–206.

Haniffa, R.M. and Cooke, T.E. (2002). Culture, corporate governance, and disclosure in Malaysian corporations. *Abacus*, 38, 317–349.

Haniffa, R.M. and Cooke, T.E. (2005). The impact of culture and governance on corporate social reporting. *Journal of Accounting and Public Policy,* 24, 391–430.

Harris, M. (1987). *Cultural Anthropology*. New York, Harper and Row.

Hofstede, G.H. (1980). *Culture's Consequences: International Differences in Work-Related Values*. Beverly Hills CA, Sage Publications.

Hope, O.K. (2003). Firm-level disclosures and the relative roles of culture and legal origin. *Journal of International Financial Management and Accounting*, 14, 218–248.

Imam, S. (2000). Corporate social performance reporting in Bangladesh. *Managerial Auditing Journal*, 15, 133–142.

Inchausti, B.G. (1997). The influence of company characteristics and accounting regulation on information disclosed by Spanish firms. *European Accounting Review*, 6, 45–68.

Ite, U.E. (2004). Multinationals and corporate social responsibility in developing countries: a case study of Nigeria. *Corporate Social Responsibility and Environmental Management*, 11, 1–11.

Jacobs, K. and Kemp, J. (2002). Exploring accounting presence and absence: Case studies from Bangladesh. *Accounting, Auditing and Accountability Journal*, 15, 143.

Khan, M.H. (2010). The effect of corporate governance elements on corporate social responsibility (CSR) reporting: Empirical evidence from private commercial banks of Bangladesh. *International Journal of Law and Management,* 52, 82–109.

Khan, M.H., Islam, M.A. and Ahmed, K. (2010). Corporate sustainability reporting of major commercial banks in line with GRI: Bangladesh evidence. Paper presented at the 6th Asia Pacific Interdisciplinary Research on Accounting (APIRA) Conference, Sydney.

Lau, C. M. and Caby, J. 2010. The effects of national culture on the role of participation in different task situations. *Advances in Accounting*, 26, 128–133.

Liu, X. and Anbumozhi, V. (2009). Determinant factors of corporate environmental information disclosure: An empirical study of Chinese listed companies. *Journal of Cleaner Production,* 17, 593–600.

Lodhia, S.K. (2003). Accountants' responses to the environment agenda in a developing nation: An initial and exploratory study on Fiji. *Critical Perspectives on Accounting,* 14, 715–737.

Mathews, M.R. (1993). *Socially Responsible Accounting*. London, Chapman and Hall

Matten, D. and Crane, A. (2005). Corporate citizenship: Toward an extended theoretical conceptualization. *Academy of Management Review*, 30, 166–179.

Mwaura, M.F. and Nyaboga, A.B. (2011). International financial accounting standards and the continent of Africa. *International Business and Economics Research Journal*, 8, 33–46.

Neu, D. and Gomez, E.O. (2006). The ethics of World Bank lending. *Accounting Forum*, 30, 1–19.

Nobes, C. and Parker, R.H. (1991). *Comparative International Accounting*. New York, Prentice Hall.

O'Dwyer, B. (2005). Stakeholder democracy: challenges and contributions from social accounting. *Business Ethics, A European Review*, 14, 28–28.

Owen, D.L. (2003). Recent developments in European social and environmental reporting and auditing practice–A critical evaluation and tentative prognosis. ICCSR Research Paper Series. Nottingham: International Centre for Corporate Social Responsibility.

Parry, M.J. and Groves, R.E. (1990). Does training more accountants raise the standard of accounting in Third World countries? A study of Bangladesh. *Research in Third World Accounting*, 1.

Patten, D.M. (1991). Exposure, legitimacy, and social disclosure. *Journal of Accounting and Public Policy*, 10, 297–308.

Patten, D.M. (1992). Intra-industry environmental disclosures in response to the Alaskan oil spill: A note on legitimacy theory. *Accounting, Organizations and Society*, 17, 471–475.

Radebaugh, L. (1975). Environmental factors influencing the development of accounting objectives, standards, and practices in Peru. *International Journal of Accounting Education and Research*, 11, 39–56.

Rene, O. (2010). Corporate social disclosures in the context of national cultures and stakeholder theory. *Accounting, Auditing and Accountability Journal,* 23, 868–889.

Rock, M.T. (2002). Pathways to industrial environmental improvement in the East Asian newly industrializing economies. *Business Strategy and the Environment*, 11, 90–102.

Salter, S.B. (1998). Corporate financial disclosure in emerging markets: Does economic development matter? *International Journal of Accounting*, 33, 211–234.

Simnett, R., Vanstraelen, A. and Chua, W.F. (2009). Assurance on sustainability reports: an international comparison. *The Accounting Review*, 84, 937–967.

Sobhani, F.A., Amran, A. and Zainuddin, Y. (2009). Revisiting the practices of corporate social and environmental disclosure in Bangladesh. *Corporate Social Responsibility and Environmental Management,* 16, 167–183.

Tagesson, T., Blank, V., Broberg, P. and Collin, S.O. (2009). What explains the extent and content of social and environmental disclosures on corporate websites: A study of social and environmental reporting in Swedish listed corporations. *Corporate Social Responsibility and Environmental Management*, 16, 352–364.

Thompson, P. (2002). Corporate environmental reporting in Singapore and Malaysia: Progress and Prospects. In Proceedings of the Corporate Environmental Reporting Conference, Kuala Lumpur.

Tsang, E.W.K. (1998). A longitudinal study of corporate social reporting in Singapore: The case of the banking, food and beverages and hotel industries. *Accounting, Auditing and Accountability Journal*, 11, 624–635.

Van Der Laan Smith, J., Ajay, A. and Rasoul, H.T. (2005). Exploring differences in social disclosures internationally: A stakeholder perspective. *Journal of Accounting and Public Policy*, 24, 151.

Van Der Molen, A. (2005). What really matters: What opinion leaders think and what others think of us? Paper presented at the Public Relations Institute of Australia (PRIA) National Conference, Brisbane.

Welford, R. (2005). Corporate social responsibility in Europe, North America, and Asia: 2004 survey results. *Journal of Corporate Citizenship*, 17, 33–32.

Wiig, A. and Kolstad, I. (2010). Multinational corporations and host country institutions: A case study of CSR activities in Angola. *International Business Review*, 19, 178–190.

Williams, S.M. (1999). Voluntary environmental and social accounting disclosure practices in the Asia-Pacific region: An international empirical test of political economy theory. *International Journal of Accounting*, 34, 209–238.

Wiseman, J. (1982). An evaluation of environmental disclosures made in corporate annual reports. *Accounting, Organizations and Society*, 7, 53–63.

Xiao, J.Z., Gao, S.S., Heravi, S. and Cheung, Y.C. (2005). The impact of social and economic development on corporate social and environmental disclosure in Hong Kong and the UK. *Advances in International Accounting*, 18, 219–243.

In: Economic and Financial Modeling
Editor: Andrew C. Worthington
ISBN: 978-1-63463-111-2

Chapter 9

MODELING FACTOR PRICE ELASTICITIES AND FACTOR SUBSTITUTION

Andrew C. Worthington [*] ***and Helen Higgs***
Griffith University, Australia

ABSTRACT

This chapter uses a multiple-input, multiple-output translog cost function to calculate Allen–Uzawa and Morishima elasticities of substitution for 36 Australian universities. The input prices are academic and nonacademic labor and capital. The six outputs are undergraduate, postgraduate and PhD completions, national competitive and industry grants, and publications. The results suggest that the derived demand for academic labor in the Australian university sector is highly price inelastic while the demand for nonacademic labor and capital is highly price elastic. This suggests that the cost drivers in the Australian university sector are presently price-related for academic inputs and technology-related for nonacademic and capital inputs. Moreover, the opportunities for input substitution are not symmetric, with the sector generally finding it easier to switch to capital than academic and nonacademic labor. Finally, while the Allen–Uzawa measures indicate that academic and nonacademic labor is a substitute, the less-restrictive Morishima measures suggest neither complementarity nor substitutability at the aggregate level.

1. INTRODUCTION

The Australian higher education sector has been subject to substantial cost pressures during the last decade. In response to burgeoning student load—from 1998 to 2006 the number of undergraduates grew from 433,498 to 524,201 (+20.92 percent) and the number of postgraduates from 80,108 to 139,716 (+74.41 percent)—and demands for greater research and research training outputs, Australian universities have substantially increased their factor

[*] Corresponding author: Department of Accounting, Finance and Economics, Griffith University, 170 Kessels Road, Nathan QLD 4111, Australia. E-mail. a.worthington@griffith.edu.au.

inputs. In evidence, the number of academic (nonacademic) staff grew from 29,775 (38,997) in 1998 to 34,971 (46,222) in 2006: respective increases of 17.45 and 18.61 percent. However, expenditures relating to labor and nonlabor inputs have increased even more rapidly, with nominal labor expenditures increasing by more than 75 percent and nominal nonlabor expenditures by more than 91 percent over the same period.

Studying the production technology of the university sector could yield useful information about the derived demand by universities for their factor inputs and their responses to changing prices in terms of input composition. For example, like universities elsewhere, Australian universities are very labor-intensive, with academic labor (salaries and salary-related costs) alone accounting for more than 30 percent of total expenditures. If the demand for academic labor is highly inelastic, then increases in salaries could result in substantial increases in production costs. One possible response to contain costs would be to substitute away from academic labor towards capital (larger lecture theatres, increased use of computer technology, etc.) or towards nonacademic labor (in providing at least some teaching, research and research training services traditionally delivered by academics). However, the precise substitution role of academic and nonacademic labor and capital in the Australian university sector is largely unknown and presently unaddressed in the existing literature (Throsby, 1986; Lloyd et al., 1993; Madden et al., 1997; Akviran, 2001; Abbott and Doucouliagos, 2003; Carrington et al., 2005; Worthington and Lee, 2008).

Accordingly, the purpose of this chapter is to estimate own-price and cross-price elasticities in the Australian higher education sector using the Allen–Uzawa and Morishima elasticities of substitution [following Blackorby and Russell (1989), Davis and Shumway (1996) and Okunade (1999]. The chapter comprises four main sections. Section 2 deals with the specification of higher education inputs, outputs and costs. Section 3 focuses on the cost function specification used to measure factor demands. Section 4 presents the results. The chapter ends with some concluding remarks.

2. SPECIFICATION

The data consist of annual observations of 36 Australian universities over the period 1998 to 2006. This is the longest period where the Commonwealth Department of Education, Science and Training (2008) (now Department of Education, Employment and Workplace Relations) has collected consistent data on university inputs, outputs and costs. The Australian Bureau of Statistics' Consumer Price Index (Education) converts all nominal monetary variables to real values (2000 = 100).

The major costs in university teaching, research, and research training are the wages, salaries, and related costs of academic and nonacademic staff. Other inputs comprise nonlabor expenditure, and these typically include the physical support of academic activities and research, libraries, other academic support services, student services, public services, buildings and grounds and administration and other general institution services. The input price of academic (nonacademic labor) for each university is determined by dividing the expenditures on academics (nonacademics) by the number of full-time equivalent academic (nonacademic) staff. We proxy the price of capital is proxied by dividing nonlabor expenditures by the stock of physical capital (measured by fulltime equivalent student load).

The total annual costs of each university are the sum of all labor and nonlabor (capital) expenditures. Five outputs are also specified: the annual number of undergraduate, postgraduate (excluding PhD), and PhD completions, the value of national competitive and industry grants (in dollars), and publications (in points) (5 points for books and 1 point for book chapters, refereed journal articles and refereed conference proceedings) [see Worthington and Lee (2008) for details and Worthington (2001) and Johnes (2006) for the specification of productive technology specifications in education].

Table 1 presents a summary of the mean costs, factor input prices, and outputs. First, between 1998 and 2006, average annual real total costs (in millions) range from \$88.1 to \$783.3 with a sector average of \$301.4. Second, in terms of real factor input prices, the means (in thousands) across the sector are \$113.2 thousand for academic labor, \$72.2 thousand for nonacademic labor and \$7.4 thousand for capital (the prices for labor are per equivalent full-time staff while the capital measure is per equivalent full-time student). Finally, over this period the typical Australian university annually graduated 3,572 undergraduates, 1,818 postgraduates, 123 doctorates, earned \$28.1 million in national competitive and industry grants and published 936 points.

3. METHOD

Starting with the assumption that the five university outputs are a function of the three inputs, the duality theory of production states that if universities purchase these inputs in competitive markets and engage in cost minimization, following Cohn et al. (1989), de Groot et al. (1991), Lloyd et al. (1993), Lewis and Dundar (1995), Hashimoto and Cohn (1997), Koshal and Koshal (1995; 1999; 2000), Izadi et al. (2002), O'Connell and Perkins (2003), Laband and Lentz (2003), Sav (2004), Stevens (2005), McMillan and Chan (2006), Lenton (2007) and Johnes et al. (2008) a dual cost function represents the production technology as follows:

$$LnC = \beta_0 + \sum_{i=1}^{8} \beta_i Lny_i + 1/2 \sum_{i=1}^{8} \delta_i (Lny_i)^2 + \sum_{\substack{i,j=1 \\ i \neq j}}^{8} \gamma_{ij} Lny_i Lny_j + \varepsilon_i \tag{1}$$

where β_0 is the fixed cost term, β_i (i = 1, 2,…, 8) are the slope coefficients of the linear term, δ_i (i = 1, 2,…, 5) are the slope coefficients of the quadratic terms, γ_{ij} (i =1, 2,…, 10, j =1, 2,…, 10 and $i \neq j$) are the slope coefficients of the cross-product terms, C is total costs and y_1 to y_8 represent the prices of the academic and nonacademic labor and capital inputs, undergraduate, postgraduate and PhD completions, national competitive and industry grants and publications.

Linear homogeneity of degree one in input prices requires the cost function in (1) to have the following restrictions:

$$\sum_{i=1}^{3} \beta_i = 1; \quad \sum \gamma_{ij} (\ln P_i \ln P_j) = \sum \gamma_{ij} (\ln Q_i \ln P_j) = 0 \tag{2}$$

where P_i is the price of the ith input (academic and nonacademic labor and capital) and Q_i is the quantity of the ith output and in addition the symmetry condition, $\gamma_{ij} = \gamma_{ji}$ for all i, j is imposed as the Hessian of the twice-differentiable cost function with respect to price is symmetrical. Using Shephard's Lemma, we obtain the factor demands by differentiating the cost function in equation (1) with respect to the input prices.

$$\frac{\partial LnC}{\partial LnP_i} = \frac{\partial C}{\partial P_i}\frac{P_i}{C} = \frac{X_i P_i}{C} = CS(P_i) \tag{3}$$

or

$$CS(P_i) = \frac{\partial LnC}{\partial LnP_i} = \beta_i + \delta_i Lny_i + \sum_{\substack{i,j=1 \\ i \neq j}}^{8} \gamma_{ij} Lny_j \tag{4}$$

where $CS(P_i)$ is the ith factor cost share and X_i is the quantity of the ith input and P_i is the price of the ith input. It is possible to improve the efficiency of the parameter estimates by estimating equation (1) with the cost share equations (3). The cost share for the three input prices must sum to one and this restriction produces singularity in the covariance of equation (4). The system of equations is estimated jointly by omitting one of the cost share equations in (4) together with equation (1) using a seemingly unrelated regression model imposing symmetry and the coefficients of the three input price coefficients to sum to one. The price of capital is the omitted input price.

In this cost function, the Allen partial elasticity of substitution (AES), which measures the effects of a change in price of the jth input on the quantity demanded of the ith input with output held constant, can be expressed as a function of the cost shares. The constant output own-price elasticity of factor demand, as well as the cross-price elasticity of factor demand are:

$$\sigma_{ii}^{A} = \frac{\delta_i + CS(P_i)^2 - CS(P_i)}{CS(P_i)^2} \tag{5}$$

for $i = 1, 2, 3$.

$$\sigma_{ij}^{A} = \frac{\gamma_{ij} + CS(P_i)CS(P_j)}{CS(P_i)CS(P_j)} \tag{6}$$

for $i = 1, 2, 3$ and $j = 1, 2, 3$, $i \neq j$.

The AES can also be used to obtain the Morishima elasticity of substitution (MES) as:

$$\sigma_{ij}^{M} = CS(P_j)(\sigma_{ij}^{A} - \sigma_{jj}^{A}) \tag{7}$$

for $i = 1, 2, 3$ and $j = 1, 2, 3$.

Table 1. Mean annual university costs, input prices, and outputs

	Total costs ($m)	Price of academic labor ($000s)	Price of nonacademic labor ($000s)	Price of physical capital ($000s)	# undergraduate completions	# postgraduate completions	# PhD completions	National competitive and industry grants ($000s)	Publication points
All universities	$301.44	$113.27	$72.24	$7.42	3573	1,818	124	$28,155	937
Australian Catholic University	$99.12	$112.33	$62.87	$3.66	1906	1,161	16	$1,284	186
Australian National University	$551.05	$128.09	$75.38	$25.07	1940	1,263	246	$68,808	2,351
Central Queensland University	$189.06	$98.07	$62.95	$7.82	2410	1,949	18	$2,010	265
Charles Darwin University	$88.50	$169.36	$118.73	$12.93	517	309	17	$4,299	123
Charles Sturt University	$185.24	$95.70	$64.25	$4.06	4792	2,276	26	$3,765	366
Curtin University of Technology	$352.80	$112.14	$69.30	$6.47	5808	1,958	111	$16,244	758
Deakin University	$307.79	$101.64	$74.54	$7.02	4552	2,432	84	$11,774	778
Edith Cowan University	$188.48	$116.02	$60.40	$4.70	3379	1,486	50	$3,136	504
Flinders University	$175.91	$101.18	$62.55	$6.43	2297	929	84	$18,990	680
Griffith University	$332.76	$103.92	$62.42	$6.42	4581	1,893	111	$20,564	922
James Cook University	$165.41	$96.62	$62.53	$7.26	1601	467	73	$8,916	441
La Trobe University	$299.35	$98.96	$70.47	$6.08	4347	2,224	143	$15,539	898
Macquarie University	$259.23	$107.70	$81.71	$6.54	3096	3,054	102	$16,759	859
Monash University	$707.25	$97.04	$70.79	$8.21	8454	3,893	309	$79,652	2,486
Murdoch University	$155.19	$99.26	$72.04	$6.87	2011	637	80	$15,508	449
Queensland University of Technology	$359.89	$101.85	$65.16	$5.64	6006	2,684	109	$15,109	996
RMIT University	$404.46	$146.85	$80.94	$5.64	5168	1,974	119	$10,390	783
Southern Cross University	$88.84	$104.62	$67.09	$5.07	1657	652	42	$3,428	165
Swinburne University of Technology	$192.25	$161.83	$115.49	$6.72	1875	938	47	$5,674	348
University of Adelaide	$330.13	$106.72	$70.14	$10.96	2808	1,048	185	$58,328	1,366
University of Ballarat	$88.13	$175.31	$84.26	$5.89	1066	724	12	$1,786	541
University of Canberra	$108.49	$117.42	$70.38	$4.98	1737	1,163	19	$3,055	237
University of Melbourne	$783.28	$106.65	$64.72	$11.31	7242	3,694	444	$137,236	2,568
University of New England	$148.74	$94.80	$59.60	$6.67	1907	1,272	77	$8,041	505
University of New South Wales	$663.54	$105.42	$86.05	$10.45	4370	3,965	338	$90,723	2,406

Table 1. (Continued)

	Total costs ($m)	Price of academic labor ($000s)	Price of nonacademic labor ($000s)	Price of physical capital ($000s)	# undergraduate completions	# postgraduate completions	# PhD completions	National competitive and industry grants ($000s)	Publication points
University of Newcastle	$264.36	$105.04	$62.25	$6.69	3254	1,324	102	$27,177	868
University of Queensland	$670.52	$97.96	$62.51	$10.79	5582	2,139	380	$106,330	2,712
University of South Australia	$280.45	$125.06	$66.56	$4.82	4597	2,259	116	$13,719	715
University of Southern Queensland	$120.18	$87.05	$57.32	$4.27	2170	1,445	21	$2,391	203
University of Sydney	$752.27	$108.98	$72.98	$9.44	6611	3,127	411	$125,695	2,762
University of Tasmania	$207.33	$103.68	$63.40	$7.69	2643	470	106	$21,082	673
University of Technology, Sydney	$279.75	$117.37	$79.43	$5.09	4174	3,775	75	$11,514	696
University of Western Australia	$378.12	$109.15	$68.06	$11.81	2758	1,016	188	$65,653	1,476
University of Western Sydney	$293.24	$109.49	$75.52	$4.54	5812	2,345	70	$6,653	698
University of Wollongong	$207.48	$102.40	$72.21	$6.98	2369	1,820	98	$16,944	798
Victoria University of Technology	$228.64	$155.36	$86.45	$6.22	2755	1,561	46	$4,457	448

At constant output, a positive AES between inputs i and j suggests the inputs are substitutes while a negative AES suggests they are complements. In equations (5) and (6), the AES $\sigma_{ij}^{A} = \sigma_{ji}^{A}$, in general the $\sigma_{ij}^{M} \neq \sigma_{ji}^{M}$. The standard errors of the estimated parameters are given as:

$$SE(\sigma_{ii}) = SE(\delta_i / CS(P_i)^2)$$
$$SE(\sigma_{ij}) = SE(\gamma_{ij} /(CS(P_i)CS(P_j)) \qquad (8)$$

Fundamentally the measures of AES and MES are quite different. The AES classifies a pair of inputs to be substitutes (complements) if an increase in the price of one causes an increase (decrease) in the quantity of the other, whereas the MES classifies a pair of inputs to be substitutes (complements) if an increase in the price of one causes an increase (decrease) in the quantity of the other relative to the quantity of the input whose price has changed. If two inputs are direct substitutes according to the AES criterion, then the two inputs must be direct substitutes according to the MES criterion. However, if two inputs are direct complements according to the AES criterion, they can be either direct complements or direct substitutes according to the MES criterion.

4. Results

The estimated coefficients, standard errors and p-values of the translog cost function are presented in Table 2. Also included in Table 2 is the R^2 for the cost function in equation (2) and Wald test statistics for the null hypotheses of no input price, output, linear, quadratic, and output cross-product effects. As shown, the R^2 of 0.9763 for the cost function is relatively high, as are the R^2 for the cost share equations (0.6225 and 0.3837) (not tabled). All other hypotheses are rejected at the one percent level of significance, indicating that all inputs, outputs, linear, quadratic and output cross-product effects should be included in estimating the translog cost function.

We use the parameter estimates of the translog cost function to calculate the AES and MES in Table 3. According to the AES, all own-price elasticities (on the diagonal) are negative and significant at the .01 level. The own-price elasticities of demand for nonacademic staff and capital, in absolute terms, are high and inelastic at –1.4554 and –1.5868, respectively. These indicate that a one percent increase in nonacademic salaries and the price of capital lead to a respective decrease in demand for nonacademic labor and capital by 1.45 and 1.58 percent. The demand for academic staff is, however, price inelastic with an own-price elasticity of –0.3406. That is, a one percent increase in academic salaries leads to only a 0.341 percent decrease in the demand for academic labor.

The off-diagonal values in Table 3 for the AES indicate that all production input pairs are potential substitutes. The cross-price elasticities show the existence of substantial substitutability between the three inputs with substitutabilities of 0.7520 between capital and nonacademic labor, 0.5990 between capital and academic labor and 0.3199 between nonacademic labor and academic labor, suggesting it is easiest to substitute capital and nonacademic labor, followed by capital and academic labor, then academic and nonacademic labor. In evidence, a one percent increase in the price of capital will decrease demand for nonacademic labor by 0.75 percent, a one percent increase in the price of capital will increase demand for academic labor by 0.59 percent, and a one percent increase in the price of nonacademic labor will increase demand for academic labor by 0.32 percent. All of the AES cross-price elasticities are statistically significant at the .01 level.

Table 2. Estimated translog cost function

	Coef.	Std. error	p-value		Coef.	Std. error	p-value
β_0	–4.0491	1.6998	0.0174	γ_{25}	–0.0052	0.0040	0.1885
β_1	0.0543	0.0497	0.2748	γ_{26}	–0.0038	0.0044	0.3896
β_2	0.4177	0.0466	0.0000	γ_{27}	0.0042	0.0037	0.2595
β_3	0.5280	–	–	γ_{28}	0.0104	0.0044	0.0191
β_4	0.9833	0.5507	0.0745	γ_{34}	0.0576	0.0813	0.4790
β_5	–0.6124	0.3557	0.0855	γ_{35}	0.0414	0.0680	0.5425
β_6	–0.7202	0.4578	0.1160	γ_{36}	–0.0658	0.0692	0.3416
β_7	0.0780	0.3832	0.8387	γ_{37}	–0.2074	0.0596	0.0005
β_8	0.7804	0.3989	0.0507	γ_{38}	0.1855	0.0897	0.0389
δ_1	0.1863	0.0098	0.0000	γ_{45}	0.0278	0.0775	0.7200
δ_2	0.0809	0.0114	0.0000	γ_{46}	0.0626	0.0829	0.4505
δ_3	0.4180	0.1161	0.0003	γ_{47}	–0.2472	0.0719	0.0006
δ_4	0.0131	0.1318	0.9209	γ_{48}	0.2166	0.0693	0.0018
δ_5	0.1047	0.0495	0.0346	γ_{56}	–0.0514	0.0529	0.3311
δ_6	–0.1947	0.0576	0.0008	γ_{57}	0.2337	0.0472	0.0000
δ_7	0.0516	0.0520	0.3213	γ_{58}	–0.3600	0.0578	0.0000
δ_8	0.0148	0.0364	0.6840	γ_{67}	0.1158	0.0442	0.0090
γ_{12}	–0.0773	0.0086	0.0000	γ_{68}	0.0819	0.0630	0.1941
γ_{13}	–0.1132	0.0076	0.0000	γ_{78}	–0.0672	0.0542	0.2157
γ_{14}	–0.0295	0.0067	0.0000	R^2			0.9793
γ_{15}	–0.0142	0.0043	0.0010	No input price effects			534.3741
γ_{16}	0.0012	0.0049	0.8121	No output effects			33.1741
γ_{17}	0.0241	0.0042	0.0000	No linear variables effects			101.4708
γ_{18}	0.0069	0.0049	0.1619	No squared variables effects			396.5424
γ_{23}	–0.0540	0.0068	0.0000	No input price cross effects			642.7557
γ_{24}	–0.0087	0.0061	0.1547	No output cross effects			70.6051

For the MES, only the cross-price elasticities between capital and academic/nonacademic labor are statistically significant at any conventional level. This would indicate that it is not possible to substitute between academic and nonacademic labor in the production of the university outputs as specified: that is, the academic labor–nonacademic labor substitutability has weakened to the point where it is no longer significant. The positive values of the remaining pairs between academic/nonacademic labor and capital show, like the AES, that these are substitutes. Compared with the AES estimates, however, the labor–capital substitutability has strengthened.

The MES offer unique insights as they are not symmetric (i.e. less restrictive in their assumptions) than the AES. In other words, for any pair of production factors, the numerical estimates of the MES depend on which of the factor prices changes. The MES show that the highest cross-price elasticity is between nonacademic labor and capital (1.7198), indicating a one percent increase in the price of nonacademic labor increases the cost share of capital relative to nonacademic labor elastically by 1.72 percent. However, the cross-price elasticity of capital and nonacademic staff (0.6532) indicates a one percent increase in the price of capital leads to only a 0.65 percent increase in the cost share of nonacademic labor relative to capital. This suggests that it is relatively easier (more than two and half times so) for universities to substitute capital for nonacademic labor than nonacademic labor for capital.

Table 3. Own and cross-price elasticities of substitution

	Allen partial elasticity of substitution (AES)			Morishima elasticity of substitution (MES)		
	Academic labor	Nonacademic labor	Capital	Academic labor	Nonacademic labor	Capital
Academic labor	–0.3406	–	–	–	0.5253	1.6073
Std. error	0.0664	–	–	–	0.4836	0.3003
t-value	–5.1261	–	–	–	1.0862	5.3525
Nonacademic labor	0.3199	–1.4554	–	0.2536	–	1.7198
Std. error	0.0757	0.1307	–	0.3090	–	0.3107
t-value	4.2232	–11.1384	–	0.8206	–	5.5351
Capital	0.5990	0.7520	–1.5868	0.6909	0.6532	–
Std. error	0.0270	0.0315	0.2147	0.1769	0.4436	–
t-value	22.2063	23.9025	–7.3913	3.9054	1.4724	–

The other statistically significant pairs of elasticities of substitution are between academic labor and capital. The cross-price elasticity of substitution between academic labor and capital (1.6073) implies that a one percent increase in the price of academic labor will increase the share of capital by 1.61 percent relative to academic labor. However, the cross-price elasticity of substitution between capital and academic labor (0.6909) suggests that a one percent increase in the price of capital is associated with only a 0.69 percent increase in the cost share of academic labor. This indicates that it is easier for universities to substitute capital for academic labor than academic labor for capital.

CONCLUSION

The findings of this chapter are as follows. First, the derived demand for academic labor in the Australian university sector is highly price inelastic while the demand for nonacademic labor and capital is relatively price elastic. While all three inputs have exerted cost pressures on universities and the sector as a whole during the last decade, this would suggest increasing prices are mainly responsible for the increase in academic labor expenditures, while the nature of the production technology is mainly responsible for the increasing expenditures on nonacademic labor and capital. Second, the opportunities for input substitution are not symmetric, with the sector generally finding it easier to switch to capital than academic and nonacademic labor. Finally, while the AES indicates that academic labor and nonacademic labor are input substitutes, the less-restrictive MES suggests that they are neither complements nor substitutes. This is likely because nonacademic labor as a whole performs both roles, and only a finer division of nonacademic labor (currently unavailable) into positions complementing teaching, research and research training and those that substitute for at least some services traditionally provided by academics would resolve this uncertainly.

REFERENCES

Abbott, M., and Doucouliagos, C. (2003). The efficiency of Australian universities: a data envelopment analysis. *Economics of Education Review*, 22(1), 89–97.

Avkiran, N.K. (2001). Investigating technical and scale efficiencies of Australian universities through data envelopment analysis. *Socio-Economic Planning Sciences*, 35(1), 57–80.

Blackorby, C. and Russell, R. (1989) Will the real elasticity of substitution please stand up? A comparison of the Allen/Uzawa and Morishima elasticities, *American Economic Review*, 79, 882–888.

Carrington, R., Coelli, T., and Rao, P. (2005). The performance of Australian universities: Conceptual issues and preliminary results. Economic Papers, 24(2), 145–163.

Cohn, E., Rhine, S. L. W., and Santos, M. C. (1989). Institutions of higher education as multi-product firms: Economies of scale and scope. *The Review of Economics and Statistics*, 71(2), 284–290.

Davis, G.C. and Shumway, C.R. (1996) To tell the truth about interpreting the Morishima elasticity of substitution, *Canadian Journal of Agricultural Economics*, 44, 183–182

de Groot, H., McMahon, W. W., and Volkwein, J. F. (1991). The cost structure of American research universities. *The Review of Economics and Statistics*, 73(3), 424–431.

Department of Education, Science and Technology (2008) Available at http://www.dest.gov.au/. Accessed June 2008.

Hashimoto, K., and Cohn, E. (1997). Economies of scale and scope in Japanese private universities. *Education Economics*, 5(2), 107–115.

Izadi, H., Johnes, G., Oskrochi, R., and Crouchley, R. (2002). Stochastic frontier estimation of a CES cost function: the case of higher education in Britain. *Economics of Education Review*, 21(1), 63–71.

Johnes, G. (1996). Multi-product cost functions and the funding of tuition in UK universities. *Applied Economics Letters*, 3(9), 557–561.

Johnes, G., Johnes, J., and Thanassoulis, E. (2008). An analysis of costs in institutions of higher education in England. *Studies in Higher Education*, 33(5), 527–549.

Johnes, J. (2006). Data envelopment analysis and its application to the measurement of efficiency in higher education. *Economics of Education Review*, 25(3), 273–288.

Koshal, R.K., and Koshal, M. (1995). Quality and economies of scale in higher education. *Applied Economics*, 27(8), 773–778.

Koshal, R.K., and Koshal, M. (1999). Economies of scale and scope in higher education: a case of comprehensive universities. *Economics of Education Review*, 18(2), 269–277.

Koshal, R.K., and Koshal, M. (2000). Do liberal arts colleges exhibit economies of scale and scope? *Education Economics*, 8(3), 209–220.

Laband, D.N., and Lentz, B.F. (2003). New estimates of economies of scale and scope in higher education. *Southern Economic Journal*, 70(1), 172–183.

Lenton, P. (2007) The cost structure of higher education colleges in England, *Economics of Education Review*, 27(4), 471–482

Lewis, D.R., and Dundar, H. (1995). Economies of scale and scope in Turkish universities. *Education Economics*, 3(2), 133–157.

Lloyd, P. J., Morgan, M. H., and Williams, R.A. (1993). Amalgamations of universities: are there economies of scale or scope? *Applied Economies*, 25(8), 1081–1012.

Madden, G. Savage, S. and Kemp, S. (1997) Measuring public sector efficiency: A study of economics departments in Australian universities, *Education Economics*, 5(2), 153–168.

McMillan, M.L., and Chan, W. H. (2006). University efficiency: A comparison and consolidation of results from stochastic and non-stochastic methods. *Education Economics*, 14(1), 1–30.

O'Connell, J.F., and Perkins, G. M. (2003). The economics of private liberal arts colleges. *Journal of Business*, 76(3), 499–514.

Okunade, A.A. (1999) Will the real elasticity of substitution 'in Norwegian dentistry' please stand up? *Health Economics*, 8, 221–232.

Sav, G. T. (2004). Higher education costs and scale and scope economies. *Applied Economics*, 36(6), 607–614.

Stevens, P.A. (2005). A stochastic frontier analysis of English and Welsh universities *Education Economics*, 13(4), 355 - 374.

Throsby, D. (1986) Cost functions for Australian universities, *Australian Economic Papers*, 25(1) 175–192.

Worthington, A.C. (2001). An empirical survey of frontier efficiency measurement techniques in education. *Education Economics*, 9(3), 245–268.

Worthington, A.C. and Lee, B.L. (2008) Efficiency, technology and productivity change in Australian universities, 1998-2003, *Economics of Education Review*, 27(3), 285–298.

In: Economic and Financial Modeling
Editor: Andrew C. Worthington

ISBN: 978-1-63463-111-2

Chapter 10

PERFORMANCE MODELS FOR INITIAL PUBLIC OFFERINGS

Nancy Vu[1], Andrew C. Worthington[2*] and Phillip Laird[1]
[1]University of Wollongong, Australia
[2]Griffith University, Australia

ABSTRACT

This chapter examines the pricing and performance of ordinary, venture capital, and private equity-backed initial public offerings in the Australian stock market. We use headline underpricing, underpricing issuer loss, underpricing loss by market value, and underpricing loss by issue price to measure underpricing, and cumulative buy-and-hold abnormal returns with equal and value-weighted market indexes, market and book-to-market value quintile adjustments, and the Fama–French three-factor model to compare performance. The measures of underpricing indicate that venture capital and private equity-backed issues are underpriced less than ordinary issues. Further, all three forms of issuance outperform the nominal performance benchmarks. However, there is no statistically significant difference in the risk-adjusted performance of initial public offerings, regardless of backing.

1. INTRODUCTION

Following the events of September 11, 2001 and the lower level of initial public offerings (IPO) in 2002, IPO activity in Australia trended strongly upwards until 2008/09 and the consequences of the Global Financial Crisis. Building on a background of strong domestic equity returns, an inundation of cash flows from superannuation (pension) funds, the T3 effect (the sale by the Commonwealth Government of its remaining stake in Telstra, Australia's leading telecommunications and information services company) and an extended resources boom, the number and value of IPOs in Australia continued to grow during this

[*] Corresponding author: Department of Accounting, Finance and Economics, Griffith University, 170 Kessels Road, Nathan QLD 4111, Australia. Email. a.worthington@griffith.edu.au.

period. In fact, equity raised during the early 2000s easily doubled that raised during the 1999–2000 dot-com boom, IPO capital collections for each of the three financial years since 2004–05 passed $10 billion, and by 2004 Australia ranked fourth in the world – after the US, Japan and China – for the total number of completed IPOs (Ernst and Young 2005). This frenetic level of activity continued with the resources boom continuing into 2007–2008 (six of the top ten IPOs were in the energy or materials sector) and a record 226 IPOs listed or are set to list on the market, up 34% from 2006/07.

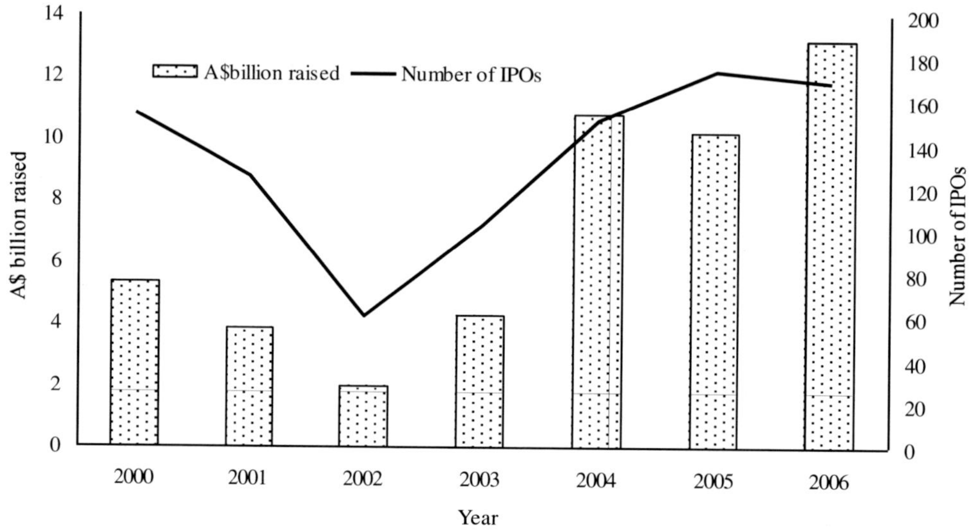

Figure 1. Summary of Australian IPO activity.

At the same time, there has been considerable growth in venture capital (VC) and private equity (PE) markets in Australia and their share of IPO activity through investment exits. For example, in 2000–01 VC-backed IPOs amounted to A$171 million; by 2003–04 this had grown to $1,460 million. Private equity has also had a role to play with A$21.7 billion invested by PE managers through the purchase of 32 listed companies in 2006, equating to about 1.4% of the total value of the Australian Stock Exchange (ASX). In time (typically seven to ten years), many of these return to the public market with "…approximately 25% of all sales of private equity investments via public offering on the ASX thereby returning the business to the listed market, usually with a more solid and profitable outlook" (APEVCAL 2006). In fact, for the first time in 2004, a significant number of PE-backed IPOs took place, demonstrating the maturing of the market (Ernst & Young 2005). By 2006, when 71 new companies listed on the ASX, eleven were the result of early-stage investors (including VC and PE) exiting their investments (PriceWaterhouseCoopers 2007). The Australian Private Equity and Venture Capital Association Limited (2006) suggests these and other changes result from the consistently high returns delivered by private equity managers, continuing growth in the global debt market allowing private equity managers (and other borrowers) to be able to borrow more, and the escalation of available funds from superannuation savings for all categories of investment.

Disturbingly, the strong performance of the Australian IPO market, as elsewhere, is often accompanied by lackluster aftermarket price performance, at least at the market level. In 2004, for example, only 44% of all IPOs during 2003–04 were trading at or above their issue price. This was 9% lower when compared to the previous year. In the following year, the percentage of IPOs trading above issue price fell to 51% down 5%. By December 2005, four of the seven largest IPOs to list in 2005–06 were trading below their issue price, including Macquarie Capital Alliance (–11%), Babcock and Brown Capital (–20%), Alinta Infrastructure (–3%) and Challenger Infrastructure (–7%), (Deloitte, 2005). Moreover, all too often a small number of outliers can strongly affect average performance. For instance, the average return increased from 11% in 2004–05 to 24% in 2005–2006. However, as in previous years this was biased by a few small-capitalization resource IPOs that experienced substantial returns (Deloitte 2006). Following earlier trends, the share price performance of the ten largest IPOs of 2005–06 was again disappointing with half trading below their issue price. Overall, the observed average performance was –2%, significantly lower than the overall market average of 24%, with 75% of all funds raised by floats in excess of $100m only achieving a return of less than 10%.

The purpose of this chpater is to consider one of the more salient features of the contemporary Australian IPO market—the growth of VC and PE-backed IPOs—within the context of the long-established focus on IPO pricing and performance. Although a substantial amount of research of this type exists in the United States and elsewhere, Australian studies concerning the pricing and performance of IPOs, not just VC and PE-backed firms, are scarce and limited in scope. This paper first aims to increase the depth of Australian research by examining the pricing and performance of initial public offers during the period June 1996 to May 2007. Then paper then extends this work by considering the differentials in pricing and performance, if any, for VC and PE firms.

The remainder of the chapter is structured as follows. Section 2 provides a brief literature review. Section 3 explains the data methodology employed in the analysis. The results are dealt with in Section 4. The chapter ends with some concluding remarks in the final section.

2. Review of the Literature

One of the more puzzling phenomena in finance is the underpricing of new stock issues. Various explanations are given, including information asymmetry, signaling relationships, cyclical behavior and third-party certification. Foremost among these, the information asymmetry hypothesis sees underpricing as an equilibrium occurrence when investors are disproportionately informed. Since uninformed investors face the consequences of poor judgment when other investors are better informed, underpricing arises to compensate uninformed investors for the risk of ending up with a less successful IPO.

Underpricing is clearly a concern for entrepreneurs, venture capitalists, and private equity investors, since it reduces the amount received by going public. However, it is argued that the extent of the entrepreneurs' concerns is limited to the influence on their net wealth. Costly action, such as employing reputable underwriters, is undertaken only where advantageous. In general, as the proportion of the company going public escalates, the existing investors in the firm attempt to reduce underpricing at an increasing rate. When informed investors believe an issue is overpriced, they discard the investment opportunity and seek issues elsewhere that are not overpriced.

An alternative rationale for underpricing is that the value of an issue depends on market demand and the underwriter's selling efforts. In general, the underwriter is typically aware of demand levels, more so than the issuer. As such, the issue price is set below its 'true value' to increase interest. Similarly, the issuer is more informed then potential investors. In an attempt to resolve problems with asymmetric information, the underwriter signals the true value of the firm by underpricing the securities and acquires a percentage of the shares. The retention of shares comes as a signaling device to the market – the higher the withholding, the higher the return expected.

Other work draws attention to the signaling relationship between the issuer's fractional holding of the firm's equity and the expected future cash flows. In response to these and other theoretical developments, a body of empirical research has arisen, largely in the US, concluding that IPOs are indeed underpriced [see, most recently, Ibbotson et al. (1994), Megginson and Weiss (1991), Hunt-McCool et al. (1996), Habib and Ljungqvist (1998; 2001), Francis and Hasan (2001), Bradley and Jordan (2002), Loughran and Ritter (1995; 2002)]. Finn and Higham (1988), Lee et al. (1996) and How et al. (1995) find similar evidence in Australian markets.

Now consider venture capital investments. Most VC organizations raise funds in limited partnerships with finite lifetimes. In the Australian context, "…venture capital organizations provide high risk capital for new or young businesses with prospects of rapid growth and high rates of return. The ultimate goal of this type of investment is to accelerate the growth of these businesses" (ABS 2001: 11). Being repeat players and regularly having to raise new funds, venture capitalists face reputational risk. There is then great pressure for young VC firms to establish a reputation in the market and to raise new funds in order to remain operational.

The literature available in the past three decades on venture capitalist funds, the monitoring processes, and the effect of having VC financing on a firm's performance in US markets is considerable. In general, venture capitalists often hold a strong equity position in the companies they finance, and bring to bear substantial influence on management (Barry et al. 1990). As venture capitalists are closely involved in the management and supervision of their investment companies, there is also a tendency to choose small, young firms with problems with information asymmetry.

Dietz (2002), for instance, argues that entrepreneurs are confronted by a trade-off between the higher costs associated with venture financing compared to bank financing and the increase in firm value due to advising. Although the costs associated with venture capitalist financing are greater than with bank finance, only risk-seeking entrepreneurs will desire VC. Accordingly, Engel (2002) shows that the decline in financial constraints due to the capital injections, monitoring and services the venture capitalist provides positively impacts on the performance of VC-backed firms. Megginson and Weiss (1991) and Barry et al. (1990) provide evidence that VC-backed firms tend to go public earlier then non VC-backed firms because venture capitalists verify the value of the offering. Gompers (1996, p. 153) concludes, "…venture capitalists repeatedly bring companies to the IPO market and … commit not to offer overpriced shares".

An IPO changes many features of a firm, but nothing more than the ownership structure. Considerable changes continue to occur as a result of the greater dispersion of shareholdings

(Brennan and Franks 1997; Mikkelson et al. 1997), have a weighty effect on managerial incentives (Zingales 1995) and influence the underpricing and underperformance of an issue (Jain and Kimi 1994; Booth and Chua 1996; Pham et al. (2003). Studies have shown that pre-IPO ownership has an effect on the pricing and costs of an issue – the smaller the proportion of pre-IPO shareholdings by management, the lower the incentive to control total issuing costs. More specifically, major decisions in the IPO process tend to favor management in firms not wholly owned before going public.

As a result, firms can suffer agency problems even before going public. Ljungqvist and Wilhelm (2003), for instance, interpret underpricing as evidence of agency costs because CEOs are required to represent pre-IPO shareholders when negotiating issue prices with underwriters. According to Habib and Ljungqvist (2001) the negative impact of underpricing on pre-IPO owners' wealth may be minimal when a smaller proportion of shares is offered to the public, or when underpricing is deliberately used as a promotional tool to reduce other marketing costs, such as underwriting fees. That is, instead of outlaying funds to promote the issue, the underwriter uses underpricing as the issue's main source of marketing. Loughran and Ritter (2002) point out that while underpricing is an opportunity cost as the ownership of pre-IPO shareholders is diluted, it is associated with an increase in the value of the retained shares.

Empirical studies generally support the value of VC financing. Gompers (1995) examines the staging and monitoring of VC investments. Gompers (1995) finds that in the lead up to an IPO venture-backed firms receive more financing and a greater number of financing rounds than venture-backed firms going bankrupt. Gompers (1995) adds that this supports the argument that VCs are better able to identify successful and unsuccessful projects through their monitoring techniques. Klausner and Litvak (2001), hypothesize that VCs can dramatically alter the professionalism of the firms in which they invest. A survey conducted by Hellman and Puri (2000) on the evolution of undeveloped, privately held, high-technology firms in Silicon Valley gives support. Lerner (1994) finds that venture capitalists time their initial public offerings so that firms are taken to market at the optimal time. A study by Megginson and Weiss (1991) in the US shows that the occurrence of underpricing in VC-backed IPOs is far less than that which takes place in non VC-backed issues. Megginson and Weiss relate this to the reputation effect, as VCs who continually take firms to the market can credibly risk their reputation that these firms are not overpriced.

In addition, VCs have the ability to attract high quality analysts to the entities going public, decreasing the level of irregular information at the time of offering. Barry et al. (1990) and Megginson and Weiss (1991) concluded from their results that VC-backing supports the quality of the IPO, leading to less underpricing. However, Habib and Ljungqvist (1999) found that the VC-backed firms in Megginson and Weiss' study issued 36 percent more shares then the other firms. This suggests that VC-backed firms are motivated to take on costly procedures in order to reduce underpricing. While VC-backed firms suffer the same wealth-loss as non-VC backed firms when the number of shares is considered, underpricing is reduced by actions taken by VC-backed firms to signal quality, rather than through VC certification.

In terms of performance, most of the extant work concurs with Moonchul and Ritter (1999) that post-IPO firms in the US generally underperform since investors are overly optimistic about their potential when listed. In terms of the aftermarket performance of VC and PE-backed IPOs, Barry et al. (1990) argues that because venture capitalists hold a strong equity position in the companies they finance and influence, their role in the success of IPOs should not be underestimated. Moreover, there is a tendency for venture capitalists to choose small, young firms where information asymmetry problems exist. For this reason, venture capitalists are able to identify successful projects through superior monitoring techniques, in addition to having the ability to attract high quality analysts to the entities going public, decreasing the level of irregular information at the time of offering and increasing aftermarket performance.

Francis and Hasan (2001) find that the initial day returns for VC-backed issues are higher than other issues. However, they attribute this to the deliberate underpricing that characterizes issues brought to the market by VCs. Lee et al. (1996) found the average underperformance of VC and PE-backed issues in the market. Conversely, Brav and Gompers (1997) conclude that although VC-backed issues outperformed non-VC backed issues; underperformance is not caused by an IPO effect. This is in line with Loughran and Ritter's (1995) conclusion that underperformance is not a trait of IPOs but rather a result of IPO firms being small with low book-to-market values.

3. METHOD

A review of the extant literature on the pricing and performance of ordinary and VC and PE-backed IPOs suggests two broad hypotheses. First, in terms of underpricing, VC and PE-backed IPOs suffer less from underpricing then ordinary IPOs. Second, VC and PE-backed firms should outperform ordinary IPO firms post-listing. In order to test the first hypothesis, four complementary measures of underpricing are calculated: headline underpricing, underpricing issuer loss, underpricing loss by market value, and underpricing loss by issue price. To test the second hypothesis, average cumulative buy-and-hold abnormal returns are calculated and performance measures from pooled Fama–French three-factor regressions are estimated.

3.1. Sample Selection and Data Sources

A list of all 1,500 IPOs undertaken during the period 1 June 1996 to 31 May 2007 is obtained from the Australian Stock Exchange (ASX). Initially, the firm's prospectus is checked to determine if venture capital (VC) or private equity (PE) backing was present prior to the IPO. For example, if the prospectus shows that a venture capitalist was a director or shareholder at the time the prospectus was issued, then the firm is VC-backed. However, due to the potential limitations of published information, all 1,500 firms were contacted via electronic mail (addressed to either the chief executive officer or the company secretary) enquiring about the presence of VC or PE activity in the firm prior to its release on the market. From the 1,500 companies, 281 replies were received (a response rate of 18.7%). This compares well with an optimal sample size of 306 for a 95% confidence internal. The sample comprises 182 (65%) ordinary firms, 54 (19%) VC-backed firms, and 45 (16%) PE-backed firms. Sixteen firms are excluded because of missing or abnormal data. Although the data set is not exhaustive, and may not necessarily comprise a pure random sample, the firms are spread over each of the years in the sample period and so meaningful results can still be drawn for the population. Regarding post-IPO performance, 91 firms only listed in 2006 and 2007. Since these firms have only two years of post-IPO data, and given they have not delisted, the strategy taken is to allow these firms to phase out as their data ends. Following Ritter (1991), Loughran and Ritter (1995), Brav and Gompers (1997), Carter et al. (1998) and Gompers and Lerner (1999), delisted firms are excluded from the performance analysis. The requisite data is collected from various sources. Daily stock prices and the market index represent ASX historical data. The issue price, secondary shares (shares already issued prior to the firm going public) and primary shares (new shares offered in the initial public offer) and the proportion of shares retained by the firm are from the company's prospectus. Information on the market value and book-to-market value are from the Aspect Huntley database.

3.2. Measures of Underpricing

The four underpricing measures used in this study are adapted from Habib and Ljungqvist (1999) and Silva Rosa et al. (2003). First, headline underpricing (*UPH*) is a traditional measure of underpricing:

$$UPH = \frac{(P_c - P_i)}{P_i} \tag{1}$$

where P_c is the closing price on the first day of trading and P_i is the issue price of the firm's stock. Second, underpricing issuer loss (*UPIL*) determines the loss to the issuer per share:

$$UPIL = (1 - \text{Retained ownership}) \times \frac{(P_c - P_i)}{P_i} \tag{2}$$

where retained ownership is the portion of ownership of the firm retained (or the proportion of shares held by the board) and all other variables are as previously defined. Third, underpricing loss by market value (*UPLMV*) is the underpricing loss standardized by the firm's market value:

$$UPLMV = \frac{(P_c - P_i) \times (\text{Secondary shares} + \text{Retained ownership} \times \text{Primary shares})}{P_c \times \text{Total shares}} \tag{3}$$

where secondary shares is the number of shares held by pre-IPO shareholders, primary shares is the number of new shares offered in the IPO and total shares is the total shares on issue for the post-IPO firm. Finally, underpricing loss by issue price (*UPLIP*) shows the loss to the issuer standardized by the value of the firm based on the issue price

$$UPLIP = \frac{(P_c - P_i) \times (\text{Secondary shares} + \text{Retained ownership} \times \text{Primary shares})}{P_i \times \text{Total shares}} \tag{4}$$

where all variables are as previously defined.

The four underpricing measures in Equations (1)–(4) are calculated for each firm in the sample. The mean and median values for the all IPOs, ordinary IPOs, VC-backed IPOs, PE-backed IPOs are also compiled. Finally, a value-weighted measure of each underpricing measures is calculated using:

$$\sum_i (\text{Total shares}_i \times UP_i) \Big/ \sum_i \text{Total shares}_i \tag{5}$$

where UP_i is respectively *UPSTD*, *UPIL*, *UPLMV* and *UPLIP*. This measure of underpricing takes into account a firm's size relative to the level of underpricing.

The following numerical example provides an illustration. Consider XYZ Ltd, a company with 1 million shares on issue prior to floatation. The company is offering 5 million new shares and 50,000 existing shares to the public at A$2.00 per share. On its initial day of trade, the closing price is $2.30 per share so headline underpricing (*UPH*) is 15.0%. *UPIL* adjusts the headline underpricing measure for retained ownership. In this case, the firm's existing owners retain 0.95 million shares of total issued capital of 6 million shares (15.8%), so *UPIL* is 12.6%.

The measure of the wealth lost to the firm divided by the market value of the firm after listing is *UPLMV*. The wealth loss to the firm comprises two parts. First, the firm loses 30¢ per share on the 50,000 shares sold ($15,000). Secondly, the firm bears a 15.8% share of the loss on the 5 million shares sold at $2.00 instead of their 'true' value of $2.30 per share. This amounts to an additional 30¢ × 5,000,000 × 0.158 = $237,000. Thus, the total loss to the firm is $252,000. When this is expressed as a proportion of the market value of the firm after listing ($2.30 × 6 million = $13.8 million), the *UPLMV* is 1.83%. *UPLIP* scales the loss to the firm ($252,000) by the value of the firm implied at issue ($2.00 × 6 million = $12 million) and is 2.1%.

3.3. Measures of IPO Performance – Cumulative Abnormal Returns

The excess return of an IPO is calculated for 24 months starting the month after the stock has listed. In common with Fama and French (1993; 1996), Brav and Gompers (1997), Lyon et al. (1999) and Silva Rosa et al. (2003), excess return is measured in six ways, with equal and value-weighted measures using market index and market/book-to-market value quintile adjustments.

Returns are defined as *CBHAR* (cumulative buy-and-hold abnormal returns) where the starting price for each company is its last price for the month of listing. The buy-and-hold return for each month up to 24 months is calculated. The *CBHAR* are then calculated by subtracting the return for the control: namely, the index, market value quintiles or book-to-market quintiles.

$$CHBAR = \left(\frac{r_{m-1} - r_m}{r_m} \right) - \text{Control} \tag{6}$$

The monthly control return is determined in the same way as the company returns. After the *CHBARs* are found for each firm, an average *CHBAR* (based on the *CHBAR* of each of the three controls) is calculated for that month for the 24-month observation period.

For the index control, the value used in the return calculation is the index itself. The value used for the return calculation of the market value and book-to-market value quintiles is the average adjusted share return of the quintile that the IPO belongs according to its market value and book-to-market value. Because of data constraints, market value and book-to-market values are only available on an end-of-year basis. Consequently, monthly market values and book-to-market values were interpolated from the end-of-year figures. The market value and book-to-market quintiles are formed on a month-end basis. This allows firms to move from one quintile to another over time.

Paired-sample *t*-statistics are calculated for each monthly *CBHAR* as there are two samples that have been matched or 'paired', namely the stock return and the control (market index, market cap and book-to-market values). First, the *BHAR* (buy-and-hold abnormal return) for month n is computed as $CBHAR_n - CBHAR_{n-1}$. The *t*-statistic for *BHAR* is:

$$BHAR\_t_{month} = \frac{\text{Average } BHAR}{\sigma(BHAR)/\sqrt{n}} \quad (7)$$

where average *BHAR* is the sample mean of each month's *BHAR* and *σ(BHAR)* is the cross-sectional standard deviation of abnormal returns for the sample of n firms. The *t*-statistic for each month's *CBHAR* is then calculated as:

$$CBHAR\_t_{month} = \frac{\sum_{month=0}^{n} BHAR\_t_{month}}{\sqrt{n}} \quad (8)$$

The size of n changes each month owing to the staggered listing of firms. Adjustments are made for n so that only firms with returns actually available for a particular month are included.

A value-weighted measure can be applied to underperforming IPOs as well as those generating excess returns. The first step taken to calculate value-weighted measures is to find the market value of all IPOs each month. The factor f for each IPO in its initial month of trade is:

$$f = \frac{\text{IPO market value}}{\text{Control value}} \quad (9)$$

The factor f can be thought of as the number of 'shares' in the index (or market or book-to-market quintile) that can be purchased, such that the value invested in the index is the same as the market capitalization of the IPO (Silva Rosa et al. 2003). As before, the control value for the index is the index itself; in market value and book-to-market value quintile calculations it is the market value of the quintile the IPO fits into for that particular month. The fixed factor f is then multiplied with the control value over the following 24 months, producing 24 values (one per month) for each IPO. For the case of market value and book-to-market quintiles, each firm has five *f*-values (corresponding to each of the quintiles). Following this, the product of the *f*-values and the control values are summed for a given month. The value-weighted return is then one minus the total market value of all IPOs in the sample for a given month.

3.4. Measures of IPO Performance – Fama–French Three-Factor Model

Recent work claims that multifactor asset pricing models can explain many pricing anomalies found in the literature (Brav and Gompers 1997). For instance, Fama and French (1996) argue that the 'value' strategies in Lakonishok et al. (1994) and the 'buying losers–selling winners' strategy of DeBondt and Thaler (1985; 1987) are consistent with their three-factor asset pricing model. In line with the models specified by Fama and French (1996), Brav and Gompers (1997), Barber and Lyon (1996) and Silva Rosa et al. (2003), regression estimates are calculated for all sampled IPOs with more than ten monthly returns. The regression equation is specified as:

$$R_{it} = \alpha_{it} + \beta_{it} RMRF_t + \gamma_{it} SMB_t + \delta_{it} HML_t + \varepsilon_{it} \tag{10}$$

where R_{it}, is the monthly return of the *i*th IPO for the *t*th month less the 90-day bank-accepted bill rate; $RMRF_t$ is the value-weighted portfolio return less the 90-day bank bill rate; SMB_t (small-minus-big) is the difference in returns of a value-weighted portfolio of small and big stocks; HML_t (high-minus-low) is the difference in returns of a value-weighted portfolio of high and low book-to-market stocks, α (alpha), β (beta), γ (gamma) and δ (delta) are parameters to be estimated, and ε is the error term. A positive value for the intercept α indicates that after controlling for market, size and book-to-market factors in returns, the IPO has performed better than the norm.

In order to determine HML_t and SMB_t, all of the firms in the portfolio are ranked on a monthly basis according to their market value (MV) as at the end of the previous month. The median firm is then used to determine the split point, sectioning the portfolio into two groups: small (S) and big (B). In a similar manner, firms within the portfolio were ranked by their book-to-market equity (BE/MV). For this analysis, book value is defined as the book value of shareholders' equity. The portfolio is then divided into three BE/MV groups based on pre-determined break points: the bottom 30% (Low), the middle 40% (Medium) and the top 30% (High). In order to establish the appropriate break points, negative book value firms were excluded. The intersection of the two ME groups and the three BE/MV groups resulted in the construction of six portfolios covering all possible combinations. These are small market value with low book value (S/L); small market value with medium book value (S/M); small market value with high book value (S/H); big market value with low book value (B/L); big market value with medium book value (B/M); and big market value with high book value (B/H). Each portfolio contains all firms with the labelled attributes.

The *SMB* variable is then determined by taking the difference between the average of the returns on the three small-stock portfolios (S/L, S/M and S/H) and the average of the returns on the three big-stock portfolios (B/L, B/M and B/H) on a monthly basis. Similarly, monthly figures for *HML* are formed from the difference in average returns of the two high-book-to-market-equity portfolios (S/H and B/H) and the low-book-to-market-equity portfolios (S/L and B/L). As defined, the corresponding coefficients beta, gamma and delta take values on a scale of 0 to 1: beta = one (zero) would be a high (low) market risk portfolio; gamma = one (zero) would be a small (large) cap portfolio; and delta = one (zero) would be a portfolio with a high (low) price/book ratio.

5. Results

4.1. Measures of Underpricing

Table 1 provides the headline underpricing (*UPH*), underpricing issuer loss (*UPIL*), underpricing loss by market value (*UPLMV*), and underpricing loss by issue price (*UPLIP*) measures for the sample of IPOs by category (ordinary, venture capital, and private equity). First, all IPOs are underpriced, on average, by 57.8% in terms of UPH. However, since the median level of underpricing is only 7.5% it is clear that underpricing is relatively low overall.

Table 1. Measures of IPO underpricing by category

Category	Underpricing	UPH	UPIL	UPLMV	UPLIP
All IPOs	Mean	0.578	0.474	–0.111	0.354
	Median	0.075	0.050	0.017	0.017
	t-statistic	4.155	3.885	–1.700	3.818
	p-value	<0.001	0.001	0.090	0.001
	Value-weighted	0.818	0.653	–0.001	0.522
Ordinary IPOs	Mean	0.707	0.605	–0.137	0.397
	Median	0.058	0.050	0.002	0.002
	t-statistic	3.448	3.304	–1.704	3.069
	p-value	0.001	0.001	0.090	0.002
	Value-weighted	0.838	0.705	–0.025	0.472
VC-backed IPOs	Mean	0.321	0.289	0.073	0.278
	Median	0.080	0.076	0.035	0.037
	t-statistic	1.921	1.744	2.733	1.864
	p-value	0.060	0.087	0.008	0.068
	Value-weighted	0.845	0.812	0.150	0.727
PE-backed IPOs	Mean	0.396	0.202	–0.225	0.285
	Median	0.075	0.039	0.034	0.035
	t-statistic	1.834	1.958	–0.950	1.482
	p-value	0.073	0.056	0.347	0.145
	Value-weighted	0.686	0.204	–0.009	0.630

Notes: UPH – headline underpricing, UPIL – underpricing issuer loss, UPLMV – underpricing loss by market value, and UPLIP – underpricing loss by issue price. VC – venture capital, PE – private equity. *t*-statistics and *p*-values are tests of null hypothesis that means are equal to zero.

Moreover, since the value-weighted mean underpricing is high at 81.8%, there is some indication firms with a higher market capitalization are disproportionately underpriced. Second, *UPIL* has a mean value of 47.4%. That is, investors holding share equity prior to the firm's initial public offer have collectively made a loss of 47.4% of their stock's share price. Once again, the observed median score for *UPIL* is comparatively lower at 5%. Since the value-weighted *UPIL* is again higher at 65.3% it is again obvious that larger firms had higher levels of loss.

An interesting observation arises with the measure of underpricing that measures the wealth loss to the firm (*UPLMV*). Unlike *UPH* and *UPIL*, *UPLMV* is –11.1% (overpriced). In the case of a negative *UPLMV*, each of the 72 firms with a negative loss did not suffer from any underpricing, rather they performed poorly on their first day of trade. Consider, for example, Extract Resources Ltd. which suffered a massive price decline on the first day of trade (29 August 2003), with prices falling from the issue price of $0.20 to $0.01 at close. This resulted in a *UPLMV* of –1024.32%. Karmel Sonix Ltd followed this with a 'loss' of –887.85%. After standardizing by issue price (*UPLIP*), the entire sample shows an average underpricing of 35.4%; when value-weighted an average underpricing of 52.2% is found. For all four measures of underpricing (*UPH*, *UPIL*, *UPLMV* and *UPLIP*) the null hypothesis that the mean is zero is rejected at the .01 level. We conclude Australian IPOs between 1996 and 2007 are underpriced in headline (57.8%), issuer loss (47.4%) and issuer price (35.4%) terms, but slightly overpriced in terms of market value lost (–11.1%). Consider now the differences between ordinary, VC-backed and PE-backed IPOs. In terms of headline underpricing (*UPH*), VC-backed IPOs are less underpriced (32.1%) than either PE-backed (39.6%) or ordinary (70.7%) IPOs. This supports the hypothesis that VC-backed firms are priced fairly. This broadly holds when the measure of underpricing is adjusted for the proportion of shares retained by the issuer is taken into account, though PE-backed firms are now less underpriced (20.2%) than their VC-backed counterparts (28.9%). This should reflect the willingness of PE investors to retain a smaller proportion of ownership in the listed entity.

Table 2. Tests for differences in variances and means of IPO underpricing by category

	Category	UPH		UPIL		UPLMV		UPLIP	
Variance		*F*-stat.	*p*-value	*F*-stat.	*p*-value	*F*-stat.	*p*-value	*F*-stat.	*p*-value
	VC-backed IPOs	4.869	0.000	3.942	0.000	28.400	0.000	2.446	0.000
	PE-backed IPOs	3.351	0.000	11.653	0.000	0.431	0.000	1.677	0.023
Mean		*t*-stat.	*p*-value	*t*-stat.	*p*-value	*t*-stat.	*p*-value	*t*-stat.	*p*-value
	VC-backed IPOs	–1.448	0.075	–1.266	0.104	2.475	0.007	–0.596	0.276
	PE-backed IPOs	–1.037	0.151	–1.909	0.029	–0.354	0.362	–0.475	0.318

Notes: UPH – headline underpricing, UPIL – underpricing issuer loss, UPLMV – underpricing loss by market value, and UPLIP – underpricing loss by issue price. VC – venture capital, PE – private equity. The null hypothesis for the two-sided variance test is that the underpricing for ordinary IPOs and VC/PE-backed IPOs have equal variances. The null hypothesis of the one-sided means test is that the mean underpricing for VC/PE-backed IPOs is less than ordinary IPOs. The variance test determines whether the means test assumes equal or unequal variances.

The null hypothesis that the mean is zero is rejected for *UPH* and *UPIL* at the .01 level for ordinary IPOs and at the .10 level for VC-backed and PE-backed IPOs. We conclude that VC-backed and PE-backed Australian IPOs suffer less from underpricing than ordinary IPOs, and that when the proportion of ownership retained is taken account, PE-backed IPOS are less underpriced than VC-backed IPOs.

However, a different picture emerges when the loss is standardised by market value (*UPLMV*) and the issuer price (*UPLIP*). In this case, neither of the mean underpricing measures is significantly different from zero for PE-backed IPOs and we may conclude these are fairly priced in the Australian market. For *UPLMV*, ordinary IPOs are moderately overpriced (13.7%) and VC-backed IPOs slightly underpriced (7.3%) and both statistics are significantly different from zero at the .10 level or higher. In terms of *UPLIP*, the differences are again significant at the .10 level with ordinary IPOs underpriced by 39.7% and VC-backed IPOs by 27.8%. Table 2 provides the results of tests of differences in variances and means between VC-backed and ordinary IPOs and PE-backed and ordinary IPOs. In all cases, the variances significantly differ. However, the mean underpricing for VC-backed IPOs is only significantly less than ordinary IPOs for *UPH*, *UPIL* and *UPLMV*, while the underpricing for PE-backed IPO is significantly less underpriced than ordinary IPOs only in terms of *UPIL*. On balance, we conclude that IPOs in Australia from 1996–2007, regardless of backing, are on average underpriced, but while strong evidence exists that VC-backed issues are less underpriced than ordinary issues, the evidence for a lower level of PE-backed IPO underpricing is weak.

4.2. Measures of IPO Performance – Cumulative Abnormal Returns

Table 2 presents the two-year equal and value-weighted abnormal returns for the IPOs included in the sample by category of backing. The mean monthly equally weighted *CBHAR* against the index is 0.01% over the whole sample. Intriguingly the corresponding value-weighted *CBHAR (VCBHAR)* for all IPOs is −1780.9%, identifying the phenomenal underperformance of IPOs to the market over the observed horizon. One inference is that the market index had a strong negative influence on IPO performance during the sample period. For example, 46 of the 132 monthly returns on the All Ordinaries are negative, with the other returns never exceeding 7.1% with a mean return of 0.75%. As a result, the *f* values calculated for each of the IPOs based on the market control are primarily below zero. Those firms that floated in a month where negative returns were recorded, acquired negative (*f x Control value)* for the remainder of its 'life' during the study.

The *CBHAR* for the sample benchmarked against market value and book-to-market value are 0.70% and 0.68% respectively. The corresponding *t*-statistics (not shown) for the *CBHAR*s benchmarked against market quintiles and book-to-market quintiles fall within the rejection region at the 5% level of significance and are thus significant. The long-run equal-weighted *CBHAR* for the ordinary backed sample against the index is –0.3% (insignificant). Market quintile and book quintile *CBHAR* are 0.34% and 0.31% (both just significant). The value weighted results express similar results as found for the whole sample except for the market value quintile score which performed quiet differently. All three measures for the ordinary sample moved in the same direction to these corresponding *CBHARs*, at 768.3%, –1.20% and 281.6%.

Table 3. Two-year abnormal returns for IPOs by category

Category	Variable	CBHAR	VCBHAR
All IPOs	Index	<0.001	9.364
	Market value quintiles	0.007	–0.410
	Book-to-market quintile	0.006	2.066
Ordinary IPOs	Index	–0.003	7.682
	Market value quintiles	0.003	–0.011
	Book-to-market quintile	0.003	2.816
VC-backed IPOs	Index	0.021	12.277
	Market value quintiles	0.028	8.331
	Book-to-market quintile	0.027	6.350
PE-backed IPOs	Index	0.019	11.330
	Market value quintiles	0.024	11.143
	Book-to-market quintile	0.025	6.988

Notes: CBHAR – cumulative buy-and-hold return, VCHAR – mean CBHAR, VC – venture capital, PE – private equity.

The results for the VC backed portfolio suggest that the portfolio performs better against all three benchmarks, even though the returns are still relatively low. Monthly returns of the VC-backed sample against the All Ordinaries Index, market value quintiles and book-to-market quintiles, all display a fluctuating trend in *CBHARs* during the 24-month period. The 24-month equal weighted cumulative buy-and-hold returns for the VC sample against the index is 2.14% and significant. Similarly, returns against market quintiles and book-to-market quintiles were 2.8% and 2.74% respectively, again both significant. As shown in Table 2, the *CBHARs* for the VC-backed firms are higher than any other sample. This is also evident in the value-weighted equivalent when tested against the index, market and book-to-market quintiles with returns of 1227%, 833% and 635% respectively. These extraordinarily large returns are partly attributable to a number of large cap firms experiencing substantial returns. The results suggest that if an investor invested in only VC-backed firms from 1996 to 2006 they would have made a positive return over a 24-month period. These results differ to Silva Rosa et al. (2003) who concluded that investors would have made a negative return if they had invested in Australian VC-backed firms from 1991 to 1999.

The final group to consider is the PE sample, which performed in a comparable manner to the VC sample. The 24-month cumulative buy-and-hold abnormal returns against the: index is 1.91% (insignificant), market value quintiles are 2.48% (insignificant) and book-to-market quintiles is 2.52% (insignificant).

It is surprising to see that these results are insignificant. Although these results suggest that PE performance is statistically insignificant, there is no denying (like for the VC sample) that if capital were invested in PE firms during the observation period, positive returns would result.

Yet again, the value-weighted figures imply that larger firms performed substantially better than smaller firms. Smaller firms were able to drag down the value weighted *CBHAR* averages from 1133%, 1114% and 699% (index, market, book-to-market) to their equal weighted equivalents of 2.14%, 2.8% and 2.74% respectively.

Table 4. Tests for differences in variances and means of IPO CBHAR by category

	Category	Index		Market value		Book-to-market	
		F-stat.	*p*-value	*F*-stat.	*p*-value	*F*-stat.	*p*-value
Variance	VC-backed IPOs	0.117	<0.001	0.158	<0.001	0.157	<0.001
	PE-backed IPOs	0.234	<0.001	0.290	<0.001	0.289	<0.001
		t-stat.	*p*-value	*t*-stat.	*p*-value	*t*-stat.	*p*-value
Mean	VC-backed IPOs	1.482	0.070	1.434	0.076	1.418	0.079
	PE-backed IPOs	1.621	0.053	1.450	0.074	1.493	0.069

Notes: CBHAR – cumulative buy-and-hold return, VC – venture capital, PE – private equity. The null hypothesis for the two-sided variance test is that the CBHAR for ordinary IPOs and VC/PE-backed IPOs have equal variances. The null hypothesis of the one-sided means test is that the mean CBHAR for VC/PE-backed IPOs are greater than ordinary IPOs. The variance test determines whether the means test assumes equal or unequal variances.

Table 4 provides tests of differences in the variances and mean CBHAR for VC-backed and ordinary IPOs and PE-backed and ordinary IPOs. All tests for equal variances reject the null hypothesis. Likewise, all tests that the mean abnormal return for VC/PE-backed IPOs are greater than ordinary IPOs reject the null hypothesis and we may conclude that VC-backed and PE-backed IPOs significantly outperform their counterparts, by three times for index returns and up to nine times for market and book-to-market value returns. In turn, VC-backed IPOs marginal outperform PE-backed IPOs.

4.3. Measures of IPO Performance – Fama–French Three-Factor Model

Table 5.4 provides the estimated coefficients, *t*-values and *p*-values for the Fama and French pooled regression. As shown, alpha is positive but insignificant. This indicates that, after controlling for market, size and book-to-market factors in returns, IPOs have not performed better then expected. The coefficient for the market factor (beta) is positive, greater than unity and significant at the .01 level. Similarly, the coefficients for the small-minus-big and high-minus-low factors are also positive and significant at the .01 and .10 levels, respectively. These result are "…consistent with the proposition that there at are least two factors that are priced in the long-run returns of IPOs", (Silva Rosa et al. 2003, p.15). The adjusted R^2 of the regression is relatively low at 4.61%.

The regression outputs for the sub samples of ordinary, VC-backed and PE-backed IPOs provide similar results. In no instance is the coefficient signifying superior risk-adjusted performance (alpha) significantly different from zero. This provides similar results on the risk-adjusted performance of IPOs to Silva Rosa et al. (2003) for 333 Australian IPOs over the period 1991-1999. The betas are all significant, with ordinary IPOs and PE-backed displaying higher market risk than VC-backed IPOs. For PE-backed IPOs particularly, this would indicate that some of their performance is associated with higher levels of market risk.

The gamma values are also significant and highest for VC-backed IPOs followed by PE-backed IPOs signifying that part of the superior nominal performance of these IPOs can bet attributed to their small size characteristics. Finally, the values for delta are highest for VC-backed IPOs and lowest for PE-backed IPOs indicating differences in performance associated with high (low) book-to-market values. In all three categories, most return variation is explained by the market, followed by size and lastly book value. However, the total percentage of variation in returns explained by the three-factor model is never more than 6.7 percent.

Table 5. Pooled Fama–French regressions

Coefficients and statistics	All IPOs	Ordinary IPOs	VC-backed IPOs	PE-Backed IPOs
Alpha	0.003	0.000	0.009	0.014
t-value	0.840	0.040	0.810	1.600
p-value	0.401	0.971	0.419	0.111
Beta	1.195	1.241	0.861	1.230
t-value	10.410	9.710	2.290	4.020
p-value	<0.001	<0.001	0.022	<0.001
Gamma	0.311	0.259	0.525	0.379
t-value	7.610	5.730	3.920	3.360
p-value	<0.001	<0.001	<0.001	<0.001
Delta	0.065	0.027	0.411	–0.166
t-value	1.950	0.710	3.680	–1.680
p-value	0.052	0.476	<0.001	0.094
R^2	0.047	0.046	0.072	0.065
Adj. R^2	0.046	0.045	0.067	0.059

Notes VC – venture capital, PE – private equity. Alpha is the constant, beta is the estimated coefficient for the market portfolio, gamma is the estimated coefficient for the small-minus-big portfolio, delta is the estimated coefficient for the high-minus-low portfolio.

CONCLUSION

This chapter examined the pricing and performance of ordinary, venture capital and private equity-backed initial public offerings in the Australian stock market from June 1996 to May 2007. Headline underpricing, underpricing issuer loss, underpricing loss by market value, and underpricing loss by issue price are used to measure underpricing. Cumulative buy-and-hold abnormal returns with equal and value-weighted market indexes, market and book-to-market value quintile adjustments and the Fama–French three-factor model were used to compare performance.

In terms of underpricing, the results indicate that Australian IPOs are generally underpriced and that VC-backed and PE-backed IPOs are less underpriced than their oridinary counterparts. All four measures of underpricing — standard or 'headline' underpricing, underpricing loss to the issuer and underpricing standardised by market value and issue price — provide some evidence that venture capital and private equity-backed issues are less underpriced than ordinary issues. However, the evidence presented of a lower level of underpricing is most strong for VC-backed IPOs. These findings support comparatively recent evidence of IPO underpricing generally in the US Habib and Ljungqvist (2001), Francis and Hasan (2001), Bradley and Jordan (2002), Loughran and Ritter (2002) along with the conjecture that venture capitalists have an incentive and means available to prevent underpricing.

In terms of post-IPO performance, the nominal performance benchmarks provide abundant evidence that IPOs outperform in terms of abnormal returns and that VC and PE-backed IPOs outperform ordinary IPOs. This supports work by Brav and Gompers (1997), amongst others, who concluded that VC-backed samples outperformed non-VC firms in the US. However, it lies counter to the only related Australia works by Lee et al. (1996) and Silva Rosa et al. (2003). One possibility is that both of these studies draw upon much earlier sample periods and that it is only relatively recently that venture capital and private equity-backed firms have begun to play a much larger role in the Australian market. However, analysis of the risk-adjusted performance of VC and PE-backed IPOs — indeed all IPOs — indicates no abnormal returns over a two-year horizon, suggesting that the superior long-run performance of IPOs mostly relates to their high level of market risk and very low book-to-market values for PE-backed firms and their small size attributes for VC-backed firms.

REFERENCES

Australian Bureau of Statistics (2005). 2004–2005 Venture capital and private equity, Catalogue No. 5678.0, Canberra. Available at http://www.abs.gov.au/.

Australian Private Equity and Venture Capital Association Limited (2006). Annual Report, Sydney. Available at www.avcal.com.au/.

Barber, B. and Lyon, J. (1996). Detecting abnormal operating performance: The empirical power and specification of test statistics. *Journal of Financial Economics*, 41, 359–399.

Barry, C., Muscarella, C., Peavy, J. and Vetsuypens, M.R. (1990). The role of venture capital in the creation of public companies: Evidence from the going-public process. *Journal of Financial Economics*, 27, 447–472.

Booth, J.R. and Chua, L. (1996). Ownership dispersion, costly information and IPO underpricing. *Journal of Financial Economics*, 41, 291–310.

Bradley, D.J. and Jordan, B.D. (2002). Partial adjustment to public information and IPO underpricing. *Journal of Financial and Quantitative Analysis*, 37, 595–616.

Brav, A. and Gompers, P.A. (1997). Myth or reality? The long-run underperformance of initial public offerings: Evidence from venture and nonventure capital-backed companies. *Journal of Finance*, 52, 1791–1821.

Brennan, M. and Franks, J. (1997). Underpricing, ownership and control in initial public offerings of equity securities in the United Kingdom. *Journal of Financial Economics*, 45, 391–413.

Brooks, R. and Dimovski, W. (2004). Initial public offerings in Australia 1994 to 1999, Recent evidence of underpricing and underperformance. *Review of Quantitative Finance and Accounting,* 22, 179–198.

Carter, R., Dark, F., and Singh, A. (1998). Underwriter reputation, initial returns, and the long-run performance of IPO stocks. *Journal of Finance*, 53, 285–312.

DeBondt, W.F.M. and Thaler, R.H. (1985). Does the stock market overreact. *Journal of Finance,* 40, 793–805.

DeBondt, W.F.M. and Thaler, R.H. (1987). Further evidence on investor overreaction and stock market seasonality. *Journal of Finance,* 42, 557–581.

Deloitte (2006). Deloitte IPO report July 2006, Sydney. Available at www.deloitte.com.au/.

Dietz, M.D. (2002). Risk, self-selection and advice: Banks versus venture capitalists (February 27, 2002). Available at SSRN: http://ssrn.com/abstract=302080.

Engel, D. (2002). The impact of venture capital on firm growth: An empirical investigation (January 15, 2002). ZEW Discussion Paper No. 02-02. Available at SSRN: http://ssrn.com/abstract=319322.

Ernst & Young (2005). Global IPO Survey 2005, Sydney. Available at www.ey.com/.

Fama, E. and French, K. (1993). Common risk factors in the returns on stocks and bonds. *Journal of Financial Economics*, 33, pp. 3–56.

Fama, E. and French, K. (1996). Multifactor explanations of asset pricing anomalies. *Journal of Finance*, 51(1), 55–84

Finn, F.J. and Higham, R. (1987). The performance of unseasoned new equity issues-cum-stock exchange listings in Australia. *Journal of Banking and Finance*, 12, 333–351.

Francis, B.B. and Hasan, I. (2001). The underpricing of venture and nonventure capital IPOs: An empirical investigation. *Journal of Financial Services Research,* 19(2/3), 93–113.

Gompers, P.A. (1996. Grandstanding in the venture capital industry. *Journal of Financial Economics*, 42, 133–156.

Gompers, P. and Lerner, J. (2001). The venture capital revolution. *Journal of Economic Perspectives*, 15(2), 145–168.

Habib, M.A. and Ljungqvist, A.P. (2001). Underpricing and entrepreneurial wealth losses in IPOs: Theory and evidence. *Review of Financial Studies*, 14, 433–458.

Habib, M.A. and Ljungqvist, A.P. (1998). Underpricing and IPO proceeds: A note. *Economic Letters*, 61, 381–383.

Hellman, T. and Puri, M. (2000). The interaction between product market and financing strategy: The role of venture capital. *Review of Financial Studies*, 13, 959–984.

How, J.C.Y., Izan, H.Y. and Monroe, G.S. (1995). Differential information and the underpricing of initial public offerings: Australian evidence. *Accounting and Finance,* 35, 87–105.

Hunt-McCool, J., Koh, S. and Francis, B. (1996). Testing for deliberate underpricing in the IPO premarket: A stochastic frontier approach. *Review of Financial Studies*, 9, 1251–1269.

Ibbotson, R.G., Sindelar, J.L. and Ritter, J.R. (1994). The market's problems with the pricing of initial public offerings. *Journal of Applied Corporate Finance*, 7, 66–74.

Jain, B. and Kimi, O. (1994). The post-issue operating performance of IPO firms. *Journal of Finance*, 49, 1699–1726.

Klausner, M.D. and Litvak, K. (2001). What economists have taught us about venture capital contracting. In M. Whincop (Ed.) *Bridging the Entrepreneurial Financing Gap: Linking Governance with Regulatory Policy*, Ashgate: Dartmouth.

Kothari, S.P and Warner, J.B. (1997). Measuring long-horizon security price performance. *Journal of Financial Economics*, 43, 301–340.

Lakonishok, J. and Shliefer, A. and Vishnv, R.W. (1994). Contrarian investment, extrapolation and risk. *Journal of Finance,* 49, 1541–1578

Lee, P., Taylor, S., and Walter, T. (1996). Australian IPO pricing in the short and long run. *Journal of Banking and Finance*, 20, 1189–1210.

Lerner, J. (1994). Venture capitalists and the decision to go public. *Journal of Financial Economics*, 35, 293–316.

Ljungqvist, A.P. and Wilhelm, W.J. (2003). IPO pricing in the dot-com bubble. *Journal of Finance*, 58, 723–752.

Loughran, T. and Ritter, J.R. (1995). The new issue puzzle. *Journal of Finance*, 50, 23–51.

Loughran, T. and Ritter, J. (2002). Why don't issuers get upset about leaving money on the table in IPOs? *Review of Financial Studies*, 15(2), 413–444.

Lyon, J.D., Barber, B.M. and Tsai, C-L. (1999). Improved methods for testing of long run abnormal stock returns. *Journal of Finance*, 54, 165–201.

Megginson, W.L. and Weiss, K.A. (1991). Venture capitalist certification in initial public offerings. *Journal of Finance*, 42, 879–882.

Mikkelson, W., Partch, M. and Shah, K. (1997). Ownership and operation performance of companies that go public. *Journal of Financial Economics*, 44, 281–307.

Moonchul, K. and Ritter, J.R. (1999). Valuing IPOs. *Journal of Financial Economics*, 53, 409–437.

Pham, K.P., Kalev, P.S., and Steen, A.B. (2003). Underpricing, stock allocation, ownership structure and post-listing liquidity of newly listed firms. *Journal of Banking and Finance,* 27, 919–947.

PriceWaterhouseCoopers (2007). Survey of Sharemarket Floats. Available at www.pwc.com/.

Ritter, J. (1991). The long run performance of initial public offerings. *Journal of Finance*, 46, 3–28.

Silva Rosa, R., Velayuthen, G., and Walter, T. (2003). The sharemarket performance of Australian venture capital backed and non-venture capital backed IPOs. *Pacific-Basin Finance Journal*, 11, 197–218

Zingales, L. (1995). Insiders' ownership and the decision to go public. *Review of Economic Studies*, 62, 425–448.

In: Economic and Financial Modeling
Editor: Andrew C. Worthington
ISBN: 978-1-63463-111-2

Chapter 11

NONPARAMETRIC MODELS OF TECHNICAL EFFICIENCY IN URBAN WATER UTILITIES

Andrew C. Worthington*
Griffith University, Nathan, Australia

ABSTRACT

This chapter models the technical operating and capital efficiency of major Australian urban water utilities using data envelopment analysis. We specify different inputs and outputs for each measure of efficiency and make allowance for the inclusion of uncontrollable contextual inputs thought to impact upon the observed efficiency of utilities but largely outside their control. The results indicate that a relatively high level of relative operating and capital efficiency prevails across the sector. Measured efficiency is even higher after we allow for the scale of operations. However, a number of utilities exhibit inefficient behavior in operations and, to a lesser extent, in capital activities, and we are able to provide target inputs, outputs, and sets of best-practice peers that these utilities can focus on when seeking to improve their performance.

1. INTRODUCTION

Starting from their essential nature as natural monopolies operating within network industries, countries around the world with initially similar settings in delivery networks and treatment systems have progressively evolved very different approaches to urban water utilities, especially in the chosen mix of privately and publicly owned entities and the extent of regulatory intervention governing pricing and standards. However, recent circumstances have added impetus to these longstanding developments. These include declining rainfall associated with climate change, pressing needs for maintaining and expanding expensive water supply infrastructure, jurisdictional, sectoral, and environmental conflicts over existing surface and groundwater supplies, and rapid population growth and urbanization.

* Corresponding author: Andrew C. Worthington. Department of Accounting, Finance and Economics, Griffith University, 170 Kessels Road, Nathan QLD 4111, Australia. E-mail: a.worthington@griffith.edu.au.

In response, governments worldwide have refocused on improving the management and delivery of urban water services. There is now concern about the ability of the urban water sector as it stands to achieve productive and efficient outcomes and thereby reassure key stakeholders, especially users, of the sustainability of the sector and this key resource, evidenced in Australia by the tasking of the Productivity Commission in 2010 to identify pathways for achieving improved resource allocation and efficiency. At least part of this relies on the conventional view that the inherent conditions of urban water utilities (supply variability, high transport costs, scale economies, and public health requirements) place significant limits on the scope for effective competition and efficient markets in urban water.

Table 1. Sampled urban water utilities

Utility	Code	Type	Utility	Code	Type
ACTEW	ACW	ML	MidCoast Water	MCW	NML
Albury City Council	ALB	NML	North East Water	NEW	NML
Aqwest - Bunbury	AQW	NMO	Orange City Council	ORC	NMO
Ballina Shire Council	BAL	NMO	Power and Water - Darwin	PAD	NML
Barwon Water	BAR	ML	Power and Water - Alice Springs	PAS	NMO
Bathurst Regional Council	BAT	NMO	Port Macquarie Hastings Council	PMQ	NML
Bega Valley Shire Council	BEG	NMO	Queanbeyan City Council	QUE	NMO
Brisbane Water	BRI	ML	Riverina Water	RIV	NML
Byron Shire Council	BYR	NMO	SA Water - Adelaide	SAW	ML
Central Gippsland Water	CGW	MO	South East Water Ltd	SEW	ML
Central Highlands Water	CHW	MO	South Gippsland Water	SGW	NMO
City West Water	CIT	ML	Shoalhaven City Council	SHL	NML
Clarence Valley Council	CLA	NMO	Sydney Water Corporation	SWC	ML
Coffs Harbour City Council	COF	NML	Tamworth Regional Council	TAM	NMO
Coliban Water	COL	MO	Tweed Shire Council	TWE	NML
Dubbo City Council	DUB	NMO	Wannon Water	WAN	NML
East Gippsland Water	EGW	NML	Water Waste Services - Mackay	WAY	NML
Gold Coast Water	GCW	ML	Water Corporation - Albany	WCA	NMO
Goldenfields Water	GFW	NMO	Water Corporation - Geraldton	WCG	NMO
Gosford City Council	GOS	MO	Water Corporation - Kalgoorlie	WKB	NMO
Goulburn Valley Water	GOU	MO	Water Corporation - Mandurah	WMN	NML
GWM Water	GWM	NML	Water Corporation - Perth	WPT	ML
Hunter Water Corporation	HWC	ML	Western Water	WSA	NML
Ipswich Water	IPS	MO	Westernport Water	WSP	NMO
Kempsey Shire Council	KMP	NMO	Wingecarribee Shire Council	WSR	NMO
Lismore City Council	LIS	NMO	Wyong Shire Council	WYS	MO
Logan Water	LOG	MO	Yarra Valley Water	YAR	ML
Lower Murray Water	LOW	NML			

Note: ML Metropolitan Large 100,000+ connected properties, MO Metropolitan Other 50–100,000 connected properties, NML Non-metropolitan Large 20–50,000 connected properties, NMO Non-metropolitan Other 10–20,000 connected properties.

Part also concerns the observation that the inefficiencies associated with current pricing arrangements, water restriction regimes, and deficiencies in supply and demand planning and investment processes, have caused additional and ongoing problems for the sector in terms of deteriorating infrastructure, threats to water quality, rising supply costs and reductions in consumer welfare. A final part draws on the apparent inability of the urban water sector to maintain a pace of reform consistent with both the rural water sector and other utilities, including gas, energy, and telecommunications.

Many early analyses designed to meet these needs have focused on the use of panel data (pooled time-series, cross-sectional data) to measure efficiency change over time and the impact of the scale and scope of urban water utilities on measured and estimated efficiency.

These include past analyses of water-only companies (Norman and Stoker, 1991; Thanassoulis, 2000; Woodbury and Dollery, 2004) and water and sewerage companies (Thanassoulis, 2002; Tupper and Resende, 2004; Erbetta and Cave, 2006) and both public and private water utilities (Lambert et al., 1993; Kirkpatrick et al., 2006; da Silva e Souza et al., 2007; Munisamy, 2010).

In this chapter, we employ a single cross section of recent data from the Australian urban water utility National Performance Reports to highlight how the 55 large water utilities listed in Table 1 could use efficiency measures from a single year to identify best-practice benchmark utilities upon which they can more closely focus. This provides, among other things, both an alternative way in which the industry can employ commonly available performance metrics and as a direction where regulators can timely identify where problems concerning the sustainability of individual utilities may arise.

Of course, we should exercise caution as one-off or unexpected events may adversely affect measured efficiency and the non-stochastic technique employed here is unable to take account of any such variation.

The purpose of this chapter is to measure cross-sectional technical efficiency assuming constant and variable returns-to-scale for Australian water utilities.

The chapter comprises five sections. Section 2 outlines the frontier approaches to efficiency measurement. Section 3 addresses the methodology employed. Section 4 deals with the specification of inputs and outputs. Section 5 presents the results. The chapter ends with some concluding remarks in Section 6.

2. Frontier Approaches to Efficiency Measurement

The recent history of microeconomic efficiency measurement begins with Farrell (1957) who defined a simple measure of firm efficiency that could account for multiple inputs.

In his approach, Farrell (1957) proposed that the efficiency of any given firm (here, an urban water utility) consisted of two components: technical efficiency, or the ability of a utility to maximize output from a given set of inputs, and allocative efficiency, or the ability of a utility to use these inputs in optimal proportions, given their respective prices. Combining the two measures provides a measure of cost or productive efficiency.

It is Farrell's (1957) suggestion that we could measure efficiency in reference to an idealized frontier isoquant—or equivalently, disturbances in an econometric model—which forms the basis of all subsequent analysis.

The essence of Farrell's (1957) argument is contained in Figure 1. Here two inputs, x_1 and x_2 (say, capital and labor) are utilized to produce a single output, y (say, treated water), under an assumption of constant returns-to-scale. The isoquant of the fully efficient utility *SS'* (showing the alternative combinations of inputs used to produce a given level of output) permits the measurement of technical efficiency. For a given utility using quantities of inputs defined by point *P* to produce a unit of output, the level of technical efficiency is the ratio *OQ/OP*. This is the proportional reduction in all inputs (i.e. by movement onto the efficient isoquant) we could theoretically achieve without any reduction in output. The technical efficiency ratio for the utility at point *P* will then be less than unity.

Point *Q*, on the other hand, is technically efficient as it already lies on the efficient isoquant. The technical efficiency ratio of the utility at *Q* is *OQ/OQ* or unity, thereby implying absolute or relative efficiency (depending upon the manner in which the efficient isoquant is constructed). If the input price ratio *AA'* is known (showing the different combinations of inputs that can be purchased with a given cost outlay), then allocative efficiency at point *P* is the ratio *OR/OQ*. The distance *RQ* is then the reduction in production costs which would occur if production occurred at *Q'*—the allocatively and technically efficient point, rather than *Q*—the technically efficient, but allocatively inefficient point. Hence, total economic (cost) efficiency is the ratio *OR/OP*, with the cost reduction achievable being the distance *RP*. Note that the cost efficiency ratio *OR/OP* is the product of the technical efficiency ratio *OQ/OP* and the allocative efficiency ratio *OR/OQ*.

The approach employed in this chapter to construct empirical measures of technical efficiency is the DEA approach. One obvious problem with DEA is that in contrast to the econometric approaches to efficiency measurement it is both non-parametric and non-stochastic. Thus, no accommodation is made for the types of biases resulting from some environmental heterogeneity, external shocks, measurement error, and omitted variables. Consequently, the entire deviation from the frontier is assessed as being the result of inefficiency. This may lead to either an under or overstatement of the level of inefficiency.

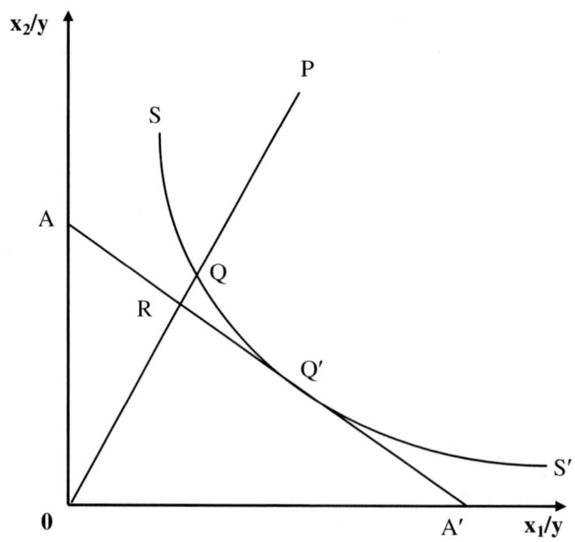

Figure 1. Technical, allocative and cost efficiencies.

However, there a number of benefits implicit in the mathematical programming approach that makes it attractive on a theoretical level. First, given its nonparametric basis, it is relatively easy to alter the specification of inputs and outputs and thereby the formulation of the production correspondence relating inputs to outputs.

Thus, in cases where the usual axioms of production activity breakdown (i.e. profit maximization) then the programming approach may offer useful insights into the efficiency of these types of industries. This is especially the case with urban water utilities.

Second, we impose considerable structure upon the data when using the econometric approach from stringent parametric form and distributional assumptions regarding inefficiency. These considerations, and the natural emphasis of DEA on the notion of 'best-practice' performance, make it an attractive choice from these two separate, though conceptually similar, approaches to the assessment of technical efficiency.

3. Model and Specification

The computational procedure used to implement the DEA (input-orientated) approach to technical efficiency measurement is as follows. Consider N urban water utilities each producing M outputs using K inputs. The $K \times N$ input matrix, X, and the $M \times N$ output matrix, Y, represent the data of all N utilities, while for the individual utility these are represented by the vectors x_i and y_i. The purpose of DEA is to construct a nonparametric envelopment frontier over the data points such that all observed points lie on or below the production frontier. The relative efficiency of each utility in ratio form (where we obtain a ratio of all outputs over all inputs) is specified as follows:

$$
\begin{aligned}
&\max_{u,v} (u' y_i / v' x_i) \\
&\text{s.t.} \, u' y_j / v' x_j \leqslant 1 \\
&\qquad u, v \geqslant 0
\end{aligned}
$$

where y_i is the vector of outputs produced by the ith water utility, x_i is the vector of inputs used by the ith water utility, u is a $M \times 1$ vector of output weights and v is a $K \times 1$ vector of input weights (the prime denotes a transposed vector), i runs from 1 to N, and j equals 1, 2, ..., N.

The first inequality ensures that the efficiency ratios for all utilities cannot exceed one, while the second ensures that the weights are non-negative. The weights are determined such that each utility maximizes its own efficiency ratio (that is, is in the best possible light). A problem with this particular ratio formulation is that it has an infinite number of solutions. To avoid this, the constraint $v' x_i = 1$ is imposed. This fractional linear program (6.1) can then be transformed into the following equivalent linear programming problem:

$$
\begin{aligned}
&\max_{\mu,v} (\mu' y_i) \\
&\text{s.t.} \, v' x_i = 1 \\
&\mu' y_j \quad v' x_j \leqslant 0 \\
&\qquad \mu, v \geqslant 0
\end{aligned}
$$

where the notation change from u and v to μ and ν reflects the transformation. Using the duality of linear programming, we use this multiplier form to derive an equivalent envelopment form of the problem:

$$\begin{aligned} &\min_{\theta,\lambda} \theta \\ \text{subject to} &- y_i + Y\lambda \geqslant 0 \\ &\theta x_i \quad X\lambda \geqslant 0 \\ &\lambda \geqslant 0 \end{aligned}$$

where θ is a scalar and λ is a $N\times 1$ vector of constants. The value of θ will be the technical efficiency score for a particular utility. This will satisfy $\theta \leq 1$, with a value of 1 indicating a point on the frontier, and hence a technically efficient utility. The value of $\theta \leq 1$ identifies the amount of any inefficiencies that may be present.

The model specified has an assumption of constant returns-to-scale and is only appropriate where all utilities are operating at an optimal scale. In other words, we compare the performance of an individual utility against both utilities of a similar size (or scale) and all other utilities. Where this assumption does not hold, scale effects will confound the measures of technical efficiency. Generally, regulatory, geographical, and institutional constraints imply that most utilities are not operating at an optimal scale, so it is inappropriate to compare utilities against other utilities that may be benefiting from scale economies and are operating at a scale that a particular may never conceivable attain.

Accordingly, we modify the linear programming problem to account for variable returns-to-scale (that is, measures of technical efficiency without scale efficiency effects) by adding the convexity constraint $N1'\lambda = 1$. As a result, no utility will obtain a lower efficiency score under variable returns-to-scale than it achieves with constant returns-to-scale and some utilities are likely to improve their scores under variable returns-to-scale. The number of 100 percent efficient utilities is also likely to be higher under variable returns-to-scale. Despite, this, the assumption of constant returns-to-scale is usually reasonable in most contexts.

DEA models can be either input (as above) or output orientated. In the input orientation, the efficiency scores relate to the largest feasible proportional reduction in inputs for fixed outputs, while in the output orientation it corresponds to the largest feasible proportional expansion in outputs for fixed inputs. It is common to use an input orientation in analyses of network utilities because the firms are generally required to supply services to a fixed geographical area, and hence the output vector (or most of it) is essentially fixed or at least not amenable to change in the short run. In this approach, urban water utilities produce physical water outputs, typically the volume of potable water (Norman and Stoker, 1991; Thannassoulis, 2000; Tupper and Resende, 2004; Coelli and Walding, 2006; Byrnes et al., 2010) and/or the number of properties supplied with water (Coelli and Walding, 2006; Saal and Parker, 2006; García-Valiñas and Muñiz, 2007).

However, the outputs can also include the length of mains supplied or the service area (Thanassoulis, 2002; Munisamy, 2010), the proportion of non-households supplied with water and/or the average pumping head (Guder et al., 2009), and indexes of water quality assessments, service outages, and customer complaints (Woodbury and Dollery, 2004; Byrnes et al., 2010).

Further, for the most part, these specifications mix operating and capital expenditure concepts as they relate to urban water utilities. The only known exceptions are Tupper and Resende (2004) and Picazo-Tadeo et al. (2008).

In this analysis, however, we take a different approach, as we are able to split the available data on inputs and outputs into operations and capital. With operating inputs and outputs, utilities are committed to providing certain qualities and quantifies of water to their customers, at least in the short run. Consequently, we use an input orientation so the natural focus is on producing a given level of outputs with the least possible inputs.

This also corresponds with the orientation used in earlier DEA studies.

As for capital-related inputs and outputs, we apply an output orientation. Conventionally, this should fit better with the longer-run objective of water utilities expanding and maintaining long-lived assets to ensure the sustainability and security of water supply.

Unfortunately, at the time of preparation of this report, data on the written down replacement cost of capital was only available for 2008–09, so this part of the analysis is necessarily restricted to a single year. Consequently, the technical assumption of a long-run output orientation does not perfectly align with the availability of data (a single year) and this potentially affects the validity of the results.

The final adjustment we make is that in our model we divide the inputs into controllable and uncontrollable inputs.

This is because many of the factors that influence the observed performance of water utilities derive from their inherent geographical, competitive, and regulatory characteristics. For instance, a utility is largely unable to alter substantially the sources of water it draws upon and the number of connected properties to which it provides water, even if it wished.

The technique we use to reflect this is to incorporate the contextual information directly into the DEA calculation.

Table 1. Inputs and outputs

Variable	Operating specification	Capital specification	Mean	Standard deviation	Skewness	Kurtosis
OXT	CI		38945.390	79807.490	4.462	26.309
CXT		CI	32143.725	69802.258	4.914	27.156
CHC	CO		89.755	21.459	–2.963	12.087
MBC	CO		97.815	7.883	–4.661	26.617
LSI		CO	1.685	1.243	3.148	16.282
WQI	CO		30.263	49.861	2.819	11.391
WMI		CO	9.373	13.161	4.904	30.591
PRP	NCI	CO	130.695	281.586	4.032	21.786
WTR	CO	CO	36005.260	77542.600	4.297	23.826
PMN		NCI	40.550	16.815	0.792	3.278
CAP		NCI	689623.891	1582023.599	4.979	17.001
BLK	NCI	NCI	30.783	43.337	0.782	1.698
GRD	NCI	NCI	14.520	27.180	2.033	5.968
REC	NCI	NCI	3.664	6.792	3.956	22.608
SUR	NCI	NCI	50.769	41.087	–0.136	1.290

Note: CO is controllable input, NCI is noncontrollable input, CO is controllable output.

In the case of input-orientated (output-orientated) models, it is then not relevant to maximize (minimize) the proportional decrease (increase) in the entire input (output) vector, rather maximization (minimization) should only be determined with respect to the sub-vector that is composed of discretionary inputs (outputs).

Thus, the contextual information contributes to the constraints placed upon decision-making units, but not the posited efficiency improvements.

As shown in Table 2, we specify two sets of inputs and outputs reflecting the different models of operating and capital behavior. The first (input-orientated) specification specifies total operating expenditure ($000) as the input along with four outputs: (i) the percentage of zones where chemical compliance was achieved (CHC), (ii) the percentage of zones where microbiological compliance was achieved (MBC), (iii) the inverse of water quality and service complaints (per 1,000 properties) (WQI) and (iv) the supply of urban water (ML) (WTR).

The inputs also include five uncontrollable (or nondiscretionary) contextual factors: (i) total connected properties (in 000s) (PRP), (ii) the percentage of water from bulk suppliers (BLK), (iii) the percentage of water from groundwater (GRD), (iv) the percentage of water from recycling (REC), and (v) the percentage of water from surface water (SUR).

The second (output-orientated) specification specifies total capital expenditure ($000s) as the input with three controllable outputs: (i) the inverse of real losses (L/service connection/d) (LSI), (ii) the inverse of water main breaks (per 100 km of water main) (WMI), (iii) total connected properties–water supply (000s) (PRP), and (iv) total urban water supplied (ML) (WTR). Lastly, we specify six uncontrollable (or nondiscretionary) contextual input factors: (i) the number of properties served per km of water main (PMN), (ii) the written down replacement cost of fixed water supply assets ($000s) (CAP), (iii) the percentage of water from bulk suppliers (BLK), (iv) the percentage of water from groundwater (GRD), (v) the percentage of water from recycling (REC), and (vi) the percentage of water from surface water (SUR).

In using this specification, we assume the utility aims to ensure a sustainable supply of networked water at the given level of capital expenditure after accounting for network density, the level of existing assets, and the sources of water. Our expectation is that by including PRP and WTR we will be able to identify surplus productive capacity that could allow for future growth and expanded delivery opportunities.

4. RESULTS

Table 3 details the technical efficiency scores for the 55 urban water utilities. The scores from four separate models are included: input-orientated technical operating efficiency assuming constant and variable returns-to-scale and output-oriented technical capital efficiency also assuming constant and variable returns-to-scale.

An efficiency score of 100 percent indicates an efficient utility (one located on the best-practice frontier) while a score less than 100 percent indicates a technically inefficient utility.

To start with, an input-orientation is used for operating efficient measurement so a score less than 100 percent indicates the extent to which inputs could be reduced while maintaining the same level of output.

Table 3. Technical efficiency scores by utility

Utility	Operating efficiency		Capital efficiency		Utility	Operating efficiency		Capital efficiency		Utility	Operating efficiency		Capital efficiency	
	CRS	VRS	CRS	VRS		CRS	VRS	CRS	VRS		CRS	VRS	CRS	VRS
ACW	100.00	100.00	100.00	100.00	GOS	80.20	80.35	92.70	92.73	SGW	100.00	100.00	100.00	100.00
ALB	100.00	100.00	100.00	100.00	GOU	100.00	100.00	100.00	100.00	SHL	100.00	100.00	100.00	100.00
AQW	100.00	100.00	100.00	100.00	GWM	62.92	62.94	100.00	100.00	SWC	100.00	100.00	100.00	100.00
BAL	100.00	100.00	95.83	100.00	HWC	100.00	100.00	100.00	100.00	TAM	100.00	100.00	100.00	100.00
BAR	87.71	87.71	100.00	100.00	IPS	100.00	100.00	97.50	100.00	TWE	100.00	100.00	81.75	82.29
BAT	100.00	100.00	100.00	100.00	KMP	100.00	100.00	81.43	100.00	WAN	93.13	93.53	80.94	84.50
BEG	100.00	100.00	100.00	100.00	LIS	93.81	100.00	100.00	100.00	WAY	100.00	100.00	100.00	100.00
BRI	100.00	100.00	87.00	100.00	LOG	100.00	100.00	100.00	100.00	WCA	100.00	100.00	92.52	100.00
BYR	100.00	100.00	100.00	100.00	LOW	100.00	100.00	100.00	100.00	WCG	100.00	100.00	100.00	100.00
CGW	100.00	100.00	100.00	100.00	MCW	100.00	100.00	100.00	100.00	WKB	100.00	100.00	100.00	100.00
CHW	44.46	44.46	41.14	43.24	NEW	100.00	100.00	100.00	100.00	WMN	100.00	100.00	100.00	100.00
CIT	100.00	100.00	100.00	100.00	ORC	100.00	100.00	97.71	100.00	WPT	100.00	100.00	100.00	100.00
CLA	100.00	100.00	100.00	100.00	PAD	100.00	100.00	100.00	100.00	WSA	100.00	100.00	100.00	100.00
COF	100.00	100.00	100.00	100.00	PAS	100.00	100.00	100.00	100.00	WSP	100.00	100.00	100.00	100.00
COL	71.46	71.68	78.15	82.27	PMQ	100.00	100.00	100.00	100.00	WSR	99.20	99.20	50.76	51.06
DUB	100.00	100.00	100.00	100.00	QUE	100.00	100.00	100.00	100.00	WYS	64.16	64.28	100.00	100.00
EGW	100.00	100.00	100.00	100.00	RIV	100.00	100.00	100.00	100.00	YAR	100.00	100.00	100.00	100.00
GCW	100.00	100.00	56.91	100.00	SAW	100.00	100.00	100.00	100.00	Mean	94.93	94.94	92.58	96.08
GFW	100.00	100.00	100.00	100.00	SEW	100.00	100.00	100.00	100.00	SD	14.07	14.05	16.56	13.42

Note: CRS Constant returns-to-scale, VRS Variable returns-to-scale. Utility names in Table 1.

For example, Barwon Water (BAR) has an constant returns-to-scale efficiency score of 87.71 percent, suggesting that based on observable best practice it could reduce its inputs to 87.71 percent of their current level (a 12.29 percent decrease) and still maintain its output at the current level (thereby moving it on to the best-practice frontier and becoming fully efficient).

Conversely, we use an output orientation for the measurement of capital efficiency. This measure thus indicates the level to which outputs must be augmented holding inputs constant to move the utility onto the efficient frontier. Consider the constant returns-to-scale efficiency score of 78.15 percent for Coliban Water (COL). This means that outputs are only 78.15 percent of their feasible level based on observable best practice, and that increasing outputs by 21.5 percent (= 100.00 percent – 78.15 percent) holding inputs constant would likewise place COL on the efficient frontier alongside its best-practice peers.

As shown in Table 3, the mean urban water utility in Australia is relatively efficient in terms of both operating and capital efficiency, with mean constant returns-to-scale operating and capital efficiencies of 94.93 and 92.58 percent, respectively. This suggests that across the sector we could reduce operating inputs to 94.93 percent of their current level while capital outputs are only 92.58 percent of their feasible level, both based on observable best practice.

Of course, we should recall that DEA scores are relative measures; the data determines the best practice frontier, not some absolute theoretical standard. Putting this aside, most utilities in the sample are 100 percent efficient. One of the three factors that may assist this achievement is the relatively large number of outputs specified in both models. All other things being equal, more outputs increase the likelihood that a utility lies on the frontier in at least one dimension, and as we have not applied a weighting to the outputs, relatively good performance in one area may effectively outweigh relatively poor performance in another.

Table 4. Best-practice reference utilities

Utility	Operating efficiency		Capital efficiency		Total
	CRS	VRS	CRS	VRS	
SEW	6	5	10	6	27
GFW	7	6	5	4	22
WMN	6	6	3	2	17
EGW	3	3	6	3	15
ORC	6	6		3	15
PMQ	4	2	6	3	15
WPT	4	5	4	2	15
WSP	6	6	1	1	14
ALB	4	4	2	2	12
BYR	3	3	4	2	12
LOG	2	1	6	3	12
SWC	1	1	6	4	12
AQW	2	2	6	1	11
HWC	6	3	1	1	11
LOW	1	1	5	4	11
RIV	3	3	2	3	11
SHL	4	4	2	1	11
BEG	1	1	4	3	9
CLA	3	2	1	3	9
NEW	2	2	2	2	8
CGW	1	1	4	1	7
QUE	1	1	4	1	7
SAW	1	1	2	3	7
WCA	3	3		1	7
GOU	1	1	3	1	6
GWM			3	3	6
PAD	1	1	3	1	6
COF	2	1	1	1	5
KMP	2	2		1	5
LIS		1	2	2	5
WAY	1	1	2	1	5
ACW	1	1	1	1	4
BAT	1	1	1	1	4
CIT	1	1	1	1	4
DUB	1	1	1	1	4
MCW	1	1	1	1	4
PAS	1	1	1	1	4
SGW	1	1	1	1	4
TAM	1	1	1	1	4
WCG	1	1	1	1	4
WKB	1	1	1	1	4
WSA	1	1	1	1	4
YAR	1	1	1	1	4
Mean	3.79	3.37	4.11	2.68	13.74
Std.dev.	1.93	1.86	2.40	1.29	4.45

A second consideration is that we have made substantive allowance for the contextual factors that impact upon observed efficiency. These contextual factors are included as part of the constraints placed on utilities, but are not included in calculating the efficiency score. A final consideration is that the outputs specified may not do a very good job at distinguishing between good and bad performance. For example, chemical and microbiological compliance are enforced by regulation and most of the utilities in the sample have performed relatively highly, if not perfectly, in terms of these outputs.

It is also noteworthy that the constant and variable returns-to-scale measures are generally the same, suggesting that the utilities included perform equally well (or poorly) regardless of whether we compare their observed behavior with utilities of a similar scale (variable returns-to-scale) or all other scales (constant returns-to-scale).

Consider, for example, the capital efficiency scores for Ballina Shire Council (BAL). As shown, BAL has a constant returns-to-scale score of 95.83 percent but this improves to 100 percent when we compare BAL only with best-practice utilities of the same scale.

The implication is that the difference in efficiency is attributable to the scale at which BAL operates (i.e. scale inefficient). Now consider the constant returns-to-scale and variable returns-to-scale operating efficiency of Gosford City Council (GOS) and GWM Water (GWM). As shown, the constant and variable returns-to-scale measures for each are almost identical, indicating inefficient behavior irrespective of whether we compare their performance with utilities of all scales or only those of a similar scale.

Table 4 provides details of the water utilities that define the best-practice frontier. Generally, but not necessarily, these utilities will be fully efficient. The values indicate the number of times that the utility serves as a best-practice performer for some other utility. Conventionally, advocates of DEA analysis would then suggest that practices in these peer organisations be looked at more closely in order to ascertain the particular source(s) of efficient behaviour. As shown, the best practice utilities are led by South East Water Ltd (SEW) with 27 references (compared to a mean of 13.74), followed by Goldenfields Water (GFW) with 22 references, Water Corporation Mandurah (WMN) with 17 and East Gippsland Water (EGW), Orange City Council (ORC), Port Macquarie Hastings Council (PMQ) and Water Corporation - Perth (WPT), all with 15 references.

As noted, utilities serving least frequently (if at all) as best-practice references for their peers are usually inefficient, and include Water and Waste Services (WAN), Gosford City Council (GOS), Coliban Water (COL) and Central Highlands Water (CHW). The bulk of the remaining utilities only occasionally serve as reference peers and this may indicate that only one or two aspects of their performance serve as a reference for another utility, sometimes the same one, and sometimes only because it is of a similar scale.

In sum, were we interested in identifying best-practice water utilities to provide possible benchmarks of behavior in the sector, we may look no further than utilities providing relatively many reference points for their peers.

Table 5 focuses more closely on the inefficient utilities and the efforts needed to bring them onto the operating efficient frontier. As shown, BAR has an operating efficiency score of 87.71 percent indicating that we could reduce operating inputs by 12.29 percent and still theoretically maintain the same level of output as determined by observable best practice. In this instance, we could attain this by reducing OXT by the entire amount.

The other main influence on BAR in terms of its efficiency gap is the fact that it is not producing enough water relative to its peers.

We must tale care here because we would not reasonably expect a utility to increase supply where demand does not exist or where water restrictions effectively constrain demand. However, it does suggest that one reason why BAR appears operationally inefficient is that it is producing less water than best-practice reference peers of a similar scale, context and operations (AQW, EGW, NEW, WCA and WPT). This may warrant a closer look.

Now consider Wannon Water (WAN) with a constant returns-to-scale operating efficiency score of 93.13 percent. As shown, in order to make WAN as efficient as its best practice peers (CLA, EGW, GFW, ORC, RIV, SHL and WPT), we would need to cut operating expenditure (OXT) by 6.9 percent, improve its chemical compliance (CHC) by 6.2 percent, and decrease the number of water quality and service complaints (WQI) by 50 percent. As with BAR, WAN is also not producing enough water relative to its peers, and though not easy to change in a highly-regulated networked sector (possibly through water trading with nearby jurisdictions or the easing of water restrictions), an increase in supply of 14 percent would help move WAN on to the efficient frontier, or alternatively, more severe cuts in operating expenditure as the key controllable input. Table 6 provides a comparable analysis for capital efficiency. Consider Brisbane Water (BRI).

As shown, when assuming constant returns-to-scale, BRI is 87 percent efficient and in order to improve its efficiency to the level of its best-practice peers (AQW, LOG, SEW and SWC) we would need to cut capital expenditure by 64 percent, and reduce water losses by 14.9 percent and water main breaks by 32.4 percent.

Table 5. Operating inefficient utilities and needed adjustment in actual inputs and outputs to achieve target inputs and outputs

Utility	Score	% OXT	% CHC	% WQI	% WTR	Reference peers
BAR	87.71	–12.3	0.0	0.0	41.3	AQW EGW NEW WCA WPT
CHW	44.46	–55.5	30.8	94.1	45.3	GFW HWC PMQ SEW WCA WMN WSP
COL	71.46	–28.5	10.1	0.0	0.0	BYR GFW HWC ORC SEW SHL WMN WPT WSP
GOS	80.20	–19.8	0.0	209.5	28.9	ALB HWC ORC PMQ SEW WMN WSP
GWM	62.92	–37.1	55.1	0.0	54.8	CLA GFW HWC KMP ORC RIV SHL WSP
LIS	93.81	–6.2	100	170.4	70.6	COF GFW LOG
WAN	93.13	–6.9	6.2	102.5	14.0	CLA EGW GFW ORC RIV SHL WPT
WSR	99.20	–0.8	100	106.4	34.3	ALB BYR GFW SEW WMN
WYS	64.16	–35.8	0.0	10.5	2.3	ALB HWC ORC PMQ SEW WMN WSP
BAR	87.71	–12.3	0.0	0.0	41.3	AQW EGW NEW WCA WPT
CHW	44.46	–55.5	30.7	83.8	45.4	GFW HWC PMQ SEW WCA WMN WSP YAR
COL	71.68	–28.3	9.8	0.0	0.0	BYR GFW ORC SHL WMN WPT WSP YAR
GOS	80.35	–19.6	0.0	211.2	28.0	ALB ORC SEW WMN WSP
GWM	62.94	–37.1	55.1	0.0	54.8	CLA GFW HWC KMP ORC RIV SHL WPT WSP
WAN	93.53	–6.5	5.9	106.9	13.8	EGW GFW ORC RIV SHL WPT
WSR	99.20	–0.8	100	106.4	34.3	ALB BYR GFW SEW WMN
WYS	64.28	–35.7	0.0	11.1	1.6	ALB ORC SEW WMN WSP

Table 5. Capital inefficient utilities and needed adjustment in actual inputs and outputs to achieve target inputs and outputs

Utility	Score	% CXT	% LSI	% WMI	% PRP	% WTR	Reference peers
BAL	95.83	0.0	4.3	384.7	4.9	4.3	BYR QUE SEW SHL
BRI	87.00	–64.0	14.9	32.4	34.8	14.9	AQW LOG SEW SWC
CHW	41.14	–30.7	143.1	143.1	143.1	192.1	GFW GWM QUE SEW SWC
COL	78.15	–53.7	28	195.8	43.1	28.0	EGW GFW GWM LOG SEW SWC
GCW	56.91	–61.4	75.7	75.7	110.0	75.7	AQW LOG QUE SEW SWC
GOS	92.70	0.0	7.9	348.6	7.9	32.5	EGW LOG LOW PMQ SEW SWC
IPS	97.50	0.0	2.6	132.3	2.6	9.4	AQW BYR GFW LOG SEW WMN
KMP	81.43	0.0	22.8	311.0	22.8	22.8	AQW BEG CGW LOW PAD PMQ WPT
ORC	97.71	–28.4	2.3	2.3	23.3	2.3	EGW GOU LOW NEW PAD PMQ
TWE	81.75	–78.5	114.4	22.3	22.3	26.6	GOU LOW PMQ SAW
WAN	80.94	–55.5	94	23.5	23.5	23.5	BEG CGW PMQ RIV SEW WPT
WCA	92.52	–9.4	8.1	8.1	8.1	70.0	AQW BEG CGW EGW WAY WPT
WSR	50.76	0.0	97	185.5	97.0	101.5	ALB BYR EGW GFW LIS SEW WMN
CHW	43.24	–34.8	131.3	131.3	131.3	183.1	BEG CLA GFW GWM ORC RIV SEW SWC
COL	82.27	–57.4	21.5	195.9	24.1	21.5	GFW GWM LOG LOW ORC SEW SWC
GOS	92.73	0.0	7.8	348.0	7.8	32.4	EGW LOG LOW PMQ SEW SWC
TWE	82.29	–78.4	114.7	21.5	22.7	27.3	LOW PMQ SAW
WAN	84.50	0.0	199.3	18.3	18.3	19.5	BEG CLA EGW NEW RIV SAW SEW WPT
WSR	51.06	–10.7	95.9	186.4	95.9	103.5	ALB BYR GFW LIS SEW WMN

However, we would also need to increase the number of connected properties by 34.8 percent and the amount of delivered water by 14.9 percent. Once again, the last two variables are not easily changed and are potentially indicative of surplus capacity and the effects of water restrictions, etc.

Now consider Gosford City Council (GOS). Here no decrease in capital expenditure is indicated, rather GOS needs to reduce the number of water main breaks and losses to a level comparable to its peers in EGW, LOG, LOW, PMQ, SEW and SWC. Clearly, once again the number of properties and the amount of water supplied are a major factor in determining the efficiency gap, even after allowance for contextual factors, suggesting that many utilities in the upper panel are operating at an inefficient scale given their circumstances.

However, because of the assumption of variable returns-to-scale, it is more difficult to explain away observed inefficiencies because we have already taken account of scale (and contextual factors).

Accordingly, we need to look more closely at the actual and target improvement. Here, the capital efficiency of GOS and WAN could be improved by augmenting their outputs in taking greater efforts to reduce water losses and preventing main breaks.

In others (CHW, COL and TWE), capital expenditures a very high relative to best-practice peers in the sector, and we would need to look at what is specifically going on in each utility to help explain this expenditure. We would then evaluate whether it is only temporary or more permanent, and judge the possible long-run impacts on the sustainable and secure supply or urban water in these areas.

CONCLUSION

This chapter examined the technical operating and capital efficiency of major Australian urban water utilities using data envelopment analysis. Different inputs and outputs were specified for each aspect of efficiency and allowance made for the direction inclusion of uncontrollable contextual inputs thought to impact upon the observed efficiency of utilities but largely outside their control. Efforts were also made to distinguish between factors that determine inefficiency and those that affect the gap in efficiency.

The results indicate that a relatively high level of relative operating and capital efficiency prevails across the sector, at least in the context of the single year of data used in this part of the analysis. Efficiency improves further when allowance is made for the scale of operations. However, a number of utilities exhibit inefficient behaviour in operations and, to a lesser extent, in capital activities, and we are able to provide target inputs, outputs, and sets of best-practice peers that these utilities can focus on when seeking to improve their performance.

Of course, not all inputs and outputs are amenable to change. While this analysis took clear account of the differences in non-controllable inputs, it also found that a major determinant of observed inefficiency is the influence of these factors, particularly the number of properties served and the amount of water supplied. This is perhaps because at least some utilities are obliged to operate at a more or less than optimal scale. One possibility is 'lumpy' investment in infrastructure (pipelines, dams, treatment plants).

As a physical network industry, it is difficult for these utilities to trade surplus capacity with any but geographically proximate utilities. At the same time, the heavy reliance on water restrictions and costly water conservation measures may be obligating urban water utilities to supply less than what is optimal given their circumstances.

One major limitation of this particular analysis is the relatively limited number of inputs able to be specified (operating and capital expenditure) and the restrictive range of possible outputs (mostly concerning regulated chemical and microbiological compliance and water quality). This acts against the ability to distinguish finely between efficient and inefficient water utilities.

REFERENCES

Abbott, M. and Cohen, B. (2009). Productivity and efficiency in the water industry. *Utilities Policy*, 17(3-4), 233-44.

Aubert, C. and Reynaud, A. (2005). The impact of regulation on cost efficiency: An empirical analysis of Wisconsin water utilities. *Journal of Productivity Analysis*, 23(3), 383-409.

Bhattacharyya, A., Harris, T., Narayanan, R., and Raffie, K. (1995). Specification and estimation of the effect of ownership on the economic efficiency of the water utilities. *Regional Science and Urban Economics*, 25, 759-784.

Bhattacharyya, A., Parker, E. and Raffie, K. (1994). An examination of the effect of ownership on the relative efficiency of public and private water utilities. *Land Economics*, 70, 197-209.

Bottasso, A. and Conti, M. (2009). Scale economies, technology and technical change in the water industry: Evidence from the English water only sector. *Regional Science and Urban Economics*, 39(2), 138-147.

Byrnes, J., Crase, L., Dollery, B. E., and Villano, R. (2010). The relative economic efficiency of urban water utilities in regional New South Wales and Victoria. *Resource and Energy Economics*, 32(3), 439-455.

Coelli, T. and Walding, S. (2006). Performance measurement in the Australian water supply industry: A preliminary analysis. In: Coelli, T. and Lawrence, D. (Eds.), *Performance Measurement and Regulation of Network Utilities*, Edward Elgar, Cheltenham, 29-62.

Cubbin, J. and Tzanidakis, G. (1998). Regression versus data envelopment analysis for efficiency measurement: An application to the England and Wales regulated water industry. *Utilities Policy*, 7(2), 75-85.

Da Silva e Souza, G., Coelho de Faria, R., Belchiar, S., and Moreira, T. (2007). Estimating the relative efficiency of Brazilian publicly and privately owned water utilities: A stochastic cost frontier approach. *Journal of the American Water Resources Association*, 43(5), 1237-1244.

Da Silva e Souza, G., Coelho de Faria, R., Belchior, T., and Moreira, S. (2008). Efficiency of Brazilian public and private water utilities. *Estudos Economicos*, 38(4), 905-917.

Erbetta, F. and Cave, M. (2006). Regulation and efficiency incentives: Evidence from the England and Wales water and sewerage industry. *Review of Network Economics*, 6(2), 425-452.

Estache, A. and Rossi, M. (2002). How different is the efficiency of public and private water companies in Asia? *World Bank Economic Review*, 16(1), 139-148.

Estache, A. and Trujillo, L. (2003). Efficiency effects of 'privatization' in Argentina's water and sanitation services. *Water Policy*, 5(4), 369-380.

Fabbri, P. and Fraquelli, G. (2000). Costs and structure of technology in the Italian water industry. *Empirica*, 27(1), 65-82.

Faria, C. R., Souza, G. and Moreira, T. (2005). Public versus private water utilities: Empirical evidence for Brazilian companies. *Economics Bulletin*, 8(2), 1-7.

Farrell, M. J. (1957). The measurement of productive efficiency. *Journal of the Royal Statistical Society*, 120, 253-289.

Filippini, M., Hrovatin, N. and Zoric, J. (2008). Cost efficiency of Slovenian water distribution utilities: An application of stochastic frontier methods. *Journal of Productivity Analysis*, 29(2), 169-182.

Fraquelli, G., Piacenza, M. and Vannoni, D. (2004). Scope and scale economies in multiutilities: Evidence from gas, water and electricity combinations. *Applied Economics*, 36 (18), 2045-2057.

García-Sánchez, I. M. (2006). Efficiency measurement in Spanish local government: The case of municipal water services. *Review of Policy Research*, 23(2), 355-371.

García-Valinas, M. A. and Muniz, M. A. (2007). Is DEA useful in the regulation of water utilities? A dynamic efficiency evaluation. *Applied Economics*, 39(2), 245-252.

Guder, J., Kittlau, B., Moll, R., Walter, M., and Zschille, M. (2009). The performance of German water utilities: A first non-parametric analysis', DIW Berlin (German Institute for Economic Research) and Dresden University of Technology Efficiency Analysis Working Papers. WP-EA-20, available at http://tu-dresden.de/, accessed May 2010.

Kirkpatrick, C., Parker, D. and Zhang, Y. F. (2006). State versus private sector provision of water services in Africa: An empirical analysis. *World Bank Economic Review*, 20(1), 143-163.

Lambert, D., Dichev, D. and Raffiee, K. (1993). Ownership and sources of inefficiency in the provision of water services. *Water Resources Research*, 29(6), 1573-1578.

Munisamy, S. (2010). Efficiency and ownership in water supply: Evidence from Malaysia. *Proceedings of the 12th International Business Research Conference, 8-9 April, Dubai, United Arab Emirates*, available at http://www.wbiconpro.com/, accessed May 2010.

Nauges, C. and van den Berg, C. (2008). Economies of density, scale and scope in the water supply and sewerage sector: A study of four developing and transition economies. *Journal of Regulatory Economics*, 34(2), 144-163.

Picazo-Tadeo, A. J., Sáez-Fernández, F. J. and González-Gómez, F. (2008). Does service quality matter in measuring the performance of water utilities? *Utilities Policy*, 16, 30-38.

Productivity Commission (2011). *Australia's Urban Water Sector, Draft Report,* April, Canberra.

Renzetti, S. and Dupont, D. P. (2009). Measuring the technical efficiency of municipal water suppliers: The role of environmental factors. *Land Economics*, 85(4), 627-36.

Saal, D. S. and Parker, D. (2000). The impact of privatization and regulation on the water and sewerage industry in England and Wales: A translog cost function model. *Managerial and Decision Economics*, 21(6), 253-268.

Saal, D. S. and Parker, D. (2001). Productivity and price performance in the privatized water and sewerage companies of England and Wales. *Journal of Regulatory Economics*, 20(1), 61-90.

Saal, D. S. and Parker, D. (2006). Assessing the performance of water operations in the English and Welsh water industry: A lesson in the implications of inappropriately assuming a common frontier. In: Coelli, T. and Lawrence, D. (Eds.), *Performance Measurement and Regulation of Network Utilities*, Edward Elgar, Cheltenham, 297-328.

Saal, D. S., Parker, D. and Weyman-Jones, T. (2007). Determining the contribution of technical change, efficiency change and scale change to productivity growth in the privatized English and Welsh water and sewerage industry: 1985-2000. *Journal of Productivity Analysis*, 28(1), 127-139.

Thanassoulis, E. (2000). The use of data envelopment analysis in the regulation of UK water utilities: Water distribution. *European Journal of Operational Research*, 126, 436-453.

Thanassoulis, E. (2002). Comparative performance measurement in regulation: The case of English and Welsh sewerage services. *Journal of Operational Research Society*, 53, 292-302.

Tupper, H. C. and Resende, M. (2004). Efficiency and regulatory issues in the Brazilian water and sewage sector: An empirical study. *Utilities Policy*, 12(1), 29-40.

Woodbury, K. and Dollery, B. E. (2004). Efficiency measurement in Australian local government: The case of New South Wales municipal water services. *Review of Policy Research*, 21(5), 615-636.

In: Economic and Financial Modeling
Editor: Andrew C. Worthington
ISBN: 978-1-63463-111-2

Chapter 12

AN APPLICATION OF CREDIT SCORE MODELING

Mohamed Habara and Andrew C. Worthington*
Griffith University, Nathan, Australia

ABSTRACT

This chapter uses three standard statistical techniques, namely, discriminant analysis, logistic regression and survival analysis, to construct and evaluate a credit-scoring model for the Al-Wahada Bank in Libya. We randomly select 400 hundred loans for the analysis and specify 21 independent variables along with measures indicating loan default. The results indicate that five independent variables are common to all three models, which we consider the most important variables affecting the probability of loan default. With regard to a comparison of model performance, the results indicate that logistic regression performs better than either discriminant or survival analysis in this particular context.

1. INTRODUCTION

In this chapter, we use discriminant, logistic and survival techniques to illustrate the modeling of credit risk in a Libyan bank. All of these techniques are parametric. Parametric statistical approaches require the use of regression analysis to discriminate between 'good' and 'bad' loans using a sample of applicants. These approaches were the first used in building credit scoring systems and still considered the most successful approaches.

All of these models attempt to estimate the probability of default based on the past data of the applicant's credit and classify them into two different groups (i.e. good and bad credit risk). In addition, survival analysis focuses on identifying the time of default.

The remainder of the chapter comprises six sections. Section 2 concerns the data collection and sample selection and discusses the specification of the variables used in the three techniques analyzed.

* Corresponding author: Andrew C. Worthington. Department of Accounting, Finance and Economics, Griffith University, 170 Kessels Road, Nathan QLD 4111, Australia. E-mail: a.worthington@griffith.edu.au.

Sections 3, 4 and 5 respectively explain the methodologies and results for the discriminant, logistic regression, and survival models. Section 6 compares the results of the credit scoring models. Section 7 summarizes the findings in the chapter.

2. DATA

2.1. Sample

We collected data from the Al-Wahada Bank in Libya, which has 62 branches and 8 agencies across the country. Of the various loans offered by the bank, long-term loans known as 'social advances' are among the most developed and have increased substantially in importance for the bank in recent years.

These social advances have the following characteristics: (i) a loan limit of two years' net salary and no more than 10,000 Libyan dinars (LYD), (ii) loan period not more than 72 months, (iii) instalments should not exceed a third of salary, (iv) no loan extensions prior to two years of the initial loan period, (v) two guarantors required that have accounts with the bank, (vi) applicant must have an account with the bank, (vii) no other loans held by the applicant, and (viii) social loans must not be exceed 20% of the bank's deposit liabilities.

We selected 1997 as the first year of the sample period as the standard loan is no more than four years, so could readily follow the state of the loan during the entire research period. We optimally sampled 400 loans from the 17,900 loans in this year using a standard method. Most of the data are included in the application form but the bank also requires applicants to provide other documents considered as evidence of the accuracy of information provided in the applications (including evidence of salary, identification cards, a copy of family records, and so on). Unfortunately, we were unable to obtain the relatively small number of rejected applications because the bank does not retain this information. This infers the potential for some sample selection bias.

2.2. Variables

The data are composed of two types of information. The first type of information comprises the dependent variable and indicates whether the borrower has a good loan or a bad loan. We divided the personal loans equally into 200 good loans and 200 bad loans. The next type of information is the independent variables used in the credit scoring models. Table 1 provides the definitions of these variables.

Most of the independent variables relate to demographic, socioeconomic, or financial characteristics. The demographic indicators include characteristics such as the applicant's age, marital status, gender, the number of children and residential status. Crook (1996) showed that demographic variables would enter both the utility function and scoring functions of lenders. For instance, Coval and Shumway (2000) found that women default less frequently on loans, while Thanh and Kleimeier (2006) showed that older borrowers are more risk averse and therefore less likely to default and Vojtek and Kocenda, (2006) concluded that homeowners are less risky borrowers because of the use of housing as collateral. The employment variable status includes the characteristics of type of occupation.

Elsewhere, Vojtek and Kocenda (2006) found that the self-employed frequently receive a lower score in the evaluation of loan applications than employed persons because of the lack of employment stability. In addition, Thanh and Kleimeier (2006) mentioned that Crook et al., (1992) found the more stable employment the higher the ability to repay a loan.

Furthermore, a study by Crook et al., (1992) used 24 predictor variables in order to compare the ranking of these variables in terms of their ability to discriminate between good and bad loan. This study, for example, concluded that more children increase the chance that a borrower is likely to default. Financial variables contain characteristics such as salary and loan amount of an applicant.

In addition, the financial variables represent the most important source of repayment for the loan. Sarlija et al., (2005) show that borrowers with higher salaries should have lower probability of default.

Table 1. Variable definitions

Variable	Definition
Borrower status	1 if borrower has a good loan; 0 otherwise
LOAN	Amount of loan (Libyan Dinar)
PUR	Purpose of loan (1 house maintenance, 2 treatment, 3 buy a car, 4 purchase furniture).
PROP	Type of property (1 unit, 2 house)
ACC	The status of accommodation (1 rent, 2 own, 3 family)
OCC_A	Occupation of an applicant (1 soldier, policeman, security, 2 professional, 3 retired, 4 private sector, 5 public sector)
AGE_A	Age of an applicant (1 "18–26", 2 "27–35", 3 "36–44", 4 "45–53", 5 "54-61", 6 "62–71")
GND_A	Gender of an applicant (1 male, 2 female)
MART_A	Marital status of an applicant (1 married, 2 single, 3 divorced, 4 widow)
CHIL	Number of children of the applicant
OPN	The opinion of credit department (1 good, 2 not applicable)
SAL_A	Monthly salary of the applicant
ONG_A	Whether an applicant's salary is ongoing (1 good, 2 not applicable)
GUR_A	Whether an applicant guaranteed another borrower (1 yes, 2 no)
EXT_A	Whether an applicant has another loan (1 yes, 2 no)
SAL_B	Monthly salary of guarantor
OCC_B	Occupation of guarantor (1 soldier, policeman, security, 2 professional, 3 retired, 4 private sector, 5 public sector)
ONG_B	Whether the guarantor's salary is ongoing (1 good, 2 not applicable)
GUR_B	Whether a guarantor guaranteed another person (1 Yes, 2 No)
AGE_B	Age of guarantor (1 "18–26", 2 "27–35", 3 "36–44", 4 "45–53", 5 "54–61", 6 "62–71")
GND_B	Gender of guarantor (1 male, 2 female)
EXT_B	Whether guarantor has another loan (1 yes, 2 no)

The importance of these variables is evident (Vojtek and Kocenda, 2006). In addition, we derived several other independent variables from the loan files of the Al-Wahada Bank. As discussed, for these types of loans, the Al-Wahada Bank requires a guarantor. Thus, the variables relating to the guarantor include the age, occupation, salary, gender, whether the guarantor has an ongoing salary, has guaranteed another borrower, and has another loan.

2.3. Descriptive Analysis

We used SPSS Version 15 for the statistical analysis of the bank data. Table 2 shows the results obtained from analyzing the categorical demographic variables for borrowers.

Table 2. Descriptive statistics for categorical borrower variables

Variable		Good Loans	Percent %	Bad Loans	Percent %
PUR	House Maintenance	140	70	81	40
	Treatment	10	5	21	10
	Buy a car	43	21	89	45
	Buy furniture	4	2	0	0
	Not applicable	3	2	9	5
PROP	Unit	76	38	120	60
	House	124	62	80	40
ACC	Rent	72	36	120	60
	Own	74	37	50	25
	Family	54	27	30	15
OCC_A	Soldier, policeman, security	32	16	30	15
	Professional	30	15	22	11
	Retired	20	10	10	5
	Private sector	22	11	60	30
	Public sector	96	48	78	39
AGE_A	18–26	32	16	40	20
	27–35	82	40	64	32
	36–44	48	24	54	27
	45–53	19	10	22	11
	54–61	9	5	12	6
	62–71	10	5	8	4
GND_A	Male	160	80	170	85
	Female	40	20	30	15
MART_A	married	123	61	118	58
	Single	70	35	46	23
	divorced	1	1	31	16
	Widow	6	3	5	3
OPN	Good	158	79	120	60
	N/A	42	21	80	40
ONG_A	Yes	172	86	130	65
	No	28	14	70	35
GUR_A	Yes	20	10	16	8
	No	180	90	184	92
EXT_A	Yes	40	20	26	13
	No	160	80	174	87

Concerning the purpose of the loan (PUR), the percentage of loans for house maintenance represents the highest at 70% for good loans while buying a car represents the highest of 89% for bad loans. In relation to the type of borrower's property (PROP), of good loans the results show that 62% of borrowers are living in houses and 38% in units.

In contrast, of bad loans, 60% of borrowers are living in units and 40% are in houses. In relation to the status of borrower accommodation, Table 2 also shows that 36% of good loan borrowers are renting and 37% own their home; both are higher than borrowers that are living with their parents 27%.

In contrast, the highest percentage of borrowers classified as bad loans are renters (60%). With respect to the borrower's occupation (OCC_A), the result shows that the highest percentage are working in the public sector for both good and bad loans of 48% and 39% respectively and the lowest percentage is retired borrowers for both good and bad loans of 10% and 5% respectively. In addition, borrowers who work in the private sector have a high percentage of bad loans (30%).

Regarding the borrower's age (AGE_A), the results show that the majority of borrowers are in the second and third categories of age (64% and 69%) in terms of good loans and bad loans respectively. Concerning the borrowers' gender (GND_A), 80% of borrowers with good loans are male and 20% are female. Moreover, 85% of borrowers with bad loans are male and 15% are female. The parentage of males with both classifications of borrowers is higher than the percentage of females. With regard to the borrower's marital status (MART_A), the majority of borrowers with both good and bad loans, 61% and 58% respectively, are married, while singles represent 35% and 23% of both good loans and bad loans. In relation to bank opinion (OPN) about a borrower, the bank provides higher percentage agreement in both classifications of loans of 79% and 60% respectively.

However, the percentage not providing opinion about a borrower for good loans is 21%, which is lower than that of bad loans (40%). Concerning whether the borrower has an ongoing salary (ONG_A), the majority of borrowers in both classifications have an ongoing salary, being 86% for good loans against 60% for bad loans. In respect to whether borrower guaranteed another person (GUR_A), the minority of borrowers in both classifications guaranteed another person; 10% for good loans against 8% for bad loans. Regarding whether the borrower has another loan (EXT_A), the minority of borrowers in both classifications have another loan, 20% and 13% respectively.

Table 3 shows the results from analyzing the categorical demographic variables for guarantors. In relation to the guarantor's occupation (OCC_B), the results show that the highest percentage are working in the public sector with good and bad loans of 57% and 77% respectively and the lowest percentage is for retired guarantors; good and bad loans of 13% and 0% respectively. With respect to whether the guarantor has an ongoing salary (ONG_B), the majority of guarantors in both classifications have an ongoing salary; 98% for good loans against 55% for bad loans. In relation to whether the guarantor guaranteed another person (GUR_B), the minority of guarantors guaranteed another person; 14% for good loans. However, about half of the guarantors guaranteed another person for bad loans. Concerning the guarantor's age (AGE_B), the results show that the majority of guarantors are in the second and third categories of age, 56% and 73% in terms of good loans and bad loans, respectively. With regard to the guarantor's gender (GND_B), 79% of guarantors classified as good loans are male and 21% are female. Moreover, 78% of guarantors classified as bad loans are male and 22% are female.

Table 3. Descriptive statistics for categorical guarantor variables

Variable		Good Loans	Percent %	Bad Loans	Percent %
OCC_B	Soldier, Policeman, Security	28	14	34	17
	Professional	31	16	12	6
	Retired	26	13	0	0
	Public Sector	115	57	154	77
ONG_B	Yes	196	98	110	55
	No	4	2	90	45
GUR_B	Yes	28	14	99	49
	No	172	86	101	51
AGE_B	18-26	25	12	30	15
	27-35	73	37	96	48
	36-44	38	19	50	25
	45-53	23	12	24	12
	54-61	26	13	0	0
	62-71	15	7	0	0
GND_B	Male	158	79	156	78
	Female	42	21	44	22
EXT_B	Yes	31	15	103	52
	No	169	85	97	48

The parentage of males for both classifications of guarantors is higher than the percentage for females. Regarding whether the guarantor has another loan (EXT_B), the minority of guarantors in the good loans category have another loan (20%). However, the majority of guarantors in the bad loans category have another loan (52%).

Finally, Table 4 shows the results from analyzing the continuous variables for both borrowers and guarantors. These variables are loan amount (LOAN), number of children for borrower (CHIL), salary for borrower (SAL_A) and salary for guarantor (SAL_B). As shown, the mean loan for good loans is LYD4,143.120 against LYD4,980.240 for bad loans which is considerably higher.

In terms of number of children, Table 4 shows that borrowers classified as bad loans have on average more children than those classified as good loans. In relation to salary for both borrowers and guarantors, the result shows that the average salary for good loans is LYD259.568 and LYD252.668 (for borrowers and guarantors respectively) and is lower than the average salary for bad loans (LYD268.051, LYD265.781 respectively). With regard to volatility, Table 4 depicts the coefficients of variation (CV) for each variable. It shows that the good loans variables are generally more volatile than bad loans variables.

The number of children exhibits the highest volatility, with 110.13% for good loans and 82.19% for bad loans. However, the loan amount is the least variable, with 31.30% for good loans and 16.49% for bad loans.

Discriminant analysis is the most common statistical technique used for credit scoring. The purpose of discriminant analysis is to classify loans into two possible groups (good loans and bad loans) based on a group of independent variables. Therefore, discriminant analysis is an appropriate technique because the dependent variable is a two-group categorical variable.

Table 4. Descriptive statistics for continuous variables

Variable	Mean		Std. Deviation		CV %	
	Good	Bad	Good	Bad	Good	Bad
LOAN	4143.120	4980.240	1296.981	821.047	31.300	16.490
CHIL	2.125	2.675	2.340	2.199	110.130	82.190
SAL_A	259.568	268.051	102.087	50.726	39.330	18.920
SAL_B	252.668	265.781	85.612	54.773	33.880	20.610

3. DISCRIMINANT ANALYSIS

The dependent variable is whether the loan is in default (in arrears more than five months) or not in default. Therefore, the dependent variable in this research is dichotomous, mutually exclusive, and exhaustive.

3.1. Assumptions of Discriminant Analysis

Normality

Normality refers to the tendency for the sample data distribution for each independent variable to have a normal distribution. In discriminant analysis, the assumption of normality is that scores on independent variables are random and the sampling distribution of any linear combinations is normally distributed (Barbara et al., 2007, p. 382). We can use histograms of frequency distributions, normal probability plots, and measures of skewness and kurtosis to test this. In addition, it can use the script for normality by substituting the logarithm, square root and inverse transformation when they make normality in a variable that is unsuccessful in satisfying the assumption for normality (Johnson and Wichern, 2007). However, Barbara et al., (2007, p. 382) suggest that there are no possible tests for the normality of all combinations of sampling distributions of means of independent variables.

Moreover, Lachenbruch (1975) indicates that discriminant analysis is relatively robust even when there is violation of this assumption. Klecka (1980) also shows that dichotomous variables, which often violate normality, should not affect conclusions based on discriminant analysis. Furthermore, because the sample for this research is large with 400 loans equally divided in the size of each group, the assessment of normality is not a matter of judgment. Thus, we do not perform this test.

Homogeneity of Variances or Covariances

The assumption of homogeneity is that the variance within each of the populations is equal. In discriminant analysis, the assumption of equal dispersion for groups defined by the dependent variable only effects the classification stage of discriminant analysis and therefore is not evaluated until we are determining the final accuracy rate of the model (Hair et al., 2006). Sharma (1996) showed that the degree to which they are affected rely on the number of independent variables and the sample size of each group.

To test this assumption, Box's M test is used to evaluate homogeneity of variance or covariances of independent variables among groups.

This test does not involve rejecting the null hypothesis. In other words, the value of F distribution in Box's M should not be significant.

Thus, the probability value of F should be greater than 0.05 to demonstrate that the assumption of homogeneity is supported. However, if the assumption is violated (heterogeneity), it can use separate group dispersion matrices at the stage of the classification. Log determinant can be used to test the assumption of homogeneity of covariance matrices between groups. This measure should be relatively equal to meet this assumption.

In addition, it can be used for quadratic discriminant analysis, which avoids over-classification into groups with greater dispersion, logistic regression or non-parametric classification (Hair et al., 2006; Barbara et al., 2007).

Multicollinearity

Multicollinearity refers to the high correlation among the independent variables. In discriminant analysis, multicollinearity is measured by tolerance and the variance inflationary factor (VIF) becomes especially critical when stepwise procedures are used (Hair et al., 2006). Tolerance refers to the proportion of the variation in the independent variables not explained by other independent variables already in the model (Hair et al., 2006, p. 273). If the tolerance value of an independent variable is less than 0.10, there is no correlation between a variable and the other independent variables. VIF is statics computed using the coefficient of determination (R^2) value of a regression model developed by predicting one independent variable of a model by other independent variables. If the VIF of an independent variable is not greater than ten, there is no significant correlation between a variable and the other independent variables. Sharma (1996) argues that discriminant analysis is inappropriate when the pattern of correlation among the independent variables varies across samples.

Linearity

In discriminant analysis, the assumption of linearity supposes that there are relationships among all pairs of independent variables within each group. According to Barbara et al., (2007), linearity is less serious than other assumptions and the violation of this assumption leads to reduced power to identify relationships instead of increased Type I error. Thus, we do not perform this test.

Outliers

Discriminant analysis is highly sensitive to inclusion of outliers. Outliers can be determined by the Mahalanabis D2 distance. First, the critical value for D2 should be determined by using the chi-square table. The number of independent variables entered in the discriminant function is used as the degree of freedom and level of significance of 0.01. The degrees of freedom can be determining by the number of independent variables in the discriminant model. Second, outlier cases can be identified by comparing the critical value for D2 with each D2 distance for all 400 cases. Cases with distance greater than the critical value for are considered as outliers.

The outlier cases must be removed from the sample, and then a new discriminant analysis is done to see if there are new independent variables that have entered or been removed from the original discriminant function.

However, if the classification accuracy rate of the new model after removing outlier cases is less than the classification accuracy rate of the original model by 2%, the original discriminant model with outliers is interpreted.

3.2. Estimation of the Discriminant Model

Estimation of the discriminant model means the process of deriving the discriminant function. This process depends on two estimation methods. First, direct (simultaneous) estimation involves calculating the discriminant function by entering all of the predictors considered simultaneously with ignoring the discriminating power of each independent variable (Hair et al., 2006). This method is used when the researcher is interested to identify a relationship without taking into consideration the best predictors of independent variables. Second, the stepwise estimation method differs from the previous method in that it involves entering the predictors into the discriminant function sequentially based on their discriminating power between the groups (Metwally, 2000). The stepwise method is useful when the researcher is interested in including a large number of independent variables in the function. For this reason, and to determine the discriminant power of independent variables, the stepwise method is used as an estimation method in this research.

Assessment of the level of significance for the discriminant function provides the information necessary to decide whether to continue on to the interpretation of the analysis or if re-specification is necessary. Assessment of the level of significance depends on different statistical criteria applied to each method of the discriminant function. This research uses the stepwise method for assessing the discriminant model.

Therefore, the Mahalanobis D^2, Rao's V measure, Wilks' lambda, and the F value are the most appropriate in applying the stepwise method.

In addition to the above measures, there are two statistics that can be used to measure the relationship between the discriminant function scores and both group of loans. The first is called an eigenvalue which is the ratio of between-groups sum of squares to the within group sum of squares. Because the dependent variable in this research has two groups, there is only one discriminant function and one only eigenvalue, which accounts for 100% of the explained variance. The criterion of this measure is the lager eigenvalue, the stronger discriminant function. The second measure is called canonical correlation, which measures the degree of association between the discriminant scores and the good loans and bad loans. It is also the ratio of the between-group sum of squares to the total sum of squares. A high canonical correlation means that the function discriminates well.

Moreover, by squaring this canonical correlation, the coefficient of determination can be obtained. This measure shows how much the total variation in the dependent variable (status of loan) can be explained by the discriminant function.

After assessment of the level of significant of the discriminant function, the overall fit of the discriminant function will be assessed. The evaluation of the overall fit involves three steps: computing discriminant Z scores for each observation, evaluating group differences on the discriminant Z scores, and assessing group membership prediction accuracy.

Computing discriminant Z scores for each observation is by applying the discriminant function equation.

The discriminant function can be stated in the form of either standardized or unstandardized weights or values. According to Hair et al., (2006) the standardized function is more useful for interpretation purposes while the unstandardized is more useful for computing the discriminant Z score. The Z score formula is:

$$Z_{jk} = \alpha + \beta_1 x_{1k} + \beta_2 x_{2k} + \ldots + \beta_n x_{nk} \tag{1}$$

where Z is the discriminant score of discriminant function j for object k, α is the intercept, β is the discriminant coefficient for independent variable, and x is the independent variable. After computing the discriminant Z scores, the overall model fit assessment should firstly be identified by the great scale of differences between the members of each group regarding the discriminant scores. This evaluation can be performed by comparing the average (centroids) discriminant Z scores for all group members.

Assessing predictive accuracy involves taking into consideration four elements that must be addressed; (i) the cutting score determination, (ii) development and construction of the classification matrices, (iii) establishing standards for assessing classification accuracy, and (iv) case wise diagnostics.

The Cutting Score Determination

The cutting score (also called the critical Z value) is the measure against which each object's discriminant score is compared to determine into which group the object should be classified. The cutting score selected is the one that minimizes the number of incorrect classifications (Sharma, 1996). The computation of a cutting score between any two groups is based on the two group centroids and the relative size of the two groups. To compute the optimum cutting score correctly, it should define the prior probabilities that affect the group sizes used in the computation. The basic formula for calculating the cutting score between any two unequal group sizes is:

$$Z_{CS} = \frac{N_A Z_B + N_B Z_A}{N_A + N_B} \tag{2}$$

where Z_{CS} is the optimal cutting score between groups A and B, N_A is the number of observations in group A, N_B is the number of observations in group B, Z_A is the centroid for group A, Z_B is the centroid for group B. For equal group sizes, the optimum cutting score is:

$$Z_{CE} = \frac{Z_A + Z_B}{2} \tag{3}$$

where Z_{CE} is the optimal cutting score value for group of equal size. The classification rule refers is that if an observation's discriminant score is less than or equal to the optimal cutting score, then assign it to group A; otherwise, assign it to group B (Metwally, 2000).

Development and Constructing Classification Matrices

Constructing classification matrices determines the predictive ability of a discriminant function. The result of this matrix is the percentage correctly classified (also called hit ratio), which measures the predictive accuracy of the discriminant function, of the estimation sample, and cross-validated and holdout sample. In addition to the percentage correctly classified, the t test determines the level of significance for the classification accuracy by applying the following equation:

$$t = \frac{P - 0.5}{\sqrt{\frac{0.5(1.0 - 0.5)}{N}}} \tag{4}$$

where P is the proportion correctly classified and N is the sample size for either the analysis sample or the holdout sample.

Establishing Standards for Assessing Classification Accuracy

The first standard that must be established for assessing classification accuracy is the percentage of chance criterion, which assumes that the costs of misclassification are equal. Where the group sizes in this research are unequal (the sample size unequally divided into analysis sample and holdout sample), the following formula of the proportional chance criterion can be used:

$$C_{PRO} = P^2 + (1 - P)^2 \tag{5}$$

where P is the proportion of individuals in the good loans group and $1–P$ is the proportion of individuals in the bad loans group. If the classification accuracy levels are higher than the proportional chance criterion, it can be said that the level of classification accuracy is acceptable. The second standard used for assessing classification accuracy is the maximum chance criterion, which is used to maximize the percentage correctly classified. The maximum chance criterion represents the percentage of the largest group, and this percentage represents performance of the model. Another criterion suggested is that the classification accuracy should be at least one-fourth greater than that achieved by chance.

The last standard of classification accuracy is Press's Q statistic. This measure compares the number of correct classification with the total sample size and the number of groups. The statistic is computed by the following formula:

$$= \frac{\left[N - (nK)\right]^2}{N(K - 1)} \tag{6}$$

where N is the total sample size, n is the number of observations correctly classified, and K is the number of groups. The formula applies for both samples; analysis sample and holdout sample.

The value that results from the application of this formula should be compared with a critical value obtained from the chi-square value for 1 degree of freedom at the significance level of 5%. If Press's Q value is higher than the critical value, the classification accuracy is significant and vice versa.

Cases Diagnostics

The final step of assessing model fit is to examine the predictive results on a case by case basis. The objective of this assessment is to understand and analyze which observations have been misclassified and are not representative of the remaining group members. The first procedure for identifying the misclassification cases is to use discriminant Z score obtained. Each case in the sample classifies as a good loan if its discriminant score is less than the discriminant Z score, otherwise, the case misclassifies as a bad loan. Each case in the sample classifies as a bad loan if its discriminant score is greater than the discriminant Z score, otherwise, the case misclassifies as a good loan. Once the misclassified cases are determined, the second procedure is to perform further analysis to understand the reasons for their misclassification. This analysis involves determining particular differences on the independent variables that may identify new variables to be added. To achieve this analysis, the cases correctly classified and cases misclassified are determined for the all independent variables per good loan and bad loan. After that, the t test is used to test the differences in the mean values of the cases correctly classified and cases misclassified. A level of significance of 5% is used to determine the classification accuracy.

3.3. Results of the Discriminant Model

The main purpose of using discriminant analysis in this research is to identify the independent variables that efficiently differentiate between good loans and bad loans in the Al-Wahada Bank. We divided the sample of 400 loans into an analysis sample of 300 loans and a holdout sample of 100 loans for validation purposes. The two group sizes of 157 and 143 loans in the analysis sample exceed the minimum size of 20 loans per group. In this section, estimation of the discriminant model and assessment of overall fit as well as the interpretation of the results are discussed. Furthermore, the assumptions of discriminant analysis are taken into consideration.

Table 5 provides the group means for each of the independent variables in the Al-Wahada loans, based on the 300 observations constituting the analysis sample. In profiling the two groups, twelve variables provide the largest differences in the group means (the amount of loan LOAN), namely, the purpose of loan (PUR), the type of property (PROP), the status of accommodation (ACC), the number of children of an applicant (CHIL), the opinion of the Credit Department at the Al-Wahada Bank (OPN), the occupation of the guarantor (OCC_B), whether the borrower's salary is ongoing (ONG_A), whether the guarantor's salary is ongoing (ONG_B), whether the guarantor guarantees another borrower (GUR_B), the age of guarantor AGE_B), and whether the guarantor has another loan (EXT_B)). We used Wilks'

Lambda and univariate ANOVA to assess the significance between the means of the independent variables for the good loans and bad loans.

Table 5. Group descriptive statistics and tests of equality in the group discriminant analysis

Variable	Group Means		Tests of equality			Minimum D^2
	Good loans	Bad loans	Lambda	*F* value	Sig.	
LOAN	4129.350	5000.049	.865	46.360	.000	.619
PUR	1.63694	2.11888	.951	15.449	.000	.206
PORP	1.62420	1.42657	.961	12.130	.001	.162
ACC	1.93631	1.55944	.943	18.140	.000	.242
OCC_A	3.61783	3.62937	1.000	.004	.948	.000
AGE_A	2.55414	2.74825	.995	1.642	.201	.022
GND_A	1.20382	1.12587	.989	3.288	.071	.044
MART_A	1.49045	1.63636	.991	2.755	.098	.037
CHIL	2.00000	2.71329	.975	7.691	.006	.103
OPN	1.23567	1.39161	.972	8.698	.003	.116
SAL_A	259.127	269.925	.995	1.416	.235	.019
ONG_A	1.16561	1.34266	.958	12.969	.000	.173
GUR_A	1.90446	1.90210	1.000	.005	.945	.000
EXT_A	1.80892	1.86713	.994	1.855	.174	.025
SAL_B	252.586	265.520	.992	2.344	.127	.031
OCC_B	3.69427	4.06993	.987	4.011	.046	.054
ONG_B	1.03822	1.48951	.749	99.814	.000	1.334
GUR_B	1.86624	1.52448	.860	48.368	.000	.646
AGE_B	2.96815	2.29371	.932	21.653	.000	.289
GND_B	1.40764	1.32168	.997	.920	.338	.012
EXT_B	1.84076	1.53147	.888	37.675	.000	.503

Table 6. Variables in the analysis following each step

Variable entered	Tolerance	Minimum	F Value	
			Value	Sig.
Step 1 ONG_B	1.000	1.334	99.814	0.000
Step 2 GUR_B	1.000	1.983	73.968	0.000
Step 3 LOAN	0.991	2.439	60.440	0.000
Step4 SAL_A	0.506	2.717	50.316	0.000
Step 5 CHIL	0.952	2.928	43.234	0.000
Step 6 GUR_A	0.873	3.177	38.966	0.000
Step 7 AGE_B	0.889	3.448	36.123	0.000
Step 8 MART_A	0.831	3.559	32.512	0.000
Step 9 PUR	0.957	3.672	29.710	0.000

These tests indicate that the twelve variables are also the only variables with significant univariate differences between the two groups.

To identify which of these twelve variables, in addition to the other variables, best discriminates between the groups, the discriminant function must be estimated. By using the stepwise method, variables with insignificant differences across the groups (more than .05) and the lowest Mahalanobis distance D^2 between groups will be excluded; and vice versa. This process continues to exclude variables in the discriminant function as long as they do not provide statistically significant additional discrimination between the groups.

Table 6 shows the steps required to select the variables that have the best discriminately power. The variable (whether the guarantor's salary is ongoing (ONG_B)) is entered as the first variable in the stepwise procedure because it has the largest significant difference between groups and the largest D^2.

As shown in Table 6, nine steps are required to select discriminately variables. These variables are whether the guarantor's salary is ongoing (ONG_B), whether a guarantor guaranteed another borrower (GUR_B), the amount of loan (LOAN), monthly salary of a borrower (SAL_A), number of children of a borrower (CHIL), whether an applicant guaranteed another borrower (GUR_A), the age of guarantor (AGE_B), marital status of a borrower (MART_A), and the purpose of loan (PUR), respectively. However, it can be noted that some variables entered into the analysis in spite of being not significant in the test of equality of the group means stage. These include the marital status of a borrower (MART_A), monthly salary of a borrower (SAL_A), and whether an applicant guaranteed another borrower (GUR_A). In contrast, the variables that were significant in the test of equality at the group means stage including the type of property (PROP), the status of accommodation (ACC), the opinion of Credit Department (OPN), whether the borrower's salary is ongoing (SAL_A), and whether the guarantor has another loan (EXT_A) do not enter in the stepwise analysis. Thus, the estimation process stops with nine variables constituting the discriminant function.

We also obtained four other results useful for our analysis. To start with, the discriminant function is highly significant and shows a canonical correlation of 0.693. By squaring this number, we obtain a value of 0.48, indicating the model including only nine independent variables can explain 48% of the variance in the dependent variable (loan status). We also obtain a large eigenvalue of 0.992, which indicates a strong discriminant function. Moreover, Wilks' lambda tests the null hypothesis that the average discriminant scores are equal for both good loans and bad loans. The Table shows that the Wilks' lambda of 0.693 has a significant value. Thus, we reject the null hypothesis and conclude that the group means of the discriminant functions appear to differ. Finally, we use the unstandardized discriminant coefficients to compute the discriminant Z score for classification. We obtain the following discriminant model to predict whether an applicant has a good loan or has a bad loan for the bank:

$$\begin{aligned}\text{Discriminant score} = & - 3.781 + 1.430(\text{ONG\_B}) - 0.992(\text{GUR\_B}) + 0.001(\text{LOAN}) \\ & - 0.006(\text{SAL\_A}) + 0.209(\text{CHIL}) + 0.907(\text{GUR\_A}) - 0.246(\text{AGE\_B}) \\ & + 0.257(\text{MART\_A}) + 0.169(\text{PUR}).\end{aligned}$$

The standardized discriminant coefficients are the coefficients obtained when all predictor variables are standardized to a mean of zero and a within-group standard deviation of one. The standardized coefficients compare the importance of the coefficient for independent variables in terms of their impact on the discriminant function. For the group means of the discriminant functions we obtain values for good loans of – 0.913 and for bad loans of 1.003. Consequently, the overall results of the model are acceptable based on statistical and practical significance.

Assessing classification accuracy requires achieving three steps; calculating the cutting score, constructing classification matrices and evaluating the achieved classification accuracy.

First, calculating the cutting scoring requires identifying the number of observations for good and bad loans in the sample. Our analysis sample includes 300 observations divided into 157 observations representing good loans, and 143 observations representing bad loans. Because we select the sample randomly, it does not reflect the population proportions. Therefore, we use the sample proportions to identify the prior probabilities for classification purposes. We then the optimum cutting score by applying (2) as follows:

$$Z_{CS} = \frac{(157)(1.003) + (143)(-0.913)}{157 + 143} = 0.0897$$

Thus, the procedure for classifying loans with an optimal cutting score is as follows: (i) if the Z_{CS} of an observation is less than 0.0897, the loan classifies as a good loan; (ii) if Z_{CS} of an observation is greater than 0.0897, the loan classifies as a bad loan. Using this approach, for the analysis sample we obtain 86% prediction accuracy, which is higher than the 77% accuracy of the holdout sample. Furthermore, the cross-validated sample achieved a prediction accuracy of 85.7%.

Table 7. Classification results

			Group	Predicted Group Membership		Total
				Good	Default	
Estimation sample	Original	Count	Good	139	18	157
			Default	24	119	143
		%	Good	88.5	11.5	100
			Default	16.8	83.2	100
	Cross-validated	Count	Good	138	19	157
			Default	24	119	143
		%	Good	87.9	12.1	100
			Default	16.8	83.2	100
Holdout sample	Original	Count	Good	38	5	43
			Default	18	39	57
		%	Good	88.4	11.6	100
			Default	31.6	68.4	100

Finally, since all of the measures of classification accuracy are quite high the evaluation process requires a comparison of the classification accuracy in a series of chance-based measures. These measures reflect the improvement of the discriminant model when compared to classification of individuals without using a discriminant function. The first measure is the proportional chance criterion, which assumes misclassifications are equal and the group sizes are unequal. The proportional chance value should be equal to 50% for both the analysis sample and the holdout sample as calculated above.

When this value is compare to all classification accuracies (hit ratios), all classification accuracies are higher than the proportional chance value. This means that the levels of classification accuracy are acceptable.

The second measure to test the acceptance of the levels of classification accuracy is that the classification accuracy should be at least one-fourth greater than that achieved by chance. Thus, the suggested threshold of these values is (50%×1.25=) 62.5% which represents the maximum chance and smaller than the levels of classification accuracy. This also means that the levels of classification accuracy are acceptable.

The final measure of classification accuracy is Press's Q, which we compute for both the analysis sample and the holdout sample. We obtain values of 155.52 for the analysis sample and 29.16 for the holdout sample. Because the values of both of Press's Q exceed the critical value of Chi-square of 3.8415, therefore the classification accuracy for the analysis sample and the holdout sample is statistically significant and better than chance. Thus, the levels of classification accuracy are acceptable.

To confirm the robustness of our results, we test for multicollinearity, outliers and homogeneity. Multicollinearity can be identified by several means including, tolerance values, variance inflation factor (VIF), condition index, and pooled within-group matrices.

Table 8 shows that even though the lowest tolerance values are indicated by the type of property and the possession of property at 0.185 and 0.183 respectively, both are more than 0.10 (as a rule of thumb).

Furthermore, the highest VIF values are 5.42 and 5.47 for the type of property and the possession of property respectively but both is still less than 10 (as a rule of thumb). On the other hand, the condition index results indicate multicollinearity. The condition indices are about 42 which exceeds the criteria (between 10 and 30).

Therefore, the solution is to remove variables causing multicollinearity represented in the type of property and the status of accommodation and whether an applicant has another loan and whether an applicant guaranteed another person. Because whether an applicant guaranteed another person is the only variable included in discriminant function, we remove whether an applicant has another loan and the accommodation status variables.

The classification output for individual cases can be used to identify outliers. To identify outliers the critical value for Mahalanobis D^2, which is the value that attains a specific level of statistical significance, should be established.

It can be assumed that a case is an outlier if the calculated D^2 exceeds the critical value. The critical value can be identified by assuming the cumulative probability, 0.99, and degrees of freedom of 9 which represents the independent variables entered in the discriminant function. The critical value calculated by the SPSS software package was 21.67. By comparing the D^2 to the calculated D^2 values we note that two cases (125 with a value of 27.794 and 185 with a value of 29.421 are larger than the critical value of 21.67, therefore these cases are outliers and they must be omitted from the analysis. After removing the outlier cases, the original cases correctly classified change from 86% to 86.6% and the cross-validated classification accuracy changes from 85.7% to 85.2%.

Table 8. Assessing tolerance and VIF values

Variable	R^2	Tolerance ($1-R^2$)	VIF ($1/(1-R^2)$
LOAN	0.561	0.439	2.277
PUR	0.159	0.841	1.189
PROP	0.815	0.185	5.417
ACC	0.817	0.183	5.470
OCC_A	0.399	0.601	1.665
AGE_A	0.634	0.366	2.729
GND_A	0.315	0.685	1.459
MART_A	0.257	0.743	1.345
CHIL	0.575	0.425	2.350
OPN	0.561	0.439	2.277
SAL_A	0.539	0.461	2.168
ONG_A	0.640	0.360	2.777
GUR_A	0.444	0.556	1.797
EXT_A	0.449	0.551	1.814
SAL_B	0.398	0.602	1.661
OCC_B	0.406	0.594	1.682
ONG_B	0.411	0.589	1.697
GUR_B	0.444	0.556	1.797
AGE_B	0.403	0.597	1.675
GND_B	0.176	0.824	1.214
EXT_B	0.419	0.581	1.720

The most common test of homogeneity is Box's M. This statistic has an F value of 358.619 with a probability of <0.001 which means the null hypothesis that the covariance matrices do not differ between groups of loans formed by the dependent is rejected and the assumption of homogeneity is violated.

However, the Box's M usually shows a significant result when the sample size is large and so can be interpreted in conjunction with an investigation of the log determination.

Therefore, we use log determinants of the group covariance matrices, as a measure of the variability of the groups, to check for homogeneity. We note that the logs of determinants are relatively equal in value (16.05 and 15.77) which indicates the homogeneity of the covariance matrices between the groups.

4. Logistic Regression

The logistic regression model is also one of the more common statistical techniques used for credit scoring. In this analysis, the purpose of the logistic regression model is to predict a qualitative variable (good loans and bad loans) from a linear combination of independent variables that maximize the likelihood of obtaining the observed probability of the sample outcome. Therefore, the dependent variable, the independent variables, and the sample considerations are identical to those in the earlier discriminant analysis.

Logistic regression does not require any additional assumptions about the distribution of the independent variables than discriminant analysis and OLS regression (Barbara et al., 2007). The reason is that the logistic regression does not assume a linear relationship between the dependent variables and the independent variables.

In addition, the dependent variable in logistic regression is not assumed to be normally distributed or have equal variance-covariance matrices across groups for each level of the independent variables. Logistic analysis also does not assume a normally distributed error term.

4.1. Estimating the Logistic Model

The specific formula for the logistic model is:

$$P(event) = \frac{e^{\beta_0+\beta_1 x_1+\beta_2 x_2+...+\beta_n x_n}}{1+e^{\beta_0+\beta_1 x_1+\beta_2 x_2+...+\beta_n x_n}} \tag{7}$$

where β are coefficients estimated from the data, x is the independent variable; e is the base of the exponential function; and P is the predicted probability that an event occurs. The linear regression equation creates the logit transformation, which is defined as follows:

$$L = In(\frac{P(event)}{1-P(event)}) = \beta_0 + \beta_1 x_1 + \beta_2 x_2 + ... + \beta_n x_n \tag{8}$$

where L is the log of the odds ratio or logit.

To estimate the logistic model, two methods can be applied, the direct method and the stepwise method. First, direct (simultaneous) estimation involves calculating the logistic model by entering all of the predictors are considered simultaneously with ignoring of the discriminating power of each independent variable (Hair et al., 2006). Barbara et al., (2007) criticize this method because of the difficulties with interpretation when the independent variables are correlated. Second, stepwise methods involve entering the independent variables into the logistic model sequentially based on their statistically significant score statistics (Cramer, 2003) using forward or backward methods. The forward method includes three types; (i) forward conditional which is based on the probability of a likelihood-ratio statistic and conditional parameter estimates, (ii) forward likelihood which is based on the probability of a likelihood-ratio statistic and the maximum partial likelihood estimates, and (iii) forward Wald which is based on the probability of the Wald statistic (Norusis, 2005). The backward method includes the same types as the forward stepwise method. However, the difference between these methods is that forward selection adds variables in order by selecting the variable with the highest score until other variables not selected show insignificant values (more than the 5% level of significance). Although Menard (1995) mentioned that both the forward and backward stepwise methods usually produce identical results, the stepwise likelihood ratio forward will be used in estimating the logistic model in this chapter.

To estimate the coefficients, we use maximum likelihood. This method requires maximizing the likelihood that an event will occur (Hair et al., 2006). Applying this method requires building a function called the likelihood function, which measures the probability of the observed data as a function of the unknown parameters.

The maximum likelihood estimators of these parameters are selected to be those values that maximize this function (Hosmer and Lemeshow, 1989). The basic criterion for selecting parameters in the logistic regression model is the log likelihood value. In the SPSS software package, the log likelihood appears as –2 log likelihood because this value has approximately a chi-square distribution and the negative sign converts this value into a positive (Menard, 1995). The rule of this value is that the lower values of the –2 log likelihood indicate a better fitting model. The log likelihood value also is also used in comparing the logistic models to measure the variation in predictive fit from one model to another. It can be used in three steps to measure this variation (Hair et al., 2006). The first step is to estimate the null model, which appears at the beginning of the logistic regression output and includes only the intercept before the independent variables are entered into the model. The purpose of the null model is to be to compare with other models, which include the independent variables. The second step is to estimate the proposed model, which includes the independent variables in the logistic model. The final step is to assess the log likelihood difference. If the difference is statistically significant, the independent variables are significant in improving model estimation fit. We use the Pseudo R^2, the Cox and Snell R^2, and the Nagelkerke R^2 to assess the overall fit of our model.

4.2. Results of the Logistic Regression

To identify which of the variables best discriminate between the groups, we estimate the logistic regression model, and by using the stepwise method, exclude variables with insignificant differences across the groups (more than .05) and the lowest score statistics. This process continues to exclude variables in the logistic regression model as long as they do not provide statistical significance. As shown in Table 9, we required eight steps to select the discriminate variables. These are whether the guarantor's salary is ongoing (ONG_B), whether a guarantor guaranteed another borrower (GUR_B), the amount of loan (LOAN), monthly salary of a borrower (SAL_A), the occupation of borrower (OCC_B), number of children of a borrower (CHIL), whether an applicant guaranteed another borrower (GUR_A), and the marital status of a borrower (MART_A). The estimated logistic equation is:

$$\begin{aligned}\text{(Loan Group)} = {} & 1.636 - 0.002(\text{LOAN}) + 0.179(\text{MART\_A(1)}) - 0.910(\text{MART\_A(2)}) \\ & - 3.074(\text{MART\_A(3)}) - 0.421(\text{CHIL}) + 0.0.14(\text{SAL\_A}) + 2.057(\text{GUR\_A(1)}) \\ & - 0.095(\text{OCC\_B(1)}) + 1.215(\text{OCC\_B(2)}) + 2.010(\text{OCC\_B(3)}) \\ & + 3.685(\text{ONG\_B(1)}) - 1.910(\text{GUR\_B(1)}).\end{aligned}$$

Table 10 presents the three different measures of R^2 for the logistic regression model. The R^2 values in the first step for Cox and Snell, Nagelkerke and Pseudo are 0.283, .377, and .240, respectively. These values eventually reach .523, .698, and .535 respectively in the final step with eight independent variables contributing to explaining the variation in the dependent variable.

Finally, we use the classification accuracy measure to test the overall fit model as shown in Table 11, which presents the classification accuracy for the eight steps. Table 11 shows the overall percentages for the first one of the logistic regression model are 74.3% and 63% for the analysis sample and holdout sample, respectively.

Table 9. Variables in the analysis following each step

	Variable	Score	df	Sig.
Step 1	ONG_B(1)	86.719	1	.000
Step 2	GUR_B(1)	36.411	1	.000
Step 3	LOAN	17.444	1	.000
Step 4	SAL_A	14.666	1	.000
Step 5	OCC_B	15.342	3	.002
	OCC _B(1)	.904	1	.342
	OCC _B(2)	1.826	1	.177
	OCC _B(3)	12.285	1	.000
Step 6	CHIL	8.614	1	.003
Step 7	GUR_A(1)	10.177	1	.001
Step 8	MART_A	9.881	3	.020
	MART_A(1)	6.923	1	.009
	MART_A(2)	2.281	1	.131
	MART_A(3)	6.042	1	.014

Table 10. Measures of R^2

Step	Cox and Snell	Nagelkerke	Pseudo
1	.283	.377	.240
2	.363	.484	.325
3	.400	.534	.369
4	.432	.576	.408
5	.472	.629	.461
6	.487	.649	.482
7	.504	.673	.507
8	.523	.698	.535

In addition, the improvement in classification from step to step indicates how well the model performs and with these improvements, the logistic regression model with eight independent variables considered acceptable in terms of classification accuracy.

Thus, the model shows the highest correctly classified in the eighth step is 87.7% and 86% for the analysis sample and the holdout sample, respectively.

As all of the measures of classification accuracy are quite high, the evaluation process requires a comparison to the classification accuracy in a series of chance-based measures. These measures reflect the improvement of the logistic regression model when compared to classifying individuals without using the logistic equation. The first measure is the proportional chance criterion, which assumes misclassifications are equal and the group sizes are unequal.

Because the two groups are equal, the proportional chance value should be equal to 50%. When this value is compared with all classification accuracy (hit ratios) shown in the overall percentage of Table 11, it can be noted that all classification accuracies are higher than the proportional chance value.

This means that the levels of classification accuracy are acceptable.

Table 11. Classification accuracy

Step	Observed		Predicted group membership					
			Analysis sample			Holdout sample		
			Group		Percentage Correct	Group		Percentage Correct
			Default	Good		Good	Default	
Step 1	Group	Default	70	73	49.0	20	37	35.1
		Good	4	153	97.5	0	43	100.0
	Overall Percentage				74.3			63.0
Step 2	Group	Default	108	35	75.5	40	17	70.2
		Good	23	134	85.4	7	36	83.7
	Overall Percentage				80.7			76.0
Step 3	Group	Default	107	36	74.8	39	18	68.4
		Good	23	134	85.4	5	38	88.4
	Overall Percentage				80.3			77.0
Step 4	Group	Default	108	35	75.5	40	17	70.2
		Good	16	141	89.8	5	38	88.4
	Overall Percentage				83.0			78.0
Step 5	Group	Default	117	26	81.8	43	14	75.4
		Good	16	141	89.8	2	41	95.3
	Overall Percentage				86.0			84.0
Step 6	Group	Default	119	24	83.2	43	14	75.4
		Good	15	142	90.4	5	38	88.4
	Overall Percentage				87.0			81.0
Step 7	Group	Default	124	19	86.7	45	12	78.9
		Good	16	141	89.8	5	38	88.4
	Overall Percentage				88.3			83.0
Step 8	Group	Default	123	20	86.0	48	9	84.2
		Good	17	140	89.2	5	38	88.4
	Overall Percentage				87.7			86.0

The second measure to test the acceptance of the levels of classification accuracy is that the classification accuracy should be at least one-fourth greater than that achieved by chance. Thus, the suggested threshold of these values are (50% × 1.25= 62.5%) which represents the maximum chance and smaller than the levels of classification accuracy. This also means that the levels of classification accuracy are acceptable.

The final measure of classification accuracy is Press's Q, which we compute for both the analysis sample and the holdout sample. Table 12 provides the results.

Table 12 shows the number of the cases classified correctly which were used in calculating the Press's Q measure for both analysis and holdout samples. Furthermore, it can be noted that the number of the cases classified correctly improved to 263 cases and 86 cases for the analysis and the holdout samples respectively. This result also improves the Press's Q measure as well. Because the values of Press's Q for both the analysis and the holdout samples exceed the critical value of Chi-square of 3.8415 the classification accuracy for the analysis sample and the holdout sample is statistically significant and better than chance. Thus, the levels of classification accuracy are acceptable.

The logistic regression model estimated coefficients for eight independent variables and the intercept. Table 13 shows the estimates for eight independent variables in the final step.

According to the Wald statistics used to assess the significance of the independent variables, six of the eight variables included exhibit significance levels of Wald statistics at the 0.05 level of significance.

The effect of guarantor's occupation (OCC_B) and marital status of the borrower (MART_A) on the group loans do not appear to be statistically significant, and neither does the intercept.

In this stage, we use the coefficients of the logistic model to assess the direction and the impact each independent variable has on predicted probability and group membership.

Table 13 shows that the independent variables; LOAN, MART_A(2), MART_A(3), CHIL, and GUR_B(1) have negative signs, which indicates a negative relationship with the predicted probability of loan therefore increasing the likelihood that the borrower will be classified as a bad loan; and vice versa. Conversely, the independent variables; MART_A(1), SAL_A, GUR_A(1), OCC_B(2), (OCC_B(3), and ONG_B(1) have positive sings, which indicates a positive relationship with predicted probability of loan therefore increasing the likelihood that the borrower will be classified as a good loan; and vice versa.

Table 12. Classification according to Press's Q

Step	Cases correctly classified	Analysis sample	Cases correctly classified	Holdout sample
1	223	71.05	63	6.76
2	242	112.85	76	27.04
3	241	110.41	77	29.16
4	249	130.68	78	31.36
5	258	155.52	84	46.24
6	261	164.28	81	38.40
7	265	176.33	83	43.56
8	263	170.25	86	51.84

Table 13. Variables in the model

Variable	Coef.	S.E.	Wald	df	Sig.	Exp(B)
Loan	-.002	.000	26.307	1	.000	.998
MART_A			8.018	3	.046	
MART_A(1)	.179	1.055	.029	1	.865	1.196
MART_A(2)	-.910	1.170	.605	1	.437	.403
MART_A(3)	-3.074	1.712	3.225	1	.073	.046
CHIL	-.421	.113	13.943	1	.000	.657
SAL_A	.014	.004	14.291	1	.000	1.014
GUR_A(1)	2.057	.688	8.952	1	.003	7.823
OCC_B			3.806	3	.283	
OCC_B(1)	-.095	.512	.035	1	.852	.909
OCC_B(2)	1.215	.650	3.497	1	.061	3.370
OCC_B(3)	2.010	.690	.8.486	1	.004	7.463
ONG_B(1)	3.685	.642	32.933	1	.000	39.858
GUR_B(1)	-1.910	.426	20.069	1	.000	.148
Constant	1.636	1.449	1.275	1	.259	5.134

In addition to using the direction of the relationship of each independent variable in interpretation of the logistic coefficients, we can also use the logistic coefficients to interpret the magnitude of the change in probability for each independent variable. For the loan amount (LOAN), the value of Exp(B) is 0.998 which implies that a one LYD increase in the loan amount decreases the odds by 0.2% [(1–0.998)×100] controlling for the other variables in the logistic model. Thus, the loan amount (LOAN) is 0.2% less likely to be in the group of good loans than in the group of bad loans. In relation to the marital status of a borrower (MART_A), the odds for a married borrower (MART_A (1)) being a good loan is 1.20 times the odds of that of a widowed borrower, while the odds for a single borrower (MART_A (2)) of being a good loan is 0.40 times that of a widowed borrower. The odds for a married borrower (MART_A (3)) of being a good loan are 0.05 times that of a widowed borrower. With regard to the number of children for a borrower (CHIL), the value of Exp (B) is 0.657 which indicates that an increase of one child decreases the odds by 34.3% [(1–0.657)×100] controlling for the other variables in the logistic model. Thus, an increase in the number of children for a borrower (CHIL) means the borrower is 34% less likely to be in the group of good loans than in the group of bad loans.

Concerning the monthly salary of a borrower (SAL_A), the value of Exp(B) is 1.022 which implies that a one LYD increase in loan monthly salary increases the odds by 1.4% [(1–1.014) ×100] controlling for the other variables in the logistic model. Thus, monthly salary (SAL_A) is 2.2% more likely to be in the group of good loans than in the group of bad loans. For whether a borrower guarantees another borrower (GUR_A), the odds of being in the good loans are 7.823 times higher for a borrower who guarantees another borrower than for a borrower who does not. In relation to occupation of a guarantor (OCC_B), the odds for a guarantor working as a police or soldier (OCC_B (1)) of being a good loan are 0.91 times the odds for a guarantor who works in the public sector. The odds for a guarantor who works as a professional (OCC_B (2)) of being in the good loans are 3.37 times the odds for a guarantor who work in the public sector. The odds for a retired guarantor (OCC_B (3)) being a good loan is 7.463 times that for a guarantor who works in the public sector. With regard to whether the guarantor's salary is ongoing (ONG_B), the odds of being a good loan is 39.68 times higher for if the guarantor's salary is ongoing than if the guarantor's salary is not ongoing. Finally, for whether a guarantor guarantees another borrower (GUR_A), the odds of being a good loan is 0.15 times higher for a guarantor who guarantees another borrower than for a guarantor who does not.

5. Survival Analysis

Survival analysis is the most common statistical techniques used for credit scoring. In this chpater, the purpose of survival analysis is to describe the proportion of cases surviving at various times for different groups and to assess the relationship between survival time and a set of independent variables to determine whether treatment differences are present after statistically controlling for the other independent variables (Barbara et al., 2007).

Therefore, the dependent variable, independent variables, and sample considerations are quite similar to those mentioned in discriminant analysis and logistic regression.

5.1. Assumptions of Survival Analysis

Survival analysis does not require assumptions about the distribution of the independent variables and concerns such as normality, linearity and homoscedasticity (Barbara et al., 2007). Nevertheless, these assumptions can improve the model of survival analysis. Therefore, survival analysis requires some assumptions as follows (Barbara et al., 2007). First, normality, linearity, and homoscedasticity assumptions are practical issue to assess the distribution of each independent variable. This can be done by applying similar procedures as linear regression. Second, multicollinearity should be absent among the independent variables. Third, outlier cases can affect the survival model, therefore we use similar techniques as logistic regression to detect outlier cases. Finally, we assume that the proportional hazard ratio is constant over time. For instance, if there are two borrowers with the same age and salary but different occupations, the ratio of their estimated hazard rates across all time points is e^B, where B is the regression coefficient for occupation.

Because the variables in this research are mixed categorical and continuous variables, an interaction term between time and independent variables can be created to test whether the coefficients significantly different from zero. An interaction term is a new variable that is the product of two other variables in the model. The effect of adding an interaction term is assessed using the partial likelihood ration test. When the proportional hazards assumption is not met with respect to a categorical independent variable, it can be used as a stratification variable instead of an independent variable to correct the problem. We estimate two separate baseline hazards functions for each level of the stratification variable, while the regression coefficients for the remaining covariates are equal across strata.

In addition to the stratification variable, the log-minus-log can assess whether the baseline hazards functions are proportional.

Survival analysis requires a minimum number of observations per independent variable. According to Elias (1989, cited in Barbara et al., 2007), each independent variable requires twelve observations to satisfy the minimum requirement. Therefore, the size of sample in this research is suitable to perform survival analysis. The independent variables specified in the survival analysis are the same as in the discriminant analysis and logistic regression. However, the dependent variable in survival analysis is divided into two elements; status, being the same binary indicator specified as the same dependent variable in the discriminant analysis and logistic regression, and time, being the number of months that has elapsed from the time of granting the loan until the time of loan failure.

Thus, loans paid off during the lifetime are censored loans, which we define as good loans. Furthermore, the end of the data collection determines the observation time, such that we consider all loans not paid by this date as bad loans with different failure times.

5.2. Estimation of the Survival Model

There are several methods to analyses survival data including Kaplan-Meier estimation, log-rank tests, accelerated failure time models, piecewise exponential models, Cox regression models, and complementary log-log models. According to Allison (1995) estimating Cox regression is considered the best method for survival analysis because the Cox regression is more robust than the accelerated failure time methods, it has good performance for time dependent covariates, it deals with both continuous and discrete time data, and is acceptable and common. Therefore, we use Cox regression to test the impact of independent variables on loan survival.

Applying Cox regression requires the use of two procedures, namely, time-constant covariates (where the independent variables do not change as function of time), and time dependent covariate (where the values change over the time) (Norusis, 2005). We assume time-constant covariates because the values of the independent variables are constant over the time. The basic model suggested by the Cox regression procedure is the proportional hazard model, which we extend through the specification of a strata variable. The proportional hazards model assumes that the time to event and the covariates are related through the following equation.

$$h_i(t) = e^{(\beta_1 x_1 + \beta_2 x_2 + \ldots + \beta_n x_n)} h_0(t) \tag{9}$$

where $h_i(t)$ is the hazard rate for the ith case at time t, β is the unknown coefficient, and $h_0(t)$ is the baseline hazard function at time t. The hazard function is a measure of the likelihood for the event to occur at a particular time t, given that the event did not yet occur. Larger values of the hazard function indicate greater probability for the event to occur. However, the baseline hazard function measures this likelihood independently of the covariates. The shape of the hazard function over time is defined by the baseline hazard for all cases. The covariates simply help to determine the overall magnitude of the function. The value of the hazard is equal to the product of the baseline hazard and a covariate effect. While the baseline hazard is dependent upon time, the covariate effect is the same for all time points. Consequently, the ratio of the hazards for any two cases at any period is the ratio of their covariate effects. This is the proportional hazards assumption (Hosmer and Lemeshow, 1999).

$$L(\beta) = \prod_{i=1}^{k} \frac{P[loan\ i\ fails\ at\ t_i]}{P[one\ loan\ from\ R(t_i)\ fails\ at\ t_i]}$$

$$L(\beta) = \prod_{i=1}^{k} \frac{e^{(\beta x_i)}}{\sum_{j \in R(t_i)} e^{(\beta x_j)}} \tag{10}$$

where $L(\beta)$ is the partial likelihood function and $T(t_i)$ is the set of borrowers at risk. In addition, maximum likelihood estimates can be used for the coefficients of the Cox model. Also, methods can be applied to estimate the Cox proportional regression model; direct method and the stepwise method (which were discussed and applied in the logistic regression section. In this research, the stepwise likelihood ratio forward will be used in estimating the Cox proportional regression model.

Once we construct the Cox proportional regression model is built, the overall test is of the hypothesis that all coefficients equal to zero. Further, as the Cox proportional regression model uses maximum likelihood to estimate the coefficients of independent variables, the likelihood-ratio test is used for assessing the goodness of fit of the Cox proportional regression model. The statistical test for coefficients in survival analysis is to test whether the Cox proportional regression model coefficients are significantly different from zero. In addition to the stepwise procedure in selection of the independent variables that should be in the model, there are three tests can be used for evaluation of the contribution of an individual independent variable to the Cox proportional regression model including Wald statistics, the likelihood ratio test, and score statistics (Norusis, 2005).

5.3. Results of the Survival Model

The survival model estimated coefficients for six independent variables. Table 14 shows the six independent variables in the final step. From Table 14, the survival model (Cox proportional hazard) is as follows:

$$h(t, X) = h(t) \exp [-0.00046(LOAN) + 0.00373(SAL\_A) + 0.81220(GUR\_A) + 2.65984(ONG\_B) - 0.55027(GUR\_B) - 0.63567(EXT\_B)].$$

We use the Wald statistics to assess the significance of the independent variables. It can be noted that the six variables have shown significance at the 0.05 level of significance. The direction of the relationship can be interpreted directly from the sign of the survival coefficients. Table 14 shows that the independent variables LOAN, GUR_B, and EXT_B have negative signs, which indicates a negative relationship with predicted probability of loan, therefore increasing the likelihood that the borrower will be classified as a bad loan and vice versa. On the other hand, the independent variables; SAL_A, GUR_A(1) and ONG_B(1) have positive signs, which indicates a positive relationship with predicted probability of loan, therefore increasing the likelihood that the borrower will be classified as good loan and vice versa.

Furthermore, the exponentiated coefficients can be used to identify the directions. It can be noted from Table 14 that the variables with values above 1.0 refer to a positive relationship and below 1.0 refers to a negative relationship. Therefore, when the loan amount increases by one Libyan Dinar the default hazard rate increase by 0.046% [(1–0.99954)×100] while for each Libyan Dinar increase in the borrower's salary the default hazard rate decreases by 0.373%. Furthermore, for dummy variables entered in the survival model, the risk ratio can be interpreted as the ratio of the estimated hazard for those with a value one to the estimated hazard for those with a value of zero.

Table 14. Variables in the survival equation

		B	SE	Wald	df	Sig.	Exp(B)
Step 6	LOAN	-.00046	.00008	31.62093	1.00000	.00000	.99954
	SAL_A	.00373	.00106	12.23978	1.00000	.00047	1.00373
	GUR_A	.81220	.25445	10.18903	1.00000	.00141	2.25285
	ONG_B	2.65984	.50725	27.49557	1.00000	.00000	14.29406
	GUR_B	-.55027	.24855	4.90149	1.00000	.02683	.57679
	EXT_B	-.63567	.22568	7.93415	1.00000	.00485	.52958

Thus, the default hazard for the borrowers who did not guarantee other borrowers (GUR_A) is 2.25 times than that for those who did. The default hazard for the guarantors who did not have a permanent salary (ONG_B) is 14.29 times than that for those who did. The probability of surviving for the guarantors who did not guarantee other borrowers (GUR_B) is 0.58 times than that for those who did. The probability of surviving for the guarantors who did not have other loans (EXT_B) is 0.53 times than that for those who did.

The aim of survival analysis is to estimate the predictive model for the Al-Wahada Bank in which the risk of an event depends on independent variables. The stepwise method is used for estimating the survival function. The survival model of the Al-Wahada Bank includes six independent variables selected using SPSS Version 15. These variables are the amount of loan (LOAN), monthly salary of a borrower (SAL_A), whether an applicant guaranteed another borrower (GUR_A), whether the guarantor's salary is ongoing (ONG_B), whether a guarantor guaranteed another borrower (GUR_B) and whether a guarantor granted another loan (EXT_B). In addition, the overall test of the survival model shows the goodness of fit by applying score statistics and likelihood ratio tests.

Moreover, the Wald statistic is used to assess significance of the independent variables. Finally, multicollinearity, proportional hazard and outlier tests are used for survival analysis of the data. The results of these tests show that all these assumptions are met.

6. MODEL COMPARISON

In this section, we compare the three credit-scoring models evaluate their performance. We employ two different methods for this purpose, the Receiver Operating Characteristic

(ROC) curve method, and the correctly classified method. First, we can apply the ROC method to assess how well credit-scoring models perform. Figure 1 depicts the ROC curve of the accuracy of the three models used in this chapter. In brief, the ROC curve illustrates the performance of a binary classifier system as its discrimination threshold is varied. We create the curve by plotting the fraction of true positives out of the total actual positives (vs. the fraction of false positives out of the total actual negatives, at various threshold settings.

The diagonal in Figure 1 divides the ROC space. Points above the diagonal represent good classification results (better than random), points below the line poor results (worse than random) and the further away from the diagonal, the better the model. As shown, all three models perform well because the curves are well above the reference line, with the logistic regression model being the best model followed by the discriminant analysis model and then the survival model. However, we should note that we fitted the logistic regression and discriminant analysis models to the definition of good and bad loans and the survival analysis model to the time to default. This infers survival models will usually perform better over time.

In addition to the visual depiction of the ROC curve, we can calculate the area under the curve numerically. Table 15 shows the result of performance of the probabilities default of the models. From the table, it is clear that the logistic regression model and discriminant analysis model have larger areas under the curve than the survival analysis model with 0.966 and .942 respectively. In our context, the area under the curve for each model represents the probability that a random good borrower has a higher value of measurement than does a random bad borrower. The table also indicates that the asymptotic significance of each model is less than 0.05, which means all models perform better than guessing would achieve.

The second method for evaluating the performance of our three credit-scoring models is the percentage of correctly classified cases. Unfortunately, this is only possible for the discriminant analysis and logistic regression. Table 6.38 shows the percentage of correctly classified cases for both the analysis sample and the holdout sample for discriminant analysis and logistic regression.

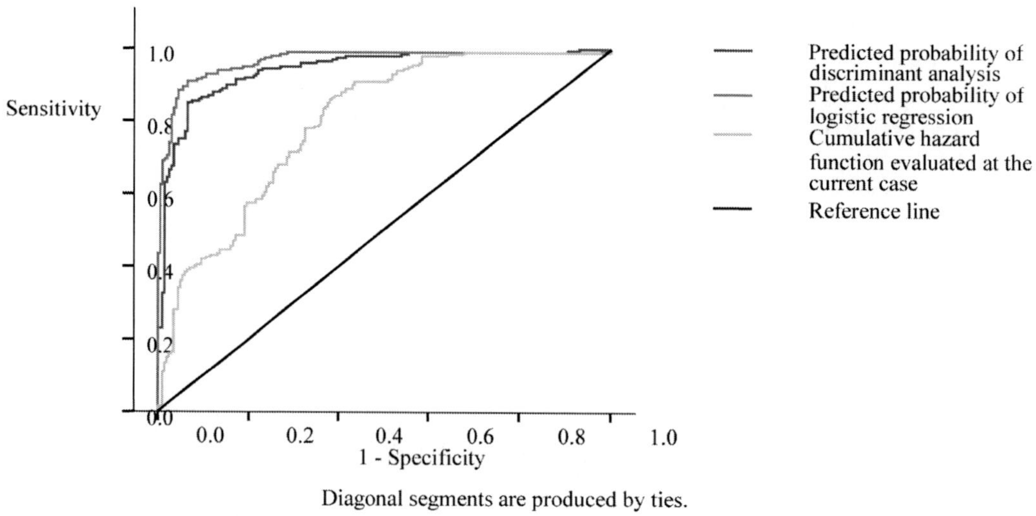

Figure 1. ROC curve for model comparison.

Table 15. Area under the ROC curves

Test Variable	Area	Std. Error	Asymptotic Sig.	Asymptotic 95% Confidence Interval	
				Upper	Lower
Predicted probability default of discriminant analysis	.942	.012	.000	.919	.965
Predicted probability default of logistic regression	.966	.009	.000	.949	.984
Hazard function of survival analysis	.797	.022	.000	.754	.840

Table 16. Modeling classifications

Performance measure	Discriminant analysis		Logistic regression	
	Analysis sample	Holdout sample	Analysis sample	Holdout sample
Percentage correctly classified	86	77	87.7	91.5

The results in Table 16, indicate the logistic regression model performs better than the discriminant analysis model in terms of percentage correctly classified cases and therefore concurs with the ROC curve in measuring performance of the models.

As a final point of comparison, we find all three models identify five common variables; (i) amount of loan (LOAN) (ii) monthly borrower's salary (SAL_A) (iii) whether the guarantor's salary is ongoing (ONG_B) (iv) whether the borrower guarantees another borrower (GUR_A) (v) whether the guarantor guarantees another borrower (GUR_B). Therefore, we consider that in this particular context, these variables are the most important factors affecting personal credit risk.

CONCLUSION

The purpose of this chapter was to analyze the data collected and discuss the results obtained by applying the credit scoring models to the loans of a Libyan bank. The three models employed were discriminant analysis, logistic regression, and survival analysis In terms of discriminant analysis. The results indicate that nine independent variables had the best discriminating power between good and bad loans. Furthermore, the percentages correctly classified appeared to be high for both the analysis sample and the holdout sample. The evaluation of these percentages resulted in acceptable levels of classification accuracy. The results also suggested that it can use interpretive measures for ranking independent variables to identify the most important discriminant variables by using discriminant loading. With the logistic regression, the model likewise produced nine independent variables. Moreover, the percentages correctly classified were high for samples and the levels of classification accuracy were acceptable according to the Press's Q measure and chi-square.

However, the results demonstrated that logistic regression is more sensitive to outlier cases. After removing the outlier cases, the logistic model added a new variable to the model.

Finally, with the survival model we used the Cox Proportional Hazard model to identify the independent variables that contribute to loan default over time. The results showed that the survival analysis model required only six independent variables. These variables effectively contributed to identification of the probability of default over the time in the Al-Wahada Bank. Finally, we compared the models applied in the chapter using the ROC curve and percentages correctly classified.

The results indicate the superiority of the logistic regression model to the other two models. In addition, the comparison indicates that five independent variables are common in to all models. However, we note that the survival model may not have performed as well as it could because of the nature of the data collected.

REFERENCES

Allison, P. D. (1995). *Survival Analysis Using the SAS System: A Practical Guide*. Cary, NC: SAS Institute.

Barabara, G., Tabachnic, B. and Fidell, L. (2007). *Using Multivariate Statistics*. 5th ed. Boston: Pearson.

Coval, J. and Shumway, T. (2000). *Do behavioural biases affect prices? Working Paper,* University of Michigan.

Crook, J. (1996). Credit constraints and US households. *Applied Financial Economics*, 6(6), 477-485.

Crook, J. Hamilton, R. and Thomas, L. (1992) A comparison of a credit scoring model with a credit performance model. *Service Industries Journal*, 12(4), 558-579.

Hair, J., Anderson, R. E., Tatham, R. L., and Black, W. C. (2006). *Multivariate Data Analysis*. 6th ed. Englewood Cliffs, NJ: Prentice-Hall.

Hosmer, D. and Lemeshow, S. (1989). *Applied Logistic Regression*. New York: John Wiley and Sons.

Hosmer, D. and Lemeshow, S. (1999). *Applied Survival Analysis: Regression Modeling of Time to Event Data*. New York: John Wiley and Sons.

Johnson, R. A. and Wichern, D. W. (2007). *Applied Multivariate Statistical Analysis*. 6th ed. Englewood Cliffs, NJ: Prentice Hall.

Klecka, W. R. (1980). *Discriminant Analysis*. Beverly Hills, CA: Sage.

Lachenbruch, P. (1975). *Discriminant Analysis*. New York: Hafner.

Metwally, M. (2000). *Applied Multivariate Statistical Techniques*. Wollongong: DE Publishing.

Norusis, M. J. (2005). *SPSS 14.0: Advanced Statistical Procedures Companion*. Upper Saddle River, NJ: Prentice Hall.

Sarlija, N., Bensic, M. and Bohacek, Z. (2005). Customer revolving credit – how the economic conditions make a difference. *Paper resented to the International Conference on Credit Scoring and Credit Control*, IX, Edinburgh University.

Sharma, S. (1996). *Applied Multivariate Techniques*. New York: Jones and Wiley.

Thanh, D. and Kleimeie, S. (2006). Credit scoring for Vietnam's retail banking market: Implementation and implications for transactional versus relationship lending. *Working Paper*, Maastricht Research School of Economics of Technology and Organization, Maastricht University.

Vojtek, M. and Kocenda, E. (2006). Credit-scoring methods. *Czech Journal of Economics and Finance,* Charles University Prague, Faculty of Social Sciences, 56(3-4), 152-167.

Editor's Contact Information

Professor Andrew C. Worthington
Department of Accounting, Finance and Economics
Griffith Business School, Griffith University
170 Kessels Road
Tel: +61 (0)7 3735 4273
Fax: +61 (0)7 3735 3719
Email: a.worthington@griffith.edu.au

INDEX

A

Abraham, 34, 42
access, 170
accommodation, 147, 220, 237, 239, 246, 248, 250
accountability, 170, 179, 180
accounting, 6, 10, 55, 102, 116, 161, 162, 163, 164, 166, 167, 168, 171, 173, 174, 175, 176, 177, 179, 180, 181, 182, 183, 186, 224
accounting standards, 175, 182
acquisitions, 79, 90
adjustment, 13, 119, 213, 223, 228, 229
Africa, 182, 232
age, 18, 81, 84, 116, 137, 138, 139, 140, 141, 142, 143, 144, 145, 146, 147, 148, 149, 150, 236, 238, 239, 247, 248, 258
agencies, 49, 55, 57, 117, 118, 166, 170, 236
aggregation, 58
agricultural economics, 172
algorithm, 124, 129, 131, 140, 141, 151
allocative efficiency, 219, 220
Al-Wahada Bank, 7, 235, 236, 238, 247, 261
American Stock Exchange, 34
amortization, 82, 83
analog models, 2
anatomy, 70
Angola, 169, 183
ANOVA, 247
Argentina, 231
arithmetic, 16, 17
artificial intelligence, 128, 131, 132
Asia, 10, 11, 42, 75, 77, 170, 174, 175, 180, 181, 183, 231
Asian financial crisis, 5, 12, 13
ASS, 81, 83, 84, 85, 86, 87, 88, 89
assessment, 14, 49, 54, 55, 56, 114, 115, 117, 131, 158, 221, 241, 243, 244, 246
assets, 48, 49, 50, 56, 58, 59, 60, 61, 70, 74, 81, 82, 83, 84, 85, 90, 123, 139, 141, 142, 143, 145, 146, 148, 223, 224
asymmetric information, 12, 200
asymmetry, 12, 77, 199, 200, 202
atmosphere, 170, 178
attitudes, 164, 175, 176
audit, 80, 165, 182
Australia, 10, 26, 30, 31, 35, 175, 180, 183, 197, 198, 209, 213, 218, 225
Austria, 70
authority(s), 47, 163, 165, 166, 168, 170, 175
awareness, 162, 166, 167, 169, 177, 178

B

balance sheet, 49, 50, 90
Bangladesh, 162, 169, 172, 179, 181, 182
bank failure, 153, 157, 158
bank financing, 200
banking, 22, 24, 25, 50, 55, 56, 68, 69, 94, 113, 130, 141, 145, 146, 151, 155, 158, 166, 170, 179, 180, 182, 265
banking industry, 24, 25, 94
banking sector, 155, 166, 170, 179, 180
bankruptcy, 50, 57, 71, 116, 123, 129, 130, 135, 139, 148, 152, 154, 157
banks, 45, 46, 47, 48, 49, 50, 51, 53, 55, 56, 57, 68, 72, 78, 89, 90, 93, 115, 116, 117, 118, 141, 145, 146, 153, 154, 155, 163, 165, 166, 167, 170, 174, 180
bargaining, 48, 78, 89, 90
base, 52, 78, 79, 102, 104, 118, 132, 252
BBB, 57, 117
beer, 143
behaviors, 7, 176
Belgium, 137, 143, 146, 147, 149, 158
benchmarks, 5, 7, 9, 16, 18, 197, 210, 213, 227

benefits, 41, 77, 78, 79, 90, 136, 147, 164, 221
beverages, 182
bias, 98, 124, 127, 133, 136, 141, 143, 144, 157, 171, 236
binary decision, 136
Bolivia, 144, 145
bondholders, 59
bonds, 49, 50, 55, 61, 70, 112, 214
borrowers, 46, 49, 50, 51, 54, 55, 57, 60, 61, 71, 89, 116, 117, 133, 137, 141, 142, 150, 154, 198, 236, 237, 238, 239, 240, 258, 260, 261
breakdown, 221
break-even, 1
Britain, 194
building blocks, 61
business cycle, 63, 99, 111, 112
business days, 5, 29, 31, 32, 35, 36, 37, 38, 39, 41
business environment, 117
business model, 90
business strategy, 15
businesses, 90, 111, 146, 174, 200
buy-and-hold returns, 5, 9, 13, 14, 15, 17, 18, 23, 24, 25, 210
buyer, 31, 49

C

campaigns, 98, 163
CAP, 223, 224
capital adequacy, 71
capital expenditure, 223, 224, 228, 229, 230
capital input, 7, 185, 187
capital markets, 43, 78, 91, 162, 171
case study, 181, 183
cash, 12, 33, 48, 54, 55, 62, 73, 78, 79, 82, 111, 142, 145, 148, 197, 200
cash flow, 12, 48, 54, 55, 62, 79, 82, 145, 197, 200
category d, 62
Census, 92
central bank, 47, 165, 166
certificate, 48, 92
certification, 12, 27, 199, 201, 215
challenges, 8, 50, 156, 182
chemical, 224, 227, 228, 230
Chicago, 72, 94, 157
child labor, 164
children, 1, 131, 137, 138, 139, 140, 141, 143, 144, 147, 150, 236, 237, 240, 246, 248, 253, 257
China, 10, 90, 198
chromosome, 131
citizens, 169, 170
citizenship, 181
City, 218, 227, 229
civil liberties, 167
civil rights, 169
civil society, 170, 178
civil war, 170
classes, 135, 155
classification, 62, 115, 122, 123, 124, 125, 126, 127, 129, 131, 132, 134, 135, 141, 143, 149, 152, 155, 156, 157, 158, 241, 242, 243, 244, 245, 246, 248, 249, 250, 251, 254, 255, 256, 262, 263
clients, 48, 145
climate, 217
climate change, 217
clubbing, 143
CNS, 85, 87
coastal region, 174
collateral, 49, 54, 137, 142, 237
colleges, 194, 195
color, 137
commerce, 177
commercial, 47, 55, 69, 71, 72, 90, 117, 132, 141, 143, 157, 166, 181
commercial bank, 47, 143, 157, 166, 181
communication, 162, 167, 169, 178
community, 148, 177
comparative analysis, 70, 153, 158
compensation, 79, 93, 110
competition, 47, 78, 218
competitive advantage, 77
competitive markets, 187
competitive process, 169
competitors, 48, 79
compilation, 15
complement, 121
complementarity, 7, 185
complexity, 8
compliance, 46, 47, 179, 224, 227, 228, 230
composition, 58, 186
computation, 66, 129, 244
computer, 3, 4, 115, 128, 132, 186
computer systems, 128
computer technology, 115, 186
computing, 56, 129, 244
conception, 171
conceptualization, 181
conference, 157, 187
confidentiality, 77, 90, 92
conflict, 123
consensus, 56
conservation, 230
consolidation, 195
construction, 21, 22, 24, 25, 87, 206, 244
consumer price index, 104, 111, 186
consumers, 47, 113, 129, 158, 162

consumption, 6, 91, 97
contextual factors, 6, 161, 162, 163, 227
continuous random variable, 65
corporate finance, 2
corporate governance, 6, 77, 79, 161, 171, 177, 181
corporate restructuring, 94
corporate sector, 55, 75, 90
Corporate Social Responsibility, 181, 182
correlation(s), 18, 24, 25, 39, 40, 51, 58, 59, 60, 61, 62, 63, 65, 66, 68, 108, 136, 143, 168, 171, 242, 243, 248
corruption, 162, 164, 165, 169, 170
cost(s), 1, 6, 7, 48, 52, 55, 68, 73, 77, 78, 79, 82, 83, 84, 89, 90, 93, 94, 95, 116, 117, 124, 127, 131, 141, 152, 164, 185, 186, 187, 188, 189, 190, 191, 192, 193, 194, 195, 200, 201, 218, 219, 220, 223, 224, 230, 231, 232, 245
cost functions, 1, 194
cost minimization, 187
country of origin, 137
covering, 49, 103, 206
Cox regression, 259
credit history, 49, 57, 115, 142, 144, 145
credit rating(s), 5, 45, 46, 51, 52, 53, 54, 55, 57, 58, 61, 62, 63, 65, 68, 69, 71, 72, 117, 118, 151
credit-scoring models, 6, 113, 114, 115, 116, 117, 118, 123, 124, 131, 133, 134, 135, 141, 148, 150, 151, 261, 262
creditworthiness, 51, 65, 89, 114, 116, 117, 137, 139, 140
crises, 10, 58
critical analysis, 124, 153
critical value, 37, 242, 246, 250, 256
criticism, 52, 68
Croatia, 148
Cross-national, 181
CSD, 179
cultural influence, 42, 181
cultural tradition, 175
culture, 91, 162, 163, 166, 170, 172, 174, 175, 176, 177, 181
cumulative abnormal returns, 5, 9, 13, 14, 25
cumulative distribution function, 119, 120, 133
currency, 13, 47, 58, 79, 143, 165
current account, 138, 139, 144
customers, 48, 90, 134, 149, 150, 223
cycles, 63, 98, 99, 110, 111, 112, 130
Czech Republic, 71

D

data analysis, 3
data availability, 68
data collection, 98, 235, 259
data distribution, 241
data envelopment analysis, 7, 194, 217, 230, 231, 232
data mining, 154
data set, 61, 68, 80, 133, 134, 202
database, 1, 14, 57, 80, 82, 89, 92, 133, 203
DEA, 220, 221, 222, 223, 225, 227, 232
deaths, 133
debts, 48, 57
decision makers, 6, 161
decision trees, 140
decision-making process, 3, 154
decomposition, 99
deficiencies, 13, 124, 219
delinquency(s), 52, 120, 142, 144, 149, 150, 152, 154, 172
Delta, 170, 212
demand, 1, 7, 12, 47, 48, 164, 165, 172, 177, 185, 186, 188, 191, 192, 193, 200, 219, 228
democracy, 111, 168, 170, 182
demography, 142
Denmark, 165
Department of Education, 186, 194
dependent variable, 19, 24, 52, 119, 121, 122, 155, 236, 240, 241, 243, 248, 252, 254, 258, 259
dependent variables, 19, 155, 252
deposit accounts, 48
deposits, 48, 146
depreciation, 82, 83
depression, 58
depth, 10, 199
deregulation, 111, 157
derivatives, 31, 49, 69, 71
derived demand, 7, 185, 186, 193
detection, 153
developed countries, 84, 162, 165, 171, 172, 177
developed nations, 173
developing countries, 94, 162, 164, 165, 171, 172, 173, 177, 179, 181
developing economies, 10
deviation, 37, 62, 107, 127, 220, 223
diffusion, 78, 151
direct cost(s), 77, 84
directors, 166, 176, 177
disclosure, 6, 29, 54, 77, 79, 95, 161, 162, 163, 164, 165, 166, 167, 168, 169, 170, 171, 172, 173, 174, 175, 176, 177, 178, 179, 180, 181, 182, 183
discounted cash flow, 3
discrete variable, 132
discriminant analysis, 7, 52, 115, 120, 122, 123, 125, 126, 127, 130, 131, 132, 136, 138, 139, 140, 143,

144, 151, 152, 153, 154, 155, 156, 157, 235, 240, 241, 242, 243, 246, 247, 252, 258, 259, 262, 263
discrimination, 137, 152, 248, 262
dispersion, 36, 91, 123, 171, 200, 213, 241, 242
distress, 125, 152
distribution, 14, 36, 48, 58, 60, 61, 62, 63, 64, 65, 66, 67, 75, 80, 81, 120, 121, 122, 123, 124, 133, 134, 136, 149, 231, 232, 242, 252, 253, 258
distribution function, 133
diversification, 58, 60, 62, 78, 90, 111
diversity, 172, 175
division of labor, 1
dominance, 90, 102, 114
donations, 98
drawing, 71
drug smuggling, 46
duality, 187, 222

E

earnings, 10, 27, 48, 55, 82, 83
East Asia, 10, 92, 182
Easter, 5, 29, 30, 31, 35, 36, 37, 38, 39, 40, 41
economic activity, 47, 63
economic change, 171
economic cycle, 46, 112
economic development, 171, 172, 173, 174, 178, 182, 183
economic efficiency, 231
economic growth, 11, 13, 77, 93
economic policy, 99
economic progress, 171
economic relations, 163
economic systems, 94, 171
economic welfare, 74
economics, 2, 52, 71, 154, 163, 195
economies of scale, 48, 194, 195
education, 140, 163, 171, 176, 177, 186, 187, 195
educational programs, 178
Egypt, 175
elaboration, 2
election, 6, 97, 98, 101, 102, 103, 104, 105, 107, 108, 109, 110, 111, 112
electricity, 84, 231
emerging markets, 9, 10, 75, 77, 80, 179, 182
emotion, 34
empirical studies, 29, 151
employees, 148, 162, 177
employment, 137, 138, 139, 140, 144, 145, 146, 147, 149, 171, 237
employment status, 137, 138, 139, 140, 144, 147
encouragement, 166
energy, 72, 157, 163, 198, 219
enforcement, 164
England, 156, 194, 195, 231, 232
entrepreneurs, 12, 73, 90, 91, 149, 199, 200
entropy, 125
environment(s), 2, 48, 134, 141, 154, 162, 163, 164, 166, 167, 168, 169, 170, 171, 172, 173, 176, 178, 179, 180, 181
environmental factors, 172, 232
environmental issues, 163, 165, 166, 167, 169, 170, 178
equality, 37, 38, 104, 107, 108, 247, 248
equilibrium, 12, 72, 93, 199
equipment, 82, 83, 84
equities, 31, 48, 50, 103
equity, 2, 7, 10, 12, 26, 48, 56, 60, 63, 67, 73, 74, 78, 79, 81, 82, 83, 84, 90, 93, 94, 98, 123, 141, 145, 146, 147, 171, 197, 198, 199, 200, 202, 206, 207, 208, 210, 211, 212, 213, 214
equity market, 10, 60, 74, 81, 90, 98, 171
erosion, 102
estimation process, 248
ethics, 182
ethnic background, 176
euphoria, 41
Europe, 156, 170, 174, 175, 183
European integration, 152
evidence, 6, 13, 25, 26, 33, 34, 35, 37, 41, 42, 43, 74, 75, 78, 79, 92, 93, 94, 97, 98, 99, 105, 110, 111, 133, 152, 163, 179, 180, 181, 186, 192, 200, 201, 209, 212, 213, 214, 231, 236
evolution, 201
execution, 31, 91
exercise, 75, 79, 111, 155, 219
exile, 91
expenditures, 82, 137, 186, 187, 193
expert systems, 51, 68, 124, 132, 151
expertise, 132
explanatory variables, 19, 52, 81, 126, 151
exploitation, 90
exposure, 31, 48, 50, 54, 55, 61, 62, 65, 66
external environment, 173
external influences, 51
external shocks, 220
extracts, 80

F

factor cost, 188
factor models, 5, 45, 59, 63
false positive, 262
families, 124
farms, 139, 157
fat, 37

federal funds, 48
Federal Reserve, 69, 70, 72, 94, 152, 153, 157
Federal Reserve Board, 70
Fiji, 176, 181
financial capital, 35
financial condition, 142
financial crisis, 5, 9, 10, 12, 13, 74, 75, 91
financial data, 2, 54, 80
financial development, 74
financial distress, 81, 154, 155, 156
financial institutions, 2, 10, 45, 46, 50, 55, 63, 67, 68, 70, 71, 115, 151, 152, 156
financial markets, 33, 57, 95
financial performance, 162, 166
financial reports, 2, 52
financial system, 47
firm size, 34, 38, 41, 56, 84, 85, 89
firm value, 53, 59, 60, 78, 200
fitness, 131
flexibility, 55, 78, 90, 130, 139
flotation, 93
fluctuations, 99
food, 22, 24, 25, 85, 87, 182
force, 2, 48, 115
forecasting, 67, 154
foreclosure, 138
foreign companies, 90
foreign exchange, 50, 79
formal education, 176
formation, 102
formula, 36, 244, 245, 246, 252
France, 33, 137, 153, 165, 180
freedom, 167, 168, 169, 170, 171, 180, 242, 246, 250
frequency distribution, 241
funding, 12, 48, 82, 84, 91, 194
funds, 10, 31, 48, 49, 50, 53, 78, 82, 83, 90, 91, 93, 197, 198, 199, 200, 201

G

genes, 131
genetic programming, 156
geography, 163
Germany, 24, 70, 71, 137, 143, 145, 146, 147, 170
global markets, 33
goods and services, 47
governance, 7, 92, 161, 170, 181
government policy, 74
government securities, 47
governments, 6, 75, 97, 98, 99, 100, 104, 107, 108, 110, 112, 163, 169, 172, 218
grades, 57, 62, 118
grading, 54
grants, 7, 185, 187, 189, 190
graph, 1, 2, 132, 133
Greece, 141
groundwater, 217, 224
group membership, 123, 244, 255, 256
group size, 150, 244, 245, 246, 250, 255
growth, 10, 12, 26, 73, 74, 75, 78, 79, 82, 83, 84, 85, 89, 116, 198, 199, 200, 214, 224
growth rate, 75, 82, 83
guessing, 262
guidance, 56, 111
guidelines, 150, 167

H

hazards, 133, 134, 158, 258, 259, 260
headline underpricing, 14, 19, 21, 203, 204, 207, 208
heterogeneity, 220, 242
heteroskedasticity, 39, 40, 108, 109, 110, 119
higher education, 167, 176, 177, 185, 186, 194, 195
Highlands, 218, 227
histogram, 241
historical data, 31, 52, 53, 62, 114, 119, 203
history, 98, 102, 133, 138, 150, 151, 163, 219
home ownership, 137, 141, 147
homeowners, 237
homogeneity, 187, 241, 242, 250, 251
honesty, 49
Hong Kong, 10, 33, 34, 75, 90, 168, 174, 183
host, 169, 183
hotel(s), 84, 182
House, 31, 99, 101, 102, 238
House of Representatives, 99, 101, 102
household income, 142, 145
housing, 139, 171, 237
human, 1, 49, 56, 115, 128, 132, 169, 174
human behavior, 1
human brain, 128
human resources, 169
Hunter, 218
hybrid, 51, 52, 68, 131
hypothesis, 12, 32, 33, 35, 39, 58, 77, 81, 84, 98, 104, 109, 133, 199, 202, 208, 211, 248, 260

I

identification, 66, 236, 264
identity, 126
ideology, 98, 99
illusions, 42
IMA, 71, 153, 154, 155, 156, 158
image, 168

imitation, 164, 165
improvements, 224, 254
impurities, 124
inadmissible, 119
incidence, 79, 174
income, 47, 49, 50, 63, 90, 93, 117, 137, 138, 139, 140, 141, 142, 143, 144, 145, 146, 147, 148, 150, 156, 171
income distribution, 171
income tax, 93, 142
independence, 33
independent variable(s), 7, 52, 108, 118, 119, 122, 133, 134, 137, 150, 151, 235, 236, 238, 240, 241, 242, 243, 244, 246, 248, 249, 250, 251, 252, 253, 254, 256, 257, 258, 259, 260, 261, 263, 264
indexing, 79
India, 10
individuality, 175
individuals, 32, 35, 54, 116, 117, 131, 145, 167, 168, 176, 245, 250, 254
Indonesia, 10, 75, 168
industrial sectors, 174
industry(s), 1, 5, 6, 7, 9, 16, 18, 19, 21, 22, 24, 25, 47, 48, 51, 55, 56, 63, 64, 65, 69, 72, 78, 79, 84, 85, 86, 87, 89, 90, 97, 113, 116, 118, 152, 157, 166, 172, 178, 182, 185, 187, 189, 190, 214, 217, 219, 221, 230, 231, 232
ineffectiveness, 162
inefficiency, 220, 221, 230, 232
inequality, 221
inflation, 47, 112, 171, 250
infrastructure, 217, 219, 230
inheritance, 170
initial public offerings (IPOs), 5, 9, 73, 89
injections, 200
inputs, 7, 48, 53, 58, 59, 60, 63, 65, 66, 67, 119, 128, 129, 185, 186, 187, 191, 193, 217, 219, 220, 221, 222, 223, 224, 225, 227, 228, 229, 230
institutions, 4, 8, 32, 34, 35, 49, 50, 51, 55, 56, 68, 117, 118, 167, 169, 177, 183, 194
integration, 34, 175
integrity, 49, 56
interest groups, 169
interest rates, 6, 47, 72, 73, 89, 99
interface, 132
internal processes, 50
International Monetary Fund, 71
intervention, 162, 217
investment(s), 2, 3, 12, 16, 49, 58, 65, 74, 78, 79, 82, 83, 84, 89, 90, 92, 93, 111, 112, 198, 200, 201, 215, 219, 230
investment bank, 65
investors, 5, 6, 10, 12, 13, 18, 34, 35, 42, 43, 48, 49, 50, 54, 55, 57, 77, 78, 79, 82, 91, 93, 97, 104, 110, 111, 165, 171, 172, 198, 199, 200, 201, 208, 210
invisible hand, 1
Islam, 181
issues, 7, 10, 11, 12, 27, 51, 53, 58, 70, 77, 94, 152, 156, 158, 164, 166, 167, 169, 172, 174, 175, 176, 177, 178, 194, 197, 199, 200, 201, 202, 209, 213, 214, 232
Italy, 79, 130, 137

J

Japan, 10, 32, 33, 43, 156, 198
joint ventures, 90
Jordan, 12, 26, 91, 172, 179, 200, 213
justification, 162, 168, 173

K

Keynes, 155
Korea, 75, 157

L

Latin America, 26
laws, 46, 152, 163, 164, 177
laws and regulations, 163, 177
lead, 47, 48, 49, 56, 57, 124, 177, 191, 201, 220
leadership, 168
learning, 94, 129, 154, 158
Least squares, 143
legislation, 47, 137, 163, 165
lenders, 6, 46, 49, 50, 51, 69, 78, 89, 113, 117, 137, 145, 148
lending, 45, 46, 47, 48, 49, 51, 56, 57, 68, 69, 70, 71, 113, 116, 117, 137, 144, 145, 148, 151, 152, 154, 155, 156, 158, 182, 265
letters of credit, 61
level of education, 139, 176, 177
Libya, 7, 235, 236
lifetime, 259
light, 7, 161, 177, 221
limited company, 75
line graph, 1
linear function, 128
linear model, 119, 156
linear programming, 115, 126, 127, 131, 132, 139, 143, 151, 157, 221, 222
linear programs, 1

liquidity, 10, 34, 35, 47, 50, 75, 78, 84, 91, 93, 137, 139, 215
liquidity ratio, 139
literacy, 177
local government, 231, 233
logistic regression, 7, 115, 122, 126, 132, 134, 135, 145, 147, 148, 149, 235, 242, 251, 252, 253, 254, 256, 258, 260, 262, 263, 264
longitudinal study, 182
lower prices, 146

M

machine learning, 153, 156
macroeconomic policy, 112
macroeconomics, 64
magnitude, 19, 24, 25, 39, 104, 110, 117, 167, 257, 259
major decisions, 201
majority, 5, 10, 79, 90, 101, 125, 239, 240
Malaysia, 10, 75, 162, 167, 168, 175, 179, 182, 232
management, 2, 15, 49, 50, 54, 56, 63, 68, 79, 114, 115, 142, 154, 155, 162, 164, 167, 176, 180, 200, 201, 218
manipulation, 1, 4, 131
manufacturing, 84
mapping, 53, 60, 65
marital status, 137, 139, 140, 141, 142, 143, 144, 145, 146, 147, 149, 150, 236, 239, 248, 253, 256, 257
mark up, 148
market access, 78
market capitalization, 10, 35, 39, 77, 205, 208
market position, 55
market share, 10
marketing, 56, 77, 201
marketing strategy, 77
Markov chain, 142, 149
materials, 198
mathematical models, 2, 3, 4
mathematical programming, 126, 127, 139, 159, 221
mathematics, 63, 123, 136
matrix, 57, 60, 62, 63, 64, 65, 68, 126, 221, 245
matrix condition, 64
matter, 74, 152, 155, 180, 182, 232, 241
measurement(s), 54, 61, 69, 114, 124, 126, 133, 155, 167, 194, 195, 219, 220, 221, 224, 225, 231, 233, 262
media, 6, 97, 170
median, 15, 37, 145, 204, 206, 207, 208
medical, 171
membership, 136
merchandise, 2
MES, 188, 191, 192, 193, 194
methodology, 10, 15, 32, 55, 58, 61, 63, 67, 72, 75, 98, 139, 151, 199, 219
Microsoft, 3
middle class, 102
Middle East, 156, 175, 180
migration, 51, 57, 62, 63, 64, 65, 66, 142
military, 91, 137, 169
Missouri, 156
modelling, 3, 4, 5, 6, 7
monetary policy, 47, 111
money supply, 47
monks, 91
Monte Carlo method, 64
morality, 49
mortality, 53, 69
mortality rate, 53
motivation, 6, 78, 90, 161, 166
multidimensional, 126
multinational companies, 90, 169, 172, 176
multinational corporations, 169
multiple regression, 5, 9, 18, 52, 134
multiple regression analysis, 5, 9
multiplier, 39, 108, 222
music, 143
mutation, 131

N

national character, 173
national culture, 175, 181, 182
national origin, 137
National Party, 101
nationality, 80, 92, 142
natural selection, 131
negative consequences, 169
negative relation, 18, 24, 84, 256, 260, 261
negotiating, 201
negotiation, 56
Netherlands, 33, 143, 145, 146, 147, 165
network density, 224
neural network(s), 124, 126, 128, 129, 130, 131, 132, 134, 135, 138, 140, 144, 147, 151, 154, 155, 156, 157, 158
neurons, 128, 130
neutral, 153
New England, 157, 189
New South Wales, 31, 189, 231, 233
New York Stock Exchange, 32
New Zealand, 99, 102, 110
Nigeria, 152, 172, 181
nodes, 124, 128, 132, 133
nonprofit organizations, 179

normal distribution, 62, 67, 121, 123, 241
North Africa, 175
North America, 170, 174, 175, 183
Norway, 165, 170
null, 20, 22, 37, 39, 40, 41, 84, 105, 107, 108, 109, 110, 191, 207, 208, 209, 211, 242, 248, 251, 253
null hypothesis, 20, 22, 39, 40, 41, 84, 105, 107, 108, 109, 110, 207, 208, 209, 211, 242, 248, 251

O

objectivity, 54, 117, 164
observed behavior, 227
obstacles, 175
oil, 10, 169, 182
oil spill, 182
one dimension, 225
openness, 168
operating system, 175
operations, 2, 7, 113, 126, 217, 223, 228, 230, 232
operations research, 113, 126
opinion polls, 98, 99, 112
opportunities, 7, 60, 73, 75, 90, 164, 185, 193, 224
oppression, 169
optimization, 58, 127, 131, 132
optimization method, 132
outputs, 7, 67, 128, 185, 186, 187, 189, 191, 192, 211, 217, 219, 221, 222, 223, 224, 225, 227, 228, 229, 230
outreach, 115
oversight, 91
ownership, 15, 26, 28, 78, 79, 80, 90, 93, 94, 95, 139, 171, 200, 201, 203, 204, 208, 209, 213, 215, 231, 232
ownership structure, 15, 80, 90, 93, 94, 95, 200, 215

P

Pacific, 10, 11, 27, 28, 42, 75, 77, 153, 175, 180, 181, 183, 215
parallel, 9, 76, 99, 135
parameter estimates, 122, 188, 191, 252
parentage, 239, 240
parents, 131, 239
parity, 32
Parliament, 101
participants, 29, 31, 35, 41, 48, 98
partition, 124
pathways, 218
pattern recognition, 125
per capita GNP, 172
per capita income, 171
percentile, 62
performance measurement, 232
permit, 13, 54
personal responsibility, 179
personality, 51
Perth, 218, 227
Peru, 182
Philadelphia, 157, 158
Philippines, 10, 75, 168
plants, 114, 230
Poland, 149
police, 257
policy, 6, 48, 72, 97, 98, 150, 152, 156, 166, 173
policymakers, 165, 167
political cycles, 98, 99, 110, 111
political instability, 6, 10, 73, 169
political party(s), 6, 98, 110
political problems, 91, 162
political system, 163, 167, 168
political uncertainty, 112
politics, 6, 97, 112, 163, 168
poor performance, 225
population, 14, 53, 114, 123, 124, 131, 144, 149, 150, 203, 217, 249
population growth, 217
portfolio, 5, 16, 17, 18, 45, 46, 50, 51, 54, 56, 57, 58, 59, 60, 61, 62, 63, 64, 65, 66, 67, 68, 69, 71, 72, 78, 90, 141, 142, 206, 207, 210, 212
portfolio credit risk, 5, 45, 59, 60, 61, 63
positive correlation, 78, 143
positive relationship, 26, 47, 84, 177, 256, 260, 261
poverty, 164
poverty alleviation, 164
predictability, 85
prediction models, 153, 156
predictive accuracy, 120, 147, 244, 245
predictor variables, 131, 237, 249
preparation, 51, 56, 223
present value, 3, 61, 62
presidency, 99
president, 170
price effect, 94, 192
price elasticity, 188, 191, 193
price index, 104
price mechanism, 29
prices, 7, 14, 29, 52, 62, 65, 79, 80, 103, 111, 112, 146, 154, 185, 186, 187, 188, 189, 192, 193, 201, 203, 208, 219, 264
prime rate, 148
principles, 131, 173, 180
private equity, 7, 12, 197, 198, 199, 202, 207, 208, 210, 211, 212, 213
private firms, 6, 73, 74, 80, 82, 83, 84, 89, 90, 93

private limited company, 75, 76
private sector, 172, 232, 237, 239
privatization, 231, 232
probability density function, 133
probability distribution, 65, 66, 124, 131, 133
probit models, 118, 119, 120
problem solving, 4
problem-solving, 3
producers, 117, 118, 167
product market, 79, 92, 214
production costs, 186, 220
production technology, 186, 187, 193
productive capacity, 224
productive efficiency, 219, 231
productivity growth, 232
professionalism, 201
profit, 81, 133, 134, 141, 143, 145, 176, 221
profitability, 6, 47, 49, 54, 56, 57, 73, 78, 81, 82, 84, 89, 94, 116, 117, 134, 137, 144, 146, 152
prognosis, 182
programming, 124, 126, 127, 135, 136, 139, 141, 143, 151, 155, 156, 174, 221
project, 3
propagation, 129
proposition, 168, 211
protection, 31, 47, 49, 55
psychology, 34, 35, 43, 122
public assistance, 137
public debt, 54
public education, 176
public health, 218
public investment, 55
public limited company, 75
public sector, 170, 195, 237, 239, 257
public service, 186
punishment, 162, 164

Q

quantitative technique, 58
Queensland, 189, 190
questionnaire, 3, 168

R

race, 41, 137, 142, 177
rainfall, 217
rate of return, 33, 50, 139
rating agencies, 55, 57, 61, 62, 117
rating scale, 57
reactions, 6, 97
real estate, 54, 85, 142
real time, 143
reality, 2, 59, 112, 213
reasoning, 168
recall, 225
Receiver Operating Characteristic (ROC), 262
recession, 46
recognition, 79, 167
recommendations, 34
recovery, 51, 59, 62, 65, 66
recycling, 224
reform(s), 111, 172, 180, 219
regression analysis, 3, 5, 6, 9, 24, 52, 97, 118, 235
regression equation, 1, 39, 40, 206, 252
regression model, 4, 85, 119, 121, 134, 141, 143, 147, 149, 188, 242, 251, 253, 254, 256, 260, 262, 263, 264
regulations, 56, 75, 79, 90, 163, 164, 165, 166, 167, 178
regulatory bodies, 166
regulatory framework, 162, 165
regulatory requirements, 166
rejection, 209
relative size, 48, 150, 244
relatives, 5, 9, 13, 14, 15, 18, 23, 25
reliability, 133, 141
religion, 91, 137
remediation, 177
rent, 142, 237
repression, 169, 170
reproduction, 131
reputation, 26, 79, 81, 92, 200, 201, 214
requirements, 6, 10, 48, 54, 55, 56, 65, 66, 67, 68, 69, 70, 73, 74, 77, 79, 80, 82, 83, 85, 90, 117, 124, 136, 164, 172, 175, 179, 218
RES, 85, 87
researchers, 6, 7, 8, 50, 113, 115, 161, 162, 166, 168, 169, 170, 172, 173, 174, 175, 176
reserves, 47, 56, 148
Residential, 54
residuals, 39, 108, 110
residues, 136
resource allocation, 218
resources, 22, 24, 25, 85, 87, 126, 141, 172, 197
response, 10, 12, 74, 112, 120, 132, 164, 182, 185, 186, 200, 202, 218
restaurants, 85
restrictions, 31, 35, 41, 187, 228, 229, 230
restructuring, 79, 180
retail, 48, 68, 75, 90, 104, 120, 134, 138, 149, 152, 156, 158, 265
retained earnings, 48, 123
return abnormalities, 5, 29
revaluation, 62

revenue, 56, 94, 146
rights, 11, 77, 79, 167, 168
risk assessment, 66, 71, 156
risk factors, 56, 67, 214
risk management, 50, 57, 118, 154
root, 105, 124, 172, 241
rules, 51, 57, 75, 114, 124, 132, 163, 165

S

sample mean, 205
sampling distribution, 241
SAS, 264
savings, 48, 91, 198
savings account, 48
scale economies, 218, 222, 231
scope, 10, 194, 195, 199, 218, 219, 232
seasonality, 31, 32, 34, 35, 214
security(s), 6, 11, 12, 26, 27, 29, 31, 32, 33, 35, 43, 48, 49, 55, 58, 65, 69, 71, 77, 79, 97, 111, 112, 139, 200, 213, 214, 223, 237, 238
self-employed, 137, 180, 237
seller(s), 10, 31, 32, 49
Senate, 101, 102
sensitivity, 4, 55, 77
September 11, 197
service organizations, 155
service quality, 232
services, 5, 9, 21, 24, 25, 26, 48, 55, 56, 85, 87, 162, 165, 171, 186, 194, 197, 200, 218, 222, 231, 232, 233
settlements, 31
sewage, 232
sex, 137
SGP, 156
shape, 47, 69, 124, 259
shareholders, 13, 14, 15, 75, 79, 80, 93, 167, 176, 201, 203, 206
shock, 104
shortage, 49, 114
showing, 133, 220
signal quality, 201
signals, 12, 128, 200
significance level, 246, 256
signs, 82, 110, 256, 260
Silicon Valley, 201
simulation(s), 4, 60, 62, 63, 67, 149, 153, 155
Singapore, 10, 75, 90, 91, 154, 167, 168, 180, 182
skewness, 36, 37, 241
small businesses, 148
small firms, 34
social activities, 91
social and environmental accounting disclosure, 6, 161, 162
social conservatives, 102
social context, 162
social group, 162
social policy, 6, 97, 111
social relations, 51
social relationships, 51
social responsibility, 164, 170, 172, 174, 175, 179, 180, 181, 183
social situations, 165
society, 1, 115, 138, 139, 144, 162, 163, 164, 166, 167, 168, 169, 170, 174, 176, 177, 178
software, 3, 61
sole proprietor, 75, 80
solution, 3, 66, 92, 127, 131, 132, 136, 250
South Africa, 147
South Korea, 10
Spain, 139
specification(s), 26, 83, 186, 187, 213, 219, 221, 223, 224, 235, 243, 259
speculation, 34
spending, 49, 149
spreadsheets, 3
SPSS software, 250, 253
stability, 11, 77, 137, 153, 164, 237
stabilization, 10
stakeholder groups, 178
stakeholders, 79, 162, 163, 168, 175, 178, 218
standard deviation, 17, 18, 36, 53, 60, 62, 104, 105, 106, 107, 205, 249
standard error, 39, 40, 108, 109, 110, 191
standard of living, 11, 77
state(s), 35, 41, 46, 47, 57, 63, 64, 65, 66, 101, 138, 151, 152, 154, 167, 170, 172, 179, 187, 236
statistics, 20, 22, 36, 37, 39, 52, 55, 84, 86, 87, 205, 207, 209, 212, 238, 240, 241, 243, 247, 252, 253, 256, 260, 261
stimulation, 6, 98
stock exchange, 25, 42, 79, 95, 172, 175, 179, 214
Stock Exchange of Thailand (SET), 9, 10, 11, 73, 74
stock markets, 42, 91, 162, 172
stock price, 14, 52, 68, 79, 80, 111, 203
stock value, 59
stockholders, 59
stratification, 133, 258
structural changes, 98
structural models, 5, 45, 59
structure, 51, 56, 59, 67, 68, 69, 70, 71, 72, 74, 78, 91, 93, 94, 98, 154, 155, 168, 194, 195, 221, 231
style, 168, 174
subgroups, 124
substitutes, 191, 192, 194

substitution, 7, 48, 185, 186, 188, 193, 194, 195
supervision, 10, 166, 200
suppliers, 48, 224, 232
supply, 1, 47, 84, 217, 218, 219, 222, 223, 224, 228, 230, 231, 232
support services, 186
surplus, 143, 224, 229, 230
survival, 7, 53, 122, 131, 132, 133, 134, 136, 140, 141, 142, 143, 145, 147, 149, 151, 152, 235, 236, 258, 259, 260, 261, 262, 263, 264
survival analysis, 7, 122, 132, 133, 134, 136, 140, 141, 147, 151, 152, 235, 258, 259, 260, 261, 262, 263, 264
sustainability, 115, 157, 162, 163, 166, 172, 181, 182, 218, 219, 223
Sweden, 33, 142, 165, 170
symbolic models, 1
symmetry, 188

T

Taiwan, 75, 153
takeover, 92
target, 7, 61, 217, 228, 229, 230
tax breaks, 6, 97
tax evasion, 169
tax incentive, 74
taxation, 2, 94
taxes, 82, 83, 142
technical change, 231, 232
technical efficiency, 219, 220, 221, 222, 224, 232
techniques, 3, 4, 5, 6, 7, 8, 25, 50, 52, 63, 113, 114, 115, 116, 117, 118, 123, 125, 126, 127, 130, 131, 134, 135, 136, 140, 141, 144, 147, 149, 151, 152, 154, 158, 159, 195, 201, 202, 235, 251, 258
technology, 7, 22, 24, 25, 87, 114, 154, 155, 185, 187, 195, 201, 231
telecommunications, 197, 219
telephone, 141
tenure, 105
test statistic, 26, 191, 213
testing, 27, 215
Thailand, 5, 6, 9, 10, 11, 13, 24, 26, 27, 28, 73, 74, 75, 76, 80, 83, 84, 89, 90, 91, 92, 93, 94, 95, 131, 168
Third World, 182
threats, 48, 219
time series, 63, 68
total costs, 187
trade, 10, 31, 78, 93, 102, 140, 141, 143, 147, 169, 200, 204, 205, 208, 230
trade union, 102, 169
trade-off, 78, 93, 200
trading days, 31, 32, 33, 34, 35, 41, 103
traditions, 115, 174
training, 125, 128, 129, 131, 163, 167, 171, 177, 182, 185, 186, 194
training programs, 167
transactions, 31, 35, 48, 50, 63, 90, 163, 165
transformation(s), 120, 129, 135, 171, 222, 241, 252
transition economies, 232
transition period, 103
transition rate, 57
transmission, 112
transparency, 79, 168, 170, 179
transport, 218
transport costs, 218
Treasury, 99
Treasury bills, 99
treatment, 217, 230, 237, 258
tuition, 194
turnover, 10, 11, 77, 79, 104, 140
Type I error, 131, 136, 242

U

underpricing, 5, 7, 9, 12, 13, 14, 15, 19, 20, 21, 22, 25, 26, 77, 197, 199, 200, 201, 202, 203, 204, 207, 208, 209, 212, 213, 214
underpricing issuer loss, 5, 7, 9, 14, 15, 19, 20, 21, 22, 25, 197, 202, 203, 207, 208, 212
underpricing loss by issuer price, 5, 9, 25
underpricing loss by market value, 5, 7, 9, 14, 15, 19, 20, 21, 22, 25, 197, 202, 203, 207, 208, 212
underwriting, 77, 142, 154, 201
unemployment rate, 138, 145
uniform, 3, 47
unions, 102, 140, 172
united, 10, 26, 32, 55, 98, 99, 102, 111, 112, 116, 138, 139, 140, 141, 142, 143, 144, 145, 146, 147, 148, 155, 157, 180, 199, 213, 232
United Kingdom (UK), 26, 32, 34, 92, 99, 102, 112, 137, 138, 139, 140, 141, 142, 143, 144, 147, 151, 155, 162, 167, 174, 183, 194, 213, 232
United States, 10, 32, 55, 98, 99, 102, 111, 112, 116, 138, 139, 140, 141, 142, 143, 145, 146, 148, 156, 157, 180, 199
universities, 7, 177, 185, 186, 187, 189, 193, 194, 195
unlimited liability, 75
updating, 159
urban, 7, 217, 218, 219, 221, 222, 223, 224, 225, 230, 231
urban water utilities, 7, 217, 218, 219, 221, 222, 230, 231
urbanization, 217

V

validation, 67, 72, 151, 162, 246
valuation, 1, 27, 59, 60, 70, 79, 94
variations, 55, 99
vector, 124, 129, 143, 221, 222, 224
vein, 176
velocity, 11, 77
venture capital, 7, 12, 26, 27, 79, 92, 197, 198, 199, 200, 201, 202, 207, 208, 210, 211, 212, 213, 214, 215
Vietnam, 10, 158, 265
volatility, 6, 33, 38, 53, 59, 60, 61, 62, 65, 97, 104, 105, 106, 108, 109, 110, 111, 240
vote, 101, 103, 108
voters, 6, 97, 101, 102
voting, 102, 167
vouchers, 142

W

wages, 186
Wales, 231, 232
war, 114
Washington, 72, 94, 116
waste, 52
water, 7, 84, 163, 217, 218, 219, 220, 221, 222, 223, 224, 225, 227, 228, 229, 230, 231, 232, 233
water quality, 219, 222, 224, 228, 230
watershed, 10
weakness, 116, 162, 165, 167
wealth, 2, 5, 9, 12, 13, 14, 15, 16, 18, 23, 25, 26, 78, 92, 169, 199, 201, 204, 208, 214
wealth relatives, 14, 15, 18, 23, 25
web, 14, 80
websites, 170, 174, 182
welfare, 219
Western Australia, 35, 190
wholesale, 48
Wisconsin, 230
workers, 114, 163
working class, 102
World Bank, 72, 94, 158, 166, 169, 182, 231, 232
World War I, 114
worldwide, 163, 218

Y

yield, 50, 52, 61, 67, 68, 122, 143, 186